Etiquette and Taboos around the World

Etiquette and Taboos around the World

A Geographic Encyclopedia of Social and Cultural Customs

KEN TAYLOR AND VICTORIA WILLIAMS,
EDITORS

GREENWOOD™

An Imprint of ABC-CLIO, LLC
Santa Barbara, California • Denver, Colorado

Library of Congress Cataloging-in-Publication Data

Names: Taylor, Ken, 1953- editor. | Williams, Victoria, editor.
Title: Etiquette and taboos around the world : a geographic encyclopedia of
    social and cultural customs / Ken Taylor and Victoria Williams, editors.
Description: Santa Barbara, California : Greenwood, An Imprint of ABC-CLIO,
    LLC, 2017. | Includes bibliographical references and index. |
Identifiers: LCCN 2017016819 (print) | LCCN 2017021772 (ebook) |
    ISBN 9781440838217 (ebook) | ISBN 9781440838200 (alk. paper)
Subjects: LCSH: Etiquette—Encyclopedias. | Taboo—Encyclopedias.
Classification: LCC BJ1815 (ebook) | LCC BJ1815 .E86 2017 (print) |
    DDC 395.03—dc23
LC record available at https://lccn.loc.gov/2017016819

ISBN: 978-1-4408-3820-0
EISBN: 978-1-4408-3821-7

21 20 19 18 17   1 2 3 4 5

This book is also available as an eBook.

Greenwood
An Imprint of ABC-CLIO, LLC

ABC-CLIO, LLC
130 Cremona Drive, P.O. Box 1911
Santa Barbara, California 93116-1911
www.abc-clio.com

This book is printed on acid-free paper ∞

Manufactured in the United States of America

Contents

Preface

Every culture on Earth has its own etiquette, by which is meant the traditional code of respectful behavior that members of a society or group are expected to follow. Etiquette is then the moderating force that balances the desire of individuals to act upon their own instincts with the need to yield to social conventions. It is necessary for individuals to uphold the etiquette of their society in order to ensure that their society functions harmoniously. Etiquette differs between societies and cultures, however, and this encyclopedia attempts to cover the "dos and don'ts" of the etiquette found in many countries and major ethnic groups around the world.

As this book concentrates on etiquette adhered to by societies and cultures worldwide, some of the entries may be familiar to American readers, such as the entries on European or African American etiquette. Other entries, meanwhile, may be less familiar to American readers, such as the entries on the Pashtuns living in Afghanistan and Pakistan, the Uyghurs of Eastern and Central Asia, and China's Hui people. While the entries contained in this book demonstrate the variety of different etiquette rules adhered to by the people of various cultures, the entries also highlight some common etiquette rules found across the world. These commonalities include the need to address people correctly during introductions and the taboo surrounding eating with the left hand found in Islamic societies across the globe.

The scope of this book takes in North, Central, and South America; Europe; Africa; Asia; the Middle East; and Oceania. The entries cover etiquette followed by men, women, and children in all manners of social situations, though they focus mainly on the etiquette of introductions and greetings, dress codes, hospitality and dining etiquette, guidelines surrounding body language and verbal communication, and the social conventions around online networking and interaction (so-called netiquette). Though the entries are obviously concerned with codes of social behavior, they also include elements of history, politics, religion, folklore, and sociology. The book's introduction looks at the history of etiquette and considers different academic perspectives (including sociological, scientific, and linguistic) on the subject.

Though this book is primarily aimed at student researchers, the writing has been kept as jargon-free as possible so that the general reader can also enjoy the book from cover to cover for entertainment or if wishing to learn about the etiquette of travel destinations. However, with the researcher in mind, every entry can be looked at as a stand-alone item and each entry is followed by a brief Further Reading list. There is also a Selected Bibliography at the back of the book.

We would like to thank our international team of dedicated contributors for their input when preparing this book, for they have provided great insight into the rich variety of world etiquette and social customs. Most importantly of all, however, the writing of this publication would not have been possible without the constant enthusiasm of Kaitlin Ciarmiello, acquisitions editor at ABC-CLIO.

Victoria Williams and Ken Taylor

Introduction

Etiquette is a code of behavior that defines expected, conventional social behavior according to contemporary norms within certain cultures, classes, and groups of people. The word "etiquette" derives from the Old French word *estiquette* (or *estiquet*) meaning "to attach," "to stick," or "to fix." Indeed the modern understanding of the word etiquette can be traced back to the royal court of French King Louis XIV (1638–1715), who employed small placards called *etiquettes* as reminders to courtiers of the behavior expected at court, such as remembering not to walk in particular areas of the palace gardens. This instance is quite unusual, however, as etiquette rules are not normally written down but rather may be collated periodically. Etiquette can shape many aspects of people's social interactions and may indicate a society's fundamental code of ethics as well as an individual's status within a society. It should be noted, however, that while the words *ethics* and *etiquette* stem from the Greek root *ethike* (meaning character), the two terms are not interchangeable. Ethics is a philosophical consideration of the morals and values that govern people's actions, whereas etiquette is the code of conventional, correct behavior that exists in a society.

The history of etiquette can be traced back much further than the time of Louis XIV. In the third millennium BCE, a collection of *sebayt* (teachings) and advice called *The Maxims of Ptahhotep* was produced, apparently written by the ancient Egyptian vizier Ptahhotep who wished to instruct his son about the subject of human relations. Four papyrus copies of the work survive, though the only complete version is the *Prisse Papyrus* dating from the Middle Kingdom that is on display at the Bibliothèque Nationale in Paris, France. In the introduction to *The Maxims of Ptahhotep*, the author explains that he wishes to pass on the knowledge of his ancestors. This knowledge appears as 37 maxims or guidelines that do not set out a complete code of morality but rather stress the importance of certain secular virtues such as the need for honesty tempered by discretion, self-discipline, moderation in all things, compassion, generosity, and integrity. *The Maxims of Ptahhotep* also suggests that it is best to learn by listening to others, and that avoiding conflict should be seen as a virtue rather than as a sign of cowardice or weakness. Other instructions included in the work relate to how to act in the presence of people of higher social ranks. At the same time, however, the maxims suggest it is necessary to practice the virtues of compassion, generosity, integrity, and so on to all human beings whatever their station in life.

Another important work in the history of etiquette is *The Book of the Courtier* by Baldassare Castiglione (1478–1529), an Italian courtier, diplomat, and humanist author. *The Book of the Courtier* is a so-called courtesy book or book of manners, by which is meant a book concerned with issues of etiquette, behavior, and morality, especially pertaining to royal courts. *The Book of the Courtier* exerted great influence in the modes of behavior in European court circles during the sixteenth century as it was printed in six languages in 20 locations across Europe. *The Book of the Courtier* influenced court etiquette for almost 500 years while also establishing a set of manners for men of wealth, privilege, and ambition. Meanwhile another notable Renaissance figure, the Dutch scholar Erasmus, published *On Good Manners for Boys* in 1530. In this work Erasmus includes etiquette advice for young children on topics such as yawning, scratching, and fidgeting.

It was arguably Louis XIV, however, who instituted the concept of etiquette as known today, for he impressed upon both the French nobility and foreign dignitaries the need for a highly codified system of etiquette that simultaneously allowed the king to assert his authority. During the so-called Age of Enlightenment a self-conscious process of imposing norms of polite society and acceptable behavior became a major symbol of belonging to the genteel classes. The aspirational, middle-class bourgeoisie strove to identify themselves with the elite and felt that by adopting the upper class's standards of behavior they somehow became a member of that class. For this reason the bourgeoisie became extremely concerned with adhering to rules of etiquette, particularly rules surrounding the expression of emotion, dress, conversation, and courteousness, especially for women.

Another of the key influences on the concept of polite society was the essays by the English writer, politician, and philosopher Lord Shaftesbury (1671–1713). Lord Shaftesbury defined politeness as the art of being pleasant company through the skillful control of words and deeds, so that other people would look upon a person favorably. It was, however, another English aristocrat, Philip Stanhope, 4th Earl of Chesterfield, who first employed the word *etiquette* in its modern meaning in his *Letters to His Son on the Art of Becoming a Man of the World and a Gentleman* (1774). This work gave advice on how gentlemen should interpret social codes while also adopting a refined demeanor in order to advance socially.

The publications of periodicals such as the British magazine *The Spectator* during the eighteenth century furthered the idea of polite society. *The Spectator* provided its readership with advice on how to conform to ideals of gentlemanly etiquette and morality while also offering its readers suggestions of how to conduct topical, yet polite, conversations. Allied to the notion of polite society at this time was the concept of civility, by which was meant a desire to interact socially in such a way as to demonstrate an appreciation of reasoned debate on topical matters. The era also saw the establishment of gentleman's clubs in London that held to their own sets of etiquette rules. These clubs were members-only private clubs that were originally established by and for English upper-class men. These clubs were still popular with English upper- and middle-class men (and women) during the nineteenth century, and by the early twentieth century had also become institutions in countries that had belonged to the British Empire, particularly the United States, India, Pakistan, and Bangladesh.

By the time of the Victorian era, etiquette had evolved into an extremely convoluted system of rules that governed everything from letter writing and dining to mourning. The Western etiquette rule of wearing black during mourning has been in operation since Victorian times when it was traditional for British mourners to wear black for an extended period of time. This period of mourning usually lasted for two years, though widows would be expected to wear black until they died. This mourning etiquette travelled far and wide throughout the British Empire so that it became the norm in countries including the United States for mourners to wear black as a sign of bereavement and to show respect for the dead. During the Victorian era, the United Kingdom's complex set of rules governing acceptable mourning behavior developed and was upheld by most people, but most especially by the upper classes. This mourning etiquette meant that when someone died, their servants and male acquaintances might wear black armbands. Men were expected to wear mourning suits consisting of black frock coats together with black trousers and waistcoats, while Victorian women were expected to wear heavy, black clothing, as well as veils made from black crêpe fabric—an outfit colloquially referred to as *widow's weeds*. Women would also wear special dark-colored mourning bonnets and caps, as well as black mourning jewelry. Victorian etiquette dictated that widows should wear their widow's weeds for at least four years; any woman deemed by society to have stopped wearing black too soon was thought to have shown disrespect to the dead and left herself open to charges of sexual impropriety. Although mourning customs relaxed slightly during the succeeding Edwardian era, it was still considered appropriate for British men and women to wear dark-colored clothing for up to one year after a death in their family. By the late twentieth century, this etiquette rule no longer applied, but black continues to be the color most associated with mourning in the United Kingdom and in former British colonies.

It is, therefore, apparent that over time every society and culture develops its own code of acceptable behavioral norms. Manners are an element of these norms of behavior and though each society has its own set of manners, many manners are common across cultures. Manners are also enforced more informally than is a society's overarching etiquette. For instance, etiquette rules may be reinforced by laws such as smoking bans in areas where smoking is frowned upon, whereas manners are rarely governed by official edicts. Manners also tend to be self-regulating in that they are policed by the society to which they apply. Manners also tend to be based on self-control for they often function as a compromise between how people would like to act or to say and what they actually do or say.

As they are central to society, etiquette and manners are of interest to people who study society, such as sociologists. In his 1939 two-volume work *Über den Prozeß der Zivilisation* (*The Civilizing Process*) the German sociologist Norbert Elias maintained that manners exist as a product of group living and act as a way of preserving social order. Elias suggested that manners thrived during the Renaissance era (the period of European history from the fourteenth to the seventeenth century) in response to the evolution of the state, that is, a time when society grew from collections of small groups of people living together to people governed by centralized authorities. According to Elias, European Renaissance morals pertaining to violence, sexual behavior, bodily functions, table manners, and speech were formed by the evolution of increasing thresholds of disgrace and disgust, until, eventually, a code of court etiquette developed. Elias also suggested that the traditions accompanying manners in English court society during the Renaissance were bound up with issues of social class meaning that, in Elias's opinion, the manners that someone demonstrates indicate the individual's social status. Similarly, sociologists Alan Petersen and Deborah Lupton in *The New Public Health* discuss manners and civility as elements that help to eradicate the boundaries between the public and the private. Petersen and Lupton argue that courteousness is an important aspect of society because participating in society relies upon individuals self-regulating both their behavior and emotions.

The sociological concept of "habitus" (a system of entrenched dispositions or tendencies that govern the ways in which people understand, and react to, the social structure around them) may also help explain the importance of manners. According to the theories of French sociologist Pierre Bourdieu, habitus is the physical embodiment of cultural capital (social assets that promote social mobility beyond financial means such as education, dress, and speech) and the entrenched habits, skills, and dispositions people possess that have been created by their life experiences. To Bourdieu's way of thinking, people's dispositions are not self-determined, nor are they predetermined by external factors. Instead dispositions operate on a subconscious level and are instilled and reproduced via experience, education, and social interactions. Manners are a central part of these dispositions as they shape people's ability to make decisions on how to act in ways that are socially acceptable.

As well as sociologists, scientists are also interested in the way people interact with each other. To this end, evolutionary biologists also research etiquette and manners, for this scientific field considers the origins of people's behavior and the processes behind people's actions. For example, famous biologist Charles Darwin suggested that the universality of people's facial reactions to disgust and shame meant that such reactions are innate in humans rather than learned behavior. Meanwhile, Professor Valerie Curtis, director of the Hygiene Centre at the London School of Hygiene and Tropical Medicine in England, has theorized that people's responses to things deemed disgusting or shameful are connected to the development of manners. Moreover, Curtis asserts that manners have an evolutionary role to play in the prevention of disease. Therefore it can be concluded that the most hygienic people also tend to have the best manners and, therefore, have the best chance of surviving and reproducing. Curtis also outlines three main types of etiquette—hygiene, courtesy, and cultural norms—that each plays a part in the complex societal role of manners. Manners related to hygiene tend to be taught to individuals when they are very young, often by parents, so that by the time the child has become an adult these manners have become second nature. These manners tend to be associated with bodily functions, such as potty training, and are likely related to ways of preventing the transmission of disease. When hygiene manners are contravened, others in society will often react with disgust. Another type of manners, so-called courtesy manners, reveal a person's ability to put the interests of other people above his or her own. This is achieved by demonstrating self-discipline in order to be trusted in social interactions. Courtesy manners are taught in a similar way to hygiene manners but are also absorbed by the individual through interactions with other people or through the cognitive processes of the brain. People often learn courtesy manners later in life than they do hygiene manners because people need to have some self-awareness and knowledge of their place in society in order to comprehend courtesy manners. The contravention of courtesy manners usually results in the disapproval of a person's peers rather than shows of disgust.

The final category of manners, cultural norms, tends to indicate an individual's identity within a certain sociocultural group. Observance of cultural norm manners permits both the distinction between sociocultural identities as well as the establishment of sociocultural limits that tell individuals who they can trust, which other people are similar to themselves, and who they should consider to be fundamentally different from themselves. People learn cultural norm manners through exposure to the society in which they exist, familiarization with what is routine in their society, as well as via experience to ways of living that are alien. Individuals who do not adhere to cultural norm manners are usually met with alienation from the society whose norms they have transgressed.

Although the etiquette and manners of people within a group tends to be similar, the etiquette of different groups varies even if they are in proximity. For example, European etiquette differs throughout the Continent on certain matters. An example of differences existing in European etiquette can be seen when considering nudity. In many European countries etiquette requires that people do not expose their genitals in public, as this may constitute indecent exposure and therefore a criminal offence. Meanwhile exposing the buttocks may be considered mooning, which though not necessarily illegal, is certainly considered insulting behavior in many European countries. However, a number of European countries (Finland, France, Spain, and Italy, for example) allow topless bathing. Thus it seems that in Europe, attitudes to public nudity vary by country. Dutch society considers nudity in a much less sexualized way than, say, does British society (and other Anglosphere nations), with the Dutch attitude to nudity echoed by attitudes found in Scandinavian countries where nudity is often customary when using saunas. Indeed in many saunas it is considered almost taboo to remain clothed. Germany also has a relaxed attitude to nudity. Though the British are seen as traditionally conservative when it comes to nudity, breastfeeding in public is permitted and indeed encouraged by British authorities though this is somewhat controversial in the United Kingdom. Despite the controversy surrounding breastfeeding in the United Kingdom, it is not uncommon to see breastfeeding occurring in cafés, shops, and so on.

European etiquette can also vary within individual countries. Indeed within these individual countries each society will demonstrate etiquette of their own where there are differences in customs and various linguistic groups. This is evident in Switzerland where French, Swiss-German, and Italian speakers live and who tend to demonstrate etiquette and social customs that hark back to France, Germany, and Italy respectively.

Despite the diversity of European etiquette, certain aspects of etiquette are similar throughout Europe, most likely transmitted via the wide spread of the Roman Empire and the travels of royalty and nobility. One aspect of etiquette that occurs frequently throughout Europe is that many European languages employ different second-person pronouns to signify formality or informality when addressing someone. This system of address is referred to as the T-V distinction by sociolinguists, and sees the T-form of "you" words such as *tu* (in Latin, Portuguese, and French) and *ti* (Croatian), used by people when addressing someone with whom they are familiar, and the V-form of "you" such as *vous* (French), *vos* (Latin), and *vi* (Croatian) used when addressing somebody with whom they are unfamiliar. In general T-forms are used when addressing friends and family, and V-forms are employed in order to show respect when addressing elders, strangers, and colleagues. It is necessary in many countries (not just in Europe but worldwide) to employ the correct form of "you," as the use of an improperly informal form of "you" can be seen as an insult.

Just as cultural and linguistic similarities mean there are common rules of etiquette throughout Europe, so religion has a significant bearing on etiquette in other parts of the world. For example in Africa, Asia, and the Middle East there are some common etiquette rules. Although these areas are enormous geographically and are inhabited by huge populations that adhere to many different cultures and customs, there are a number of etiquette commonalities, many of which are based on religion. A number of countries in Africa and Asia have traditions based on Islam and therefore to at least some degree share values with other parts of the Muslim world, such as the Middle East. This is true particularly in countries that have Muslim majority populations such as Senegal, Chad, and Mali in Africa and Pakistan and Indonesia in Asia. In the Middle East, Africa, and Asia many etiquette norms are related to Islam and the way in which the Koran has been understood and practiced for millennia. Prescribed Islamic etiquette is referred to as *Adab*. *Adab* has a twofold meaning. On the one hand *Adab* refers to a hand gesture of greeting conferring respect, but *Adab* also describes approved Islamic etiquette that requires Muslims to behave in a way that suggests refinement, good manners, morality, restraint, dignity, and humanity. While Muslims interpret *Adab* in a variety of ways, *Adab* rules of etiquette pertain to everyday life meaning that many Islamic etiquette rules are common across the Islamic world.

Common etiquette rules found in Islamic nations include not eating pork or drinking alcohol, the need for women to wear clothes that are not revealing, not eating with the left hand, respecting elders, refraining from public displays of affection between people of the opposite sex, removing shoes when entering certain places, and offering hospitality to guests. Some Islamic taboo actions may seem completely innocuous to people who are not Muslim. For example in the West there are no taboos around displaying the sole of the foot, while being touched by a shoe is not considered an insult (shoes being considered unclean in Islam). That being touched by a shoe is an insult in Islamic cultures was evinced in 2008 when

Iraqi journalist Muntazar al-Zaidi threw his shoes at then U.S. president George W. Bush in protest of U.S. actions in Iraq. Conversely, gestures that have a positive connotation in the West may be viewed negatively elsewhere. For example, during the inauguration of President Donald Trump in January 2017 the president made a thumbs-up gesture. In many parts of the Middle East, western Africa, Bangladesh, South America, Italy, and Spain, this gesture is considered highly offensive. Similarly, the "okay" gesture (made by someone connecting their thumb and forefinger in a circle while keeping the other fingers straight) conveys a message of confirmation and that everything is well in Britain and North America, while in parts of South America and southern Europe this is a distasteful gesture.

The fact that President Trump's thumbs-up gesture was seen around the world in countries where the action suggests positivity as well as in other areas where the gesture is insulting highlights the fact that in today's multimedia age, gestures can be beamed around the world instantaneously. This is one of the reasons that understanding etiquette is very important. Also in a world where people travel more often and further afield than ever before, knowing the correct way to behave is imperative if one is to avoid causing offence or incurring the wrath of other people.

In the modern world it is easy to think that etiquette is an outmoded concept based upon class distinctions about which very few people care. Some critics consider etiquette to be an unwelcome relic of previously class-conscious times and nothing more than a leftover code of behavior that was used by medieval societies to distinguish between rich and poor, and to make socially acceptable the conduct of battle-scarred knights when attending royal courts—some medieval books exist that explicitly instruct returning knights to refrain from blowing their noses on tablecloths when at court, as such uncouth behavior was frowned upon. When seen in this light it could be argued that etiquette rules are little more than ways to force people to act contrary to their true nature. Moreover, critics of etiquette contend that etiquette tends to be misogynistic, as etiquette creates rules surrounding the minutest details of social behavior that more often than not particularly affect women. For instance traditionally British etiquette has rules concerning when women are permitted to remove their gloves in public, while many societies around the world govern what women should wear. This is seen in the number of cultures that frown upon women revealing too much skin and the number of religions that rule women should be covered by veils and the like. Other commentators also suggest etiquette is a remnant of colonial days with the rules of etiquette existing as a way to differentiate between the civilized behavior of colonialists and native modes of behavior. Hence the phrase "going native" means that someone has stopped using the prevailing etiquette of the civilized colonials and has instead adopted the etiquette rules of local people.

Today etiquette is indeed bound up with politics to an extent, though not necessarily the politics of colonialism but rather the politics of Left and Right. For example, while some people (usually with Left-leaning political tendencies) deliberately avoid using certain words or phrases so as not to offend other people, the very act of deliberately not causing offence is labeled political correctness by others, typically those whose politics tend to the Right. The Left argue that avoiding certain terms found insulting by some is actually what was once deemed good manners or etiquette, not so-called political correctness. Moreover those who are dubbed politically correct contend they are merely being civil by not causing somebody else offence. On the other hand, those people who object to what they consider political correctness feel that their right to free speech is being eroded by not being "allowed" to use certain terms. Recently those who are anti–political correctness have started using the term *snowflake* to describe people whom they consider to be politically correct and prone to being offended. Meanwhile the so-called snowflakes increasingly accuse those who do not moderate their language so as not to cause offence of being racist, sexist, misogynistic, and so on. Thus it is apparent that the line between what some people consider good manners and what others see as political correctness is both blurred and contentious. Much of the controversy surrounding snowflakes, political correctness, and free speech is played out on social media. Therefore, while critics of etiquette may consider the idea of etiquette out of date, it is actually to the fore in the modern realm of the Internet. Indeed the very interconnectedness of the modern world has provoked a surge of interest in how to behave correctly across all media and situations. For example, Debrett's (a specialist British publisher and authority on etiquette), whose *Peerage* was first published in 1769, now issues guides on modern manners and last year teamed up with high-society magazine *Tatler* to create a course on modern etiquette that promised to teach students how to be graceful and effortlessly charming at all times. The course addresses how to act correctly in extremely modern situations about which there is no existing etiquette, including how to act when taking a so-called selfie with a celebrity. The desire to create selfie etiquette arises because selfies necessarily involve intruding on a stranger's personal space, and the issue also arises as to whether it is correct to hug the celebrity whose space has already been encroached. Another influence on modern etiquette is that with increased levels of affluence, more people are entertaining at their homes, with hosts thus wishing to learn how to behave toward their guests.

The prevalence of social media is a minefield of new etiquette as users try to determine what actions constitute accepted norms of, for instance, Twitter and Facebook use. This is where so-called "netiquette" comes to the fore. Where once etiquette was primarily the preserve of the upper classes, social media is not limited to the elite but rather is democratic with everyone from the royal family in England and the president of the United States to children in war-torn Syria having Twitter accounts. For this reason social interactions and, by extension, etiquette have also become democratic and to a degree self-governing. Indeed, the rise in online business and social media has to a certain extent seen the creation of a new worldwide online society, which by necessity has created its own code of conduct, so-called *netiquette*. The rules of netiquette govern the correct protocol for communication on social media, by e-mail, in online forums, and on blogs. Moreover, just as social media is constantly evolving, so netiquette is developing continuously.

The etiquette of business is often bound up with netiquette. Office etiquette applies to interactions between coworkers, but does not extend to interactions with external associates such as customers or suppliers. When conducting group meetings in the United States, the assembled people might follow Henry Martyn Robert's *Robert's Rules of Order*, in lieu of company etiquette policies. First published in 1876, *Robert's Rules of Order* is a guide for conducting meetings and making group decisions. The book is revised frequently, with the most recent version published in 2011 as *Robert's Rules of Order Newly Revised*. In today's interconnected world, which sees people travel at short notice to foreign countries, it is important to note that business etiquette can vary greatly geographically. For example, the etiquette associated with conflict resolution differs greatly between the West and China. Chinese businesses tend to rely upon personal relationship management to side-step conflict. This reflects Chinese business culture's dependence on *guanxi* (meaning "connections" or "relationships"). The Chinese believe that good *guanxi* results in the formation of networks of mutually beneficial relationships that evolve outside of the workplace (at social dinners, drinks, and the like) that result in amiable, conflict-free business relationships. In contrast, Western businesses, when faced with conflict or problems, tend to resolve issues by instructing lawyers and by implementing contracts.

Another aspect of social media is that actions performed in private can become public knowledge, while private, controversial thoughts if aired on social media can "go viral," meaning transgressions can be known worldwide. For instance, if someone picks their nose at home in their bedroom, nobody need know about it except the nose-picker. However, as soon as the nose-picker posts a photo of themselves picking their nose on, say, Instagram, suddenly the nose-picking incident becomes known to many more people. Moreover, in an era of trolling, fat-shaming, and so-called left-swiping (having your online photograph judged unattractive by others), some people do feel there is a need for some kind of self-imposed etiquette for users of social media. Therefore, while traditional rules of etiquette may not hold the influence over daily life they once did, it could be argued that the need for etiquette is as important in today's multimedia age as it ever was.

Victoria Williams

Further Reading

Amelia, William. "Castiglione and 'The Courtier'." *History Today*, vol. 28, no. 9 (September 1978). http://www.historytoday.com/william-amelia/castiglione-and-'-courtier'. Accessed January 22, 2017.

Axtell, Roger E. *Gestures: The Do's and Taboos of Body Language Around the World*, rev. and exp. ed. New York: John Wiley & Sons, 1998.

Curtis, Valerie. *Don't Look, Don't Touch: The Science Behind Revulsion*. Oxford: Oxford University Press, 2013.

Denny, Frederick M. "Ethical Dimensions of Islamic Ritual Law." In Edwin B. Firmage, Bernard G. Weiss, and John Woodland Welch, eds., *Religion and Law: Biblical-Judaic and Islamic Perspectives*, 199–210. Winona Lake, IN: Eisenbrauns, 1990.

Gander, Kashmira. "The Etiquette of Celebrity Selfies, and Other Modern Dilemmas." *The Independent*. May 26, 2016. http://www.independent.co.uk/life-style/the-etiquette-of-celebrity-selfies-and-other-modern-dilemmas-a7050271.html. Accessed January 22, 2017.

Hope, Katie. "Doing Business the Chinese Way." *BBC News: Business.* October 8, 2014. http://www.bbc.co.uk/news/business-29524701. Accessed January 24, 2017.

Johnson, Ben. "British Etiquette." *Historic UK.* http://www.historic-uk.com/CultureUK /british-etiquette/. Accessed January 22, 2017.

Lichtheim, Miriam. *Ancient Egyptian Literature: Volume I: The Old and Middle Kingdoms.* Berkeley: University of California Press, 2006.

Peron, James. "Courtesy Is Not Political Correctness." *The Huffington Post US Edition: The Blog.* July 1, 2014. http://www.huffingtonpost.com/james-peron/courtesy-is-not-political_b _5250744.html. Accessed January 22, 2017.

Petersen, Alan, and Deborah Lupton. *The New Public Health: Health and Self in the Age of Risk.* London: SAGE, 2000.

Rossi, Patricia. *Everyday Etiquette: How to Navigate 101 Common and Uncommon Social Situations.* New York: St Martin's, 2011.

Williams, Victoria. *Celebrating Life Customs Around the World: From Baby Showers to Funerals.* Santa Barbara, CA: ABC-CLIO, 2017.

Wise, Hilary. *The Vocabulary of Modern French: Origins, Structure and Function.* London: Routledge, 1997.

A

AFRICAN AMERICAN

African American cultural etiquette is a culmination of traditions that span two continents and four centuries. Values and behaviors transported from Africa to North America have been molded by the experiences of enslavement, as well as innovation under the oppression of Jim Crow laws and positive affirmation of blackness in the post–Civil Rights era. Most African Americans practice social protocol that reflects mainstream norms. Nevertheless, the individuality of the African diaspora and subsequent challenge to reinvent communities in the United States created a unique cultural legacy that endures within black America.

African American cultural etiquette bears many similarities to standard American norms that are all rooted in nineteenth-century Victorian values. However, social graces that millions of African Americans exhibit today are part of a political legacy designed to protect and uplift the entire African American race. In the years following Emancipation and Reconstruction, the African American church stood as the lone black-controlled institution that provided spiritual *and* social support. African American Christians generally belonged to denominations such as the elite African Methodist Episcopal church (AME), middle-class Baptist and Methodist congregations, and the working-class Church of God in Christ (COGIC). Each denomination promoted etiquette standards and values that reflected the disparate social and economic standings of its congregants. While African Americans have never represented a social monolith, cultural etiquette across class lines emphasized property ownership when possible, liberal arts or industrial education, physical and spatial cleanliness, temperance, thrift, staid Christianity, proper attire for men and women, and impeccable manners. This concept, called the "politics of respectability," served as a foundation for economic and social uplift, as a protective mechanism against hostility and violence, and has endured in African American communities to the present day. These etiquette standards promoted strict adherence to Victorian conventions but also reflected the legacy of enslavement and social necessities that were exclusive to black Americans. Enslavement forced a counterculture that redefined notions of masculinity and femininity based upon black experiences that inevitably deviated from white standards. Forced to perform physical and "masculine" labor, enslaved women who were equated with men by slave owners asserted gender equity within their communities that was unthinkable in free white society. Similarly, enslaved men who were denied citizenship and male privilege cooperated with women to sustain parental and familial relationships, provisions, cultural life, and leadership within the hidden world of enslaved people. This led to a kind of sexual equality born in enslavement that affected African American social, economic, and political culture even as black men and women ascribed to etiquette standards that emphasized separate roles for men and women. Economic discrimination meant that the majority of black women, regardless of class status, worked outside the home. Historians have estimated that 73 percent of elite and middle-class black women were employed at the turn of the twentieth century, where such a figure never applied to white women of similar standing. Working-class black women generally worked as domestic laborers and sometimes in agricultural labor that often placed them beside their husbands and other men. Nevertheless, African American communities strived to embody unyielding adherence to respectability standards that reflected their values and cultural expectations.

Historians and sociologists theorize that African American communities and cultural practices are rooted in the fragmented societies represented when captive men, women, and children were sold to European slave traders and transported across the Atlantic to North America. Inside of the ships, enslaved people confronted the linguistic and social barriers that disparate cultural regions presented. To cope with the terror and isolation of bondage, African people formed "fictive kin" relationships to establish nuclear and extended familial roles that comforted and empowered black people in the New World. These connections served as substitutes for severed blood ties and bound people within enslaved communities across colonial America and in the United States. Today, "relationships of appropriation" and adjacent titles that denote parental, grandparental, and sibling connections are sustained in African American communities as hallmarks of extended families and kinship networks that render black family structures exceptional. This legacy is reflected today through the ways by which millions of African Americans interact with one another, as men and women frequently afford loved ones familial titles such as "Aunt," "Uncle," "Brother," "Sister," or "Mama." These names do not necessarily assume blood ties, but are offered as markers of respect to an individual and serve as indicators of a man or woman's close association with a particular family.

While respectability politics dictated African American dress standards from Reconstruction until the 1960s, distinctly black American style rose to national consciousness during the civil rights movement and the decolonization of Africa. Fashion trends for African Americans veered away from mainstream, Eurocentric clothing norms and beauty standards to incorporating West African fabrics, patterns, and dress styles that young men and women celebrated as culturally specific. Throughout the 1960s and 1970s, kente cloth and dashikis earned acceptance, as well as debate, among all age groups of African Americans as markers of black pride and cultural symbolism. Hairstyles also reflected shifting and sometimes contrasting attitudes among African Americans as to proper appearance. Hair has played an important social and political role in African American culture and etiquette since the arrival of the first Africans in North America. Complex braid and row patterns indicated the community or region to which a man or woman might belong, and served as a marker of power. In the instance of the Wolof society within West Africa, men and women believed women's hair to be imbued with

Culture Shock! ⊕

Kente Cloth

Kente cloth is one of the most famous African fabrics. Ghana's Ashanti people developed the cloth around 375 years ago when, according to legend, two brothers from the village of Bonwire, Kurugu and Ameyaw, came across a spider spinning a web and were so transfixed by the web's beauty that they wove a fabric to resemble the web. The first cloth was woven from the black and white fibers of a raffia tree. Nowadays Bonwire is the most famous center for the production of kente cloth. The cloth's colors, patterns, and symbols hold specific meanings relating to the history and faith of the Ashanti people. Before becoming a master kente cloth weaver, a person must learn the symbolic meanings of all of the patterns.

Victoria Williams

spirits to drive men insane. The significance of black hair carried through as African Americans struggled for acceptance and adopted the Victorian fashion conventions that placed European preference for straight hair over the organic ways that African Americans' hair grew. In the 1960s, however, time-consuming and often painful perms for men and women gave way to some African Americans electing to wear naturally curly hair, or Afros and cropped looks that recalled traditional African hairstyles worn on the continent. Throughout the 1980s and into the twenty-first century, cornrows, braids, and dreadlocks are worn by African Americans of all ages.

Today, African American communities still debate what constitutes appropriate attire. Particularly in urban areas, oversized clothing, bright patterns, body art, facial jewelry, and theatrical cosmetics reflect the popularity of hip-hop and rap music culture that is integral to fashion choices among men and women who argue that respectability politics demand a conservative appearance at the expense of authentic blackness. The success of clothing lines such as Sean John (created by music mogul Sean Combs), House of Dereon (Beyoncé Knowles Carter and Tina Knowles), and the brand F.U.B.U. (For Us, By Us) highlight the acceptance and promotion of fashion choices created specifically for African American consumers. Millions of African Americans debate what kinds of aesthetics are culturally acceptable and what choices breach social etiquette. However, a general consensus indicates that the appropriation of specifically African or African American dress styles or traditions, labels, jewelry and body art, and hairstyles are inappropriate for nonblack Americans and are viewed by African Americans as vapid consumption of their culture without acknowledgment that such style markers typically spring from political and social frustrations as traditionally marginalized people within American society.

Culinary etiquette is perhaps among the most defining characteristics of African American communities for nonblack Americans. The phrase "soul food" is commonly

Young African American men in New York City exhibiting culturally appropriate fashion. A distinct urban way of dressing is widely accepted in the African American community. (sx70/iStockphoto.com)

understood as dishes prepared by Southern African Americans, though these hearty foods are enjoyed in communities throughout the United States. This style of cooking emphasizes innovation and using available ingredients to create meals. Soul food represents the privations of enslavement, where black families were allotted the poorest cuts of meat and leftovers from owners' tables, while any supplements of fresh vegetables, fruits, or breads were provided by enslaved people's own stoves or gardens that they worked after returning from tasks. Richly seasoned dishes such as collard greens or catfish and cornbread cooked with cornmeal and oil that are staples of soul food restaurants and African American kitchens were born out of subsistence diets and were originally derided as lower-class forms of cooking. Today, however, soul food is a cherished form of connection between individual African Americans and black communities. Not only do certain foods recall a connection to the unique legacy of enslavement, but other dishes that are African American hallmarks represent the survival of African customs in North America. Vegetables such as sweet potatoes and okra, certain grains of rice and sorghum, and fruits like watermelon derived from Africa and became integral to Southern kitchens and regional cuisine alike, including Creole and Low Country fare where dishes such as gumbo, hoppin' john, and biscuits and cane syrup are standard items.

African American food is not merely eaten, but celebrated as a link to the past, between people and communities. Therefore, table manners and general etiquette at daily meals, formal gatherings, or milestones such as weddings and funerals demand appreciation for meals that are actually cultural markers. Refusing dishes is often viewed with suspicion or as an affront to the cook or community. Some foods, however, are generally considered taboo among African Americans and their culinary traditions. For example, pastas served with tomato sauce are historically rejected as masks for spells, a tradition born out of West African Voudon and Santeria practices that used menstrual blood in foods to manipulate an individual and that reportedly remain in practice by priests and priestesses along the Gulf Coast.

The style of language used in African American communities across the United States echoes the adaptation and innovation of African ancestors from the diaspora. Language barriers presented challenges to Africans who struggled to understand one another as well as white colonists and settlers. As a result, pidgin languages developed among black communities throughout colonial North America. Composed of two or more tongues, pidgins allowed Africans and subsequently African Americans to communicate with one another while establishing a rich linguistic tradition among speakers. African American Vernacular English (AAVE) further reveals the exceptionality of African American innovation in communication. A recognized dialect of Standard American English, AAVE highlights the adaptations of African Americans who live or have lived in largely segregated communities. AAVE grammar includes use of negative concord and dropping of final consonants that are similar to Southern and New England dialects in the United States. Yet this particular dialect also showcases pidgin markers that reflect its African origins. Though not all African Americans use AAVE, this dialect is often spoken in communities and by individuals to indicate comfort, familiarity, and a sense of place between black Americans, while Standard American English may be used with outsiders. Generally, African American cultural etiquette discourages speaking AAVE with nonblack acquaintances, and the appropriation of black American dialects by nonblack people is widely considered offensive.

Misti Nicole Harper

Further Reading

Billingsley, Andre W. *Climbing Jacob's Ladder: The Enduring Legacy of African American Families.* New York: Simon and Schuster, 1992.

Bower, Anne. *African American Foodways: Explorations of History and Culture.* Champaign-Urbana: University of Illinois Press, 2009.

Byrd, Ayana D., and Lori L. Tharps. *Hair Story: Untangling the Roots of Black Hair in America.* New York: St. Martin's, 2001.

Higginbotham, Evelyn Brooks. *Righteous Discontent: The Women's Movement in the Black Baptist Church.* Cambridge, MA: Harvard University Press, 1993.

Morgan, Philip D. *Slave Counterpoint: Black Culture in the Eighteenth-Century Chesapeake and Lowcountry.* Chapel Hill: University of North Carolina Press, 1998.

Pullum, Geoffrey K. "African American Vernacular English Is Not Standard English with Mistakes," in Rebecca S. Wheeler, *The Workings of Language: From Prescriptions to Perspectives.* Westport, CT: Praeger, 1999.

ALGERIA

Algeria, located in North Africa, lies at the crossroads between Europe, North Africa, sub-Saharan Africa, and the Middle East. Over 90 percent of the inhabitants live along the Mediterranean coast, and almost 50 percent of the population is urban. The Algerian constitution declares Islam to be the state religion, and over 99 percent of Algerians are Sunni Muslim. Algeria depends heavily on its oil and natural gas reserves. Since the 1980s, the country has attempted to move from a socialist economy to a market economy. Algerians are warm and hospitable people and tend to offer a friendly welcome to guests and visitors. Each region has its own language, customs, and traditions, yet the Algerian people share a common religious heritage based on Islam. While many of the traditional customs and rules of social etiquette are still in practice, it is important to remember that Algerian society, just like most societies today, is transforming rapidly.

When greeting each other, most people in Algeria, including among men, exchange kisses on the cheeks (usually four times). Handshakes are also used, and sometimes people hold hands for a moment while talking as a sign of goodwill. Similarly, some people will also bring their right hand to their heart after a handshake as a sign of respect and sincerity. It is also customary among Algerians to ask each other about family, children, work, health and well-being, and the weather, among other concerns. In Algerian society the individual counts for less than the family or the group in which he or she lives. Even though this tendency is gradually disappearing, the family remains the most important unit in Algerian society. Unlike the Western concept of family, which tends to focus on the nuclear family, the Algerian family is extended to include other members of the group, such as grandparents, uncles, aunts, and cousins.

When meeting Algerian women for the first time, it is proper to nod and wait to see if they initiate a handshake or even kisses on the cheeks. Women visitors should also note that religious men, out of respect, might not shake their hand. The relationship between men and women has changed a great deal recently in Algeria. Overall, however, people of the opposite sex do not interact openly, especially in rural areas. Talking to, or trying to flirt with, a woman in a public space is frowned upon. Similarly, for a man to make prolonged eye contact with a woman might be interpreted as disrespectful or as a sign of flirting with her. In Algeria it is always proper to greet older people first. The elderly, both men and women, are placed at the top of the hierarchy in terms of respect. Algerians have a different relationship to personal space than is accepted in the West. To this end in Algeria it is normal for people to stand very close together, perhaps even touching. Gift giving is performed as a sign of love and respect. It is also normal for people to offer a gift as a thank you gesture on receiving service or assistance. This gift does not have to be a valuable item as it is simply a gesture intended to show gratitude. In rural areas, for example, people will offer farm products or even live animals to their doctors or schoolteachers.

Dress codes in Algeria vary from one region to another, from one class to another, from one ethnic group to another, and for a variety of reasons. For example in Berber-speaking Kabylia, women, especially in small villages, tend to wear a traditional dress patterned with multiple colors and ancient motifs in order to demonstrate their attachment to the Berber identity and local culture. Meanwhile men belonging to the desert-dwelling Tuaregs wear a veil. Men do not wear a veil in any other part of Algeria, and the Tuareg men are sometimes referred to as the blue men because the color of their clothing is often blue. Tuareg men wear the veil as a protection from sandstorms. There is a tendency nowadays among women throughout Algeria to wear the religious veil, the hijab. Not every pious woman wears a hijab, however. It depends on the woman's interpretation of the Koran and the degree of conservatism within her household or community. Older women also wear another type of veil called *haïk* that is unrelated to religion. This is a traditional veil, usually white in color, that is intended to keep the anonymity of women in public spaces. The *haïk* resembles the toga that Greek and Roman women wore in antiquity. Educated Algerian women or those from the upper classes tend to dress in Western-style clothing. As for men, most dress in Western style (pants and shirts or T-shirts), except for the strongly religious who tend to wear a djellaba. Shorts are not usually accepted in public spaces such as schools and administrative offices. People (both men and women) do, however, wear them in the streets or on the beach, especially during the summer.

Algerian families usually eat their meals together, especially dinner. Algerians love entertaining guests and usually treat their guests very well. Usually men and women are seated separately except when they are family members or very close friends. Guests are supposed to stay in the living room (or the dining room when it is time to eat) and should not venture into the kitchen. Unless hosts partake of alcohol, guests should not bring alcoholic drinks with them when invited to someone's house. Instead it is better to bring pastries or any homemade food. Hosts tend to insist that their guests take more and more food, so it is advisable to start with small portions and then take more when urged to do so. The expression *Bismillah* (In the name of God) is most often said before a meal, even by nonreligious people. *Alhamdollah* (Thank God) is pronounced at the end of the meal. These pronouncements are intended to show politeness and humility. It is also advisable for guests to ask if shoes must be removed at the entrance when they arrive, and guests should wash their hands before eating. In Algeria, guests do not have to arrive on time when they are invited to someone's house. Punctuality does not have the same importance and relevance as in countries such as the United States.

One of the most striking aspects of Algerian society is code-switching, during which people mix several languages into their conversation. For example, Algerians may use Algerian Arabic, called *derja*, together with French, standard Arabic, and, in some regions, a variety of Berber. Another notable aspect of Algerian verbal communication is the Algerian love of jokes and anecdotes. These might seem trivial, but the jokes and stories often carry a political or social connotation. Algerian culture is mostly oral and therefore meaning is usually hidden in puns, allusions, proverbs, and other figures of speech. People also like to talk about sports, traveling, education, cuisine, politics, and especially family.

There are several taboo topics in Algerian society. Some of these taboos are related to religion and others have more to do with cultural tradition. Pork and alcohol are proscribed in Islam, and that is why most Algerians do not consume these products. While one can easily find alcoholic drinks in stores, pork is rarely found in markets. Wild boars, however, are hunted in some places and some people indulge in eating boar meat. In addition, during Ramadan, the holy month of Islam, people are not allowed to eat in public from sunrise to sunset. Sex is another taboo topic in Algeria, so any discussion of sex is seen as very impolite and might even be taken as an insult. Cursing is generally frowned upon too.

Most Algerians are practicing Sunni Muslims and might easily take offense if their faith is criticized. As Muslims, Algerians are expected to pray five times every day. Men in particular are supposed to visit the mosque. Women have only just recently been allowed to go to mosques in Algeria. In addition, during the month of Ramadan Muslims should fast, give to charity, and accomplish the duty of pilgrimage to Mecca, called hajj, if financial means and health allow them to do so. Religion also influences modes of correct behavior at Algerian funerals. Most Algerians follow Islamic Sunni rites for death-related matters, such as funerals and burials. It is considered correct for men to accompany the deceased to his or her resting place in the cemetery and say religious chants throughout the procession. While at the cemetery, the imam stands by the corpse and reads the Koran, with mourners expected to listen and repeat some of the words and gestures performed by the imam. Women, on the other hand, are allowed to visit the tomb only on the day following the funeral.

Nabil Boudraa

Further Reading

Heggoy, Alf Andrew, and Philip Naylor Chiviges. *The Historical Dictionary of Algeria*, 2nd ed. Metuchen, NJ: Scarecrow, 1994.

McDougall, James, ed. *Nation, Society and Culture in North Africa*. London: Frank Cass, 2003.

Ruedy, John. *Modern Algeria: The Origins and Development of a Nation*. Bloomington: Indiana University Press, 2005.

Stora, Benjamin. *Algeria, 1830–2000: A Short History*. Ithaca, NY: Cornell University Press, 2001.

ARABIAN PENINSULA

The Arabian Peninsula is located in Western Asia and is composed of seven countries: the United Arab Emirates (UAE), Qatar, Bahrain, Kuwait in the east, Oman in the southeast, Yemen in the southwest, and Saudi Arabia in the middlemost region. Inhabitants of the Arabian Peninsula speak Arabic and have tribal Semitic ancestry. Because it is flanked by the Arabian Gulf, the Arabian Peninsula is often referred to as the Arabic word for "gulf"—*khaleej*, and Arabian people are commonly called *khaleeji*. Home to Mecca and Dubai, the Arabian Peninsula epitomizes both sacred tradition and modern invention. Arabs predominantly practice Islam, although the majority of the world's Muslim population is not Arab. Though the people of the Arabian Peninsula are often conceptualized as a monolithic group—and while there certainly are prevailing conventions throughout the region—each of the seven countries possesses its own unique kaleidoscope of historical legacies, present realities, and local customs.

Though generally viewed as more reserved and less outgoing than their North African neighbors, *khaleeji* people are well known for their warmth and exceptional hospitality. Two of the most common greetings in the Arabian Peninsula are *Hala w'ghala*, which is similar to saying "Hi," but directly translated means "Hello, you are precious," and *Hala w'marhaba,* meaning "Hello, welcome." *Asalaamu alaikum* (Peace be with you) is the most significant greeting in Islam, and although it is not the primary way Arabs greet each other in informal settings, it is also used quite regularly, particularly in more formal contexts. Due to extensive foreign language education in public and private schools and very large expatriate communities throughout the Arabian Peninsula, many *khaleeji* people speak English and will often greet foreigners in English. While titles of respect based on age and social class are very important in places like Egypt, they are far less common in the Arabian Gulf. It is extremely common, however, for individuals to be addressed in reference to their oldest child. For example, a man whose oldest child is a son named Ahmed will be almost exclusively referred to as *Abu Ahmed* (father of Ahmed). Ahmed's mother would be called *Umm Ahmed* (mother of Ahmed). *Khaleeji* people extend this tradition to their non-*khaleeji* friends and associates, and it is not uncommon for Europeans and North Americans living and working in the Arabian Gulf to also be called by their oldest child's name—Abu James, for example. In general, in the Arabian Gulf handshakes are reserved for people of the same sex. It is very common for Arabs to greet by kissing both cheeks, though this is also exclusively for individuals of the same sex. In some Arabian countries people kiss cheeks three times—right, left, right. Arab men also greet by touching noses, something very unique to the region. To show respect when greeting someone older or of high esteem, a man will touch his nose to the shoulder of the older, more esteemed gentleman.

The Arabian Gulf is famous for its traditional clothing practices. The majority of Arab men wear *thobes*, floor-length garments that are usually white in color. *Thobes* are accompanied by the *ghutra*, a male headscarf. A *ghutra*'s color, print, and the way it is draped indicate which Arabian country a man is from. For example, the Saudi Arabian *ghutra* is white with a red checkered pattern, while many Emirati men wear solid white scarves. Each country has different norms in how the scarves are tied, with Omani men normally wearing the scarf tight around the top of their head, while Kuwaiti men often wear their scarves long and loose. In all Arabian Peninsula countries, there are formal and informal versions of the *thobe* and *ghutra* with choice of fabric, fit, and draping dependent upon the occasion. Leather sandals are also commonly worn by *khaleeji* men. These sandals have a unique loop for the largest toe, then a large flap that crosses the body of the foot. Sandals are often made out of camel leather and custom crafted by local cobblers.

Similar to men in the Arabian Gulf, *khaleeji* women also wear traditional clothing. Like the *thobe*, Arab women typically wear the abaya, a floor-length garment often black in color. Abayas are usually accompanied by the hijab, a female headscarf. *Khaleeji* women are known for wearing black scarves and black abayas, though colorful scarves are becoming more popular in certain locations. Also like the *ghutra*, the way a woman wears her hijab is often a strong indicator of which country she is from. The niqab (face veil) is worn by some *khaleeji* women, though is only standard practice in Saudi Arabia, where it is considered part of Saudi cultural tradition. Though the vast majority of Arabs wear some variation of their traditional dress while in their home country, many adapt their clothing style when traveling abroad. *Khaleeji* people do not expect foreigners to wear traditional Arabian clothing when in the Arabian Gulf. In Saudi Arabia, however, it is customary for all women, including non-Saudis, to wear an abaya when in public.

The Arab peoples are famous for their remarkable levels of hospitality. Guests are treated with profound respect and generosity. Guests usually remove shoes upon entering an Arab home and bring chocolates or baked goods for the host and a small toy for children. Many Arabian homes have ornate, custom couches that sit very low to the ground. While most Arabian homes and newer commercial buildings have Western toilets, squat toilets are not uncommon. In accordance with Islam, most Arabs eat strictly with their right hands and do not drink alcohol or eat pork. It is common for Arabs to eat with their hands and to serve food on a large communal platter. Though this community style exists in some Arab restaurants, the majority of restaurants in the Arabian Gulf serve food based on Western traditions. Food is an important currency, and visitors are showered with large meals and a variety of desserts and drinks. Arab hosts will repeatedly try to feed guests, even if the guests insist they are full. Eventually the guests relent and eat more. Similarly, guests often tell their hosts they are ready to leave, only to have the hosts insist they stay longer. Rituals like these are a kind of game that allows guests and hosts to demonstrate their appreciation for one another. Unlike in some societies where it would be considered rude to force guests to eat when they are full or stay after they've expressed a desire to leave, in Arab countries and other parts of the Middle East, it is inhospitable not to do these things.

It is common for Arab men to be affectionate with each other, often holding hands, as a sign of friendship. When it comes to public norms, many non-Arab visitors are surprised to find the absence of line or queue systems for waiting in groups. People in the Arabian Gulf often form crowds and are served based on whoever is able to get to the front of the crowd first. Though this can be experienced as rude by those used to strict turn-taking practices, the lack of adherence to lines in *khaleeji* countries is not intended to offend, nor is it locally viewed as cheating.

Arabs of all ages and backgrounds use social media to keep in touch with friends and relatives and to stay abreast of current events. Arabs rely on social media, more than television, to obtain most of their political news and sports information. *Khaleeji* people, like many others in the Middle East, adore the sport of soccer and often have massive, impromptu celebrations in the streets if a beloved team wins a big match. Gulf people are also very nationalistic and national holidays are major, countrywide events. Due to these strong nationalistic sensibilities, locals can be easily offended by disparaging remarks about their home country, particularly if a foreign guest makes the remarks.

Marriage is the most important rite of passage in Arab society. Once someone reaches marital age (early to mid-twenties) their friends and family get very involved in the spouse selection process. In Arabian societies tribal affiliation is still extremely important. Though Arab societies are not generally constructed based on social class relating to wealth, Arab society is organized based on tribes. Arabs marry within their own tribe or from other tribes deemed compatible with one's own tribe. Young people are set up on blind dates until the right match is made. Based on the strong roles Islam plays in Arab culture, premarital sex and general physical affection outside of marriage are taboo. Instead of spending time together as boyfriend and girlfriend, men and women engage in a somewhat formal courting process before marriage, often in group settings with other friends and family members present.

Arab weddings are extremely lavish events. Brides wear ornate dresses and heavy makeup. Grooms wear formal *thobes*. Female wedding guests often have dresses specially made for the occasion. Weddings in the Arabian Peninsula are similar to what would be considered a wedding reception in the West. The religious ceremony takes place separately and the wedding is normally held in the evening as a joyful, raucous party. In some Gulf societies men and women are separated for the wedding party, with the bride and female guests wearing more revealing clothing than they would in public. Music and dancing are very important, with female guests generally dancing with each other, and male guests dancing together in groups. In the Arabian Gulf marriage and a new home go hand in hand, and couples often delay marriage until they are able to purchase a nice house.

In Arabia it is not uncommon for cousins to marry each other. Though this practice is highly taboo in many parts of the world, it is viewed as quite normal in the Middle East. It would be offensive for tourists or other visitors to express disapproval or make jokes about cousin marriage. Parents are highly respected in Arabian society. It is considered profoundly offensive to insult or joke about parents, especially mothers. It is also considered very disrespectful to make jokes about a man's wife or to tell a man his wife is attractive. It is less taboo for a woman to compliment or joke about someone else's husband. Additionally, inflammatory remarks or negative statements about religion, religious figures, or tribes are highly taboo. Although they strongly adhere to their own cultural norms, *khaleeji* people are generally very accustomed to foreigners and are not easily offended by a well-intended faux pas.

Emily R. Sutcliffe

Further Reading

Al-Semmari, Fahd. *A History of the Arabian Peninsula*. London: I. B. Tauris, 2009.
Hourani, Albert. *A History of the Arab People*. Cambridge, MA: Harvard University Press, 2002.
Nydell, Margaret. *Understanding Arabs: A Guide for Modern Times*. London: Intercultural Press, 2005.
Said, Edward. *Orientalism*. New York: Random House, 1978.

ARGENTINA

Argentina is a federal republic located in the southern half of South America. The country shares land borders with Chile, Bolivia, Paraguay, Brazil, and Uruguay, while it is also bordered by the South Atlantic Ocean to the east and the waterway known as the Drake Passage to the south. Argentina also claims sovereignty over part of Antarctica, the Falkland Islands, and South Georgia and the South Sandwich Islands. Argentina has a mainland area of 1,073,500 square miles, making it the eighth-largest country in the world. Argentina is also the second-largest country in Latin America and the largest Spanish-speaking country in the world. The Spanish colonized Argentina during the sixteenth century but the country gained independence in the nineteenth century. In that century Argentina also experienced a civil war, after which the country was established as a federation of provinces with Buenos Aires enshrined as the capital city. After this Argentina enjoyed relative stability and experienced waves of European immigration that shaped the country's culture and society. Today Argentina is one of the world's top developing nations and a member of the G-20 major economies. The majority of Argentinians are Roman Catholics, though many do not actively practice their religion. There are also significant numbers of Jews and Protestants in Argentina, while New Age and Eastern religions are also becoming popular among Argentina's middle and upper classes. In particular, Islam is gaining in popularity in Argentina.

An air-kiss on the cheek (without touching skin) is the standard greeting for both men and women in Argentina, though in very formal situations people shake hands. Handshakes between Argentinian men tend to be brief and firm, while handshakes between a man and a woman or between two women should be softer. Men should never instigate a handshake with a woman and must remove their gloves if they wish to shake a woman's hand. Conversely, a woman may keep on her glove if shaking a man's hand. In informal situations, a hug may take place between Argentinians.

When meeting, Argentinians will usually greet the oldest or most senior person first. It is essential to employ the correct title when making introductions, using *Señor* (Mr.), *Señora* (Mrs.), and *Señorita* (used for unmarried, young women) followed by the person's family name. If a woman's marital status is unknown, then she should be addressed as *Señorita*. First names should not be used to refer to someone, unless the person has stated it is okay to do so. However, if meeting an older person or someone who is well respected, then the term *Don* (masculine) or *Doña* (feminine) may be used followed by the person's first name. This form of address is used to demonstrate that the person is greatly revered, and it is imperative to use the form of address followed by the person's first name, such as Don Manuel rather than merely Don. Argentinians often practice third-party introductions, meaning a host/hostess will introduce visitors to other people present rather than allowing guests to introduce themselves. Typical greetings include "Buenos dias" (Good morning), "Buenas tardes" (Good afternoon), and "Buenas noches" (Good evening). When leaving, it is considered courteous to bid farewell to each person individually.

Argentinians tend to place great significance on appearance, and may judge people on their personal presentation. Business clothing is considered to be stylish, but also formal and somewhat unadventurous. Men typically wear dark business suits, while women sport business suits or more formal dresses. Both men and women carry good-quality accessories. Guests, when invited to someone's home for a meal, should wear dressy clothing. Men should wear a jacket and tie while women should wear either a skirt and blouse or an elegant dress. Guests to a dinner party should aim to arrive 30 to 45 minutes late, as punctuality is not usual in Argentina. The host/hostess will indicate where a guest should sit, and there may also be a seating plan. Table manners are Continental style, meaning that when eating, Argentinians hold their fork in the left hand and their knife in the right hand. It is considered polite to refrain from eating until the host indicates that dining should commence. Similarly a toast will be said before guests can start to drink. It is thought fairly bad mannered for guests to pour wine, so if possible a guest should let the host pour the drinks.

When eating, hands should be visible and elbows should be kept off the table. Argentinians also consider it proper to leave some food on the plate when finished eating. To indicate that one has eaten enough, he should lay his knife and fork across his plate with the tines facing down and the handles facing towards the right.

To thank an Argentinian for their hospitality, it is typical for guests to bring a small gift for the hostess. Gifts of alcoholic spirits are often well received because Argentina places high import taxes on bottles of imported spirits. Conversely, it is considered rude to bring a hostess knives or scissors, as these are symbolic of a severed relationship. The day after the dinner party, guests should telephone their host to say thank you.

Argentinian cuisine is very keen on beef and pasta with most restaurants offering a number of beef and pasta dishes. Many Argentinians serve fresh pasta for Sunday lunch, which is usually a family event to which extended family are invited. In Argentina, lunch is typically served between 12:30 p.m. and 2:00 p.m. In the past, lunch was the main meal of the day, but because of modern work schedules Argentinians are eating increasingly lighter lunches. Argentinians tend to take an afternoon break for tea or coffee that they accompany with sandwiches, cakes, cookies, and pastries. Dinner is typically served from 9:00 p.m. to 10:00 p.m. Popular Argentinian meeting places include the cafés that lie at the heart of modern Argentinian urban culture. Here people meet to enjoy espresso coffees and tea as well as to discuss politics and soccer. Argentinians often attend barbecues where dishes such as *locro* (a stew of corn, meat, chorizo sausage, pumpkin, and sweet potato) and empanadas (filled bread or pastry) are served. The Spanish savory rice dish paella is also served at social gatherings. As a wine-producing nation, Argentinians typically serve wine at social events and festivities. The South American drink, maté, may also be served at social gatherings in Argentina. Maté is a caffeine-rich infusion prepared by steeping dried leaves of yerba maté in hot water and is defined by Argentinian law as the national infusion.

Spanish may be the main language of Argentina, but this form of Spanish is heavily influenced by Italian, which is the second language of Argentina followed by German and English. Argentinians typically address each other using the colloquial form of the singular "you," *vos*. This is the equivalent of *tu* that is used in other Spanish-speaking countries. In order to show respect to superiors and elders, Argentinians may also use the more formal form of "you," *usted*. When conversing, people tend to stand much closer together than they do in the United States. People may also make physical contact with each other when talking, while also making direct eye contact. The direct glance is used to indicate that they are giving the

A scene in the historic Café Tortoni in Buenos Aires, Argentina. The café is an important meeting place in Argentinian urban culture. (Sergio Schnitzler/Dreamstime.com)

Culture Shock! ⊕

Pato: Playing Polo with a Duck

Pato (Spanish for duck) is a team ball game similar to polo, basketball, and rugby, played on horseback. In 1953 President Juan Perón declared *pato* the national sport of Argentina. Today the sport is popular with *gauchos* (the Argentinian equivalent to cowboys) and among Argentina's upper classes. *Pato* developed in 1610 when people in rural Argentina held competitions in which two teams on horseback from neighboring ranches would meet at the boundary of their properties and maneuver a live duck toward a predetermined point serving as a goal. *Pato* thrived despite being banned many times by the clergy and politicians. These bans were lifted eventually and in 1941 the sport's governing body was established. Nowadays two teams of four players on horseback maneuver a six-handled leather ball through hoops instead of manhandling a duck.

Victoria Williams

other person their undivided attention. Furthermore, Argentinians often gaze into each other eyes, and it is quite usual for Argentinian men to make flirtatious remarks (*piropos*) to women who are walking past.

Argentinian society is focused on relationships, so people build and maintain networks of business contacts and family and friends whom they call upon for help. It is customary in Argentina that if a person requests help from someone else, then the first person will need to repay the favor at some time in the future. Part of the Argentinian focus on networking results in name dropping and even nepotism. In Argentina, these do not carry the negative connotations that they may elsewhere. Instead, Argentinians see name dropping and nepotism as demonstrating that they like to do business with people that they know. On the whole, Argentinians prefer to interact in person rather than in writing, online, or on the telephone.

Argentinians may often seem to make very personal, teasing yet somewhat disapproving comments regarding people's weight, appearance, age, and habits. While such comments may not be welcome and might be taboo in the West, the comments are not intended to cause offense. Instead the comments are the Argentinian way of making amiable conversation. In general, Argentinians also love to talk about opera, food, children, and soccer, while women also like to discuss fashion. Argentinians also like to talk to visitors about the tango—the dance that originated in the slums of Buenos Aires. Taboo topics of conversation include asking an Argentinian if they belong to an indigenous group (Argentinians are proud of their European heritage), work colleagues, politics, and Argentina's relationship with Chile and Bolivia. It is also best to avoid discussing the British with Argentinians, due to the disputed sovereignty of the Falkland Islands, over which the two countries fought during the 10-week long Falklands War in 1982. Indeed, it is worth noting that Argentinians refer to the disputed archipelago not as the Falkland Islands, but as Islas Malvinas.

Victoria Williams

Further Reading

Commisceo Global Consultancy Ltd. "Argentina Guide." *Commisceo Global*. 2016. http://www.commisceo-global.com/country-guides/argentina-guide. Accessed January 5, 2017.

Ferradas, Carmen Alicia. "Argentina." *Countries and Their Cultures: Culture of Argentina.* http://www.everyculture.com/A-Bo/Argentina.html. Accessed January 5, 2017.

Foster, Dean. *Global Etiquette Guide to Mexico and Latin America.* New York: John Wiley & Sons, 2002.

ARMENIA

Located in the heart of Transcaucasia and landlocked within the 440-mile-wide strip between the Black Sea and the Caspian Sea, Armenia has long been a crossroads of culture. Accordingly, the etiquette and taboos of Armenia simultaneously look both east to Asia and west to Europe, frequently combining the two, while also displaying considerable variation. For instance, customs will vary in rural villages versus urban centers and within the Republic of Armenia versus throughout the Armenian diaspora.

In Armenia, friendships—like family ties—typically last a lifetime, and first impressions are important. When two men meet, they will shake hands and then exchange a kiss on the cheek or an air-kiss (without touching skin) if they know each other well. Otherwise they will simply shake hands. When two women meet, they will typically greet each other not only with a hug, even if they are not yet well acquainted, but also with a kiss on the cheek, especially in traditional households. When men and women meet, the man will, typically, initiate the handshake. Men and women who know each other well or who are related will often hug each other lightly, followed by a discreet kiss on the cheek. In conversation, most Armenians will use each other's first names unless they are addressing a person in authority or someone who is much older and wish to show more respect. The suffix *jan* (meaning "dear" and pronounced like *djohn*) is often attached to a first name—e.g., *Arsen jan* or *Hasmik jan*—as a term of endearment. When getting to know someone, it is wise to avoid discussing issues of politics, gender, or religion. However, personal matters, such as one's family background or marital status, are not considered taboo topics even when talking with someone for the first time. When meeting foreigners, Armenians often display great pride in their history, language, culture, food and drink, and land. Foreigners should never dispute such claims.

Looking good is an important value of Armenian cultural identity, so Armenians typically wear clothing that is always immaculately clean and respectably conservative. Armenians believe that the way one appears in public represents not only one's personal values, but also the values of one's family and culture. Accordingly, many Armenians would never go out in public wearing torn jeans or looking sloppy. Traditional ethnic attire—such as long-skirted dresses and head adornments or colorful sashes around the waist—may be worn on special occasions, especially in rural areas, but not frequently; contemporary Western-style clothes are the norm.

Socializing in groups and making friends are two extremely vital aspects of Armenian life. In particular home hospitality is important to Armenians. Guests should plan to arrive on time or just a few minutes late and should bring a small gift, such as cognac or chocolate. If taking flowers as a gift, guests should bring only an odd number because even numbers are associated with death and funerals. Moreover yellow flowers specifically mean "I miss you." Outdoor shoes are typically removed when entering a private home, but this is not a hard and fast rule. Formal meals with guests often include predinner snacks, such as nuts; *dolma* (cabbage leaves or grape leaves stuffed with meat); soup, such as *bozbash* (lamb soup); *lavash* (flat bread); a main meat course, such as *khoravats* (meat that is marinated and grilled); fresh fruit; and dessert—all washed down with frequent toasts of vodka, wine, or Armenian cognac. The diners are seated at a table and employ the standard European method of fork in left hand and knife in right hand. Touching food with the left hand is discouraged, but eating plenty of food—and all of the food on one's plate—is strongly encouraged. If there is any food left on the table, it may be given to guests to take home as leftovers.

In more Western cultures, keeping an "arm's length" distance is considered polite among individuals. However, Armenians typically move closer to one another—especially among friends and family—and may often touch each other without intending to convey a physical attraction. Members of the same sex may hold each other's hand on the street, even in large groups, without the slightest hint of homosexuality. In contrast, Armenians who are gay or lesbian would not hold each other's hand in public because traditional attitudes in Armenia are still somewhat resistant to acknowledging same-sex couples. Indeed gender distinctions and family ties affect many aspects of etiquette in Armenia. Since marriage and raising a family are expected of every Armenian, young men and young women will go out on formal dates, rather than the casual "hanging out" that is more common in the United States. Also, because Armenia is predominantly patriarchal, men customarily initiate the dates. If a couple continues dating beyond 12 months, marriage is regarded as inevitable. Although arranged marriages are now relatively rare in Armenia, the parents of a prospective bride and groom are still very much involved in wedding preparations. These may include the engagement negotiations, a formal party to celebrate the engagement, the wedding service itself (typically taking place in the sacred space of an Armenian Apostolic Church), and a postservice celebration in the groom's home—all of which are designed to reinforce family status and traditional gender roles.

James I. Deutsch

Further Reading

Abrahamian, Levon, and Nancy Sweezy, eds. *Armenian Folk Arts, Culture, and Identity*. Bloomington: Indiana University Press, 2001.

"Armenia." 2008. Culture Crossing Guide. http://guide.culturecrossing.net/basics_business _student.php?id=11. Accessed May 10, 2015.

Dresser, Norine. *Multicultural Manners: New Rules of Etiquette for a Changing Society*. New York: John Wiley & Sons, 1991.

Monger, George P. *Marriage Customs of the World: An Encyclopedia of Dating Customs and Wedding Traditions*, 2nd ed. Santa Barbara, CA: ABC-CLIO, 2013.

Petrosian, Irina, and David Underwood. *Armenian Food: Fact, Fiction and Folklore*. Bloomington, IN: Yerkir Publishing, 2006.

Solomon, Susan. *Culture Smart! Armenia: The Essential Guide to Customs & Culture*. London: Kuperard, 2010.

AUSTRALIA

Australia's history as both a penal colony and a remote outpost of the British Empire attracted immigrants with a sense of adventure and a desire to succeed based on one's own merits, as well as not a few individuals who disliked law and authority. This particular history has shaped the modern Australian's attitude towards life as well as the country's culture and etiquette. Australians tend to be strong individualists and dislike standing on ceremony, and they possess a fierce egalitarianism in which everyone, no matter what their social status, is considered equal. These attributes make Australia a country where people are typically polite but not formal, and where individuality, directness, and equality are all highly valued. This is reflected in the way that although Australian business cards will often contain a long list of titles and postnominals (initials of degrees and titles placed after the name), Australians tend to avoid titles in speech and quickly move to a first-name basis. It may be considered pretentious to refer repeatedly to one's title.

Australians value politeness, and appreciate proper greetings, responses, and words used in making and acknowledging requests. This means, in most situations, the use of greetings such as "Hello" or "Good day," and words such as "please," "thank you," and "excuse me." Nevertheless, Australians might dislike requests that seem to be too imploring, whiny, or demanding. To this end it is perhaps best for people to be polite, but not overly fawning. "G'day," the quintessential Australian greeting, is commonly used by Australians, but non-Australian visitors should avoid using this term as doing so sounds too much like one is pretending to be Australian. Australians shake hands when meeting, and handshakes are normally expected to be firm. In Australia it is considered impolite to make eye contact when shaking hands and when speaking to someone. Australians do not normally resort to other physical greetings, and gestures such as backslapping should be avoided.

As befitting their relaxed lifestyle and generally warm climate, Australians tend to dress very casually outside business and professional settings. In business and professional circumstances more formal clothing, such as suits and ties for men, are used. In casual situations in warmer areas it is common to see people dressed very skimpily indeed. In general, Australians dress very much like Americans, with shorts, T-shirts, sleeveless shirts, and work wear being commonly seen.

Table manners in most situations resemble those of the United States, with the notable exception of holding fork and knife, which is done in the European way, with the fork held in the left hand and the knife in the right. Australians often host dinners and barbecues, and these are usually of the potluck kind, where guests are expected to bring their own meat and drink. Invitations to such events, especially to barbecues or cookouts, will usually specify this if applicable. At such gatherings, the host will provide side dishes, while the guests bring their own meat and beverages. It is customary to leave any unused food or beverages with the host. If one is invited to a dinner where the host provides all of the food, it is still polite to bring a bottle of wine or other gift. In restaurants, each diner usually pays for his or her own meal, reflecting Australians' sense of individualism and desire not to be in debt to anyone. If given poor service in a restaurant, Australians are unlikely to complain, as this will sound too much like whining; instead, people will avoid that restaurant in the future. Tipping is not very common in Australia, as service staff are paid well, and thus diners should not expect that the promise of a large tip will predispose service staff in their favor.

Australia is a country where both beer and wine are drunk frequently, and these beverages often form a bonding element in social life. Australian pubs, or bars, are centers of social gathering. When drinking at a pub, one member of the group will pay for, or "shout," the first round of drinks. Another member will shout the second round, and so forth until all group members have paid for a round of drinks. Not to shout a round is considered very antisocial. Beer glasses come in various sizes in different Australian states, so one should learn what the names of these glass sizes are before ordering.

Australians speak English, but it is of a distinctive, very direct and unique kind filled with slang expressions. Australians tend to use British words and spellings (such as "bonnet" instead of "hood" on a car, and "lift" instead of "elevator"). They also have their own unique words, such as "ute" (short for utility vehicle) instead of "pickup truck," "arvo" as a slang expression for "afternoon," and "crook" as an expression meaning "sick." Some words and expressions commonly and properly used by Americans can have obscene meanings in Australia: "stuffed," "fanny" (as in fanny pack), and "root" (meaning to cheer for a team) should all be avoided. Likewise, the gesture of two fingers held up in a "V" position should only be done with the palm facing out; to make this gesture with the palm facing in is the equivalent of "giving someone the finger" in the United States. Most Australians very much dislike any talk that can come across as bragging or whining. Anyone who does so is usually cut down to size with a sarcastic response. Australian humor is itself quite sarcastic and biting, and visitors should be aware that Australians enjoy teasing others and should not be offended by this. The proper response to such teasing is to respond in kind. Australians often call each other "mate," a term usually (but not always) indicating friendliness. Visitors should avoid this term unless they understand the intricacies of its use.

Australia's indigenous population is collectively known as Aboriginal people, the term "Aborigine" being dated and vaguely impolite. If visiting an Aboriginal community or site, visitors should always show respect and follow the guidelines suggested by the locals. It is taboo to refer to dead people by name. Visitors should always ask permission before taking photos of people or sites, and should avoid touching things or climbing in places where this is prohibited by Aboriginal custom.

Michael Pretes

Further Reading

Broome, Richard. *Aboriginal Australians: A History Since 1788*. Sydney: Allen and Unwin, 2010.
Bryson, Bill. *In a Sunburned Country*. New York: Broadway Books, 2001.
Dewi, Thomas Ap. *A Is for Australia: The Essential A to Z Guide to the Culture, Customs, People, and Paces on the World's Deadliest Continent*. Amazon.com (digital book), 2014.
Morgan, Kenneth. *Australia: A Very Short Introduction*. Oxford: Oxford University Press, 2012.
Penney, Barry. *Culture Smart! Australia: The Essential Guide to Customs & Culture*. London: Kuperard, 2016.

B

BALKAN PENINSULA, WESTERN

The Balkan Peninsula is immediately recognizable by its mountainous landscape and the ruins of Roman and Hellenic arenas, baths, and colonnades lying next to Renaissance palaces and minarets. In this instance the Western Balkan Peninsula is defined as including the countries of Albania, Bosnia and Herzegovina, Croatia, Macedonia, Montenegro, Serbia, and Slovenia. It may seem an impossible task to define the term "Western Balkans," however, for Slovenes do not consider themselves as belonging to a Balkan nation, and neither do many Croatians. They may be right. A glance at the origin of the name "Balkan" could provide a key to understanding the problem. In Turkish, *balkan* means a mountain, which would suggest that the Balkans cover the European territories of the former Ottoman Empire. Yet, Slovenia, Croatia, and Montenegro were never a part of the empire. The complexity of this western part of southeastern Europe is truly amazing. A hundred million people live there; of this population, a third speak Slavic languages; 24 million speak Romanian; Greek, Hungarian, and Turkish are spoken by 10 million each; and 6.5 million speak Albanian (an ancient Illyrian language). Three million Roma people speak their own language. In other words, this is a region with a population of 70 million people of Slavic, Illyrian, Greek, and Turkish origin, professing Roman Catholicism, Orthodox Christianity, or Islam, writing in three different alphabets—Greek, Latin, and Cyrillic—and speaking languages belonging to five different language families. There is no other place in Europe boasting such a kaleidoscope of ethnicities and cultures, yet there is no other place torn by such historical rivalries and animosities, either. This is a region influenced by the Roman Empire, Byzantium, the Slavic kingdoms, the Ottomans, Austro-Hungarians, and Russia. Now it is undergoing a return to its European roots and becoming a member of the global family of nations. Some of the Balkan countries like Slovenia, Romania, and Bulgaria have already joined the European Union, while the rest are aspiring to membership.

The Balkan region is a hospitable place, and the people tend to be warm and helpful. Most young Serbs, Macedonians, Croatians, Slovenes, and Bosnians speak English, while the educated citizens of the Albanian cities speak Italian and Greek, so communication is not difficult. When meeting people in informal environments, common greetings used are "Hello" and "How are you?" while in more formal settings people would say "Good day" or "Good evening," shake hands, make eye contact, introduce themselves with their full name, and say "Pleased to meet you." Firm handshakes are almost obligatory when meeting casually or formally. When seated, it is polite to stand up when greeting other people, particularly women and older individuals. Kissing is a widespread form of greeting among friends, both men and women. For example, in Serbia the custom is to give three kisses on alternating cheeks, or to kiss only once when you meet someone regularly. Making and maintaining eye contact is very important in any greeting situation; lack of eye contact is often considered rude. It is considered polite to chat with strangers on a bus, a bus stop, or a park bench. Offering personal information and asking personal questions is considered a gesture of politeness and good upbringing. Balkan people might appear quite straightforward and blunt to Westerners; however, this is not nosiness but rather curiosity and desire to learn about other cultures.

In a multiethnic, multicultural region like the Western Balkans it is natural to expect a variety of clothing styles. Before World War I one could determine a person's ethnic background by their typical attire. For example, rural Greeks and Albanians wore *fustanela*—a short, pleated skirt over tight pants, while women wore elaborately decorated and embroidered aprons and jackets on top of loose white robes. Macedonians, Serbs, and Montenegrins were recognized by the cuts and colors of their richly embroidered clothes. However, with the advent of ready-made clothes and fashions coming from Europe, Balkan people started to dress just like the rest of their European peers. Women are typically proud of their beauty and are always very well dressed, especially those living in the cities. Men also like to dress fashionably. Designers like Bosnian Haad and Croatian-born Ottavio Missoni have made a name for themselves and the region as a whole.

Culture Shock! ⊕

Besa: How Albanian Hospitality Saved Jewish Refugees in World War II

Albanians have a very strong code of ethics based on the concept of *Besa*, literally meaning "to keep the promise." The key tenet is that anyone acting according to *Besa* keeps their word to the extent that they can be trusted implicitly, even in life and death situations. To this end Albanians offer help, kindness, and courteousness to guests. *Besa* is also based in part on the Islamic tenet that saving a life is a blessed act. After Hitler's rise to power, many Jews fled to Albania, which at that time had a tiny Jewish population. During the German occupation of Albania, the Albanian people refused to comply with German orders to turn over lists of Jews residing in their country. Furthermore, various Albanian government departments gave Jewish families fake documents that allowed the families to blend in with the rest of the population. The help afforded the Jews by Albania was based on the belief in *Besa*. According to Yad Vashem, Israel's official memorial to Holocaust victims, no Jew was turned over to Nazi authorities in Albania during Albania's occupation. To date Yad Vashem has given the title Righteous Among the Nations to 68 Albanians. This title is used by Israel to describe non-Jews who risked their lives during the Holocaust to save Jews from the Nazis.

Victoria Williams

The Western Balkan region is predominantly secular and nonreligious despite the huge diversity of faiths—Catholics, Orthodox Christians, Protestants, Sunni, the Albanian Muslims, atheists, and Jews. In 1967 Albania became the only country in the world to be legally proclaimed atheist, yet the Orthodox Church is respected throughout the region as the guardian of tradition and the defender of national identities. For this reason it is important that people dress and act respectfully when visiting churches in the Balkan Peninsula. For instance, when visiting churches or monasteries women should wear long sleeves and long skirts and cover their hair. Men should remove their hats and all visitors are expected to be modest, quiet, and refrain from loud conversations, laughter, or shouting. Taking photographs is generally unacceptable; one might need to seek special permission to do so. There is an old tradition of buying a few candles and lighting them. In addition to religious motivations, this generates income for the custodians. Also, before entering mosques visitors should remove their shoes and socks. Additionally, visitors should not walk in front of worshippers who are in the act of praying.

Balkan hospitality is fabled. For example, Albania has adhered for centuries to an ancient code of conduct, called *kanuns*, based on honor and hospitality. The *kanuns* postulated 38 rules on how to treat a guest, even including blood revenge if the guest was murdered while under the host's roof. Hospitality is still highly regarded everywhere, and people are great hosts. It is important to offer the best

An Albanian family celebrates Dita e Verës, the Summer Day festival, in Elbasan, Albania. Social events in Balkan countries are typically marked by eating, drinking, and entertainment. (Luis Dafos/Alamy Stock Photo)

food and drink, and the best room will be at the disposal of the valued guest. This emphasis on eating, drinking, and entertainment is a key feature of Balkan identity and the pillar of all sociocultural rituals like weddings, funerals, and everything in between. When a group of people goes out to a bar or a restaurant, the bill is usually paid in rounds, or split roughly among everyone. If a guest is invited to dinner, the host will pay the whole bill; any attempt to share it will be considered rude and offensive. However, as the Balkan countries have been opening up to the rest of the world, these customs change, too.

The cuisine of the region is a mix of Mediterranean, Turkish, and Central European influences and is very rich in proteins. Pork is the meat of choice in Serbia, Macedonia, and Montenegro, while beef and lamb are favored in the other countries of the region. Horsemeat is eaten in Slovenia and Serbia, but not in the other countries. The Balkans is an agriculturally rich region, and local ingredients are mostly organic. Poor countries like Albania and Macedonia have no money for pesticides, and there is no industrial meat farming in the region. Locally made beer, wine, and the widely popular plum or grape brandy (*rakija*) are served everywhere, and usually accompany lunch and dinner. However, getting drunk, especially for women, is highly objectionable despite the fact that alcohol flows freely almost anywhere in the Balkans. The evening stroll in the city square, hanging out with friends, and heated group discussions in bars and cafés are characteristic features of Balkan culture. Men often sit, talk, and have coffee while women tend to do the shopping, cooking, and housekeeping. The younger generation may be as trendy as their peers anywhere in the West, but family life tends to be very traditional, with male and female roles clearly separated. Balkan societies are family oriented and the extended family forms a tight-knit and highly dependable network of support. What would look like nepotism to members of meritocratic cultures is just the normal way of society in the Balkan region. Extended families maintain close relations at all times; they always come together at three important life events: marriages, births, and deaths in the family. It is considered highly disrespectful not to invite all relatives to a wedding, or to fail to inform them of the birth of a child or the passing of an immediate family member. Weddings tend to be flashy, noisy, and high spirited with both families expected to demonstrate their generosity by overspending and providing endless amounts of food and alcohol, live orchestras, and expensive gifts for the newlyweds.

The conservative, macho culture of the Balkans has traditionally supported sex taboos, from the Albanian cult of virginity and its sworn virgins to the sex workers lured by criminals with the promise of a decent job and a decent life in the West. Strictly supported by a culture of prejudice, silence, and shame, sex taboos are still the predominant attitude. From sex before marriage to children out of wedlock to decisions not to have children—many traditional prohibitions retain much of their power. Yet, with the dissolution of socialist Yugoslavia and the democratization of communist Albania, Balkan peoples have started to lose their reticence, and this is quite visible in the spheres of entertainment and advertising where scantily clad, silicone-enhanced beauties adorn the pop stage, billboards, and magazines throughout the region. Homosexuality has always been looked down upon in the

Western Balkans, and is still considered to be taboo. There are three reasons for this: the region's history, the conservative traditions, and the strong macho culture. For centuries the only outlet for individual expression and a sense of freedom was the traditional family unit where a person felt safe, spoke their mind, and built traditional relationships. Everything outside that unit, whether an individual or an institution, had to be treated with caution. Although times have changed, political and economic troubles have kept Balkan families very tight and conservative. However, Slovenia is an exception, for in March 2015 the country adopted a law allowing same-sex couples to marry and adopt children.

Other taboos focus on the Balkans' troubled history. Painful memories from the distant and more recent past have turned the subject of local politics into one of the Balkans' conversational taboos. Serbs still feel uneasy about their Croatian neighbors; more than 200,000 Serbs were expelled from their homes in Croatia during the 1992 war and still live in subsidized dwellings. Kosovo is another very sensitive issue for Serbs as it is largely considered to be the historical heartland of Serbia. Another grudge Serbs have is against Western media and coverage of the turmoil in the wake of the disintegration of the Yugoslavian federation in the 1990s. Many Serbians feel demonized and inaccurately portrayed. On the other hand, Croatians, Bosnians, and Slovenes still remember the devastation of the wars in the wake of Yugoslavia's disintegration.

For Balkan people uttering the word *death* was feared to cause someone to die, so it became taboo to say the word. The turbulent history of the region—invasions, wars, famine, migrations—left many widowed and orphaned. "Black," as death is called there, has been one of the strongest taboos. The name likely originated in ancient times, when the Thracians placed white and black stones under the head of the deceased, white for their happy days and black for their ill-fated days. It is a custom that still survives in countries like Albania and Romania. Death was described as a wedding, especially if the deceased was single. In Albania widows were not allowed to remarry.

Taboo words are often quite bizarre. Albanians, for example, never use the word for wolf, for fear that one might turn up. Instead, they use a contraction of a sentence meaning "May God close his mouth." Another Albanian taboo-contraction is the word used for fairy, which means "May God increase their round-dances."

Juliana Tzvetkova

Further Reading

Hemon, Aleksandar. *The Book of My Lives*. New York: Farrar, Straus and Giroux, 2013.

Kadare, Ismail. *Chronicle in Stone*. Melbourne: Arcade Publishing, 2011.

Kaplan, Robert. *Balkan Ghosts: A Journey Through History*. New York: Picador, 2005.

Merrill, Christopher. *Only the Nails Remain: Scenes from the Balkan Wars*. Lanham, MD: Rowman and Littlefield, 2001.

West, Rebecca. *Black Lamb and Grey Falcon: A Journey through Yugoslavia*. New York: Penguin Classics, 2007.

Zmukic, Lara. *Culture Smart! Serbia: The Essential Guide to Customs & Culture*. London: Kuperard, 2012.

BANGLADESH

Historically, people of different cultures arrived and settled in Bangladesh, located in southeast Asia and almost entirely surrounded by India. As a result, Bangladeshis developed a highly diverse culture embodying norms, values, beliefs, and practices from many sources. Religions, particularly Islam and Hinduism, stand out as the most influential sources of cultural elements in Bangladesh. Another important source is the hierarchical social organization based on the caste system. Not only do these religious and social categorizations dictate what is allowed, encouraged, and awarded, but also what is prohibited, discouraged, and punished. This fact is apparent in the etiquette and manners among the Bangladeshis.

Meetings generally involve persons of the same sex unless it is a formal meeting. Bangladeshis are known for not showing up on time regardless of whether the meeting is informal involving family and friends or formal with professional people. Also, there is a cultural pattern that those relatively more powerful would be the ones delaying, as this indirectly demonstrates their higher social status. Those waiting are usually people with lower status, vis-à-vis the guests. The hosts keep waiting without complaint as a way to show honor to the guests. Except formal meetings outside of the house, guests usually bring sweets as gifts. Since the majority of Bangladeshis are Muslims, it is customary to exchange greetings by saying *As-salamu-alaikum* and replying with *Oalaikum-as-salam*. Those of Hindu religion use *Nomoskar* to welcome guests. Relatives and friends of the same sex often hug each other. Handshaking is also practiced, especially in formal settings. This involves individuals of the same sex. However, handshaking with a Bangladeshi woman is sometimes permitted only if initiated by the woman. Unlike in Western cultures, the perception of personal space is less of an issue in Bangladesh. Bangladeshis usually stand close when speaking to someone of the same gender and often touch hands. Addressing others by name is a privilege of older individuals. Bangladeshis use various suffix endings referring to their relations (e.g., uncle, aunt, brother, sister, etc.) when addressing older people. They often address educated and wealthy men as "Sir" and women as "Madam" to denote respect. Calling by first name is generally practiced when elder relatives address the younger ones, and also among peers.

The tropical climate characterized by torrential rains and high humidity has left its marks on the appearance and dress of the Bangladeshis. Men generally wear *kurta* or *fatua* (two pieces of semicasual clothing traditionally for men) on social, cultural, and religious holidays. At home, most wear *lungi* (a long, skirtlike cloth covering body parts below waist level) as casual wear both in the villages and towns. However, wearing *lungi* outside of the house is not considered proper except by the farmers and the poor. Most men wear shirts and pants or suits on formal occasions. The most common dresses for girls and women are *shalwar kameez* and saris. Unmarried girls generally wear *shalwar kameez* and married women wear saris, although all of them wear colorful saris on social and cultural occasions. Recently, many professional women have begun to wear formal suits instead of saris in their workplaces.

Contrary to the identity of Bangladesh as a poor nation, Bangladeshis are very generous in treating their guests. This is due, perhaps, to the cultural belief that guests bring blessings from God. There is a saying among the Bengali Hindus, *Atithi narayan*, meaning the guest is one of the supreme gods in Hinduism. Even if a stranger asks for drinking water, Bangladeshis offer sweets or other home-made snacks in addition to the water. Generally, Bangladeshis offer a range of spicy dishes prepared with rice, fish, lentils, and vegetables on the dinner table. The number of dishes often goes beyond what the guests can manage to eat in one sitting.

Bangladeshi culture involves a number of unique table manners. Generally, men and women eat separately. Rather than spoons and forks, they use their fingers to eat food. Therefore, they wash their hands before and after eating. Main courses are offered in large dishes to share. Customarily, the guests are served first. If there is no guest, the elders are served first and everybody waits until the guests or the elders begin eating. While multiple servings are offered, it is considered good to refuse the second offering. It is expected that one finishes all the food on one's plate. Although a few Bengalis may be found licking their hands after eating, it is considered to be bad manners. Unlike many cultures, Bangladeshis offer fruits as soon as the guests arrive. The dinner ends with varieties of sweets and desserts made primarily of rice and milk products.

Bengali is the mother tongue of Bangladeshis. However, English is widely spoken in the big cities. In most social interactions, Bangladeshis adhere to the social hierarchies in both verbal and nonverbal communications. For instance, it is considered improper to outright refuse to obey orders or to accept suggestions from older persons. Showing a stern face without a smile is regarded as a sign of maturity and seriousness. Consequently, Bangladeshis use varieties of indirect techniques in effective communication. For example, they often use phrases like "We will try," "That may be difficult," or "We will have to give that some thought," which sound positive, but the actual meaning is negative. Similarly, they sometimes use silence as a way to communicate their disapproval or disagreement. Therefore, it is important to keep asking different questions to understand their true response. Expression and display of emotion and affection in public is generally acceptable. However, kissing in public is highly frowned upon and disapproved. As Bangladeshis value religion highly, they often ask strangers about their religious affiliation while engaging in conversation.

Bangladeshis use a variety of nonverbal communication techniques as well. Soft-spoken in nature, Bangladeshis usually speak in low tones and avoid loudness and intense expressions. They pay special attention to avoiding eye contact as it is considered impolite and arrogant. Blinking of eyes is considered naughty and therefore should be avoided. Facial expressions should be as normal as possible, since Bangladeshis believe that the face mirrors the state of mind. While a thumbs up indicates approval in the Western cultures, it is an insult to the Bangladeshis. Bodily postures are also important in demonstrating humbleness and respect to the elderly.

As a global technology, cyberspace has its own culture and has developed its own rules. However, Bangladeshis have developed some unique netiquette in accordance to their culture. Without being aware of these unspoken rules, one is likely to commit social blunders. For instance, using a first name to address some-one in an e-mail is regarded as highly disrespectful and unwelcome among the Bangladeshis. Much the same way as in face-to-face communication, Bangladeshis do not use each other's first names, but use suffixes based on social relations and seniority of individuals in Internet communication. They also tend to delay in re-plying to e-mails. While official appointments may be accepted through e-mail, the same does not work in inviting Bangladeshis to private parties. This is perhaps because the Internet cannot embody the cultural subtleties involved in the Bangla-deshis' communication.

Any food that is not halal is taboo in Bangladesh, such as pork. No meat stores in Bangladesh sell pork or any food with pork substances. While beef is prohibited among Hindus, it is widely popular among Muslim Bangladeshis. For most Bang-ladeshis, drinking alcohol is a taboo. Using the left hand to eat is strictly forbidden, as is going to the restroom while dining. It is considered rude to turn down an invitation to a meal directly. Instead, one should use less direct and polite language suggesting that attending the invitation would be difficult by using phrases like "I will try," or "I will have to see." Guests should never begin eating before the sen-iors in the party.

Bangladesh is a predominantly Muslim country with a notable Hindu popula-tion. Thus, both Islam and Hinduism play very important roles in shaping the patterns of association, marriage, and family of Bangladeshis. For instance, it is strictly forbidden for both Muslims and Hindus to associate with the outcasts in any kind of socializing. Unmarried boys and girls are not allowed to socialize out-side of the house unless they are accompanied by somebody to watch over them. While interactions across religions are allowed, those in the untouchable castes (such as the cleaners or the cobblers) are frowned upon.

Marriage among Bangladeshis strictly follows religious precepts, and breaching those is considered taboo. For instance, marrying first cousins among Hindus is strictly prohibited, although Muslims sometimes allow such marriage. Since ar-ranged marriage is the norm, individuals are discouraged to arrange their marriage by themselves without involving their respective families. While the individual's preference is becoming increasingly important with the acceptance of love, it is taboo for a girl to propose and initiate her marriage. Marrying outside of one's own religion is also a taboo. Adult men are allowed to marry much younger girls, but older women cannot marry younger boys. Same-sex marriage and romantic relations are forbidden and those caught in such relations are severely punished. If a groom decides to live with his wife at his in-laws' residence instead of taking the bride to his parental residence, he suffers from severe ridicule and public shaming.

Religion defines the major social and cultural practices as well as identity of Bangladeshis. Therefore, having no religious affiliation is a big disadvantage for Bangladeshis. Showing disrespect to prophets, religious figures, and holy scriptures is a taboo among people of all religions. For Muslims, idolatry and polytheism are taboo. However, visiting the shrines of and making offers to dead religious gurus are tolerated. While Muslims are fond of beef, it is a taboo among the Hindus to kill a cow for any reason. Homicide and suicide are taboo in both Islam and Hinduism. Women of reproductive age face various religious taboos restricting their social lives, especially in rural areas. Graveyards are considered sacred and therefore dwelling in, walking through, or cultivating graves are strictly prohibited.

Both Islam and Hinduism prescribe elaborate burial rituals and consider it taboo not to hold those rituals for the dead. Cooking food by the family of the deceased on the day of death is strictly prohibited. Both religions prohibit women to participate in washing and preparing the dead body for the rituals. The families of those who commit suicide encounter a number of restrictions due to the stigma and superstitions associated with suicide. Places of burial and graveyards are considered taboo for everybody.

There are dozens of words and expressions in Bengali that are considered taboo, such as calling someone a *rajakar* (war criminal) or *dalal* (collaborator) or calling a young boy "feminine." Using slang is common among peer groups, but doing the same is taboo in conversation with elders and seniors. Making derogatory comments about someone's family is taboo. Calling someone a *kafir* (disbeliever) is a taboo among the Muslims.

Beckoning with the index finger and whistling or winking in public are considered very rude. It's also impolite to cross one's legs or smoke in the presence of an elder. Pointing the bottom of one's shoe at someone is believed to lower their worth. While mourning loudly is allowed for women, crying in public is a taboo for adult men. A facial expression of contempt or disapproval to elderly and senior citizens is prohibited.

Hasan Mahmud

Further Reading

Kasem, Akhtar Sanjida. *An Executive's Hand Book of Etiquette and Manners*. Dhaka: Oitijjha, 2014.

Rahman, Urmi. *Culture Smart! Bangladesh: The Essential Guide to Customs & Culture*. London: Kuperard, 2014.

Sahukar, Nimeran, and Prem P. Bhalla. *The Book of Etiquette and Manners*. Kolkata: Pustak Mahal, 2003.

BASQUE

The Basques are a group of people living in northeastern Spain and southwestern France. So-called Basque Country consists of four areas on the Spanish side of the Pyrenees (Vizcaya, Navarra, Guipuzcoa, and Alava) and three areas on the French side of the Pyrenees (Labourd, Basse-Navarre, and Soule). Basques call these territories *Euskadi*. There are around 3 million Basques (2.5 million living in Spain and 0.5 million living in France). Many Basques have migrated from the Basque Country and settled in the rest of Spain and France as well as the United States, Canada (particularly in New Brunswick and Quebec), South America, South Africa, and Australia. The Basque language, also known as Euskara, is unrelated to Spanish, French, or any other Romance language and is Europe's oldest living language.

Nearly all Basques are Roman Catholic. Basque society values women, and while not actually matriarchal, a great deal of responsibility is traditionally placed on the role of the wife (*etxekoandre*) or homemaker as well as on the institution of the family itself.

The Basque people use a number of phrases when greeting each other. Basques have specific greetings for each time of day—*Egun on* (Good morning), *Arratsalde on* (Good afternoon), *Gabon* (Good evening)—as well as a greeting used at midday (*Eguerdion*). On being introduced to someone a Basque person will often say *Urte askotarako*. This translates as "For many years" and is the Basque equivalent of saying "Pleased to meet you." The phrase is also used after congratulations in order to express the wish that someone's happiness lasts many years.

Basque people typically dress in modern Western styles. The one uniquely Basque item of clothing is the flat, wide, black beret worn by Basque men.

Basque people often join organizations—everything from formal business cooperatives to *cuadrillas* (groups of friends who spend their leisure time in each other company). According to 2006 figures there were 6,533 sports clubs in the Basque Country, 2,428 political/socioeconomic organizations, and 5,035 cultural societies.

On the whole Basques are very sociable and enjoy interacting with other people. Basques take food and hospitality seriously, with traditional Basque recipes being simple enough to highlight the high quality of their ingredients. Basques often invite family and friends round to enjoy a long dinner accompanied by lots of red or rosé wine from Rioja or Navarre, *txakoli* (a semisparkling, very dry white wine with high acidity and low alcohol content produced in the Basque Country), or still apple cider. The Basques are famous for their cuisine, much of which is based on seafood. A Basque specialty, *ttoro*, is fish stew containing mussels, crayfish, eels,

---

Culture Shock! ⊕

Pelota

Pelota is a Basque folk court game akin to handball. Although Basque folklore suggests the sport originated when *jentilak* (giants who had rejected Christianity) used the boulders of the Pyrenees as balls (*pelotas*), historians theorize that pelota may have developed as a result of Basque people combining elements of Aztec ball games brought to the area by returning conquistadors and French *jeu de palme*. In the Basque region pelota has been documented since the thirteenth century. In the Basque Country, pelota rivals soccer in popularity and is also popular in Latin America, the Netherlands, India, and the Philippines. In 1900 pelota was included in the Summer Olympic Games held in Paris. The first official professional pelota championship was held in 1925, while the first amateur pelota World Championships took place in San Sebastián, Spain, in 1952 and now takes place every four years.

Victoria Williams

and cod heads. Other specialties include *txangurro* (spider crab), *kokotchas* (the flesh found under a hake's jaw), and *gateau Basque* (Basque cake), which is made from eggs, flour, sugar, and rum. Other classic Basque recipes include the sauces *pil-pil* (made with cod gelatin); a green sauce made from parsley, garlic, and onion; red *salsa vizcaína* (made from dried red peppers); and a black sauce made with squid ink. Gazpacho, a cold soup consisting of tomatoes, peppers, cucumbers, and olive oil that is popular across Spain, is also a Basque favorite. Another type of social get-together enjoyed by Basques is the *txikiteo*. This involves a group of friends going for a leisurely walk and stopping at bars for *pintxos* (tapas dishes) washed down by small glasses of wine called *txikitos*. Friends will also often meet at a *sagardotegi* (ciderhouse) where they eat cod omelettes, fried cod with green peppers, grilled steak, and Idiazabal cheese served with walnuts. When at a *sagardotegi* Basques drink apple cider served fresh from the barrel. In a traditional *sagardotegi*, each person will pay for a glass that they may fill with cider an unlimited number of times. Then at intervals, the word *txotx* (the word refers to a Basque cider barrel) is shouted out within the *sagardotegi*. When they hear this everyone who has paid for a glass leaves their seat and heads to the back of the *sagardotegi* where the barrels are located. The cider barrels are large and have a small tap in the lid at a reachable height. When everyone is assembled the owner of the *sagardotegi* (or the first person to reach the barrels) reaches up and undoes the barrel tap. As the cider is not carbonated, the angle of the barrel and force of the liquid makes the cider shoot from the barrel when the tap is undone. All the drinkers then catch the cider in their glasses. The shooting action also adds bubbles to the cider. When everyone has cider in their glass they drink in unison, all the while cheering loudly.

Many Basque people speak Euskara in social settings and to express themselves. However, Euskara's survival as a living language is not guaranteed, despite efforts made during the 1970s to ensure the language is spoken by Basques. Euskara is promoted in the media, and is the language of public communication. Basques are keen on using the Internet and on digitization, which many Basque cultural organizations consider a key way of preserving Basque cultural heritage.

Victoria Williams

Further Reading

Advameg. "Basques." *Countries and Their Cultures*. 2017. http://www.everyculture.com/wc/Rwanda-to-Syria/Basques.html. Accessed January 11, 2017.

Eusko Jaurlaritza—Gobierno Vasco. "Try Out Your Basque." *Basque Country*. 2015. https://tourism.euskadi.eus/aa30–12377/en/contenidos/informacion/atrevete_con_el_euskera/en_def/17_palabras_y_expresiones_para_desenvolverte_en_euskera.html. Accessed January 11, 2017.

Zallo, Ramón, and Mikel Ayuso. *The Basque Country: Insight into Its Culture, History, Society and Institutions*. January 2009. Eusko Jaurlaritzaren Argitalpen Zerbitzu Nagusia Servicio Central de Publicaciones del Gobierno Vasco Donostia-San Sebastián 1. San Sebastian, Spain. http://www.kultura.ejgv.euskadi.eus/r46–714/es/contenidos/informacion/ezagutu_eh/es_eza_eh/adjuntos/eza_en.pdf. Accessed January 11, 2017.

Zubiri, Nancy. *A Travel Guide to Basque America: Families, Feasts, and Festivals*, 2nd ed. Reno: University of Nevada Press, 2006.

BEDOUIN

The Bedouin (also spelled Beduin) are an Arabic-speaking seminomadic indigenous people living in the Middle East and North Africa, particularly in Egypt, Syria, Israel, Jordan, Saudi Arabia, Yemen, Oman, Iraq, Morocco, Sudan, Algeria, Tunisia, and Libya. It is not known exactly how many Bedouin people live in these countries because Bedouin populations are not always included in official population statistics. However, estimates suggest that the Bedouin number around 4 million people. The Bedouin therefore make up only a small percentage of the total population of the countries in which they live. Though traditionally thought of as desert dwellers, today significant numbers of Bedouin live in urban areas. That said, many Bedouins are animal herders who migrate to the desert in winter before returning to cultivated land in summer. Bedouin society is polygamous and patriarchal. The majority of Bedouins are Sunni Muslims, although there are a few Christian Bedouins living in Jordan. The Bedouin people follow a rigorous code of honor that demands correct behavior on the part of all members of Bedouin society. This means that all Bedouin men, women, and children must live according to society's myriad rules.

The Bedouin are famous for their greeting etiquette. When Bedouin acquaintances meet often they will rub the palms of their hands together before kissing the tips of their fingers, while when close Bedouin friends meet they will shake hands and kiss each other on the cheek. Most famously when Bedouin family members greet each other they shake hands, rub their noses together, and kiss each other on the cheek. A healthy younger person is always expected to stand up in order to greet an older person. Bedouins always start by first greeting the person to their right and then going on moving right until they have greeted everyone present. Similarly, Bedouins always serve food first to the person on their right, even if that person is a child.

Bedouin men typically wear a long djellaba (a loose-fitting robe with full sleeves) together with a *smagg* (a red and white draped head covering), *aymemma* (a white head covering), or a smaller white head covering that is held in place using a length of black cord called an *agall*. Bedouin women tend to wear colorful, long dresses when indoors but when they venture outside the women wear an abaya (a thin, long black coat). When outdoors, Bedouin women also cover their hair by placing a black shawl called a *tarha* over their hair. Traditionally, Bedouin women covered their faces with a highly ornate *burqa'ah* (an all-enveloping face veil), though this tradition is dying out gradually. Today younger women tend to hide their faces behind their *tarha*.

A tradition of hospitality is deeply rooted in many Arab societies, including that of the Bedouin. In times past the Bedouin culture of hospitality was influenced by the fact that not allowing a stranger to stay in a Bedouin desert settlement could mean the difference between the visitor living or dying, due to the harsh desert environment. Thus the hostile desert environment led to the Bedouin's belief in the total dependency of individuals on the hospitality of others. Hospitality also has a religious importance to the Bedouin people, for they see hospitality as a way both to honor God and to receive God's grace. Bedouin hospitality is heavily ritualistic.

It is often the case that an animal will be sacrificed in a guest's honor in a manner in accordance with Islamic law. Guests are incorporated into their host's household symbolically because it is believed that if armed fighting breaks out while a guest is present, then the guest must be protected as if they were a member of the host's family. When a guest arrives, they may be welcomed by a rug being spread out on the floor in front of them before being served a glass of sweet tea. Since the Bedouin take hospitality so seriously, it is important that a guest show his or her host respect and gratitude before taking their leave.

At meal times men and women eat separately, with children sitting with the women; once boys are older they sit with the men. Non-Bedouin visitors (whether male or female) sit with the men too. Bedouin people typically sit on the floor to eat, either sitting with their legs crossed or adopting a one-legged squatting position. Before they sit down to dine, Bedouin diners wash their hands and say *Bismillah al Rahman al Raheem*, which translates as "In the name of God, the Beneficent, the Merciful." When eating, Bedouins eat from one large plate around which they sit. Bedouins take food from the section of the plate that lies in front of them. It is a welcoming gesture for a Bedouin to place a tasty hunk of meat in the section of the plate that lies in front of a guest. Conversely, it is a breach of Bedouin dining etiquette to eat from the section of the plate that is in front of a fellow diner. Bedouins only use their right hand to transfer food from the plate to their mouths.

Men belonging to the Tarabin Bedouin tribe in Ain Um Ahmad, Egypt, gather for *iftar*. *Iftar* is an evening meal that constitutes the ritual breaking of the fast each night during the Muslim holy month of Ramadan. (AP Photo/Ruth Fremson)

Many Bedouin eat with their hands, as this is thought to improve the taste of the food and ensure that food is not so hot that it will burn the mouth. If eating with their hand a Bedouin may roll a little of the food into a small ball and slide it into their mouth using a finger. It is thought to be very rude for someone to lick their fingers and then continue to eat. It is also considered rude for someone to eat all the food in his or her section of the plate, as this is seen as a sign of greed. Instead, diners should ensure that some food is left on the plate at the end of the meal.

Once a Bedouin diner has finished eating it is usual for the diner to say *Al Hamdulillah*, meaning "All praise and thanks be to God." The diner will then stand up and go to wash his or her hands whether or not anyone else is still eating. Guests should make sure that they are not the first to finish their meal, because once a guest finishes eating everyone else who is dining will be expected to stop eating.

After everyone has washed their hands, the diners return to the seating area and sit down to relax. A short while after everyone has returned to sitting, tea is served in glasses. When a guest has had enough tea it is customary for the guest to signal their satisfaction by placing their hand over the top of their tea glass or to turn the glass upside down. Sometimes after a meal, freshly prepared, cardamom-spiced Bedouin Arabic coffee is drunk. The preparation of this coffee is complex, with the coffee beans roasted over an open fire before being ground in an ornate mortar. The coffee is ground by being pounded to a special rhythm that is audible for some distance, thus allowing nearby neighbors to know that coffee is being prepared and that they should drop by the tent for a drink. The coffee is poured from the mortar into a brass coffee pot that is filled with water and to which a few cardamom pods are added. The resultant mixture of ground coffee, water, and cardamom is then boiled three times before being left to settle for a little while. According to tradition the coffee is served in very small, ceramic cups called *feenghal*. The cups are usually only half filled with coffee, but each person is served three cups of coffee. After drinking the third cup it is important for the drinker to announce *Da'imeh*, meaning "God preserve you." If a guest is present then the first cup of coffee (*al heif*) is poured and tasted by the Bedouin host as this shows a guest that the coffee is safe to drink. The second cup of coffee (*al keif*) is given to and tasted by the guest, and then the third cup of coffee that is intended for the guest is poured. The guest then drinks this cup of coffee, which is known as *al dheif*. The guest should drink at least one cup of coffee and when he or she has had enough coffee they should place their hand over the cup and twist the cup a few times. This signals to the host that the guest has had their fill of coffee. If a Bedouin family wishes to show the utmost hospitality to their guest, then they may serve three rounds each of both tea and coffee. Bedouin people view tea as an everyday drink and serve it during discussions. In contrast, great ceremony attends the preparation and drinking of coffee, which is served when a deal has been reached, or an arrangement such as a marriage proposal or land acquisition has been agreed.

Women are protected by the Bedouin code of honor. Under this etiquette code, a man must not touch any woman to whom he is not closely related. This preclusion extends to even the slightest of touches. For example, a man may not allow his fingertips to brush against a woman's hand when passing her something, for

---

Culture Shock! ⊕

Camel Racing

The sport of camel racing is extremely popular on the Arabian Peninsula but also takes place in the desert regions of Sudan, Egypt, Kenya, India, and Australia. The history of the sport can be traced to the Bedouin living on the Arabian Peninsula during the seventh century, for the Bedouin included camel racing at their social gatherings and festivals. The Bedouin cared greatly for their camels and treated the animals with great respect. To the Bedouin camels represented both a mode of transport and a symbol of wealth, with camel racing and riding a major hobby among Bedouin children. During the latter half of the twentieth century camel racing became much more formalized and is now both a major tourist attraction and a source of employment.

Victoria Williams

---

any such physical contact is thought to dishonor the woman. The Bedouin consider any loss of a woman's honor (*ird*) to be a very serious matter. Moreover, some Bedouin tribes feel that if a woman loses her *ird* then she brings dishonor not just upon herself but upon her entire family, since *ird* is held by whole families rather than by individuals.

Bedouin men and women are allowed to choose their life partner, although romantic love is often not seen as important by Bedouin society and Bedouin parents can exert pressure on their children to ensure that their child marries a preferred person. If there is no father to speak for a woman, then a brother or other male relative will arrange marriage matters on her behalf. Bedouin couples go through an engagement period lasting around one year, during which the Bedouin man may visit his future bride at her family home. During these visits the couple are allowed to talk together, though they are rarely left alone with each other. If an engagement does not go well, then it can be ended. The Bedouins live in a society with a patriarchal system. According to Islamic custom polygamous marriage is permitted as long as the husband can provide equally for all of his wives. Today, however, plural marriage occurs more infrequently than it once did. Instead many Bedouins tend to divorce and marry again as divorce is regarded as normal and does not carry a social stigma.

Bedouin death customs and etiquette are in line with Islamic traditions. A corpse will be buried as soon as possible and certainly within 24 hours of death occurring. Some Bedouin groups try to bury all their dead in one location, but this may not be possible if a Bedouin person dies somewhere that lies more than 24 hours travelling time away. Bedouin funeral rituals are extremely simple. Similarly, Bedouin graves are denoted simply by placing a stone or board at the head of the grave. It is considered correct for the deceased's family to place a fresh palm leaf at the head of the grave too. When a Bedouin family visits a grave, etiquette demands that everyone present remove their shoes and pray, before sitting around the grave and eating fruit while children are given candy.

Victoria Williams

Further Reading

"Bedouin Culture." Bedawi.com. 2007. http://www.bedawi.com/Bedouin_Culture_EN.html. Accessed January 2, 2017.

"Bedouin Mealtime Customs and Etiquette." Wadi Rum Nomads. 2014–2017. https://www.wadirumnomads.com/bedouin-mealtime-customs-and-etiquette/. Accessed January 2, 2017.

Bent, J. Theodore, and Mabel Bent. *Southern Arabia*. London: Routledge, 2011.

Bouchara, Abdelaziz, and Bouchra Qorchi. *The Role of Religion in Shaping Politeness During Greeting Encounters in Arabic: A Matter of Conflict or Understanding*. Hamburg: Anchor Academic Publishing, 2016.

Jones, Jeremy, and Nicholas Ridout. *Oman, Culture and Diplomacy*. Edinburgh: Edinburgh University Press, 2012.

Shoup, John A. *Culture and Customs of Jordan*. Westport, CT: Greenwood, 2007.

Webster, Donovan. "Empty Quarter." *National Geographic*. February 2005. http://ngm.nationalgeographic.com/features/world/asia/saudi-arabia/empty-quarter-text/1. Accessed January 2, 2017.

BELGIUM

Belgium is a sovereign state located in Western Europe that is bordered by France, the Netherlands, Germany, and Luxembourg, with a northwestern coast on the North Sea. Belgium is a small and densely populated country covering an area of 11,787 square miles. The population numbers some 11 million people. Belgium is divided into three regions and three communities that coexist. Belgium's two largest regions are Flanders, which lies in the north and where people speak Flemish (a variety of Dutch), and Wallonia, which is located in the south and has a French-speaking population. The Brussels-Capital Region lies within the Flemish Region and is officially bilingual (French and Flemish). There is also a German-speaking community that lives in Wallonia. Belgium's language complexity is the result of a troubled history that has seen Belgium invaded, occupied, and colonized multiple times. This tumultuous history has also resulted in Belgium having a liberal society that is tolerant of various races, cultures, and religions with people of different nationalities, races, and faiths living together in relative harmony. Belgian culture is influenced by both Germanic and Latin Europe.

In many ways Belgian etiquette is much like that of the rest of Western Europe. Belgians are fairly reserved and tend to greet people that they do not consider to be friends with a handshake. In French-speaking areas of Belgium, it is common for people to kiss each other on the cheek as a greeting. Usually Belgians greet close friends with three air-kisses (without touching skin) to alternating cheeks starting with the left cheek. In business meetings the protocol is more formal. Greetings start with attendees saying something along the lines of "Good day" and shaking hands while maintaining eye contact. In Belgium handshakes should not be too vigorous and backslapping should be avoided. If a woman wishes to shake hands, then she will initiate the gesture. After the handshaking, everyone present usually swaps business cards. It is important to bring lots of business cards to meetings in Belgium, as it is considered very bad form to run out of cards during a meeting. It is also a good idea to present business cards printed in French on one side and in Flemish on the other side, as this shows respect and understanding of Belgian society. Alternatively, one side may be printed in English and the other in French, German, or Flemish.

When addressing people, the English titles Mr., Mrs., and Miss may be used for people who speak English or German while the French appellations *Monsieur* (Mr.), *Madame* (Mrs.), or *Mademoiselle* (Miss) should be used for French speakers. When addressing Flemish Belgians it is appropriate to use *Meneer* (Mr.), *Mevrouw* (Mrs.), or *Juffrouw* (Miss).

Smiling when greeting someone suggests positivity, but smiling too much should be avoided. Sometimes, if a meeting has a lot of attendees, the person chairing the meeting might go around the room inviting each person to introduce themselves by stating their name and job title, and, if they are from an external organization, the company for which they work. In Belgium English is used increasingly in business with directories and salespeople often starting conversations in English. However, French-speaking Belgians are usually pleased if visitors begin conversations by speaking to them in French.

Belgians tend to dress essentially the same as other people in Western Europe, though in social situations French-speaking Belgian women tend to dress quite formally and do not wear tracksuits or sneakers often. In business situations it is normal for men to wear a jacket, though not necessarily a suit. Indeed, if a man wears a full suit he may be seen as rather stuffy. Younger men working in tech companies are generally allowed to wear an open-neck shirt and jeans to work. Clothes should not be too brightly colored, however, and shoes (never too-casual loafers) should be well polished and clean. Cleanliness is very important to Belgians, who are often found cleaning the front of their homes. Women may wear trousers, particularly trouser suits, to work. If in doubt regarding dress code for a business meeting, it is better to be well dressed rather than dressed too informally. Uniforms are rarely worn except for chefs, cleaners, and so on. When arriving for a business meeting it is important to bear in mind that Belgians are very punctual and expect people to arrive on time. Failure to do so may scupper a business deal before negotiations even begin.

Belgians tend to socialize at highly regarded restaurants (of which there are many) and in their homes, though the home is reserved more often for visits from family and close friends. When eating in a restaurant in northern Belgium, only one form of starchy food will be served at a meal. For example, if potatoes are served then bread will not be provided. In this case it is not appropriate to request bread to accompany the meal. Meanwhile in southern Belgium, bread is usually served with a meal—but butter will not be served and should not be requested. In Belgium waiting staff are comparatively well paid and do not rely on tips to make up their income. Furthermore, restaurant, taxi, and hairdressing bills include a service charge, so tipping is not customary. If a visitor feels he would like to leave a tip, then it is acceptable to round the bill up to the nearest Euro or to leave 10 percent of the bill as a gratuity.

In Belgium, if a person receives a written invitation to an event, it is deemed correct to reply in writing. Business lunches, which often take place in restaurants, are an essential part of Belgian work practices and tend to last for about two hours from 1 p.m. to 3 p.m. When arriving as a guest at a home or restaurant it is considered courteous to arrive on time because Belgians see punctuality as a sign of respect. The host will typically introduce guests to each other and indicate where guests should sit, with women taking their seats before men. As Belgium is a country of Western Europe, table manners are Continental style with the fork held in the left hand and the knife in the right, and wrists are kept above the table while eating. In Belgium it is considered rude not to eat all the food on the plate as this is seen as both inconsiderate and wasteful. To indicate that one has finished eating, one should place the knife and fork parallel on the plate, with the prongs of the fork facing upwards and the handles facing to the right. Alternatively the guest can form the knife and fork into an X shape with the tines of the fork facing upwards. Food is very important to Belgians, who take great pride in their cuisine. For this reason it is considered a sincere compliment to the host to praise the food served. When invited to a person's home it is good form to give flowers to the host and chocolates to the hostess. It is never acceptable to give a host white chrysanthemums, however, as in Belgium these symbolize death and are associated with funerals. Similarly, an odd number of blooms should be given but never give 13 flowers, as this number is considered unlucky.

Belgians tend to be very keen on alcohol, especially beer, with toasts often said at meals. It is a good idea for a guest to see if the host or guest of honor is going to say a toast before starting to drink. If a toast happens, everyone should stand. Also note that Flemish Belgians raise their glasses twice for a toast. The first raising of the toast marks the start of the toast while the second signals the toast's completion. When making a toast Flemish Belgians will say *Op uw gezondheid* (A toast to . . .), while French speakers will proclaim *Á votre santé* (To your health).

Technically it is illegal to drink on the street in Belgium, but in practice, as most bars have outside smoking areas, this law is rarely enforced and it is usual to see Belgians drinking beer on the street. Unlike in some other Western European countries, smoking is socially acceptable in Belgium. Another area in which Belgium differs from other Western European nations is that prostitution is legal, as it is in its neighbor the Netherlands. Many Belgian cities, such as Antwerp, have an unofficial sex district (a so-called red light area) where lingerie-clad women advertise their services from windows lining the streets.

Belgians tend to employ restrained body language, and as they like their own personal space, they usually do not enjoy people standing too close to them during conversation or being touched while talking. Typically Belgian men hold doors open for women and stand when women enter the room. Belgians consider it rude to point using the index finger (the whole hand should be used for this), to yawn, to place feet on seats, to blow the nose in public, and to talk with your hands in your pockets. Snapping fingers is considered an obscene gesture.

Verbal communication in Belgium is something of a linguistic minefield as Belgians switch between languages until they discern which language is most suited to a conversation. On the whole Belgians speak excellent English, with business meetings often conducted purely in English. Flemish-speaking Belgians prefer to speak English rather than French, but are normally fluent in all three chief languages spoken in Belgium (Flemish, French, English). If in doubt as to which language to employ, it is safest to speak in English for there is nowhere else in Europe where a visitor can get into more trouble for using the incorrect language than Belgium. It is also a good idea to avoid discussing religion or politics when visiting Belgium, and criticizing the monarchy is taboo. Belgians also greatly dislike being compared to the French, about whom Belgians often make highly disparaging remarks.

Victoria Williams

Further Reading

Commisceo Global Consultancy Ltd. "Belgium Guide." *Commisceo Global*. 2016. http://www.commisceo-global.com/countryguides/belgiumguide?highlight=YToxOntpOjA7czo2OiJmcmFuY2UiO30. Accessed January 2, 2017.

David. "Culture Shock in Belgium." *ExpatArrivals*. 2016. http://www.expatarrivals.com/belgium/culture-shock-in-belgium. Accessed January 2, 2017.

Elliott, Mark. *CultureShock! Belgium: A Survival Guide to Customs and Etiquette*, 4th ed. Tarrytown, NY: Marshall Cavendish Corporation, 2011.

Gulliver. "Mind Your Manners in Brussels." *The Economist*. August 9, 2008. http://www.economist.com/blogs/gulliver/2008/08/mind_your_manners_in_brussels. Accessed January 2, 2017.

Martin, Jeanette S., and Lillian H. Chaney. *Passport to Success: The Essential Guide to Business Culture and Customs in America's Largest Trading Partners*. Westport, CT: Praeger, 2009.

Passport to Trade 2.0. "Business Etiquette." *Passport to Trade 2.0*. 2014. http://businessculture.org/western-europe/business-culture-in-belgium/meeting-etiquette-in-belgium/. Accessed January 2, 2017.

BERBERS

Morocco's Berbers, often referred to as Imazighen (sing. Amazigh), form a sizeable component of the country's population. Whereas they were formerly found solely in the mountainous and southern desert regions of the kingdom, nowadays many inhabit urban areas of the Atlantic plain, or Gharb. Being a Berber is not a racial distinction, but rather a linguistic or social one. In fact, whether they speak one of three main Berber dialects (Tarifit, Tamazight, or Tashelhit) is the best means of distinguishing them from their fellow countrymen. Our focus will be on the Tamazight-speaking Berbers of central Morocco.

Imazighen usually greet each other with *May teɛnit* (How are you?), or more poetically with *Tifawin tildjiyin* (Flowery mornings). When meeting an old friend one will prefer the somewhat more intimate *Mani-š?* (Where have you been?) or

Is thenna šwi? (Is everything OK?). A typical rejoinder to the effect that all is well would be *Thenna γuri* or *Thenna ddunit*. When taking leave in the evening, the equivalent to "Good night" is *Timensiwin*. Leave-taking at other times will often be limited to a perfunctory *Mun d lman* (Go in peace), or *Mun d wayd*, assorted with *Ar tikkelt yadnin* (Until next time), or *Al nmyannay* (Until we meet again). Also at this point a suitable gap-filler would be *Siwd-asn sslam i ayt uxam-nneš* (Say hello to your family). If the other person has just arrived from a journey, one should greet them with *May teɛnit d ubrid* (How was it along the way?). Nowadays, however, given widespread cell-phone ownership, on reaching some remote village, one may hear *Is tumzd rizu adday texlid tizi?* (Did you get a signal as you were coming over the pass?).

The handshake, when greeting a fellow Amazigh, is de rigueur. Sometimes the index finger is then raised to one's lips and kissed. Men meeting intimate friends will usually embrace Mediterranean-style. Men, however, refrain from kissing their womenfolk in public, though a woman may kiss a man's forehead if he has done her a good turn, or as a sign of respect.

Regarding men with whom one is at odds, any risk of a chance encounter along the way developing into violence can be averted by avoiding eye contact. An old proverb, which actually was an antidote against falling foul of a panther in the forest, supports this: *Allen imyannayn mezlaγent, allen ur imyannayn mmezγalen* (When eye contact is established they fight, when there is no eye contact they go their separate ways).

Traditionally, until about 20–30 years ago, rural Berbers dressed in flowing white robes with a light cloak (*selham*) or a heavier woollen homespun garment (*azennar*). At one time, for example, the ex-French army greatcoat (*kabut*) was popular. The head would be shaved and covered with a turban. Today, many men are to be seen wearing Western-style cast-offs. Young men will often grow a moustache, rarely a bushy beard, except among deeply religious believers. Usually, side-whiskers and a small tuft of a beard are considered adequate. Footwear consists of a pair of sandal-like *idušan*. In winter, shepherds used to wear woollen trousers (*aserwal n ifilan*) and greased gaiters and sandals of similar material.

Women don cotton dresses in summer, or an ample winding-sheet kind of garment held in place by a safetypin or ornamental brooch (*tisiγnest*); over that would be a woollen cloak (*tamizarth*) and tribal headdress and scarf, while facial tattoos would proclaim which tribe they came from. Nowadays, many young women wear the hijab and are no longer tattooed, this practice having been denounced as *bideɛ* (unbecoming) by Salafi preachers who were active in tribal areas in the late 1990s. In the home, women usually go barefoot, putting on light sandals or plastic galoshes outside.

Berbers are justly renowned for their hospitality. Nowadays, guesthouses (*gîtes*, Fr.) dot the tourist routes frequented by trekkers and backpackers. Except in some remote backwaters, this has effectively killed off the traditional form of Berber hospitality (*tinubga*). In the old days, however, a traveler putting up for the night in a village would find lodging in one of the local households according to a roster system (*afalis*). Usually, pronouncing the two words *Anebji rebbi*

A Berber family entertains a guest at their home in Tunisia. Typically, guests are not seated at a table but recline on a carpet and cushions. (Andrew Woodley/Alamy Stock Photo)

(God's guest) would be sufficient to be taken under someone's roof. In between bouts of tea drinking he would be expected to tell his host about his journey, or entertain him with brief anecdotes. Berbers set much store by conversation, and one must know how to be suitably talkative. Silence on the part of a guest is unthinkable. The tea ritual is a complex one, the guest often being asked to preside over this ceremony himself; he must bring the water to boiling point in the teapot and prepare the brew, correctly measuring sugar, mint, and tea. The host, too, must look after his guest, never leaving him alone. That would be the height of bad taste. Barring certain circumstances, the head of the household is present all the time; sometimes one of his sons can stand in for him. The spouse is usually absent as she is busy cooking the evening meal. Women, however, will preside over tea and/or dinner if the husband is sick or otherwise incapacitated.

Guests are not seated at a table but recline (*senned*) on a mat, carpet, and cushions. Dinner (*imešli*) is served on a low table in a large bowl. After hand washing, one eats with the fingers of one's right hand (the left hand is unclean), with a spoon if *kus-kus* is provided. For meat and vegetable stew (*tajin*), it is customary to dip pieces of flapjack barley bread in the sauce. The paterfamilias usually removes pieces of meat and then cuts them down to size with a pocket knife before handing them to guests. One is supposed to accept these choice morsels—a difficult task when the meat is tough. Any water served during the meal is drunk from a collective drinking mug. Belching at the end of a meal is an acceptable means of expressing satisfaction. Mouths will then be rinsed, hands soaped and washed in a portable washbasin, then dried with a towel (*futa*).

Berbers tend to be very expressive, as much with their mouths as with their hands. An outward upward movement of the palms of both hands means "What's up?" The right hand extended then inflected towards the body signifies "Come here!" Stroking one's nose and face in a downward movement of the right hand is an oft-repeated gesture, though its actual significance is not always obvious. Holding the right hand of an intimate friend appears quite acceptable, especially when striving to make a point in conversation. Avoiding an argument or hiding one's true feelings in public are outward signs of intelligence and self-control, and a man capable of such behavior is admired by his peers. The following verse emphasizes this: *Ul-inw ag enn illa umyayar; ma t uymas tessant i wenna rix d wadda wr hmilx!* (In my heart lies the distinction when I smile at my friend or my enemy!).

Girls especially are taught to avoid eye contact with men other than close relatives. Downcast eyes are seen as a sign of submission and good manners on their part. Otherwise, a girl with whom one is more intimate can roll her eyes to express surprise or indignation.

As with many other things in Morocco, there is a gap between theory and practice. As Muslims, of course, Imazighen are not supposed to eat pork or indulge in intoxicating drinks. However, it is a well-known fact that in winter in the mountains they sometimes kill and eat wild boar (*abulxir*), the more so as this animal devastates their crops. A similar two-sided situation occurs with alcohol. Apart from some educated, town-dwelling Berbers who may have a fancy for wine or whisky, mountain Berbers are partial to fig brandy (*mahya*) that the Jewish community used to prepare in the old days—a tradition the Berbers have perpetuated. Officially, however, they will not publicize their drinking habits in a society governed by a certain amount of hypocrisy. Nonetheless, Berbers who have access to bars will often drink beer, which, compared to wine or spirits, is seen as a less innocuous, marginally acceptable form of alcohol.

Basically, the Berbers are a bread-eating people. In fact, bread and tea (*aɣrum d wattay*) constitute their staple diet, at a pinch bread and butter; this is what is usually served to passing travelers (*inejda*). Made from wheat or barley, bread is their basic foodstuff—even more so than the potato. Dipping bread into a bowl containing oil and honey is seen as a great delicacy. Such food will be supplemented by pancakes, dried dates, bean soup, skewered meat, and *tutliwin* (mutton, goat, chicken, etc.) grilled over glowing embers (*tirgin*) kebab-fashion. Whatever the meat, the animal must be slaughtered with a knife in the approved Muslim style; otherwise it is not seen as *hellal* (halal, permissible). For breakfast they drink tea and/or coffee containing ground pepper beans. Although there are trout streams in the Atlas Mountains, there is no great fish-eating tradition among the Berbers. Fresh fish is somehow apprehended as an unclean, unsuitable source of food, though preserved fish, especially sardines, appear acceptable to some Berbers. Likewise, frogs or snails are not fit for eating.

The family is a close-knit institution as in similar segmentary tribal communities, governed by an all-encompassing, all-pervading form of solidarity and loyalty, right or wrong. In simplified form this may be summed up by the following notion: "Me and my brother against the rest of my family; my family against the rest of the world."

Family life is also closely linked to the notion of honor, *tsart* or *nnifs*. Family honor, in this case, is enshrined in a girl's virginity. Needless to say, this is seen as some kind of ultimate sanctuary (*horm*) that should be preserved until her wedding night. There are cases of bridegrooms interrupting their nuptials on discovering that their wives-to-be are not virgins, dousing the house fire, and leaving in high dudgeon. This is because any sexual relation outside of wedlock is *ur ieɛdil* ("not done")—in fact, totally taboo. The offenders risk being turned to stone by God, as vividly illustrated by the grotto of Akhiam n Imsegh Rebbi in Ayt Hadiddu country, where subterranean stalactites are said to represent an overhasty young couple. In that tribe, in particular, the women are said to be good mothers. Although there may be instances of sodomy between teenagers, homosexuality is definitely frowned upon.

While visualized by some as lukewarm Muslims because of a not totally unjustified reputation for animism and heresy, tribal Berbers are actually quite serious about their religion. The month of fasting (*Remdan*, Ramadan) is more diligently observed than in most of urban Morocco. However, due to the presence of *igurramn*, or local saints—representatives of Moroccan Sufism at its purest who act as go-betweens with God—some Berbers retain credulous attitudes regarding miracles such as levitation, flying to Mecca, and the "sleeping child" (*amjun*) who is suddenly born to a mother whose husband has been absent for over nine months.

Although there is a very sensible, open awareness about death, great pains are taken to alleviate the sufferings of terminally ill people. For example, the devoted housewife will tenderly nurse the male head of the household at death's door; in summer she will send for snow that will be administered to the dying one via a thread of wool (seen as a highly positive substance) to facilitate his passage into the hereafter (*lixra*), a ceremony known as *nemsifad* (leave-taking). Interment will usually follow within 24 hours of death. Later, if an owl (*tawušt*) hoots at night, it is said to be the soul of a dead relative coming back to haunt the living.

Rude language is considered distasteful among Imazighen. In poetry, use of synonyms works around this difficulty. Otherwise, several word taboos are enforced. The jackal is rarely called by its name, *uššen*, but instead *war iberdan* (the pathless one). Likewise the kettle is referred to as white rather than black. In similar vein and as a propitiatory gesture, the Ayt Hadiddu of the Imilshil region call their main river *asif mellul* (white river), although sorely tempted to name it *asif abxuš* (black river) because of its propensity to flood its banks and ravage their fields. If reciting a folktale, any allusion to a monkey, a dog, or a Jew will be accompanied by the expression *Haša leɛbad* (Begging your pardon). However, a black man, possibly referred to as *aqebli*, may accept the nickname *ahaqqar* (raven) in good faith; the expression *ismeɣ* (negro) is impolite in public, in a society where attitudes toward color and race remain ambiguous.

Michael Peyron

Further Reading

Brett, M., and E. Frentress. *The Berbers*. Oxford: Blackwell, 1996.

Gellner, E. *Saints of the Atlas*. London: Weidensfeld & Nicolson, 1969.

Gellner, E., and C. Micaud. *Arabs and Berbers*. London: Duckworth, 1973.

Hart, D. M. *Dadda 'Atta and His Forty Grand-sons*. Wisbech: MENAS Press, 1981.

Hart, D. M. *The Ait 'Atta, Daily Life and Recent History*. Wisbech: MENAS Press, 1984.

Hart, D. M. *Tribe and Society in Rural Morocco*. London: Frank Cass, 2000.

Kasriel, M. *Libres Femmes du Haut-Atlas*. Paris: L'Harmattan, 1989.

Laoust, E. *Mots et Choses Berbères*. Rabat: S.M.E., 1983 [1920].

Maher, V. *Women and Property in Morocco*. London: Cambridge University Press, 1974.

Peyron, M. *Rivières Profondes*. Casablanca: Wallada, 1993.

Peyron, M. *Women Braver than Men, Berber Heroines of the Moroccan Middle Atlas*. Ifrane: Al Akhawayn University in Ifrane Press, 2003.

Peyron, M. (ed.). *The Amazigh Studies Reader*. Ifrane: Akhawayn University in Ifrane Press, 2006.

BOLIVIA

Bolivia is a culturally diverse and eclectic country located in the heart of South America. It has been landlocked since 1879, when Bolivia entered into war with its neighbor Chile. The resultant loss of coastal territory has led to a national belief that one day the country will reclaim the land of its former coast. Bolivia has a diversity of religions, with Catholicism representing a large percentage of the population. Among the minority religions are Evangelism, Islam, Judaism, Jehovah's Witnesses, and ancient folk religions. Bolivians who practice these ancient religions traditionally rehearse rituals in honor of the heavenly Astros, including the worship of the motherland known as *Pachamama*, the sun *Inti*, and the moon *el puma Punku*.

Culture Shock! ⊕

Pachamama: The Earth Goddess

Pachamama is a goddess worshipped by the indigenous people of the Andes as the wife of Pacha Kamaq (the Creator of the World) and mother to Inti, the sun god, and Killa, the moon goddess. In Incan mythology Pachamama is the goddess of fertility who presides over sowing and harvesting, personifies the region's mountains, and causes earthquakes. Pachamama is also considered omnipresent, self-sufficient, and powerful enough to sustain life on Earth. Shrines to Pachamama are found in rocks and trees, and priests sacrifice llamas and guinea pigs in her honor. After the Spanish Conquest, which forced indigenous people to convert to Catholicism, the figure of the Virgin Mary blended with that of Pachamama in the minds of many indigenous people. Today many South Americans think that issues arise when people take too much from nature, thereby depleting Pachamama.

Victoria Williams

Climates and landscapes are also varied in Bolivia and play important roles in Bolivian customs and etiquette. The warm climate of the eastern lowlands is reflected in its people's greetings. Lowlanders tend to be very open people and are likely to acknowledge others around them. It is customary for lowlanders to acknowledge other people whenever they come into their presence or leave. Even if a person enters a large gathering of people, that person will be expected to greet each person. When a man is greeting a woman, a handshake and a kiss on the cheek are acceptable. When a woman greets a man, a handshake is acceptable and the kiss on the cheek is optional (it will depend on the closeness of the relationship for the kiss on the cheek). The woman will not initiate the kiss, so it will be up to the man. When a man is greeting another man, a handshake using the right hand is a must, with a quick hug and pats on the back, followed by a second handshake. For men in a close relationship a pat on the chest is an expression of cordiality and friendship. Greetings among the typically more reserved highlanders are more inconspicuous. Highlanders often take a calmer attitude towards people around them, acting more cautiously with strangers until they feel they are able to trust that person. Man-to-man greetings will consist of a handshake using the right hand and a pat on the shoulder using the left hand. It is not acceptable to pat on the chest, as this can be viewed as a hostile gesture. When women meet, a handshake is acceptable until a friendship has been established, at which time they may exchange up to four kisses to the cheek.

In Bolivia appearance and attire varies depending on the climate of the state (*departamento*). The warm climate in the eastern lowlands sets the tone for the attire not only for men, but also for women. Men who hold office jobs usually wear pants and white or light-colored short-sleeved shirts, rarely with a tie. Women wear blouses and skirts, or light-colored dresses, and open-toed shoes. Jeans, T-shirts, shorts, and spaghetti strap tank tops are very popular among young adults. The climate of the western highlands is cooler, so men and women tend to wear more formal attire for office jobs. Both men and women might wear suits and ties to work, and for some schools, ties are required. Young adults wear pants and long-sleeved shirts and, most of the time, jackets. It is also common for men to wear colorful jackets made from *aguayo* (woven thread), alpaca, or wool, while women wear big pleated skirts (also known as *polleras*) accompanied by hats worn on either the side or top of the head.

Bolivians are typically very hospitable, and throughout Bolivia an invitation to a home carries a lot of importance. Bolivians invite others to their homes when they like and trust them, and take pride in introducing their family members to new visitors. Social parties and family gatherings always involve a large amount of the best possible food.

In Bolivia it is still customary for men to work while women stay at home to prepare meals, keep the home, and care for the children. It is not common for a man to prepare his own food, but there are a few exceptions. Some men are taking up the art of cooking. In some places the man might wait for his food, either at the table when he is at home, or, depending on his job, the children or the wife may deliver the food to him. If the man is at home, he usually sits while the wife or the children serve him. Bolivians tend to consume large quantities of food either for breakfast, lunch, or dinner depending on the *departamento*. The most important meal in the bigger cities is lunch. Children are typically taught at an early age to eat everything on their plates, so it is quite common and expected that people eat everything served to them. If a person is invited for a meal at someone's home, the visitor is expected to eat the portions of food given by the host. The host will take the empty plate as a sign of enjoyment and gratitude. It can be a tricky situation for a visitor who is not used to either the flavors or the amount of food served. If someone has eaten all the food on their plate, it is taken to mean that they really enjoyed the meal and that they probably want some more food.

The lifestyle in the big cities around Bolivia is busier and more modern than in the small towns. Even though life can get busy for Bolivians, they are still people oriented instead of time oriented. Not being overly concerned about time, Bolivians will often show up late for events. Events will often start between 30 minutes to an hour later than the stated starting time.

Respect should be shown to elders at all times, not only in words, but also by actions, especially from younger people. It is considered impolite to call an older person by his or her first name. Public buses are the main means of transportation, and people from all walks of life take them. Younger passengers are expected to give up their seats to older passengers. If a younger person neglects to provide their seat, the rest of the passengers will voice concern. The same rule applies to pregnant women or women with children. The family is the nucleus of Bolivian society, so time with family is very important. Young adults often wait until they are married to move away from their parents' home, and sometimes they stay with their families even after marriage. Some couples live together, have children, and never marry.

Death is not a topic of conversation for Bolivians and is considered a taboo subject. When someone dies, there is a lot of crying, and often screaming. Family and friends wear black or dark clothing as a sign of mourning. Children are not usually allowed to attend wakes, nor are they present at cemeteries for the funeral. This is due to the Bolivian belief that the ground in cemeteries is contaminated, thus it is feared that children might become sick if they visit a cemetery. In Bolivia it is customary to remember the dead for nine days after burial. This practice (known as a novena) sees family and friends come to pay their respects to the grieving family. On the last day of the novena, the family offers a small party in remembrance of the life that has passed, and they serve the dead's favorite meals. Further, November 1 and 2 are holidays set apart to remember the dead. On November 1 those who die at a young age are remembered, while November 2 is designated for those who died in adulthood. On these special days families clean the tombs of loved ones and spend the day at the cemetery receiving those who come to pay their respects to the family by bringing candles, flowers, or offering prayers. In return the host family usually feeds visitors the deceased's favorite meals or snacks.

Bolivians also consider sex to be a taboo subject, and parents often do not teach their children about sex. If a young girl gets pregnant, the family might either hide the girl or try to marry her quickly so that the family is not disgraced. Also, it is understood that while men work outside, the women take care of the house. The man makes most of the family decisions, and sometimes can even be in an adulterous situation without his wife knowing. If the wife does find out, the husband will often go to be with the other woman, leaving his wife to provide for his children alone. Domestic abuse against women is another part of the gender battle, and usually other people do not get involved in these situations.

Blanca Montero-Phillips

Further Reading

Galvan, Javier A. *Cultures and Customs of Bolivia.* Santa Barbara, CA: Greenwood, 2011.

Hudson, Rex A., Dennis Michael Hanratty, and Thomas E. Weil. *Bolivia: A Country Study.* Washington, D.C.: Federal Research Division, Library of Congress, 1991.

Read, James. *The Rough Guide to Bolivia.* New York: Rough Guides, 2008.

BRAZIL

Brazil is an immense country of continental dimensions, with a landmass greater than that of continental Europe or the continental United States. Each region in Brazil is famous for a distinct element of the nation's cultural identity. The most famous city in Brazil is Rio de Janeiro, the former political capital of the country and the nation's undisputed cultural capital. Rio de Janeiro's population of about 6.5 million inhabitants (called *cariocas*) is famous for its love of leisure, but while the residents of Rio de Janeiro never seem to worry about business or work, in truth they are industrious and simply know when it is time to work and when it is time for leisure. Contrastingly, São Paulo, one of the largest cities in the world, prides itself on being the economic engine of the country, and the city's residents (*paulistasi*) have a reputation of being all business. The playful criticism between Rio de Janeiro and São Paulo is that the latter city lives to work while the former lives to play. Brasilia, the country's capital city, was inaugurated in 1960 after a five-year building frenzy that ultimately linked the distant Brazilian states by highway, thereby ushering in a period of strong economic growth and development for Brazil. Despite national pride in Brazil's modern, planned capital city, its inhabitants (*brasilienses*) have the reputation of being bureaucrats and politicians, and often bear the implicit accusation of being corrupt. The Amazon rainforest extends across most of the northern part of Brazil, an expanse almost as large as the contiguous 48 states of the United States. Manaus, situated in the northwest of the country at the confluence of the Preto and Solimões Rivers, where they become the Amazon, is home to 2 million people who work in manufacturing and increasingly in ecotourism. Along the coast of Brazil lie other large metropolises like Recife and Salvador, the latter being the Afro-Brazilian cultural capital of the country. The south of Brazil is home to the *gaúchos*—Brazil's cowboys and ranchers are a cultural and economic similarity that Brazil shares with its neighbor and longtime rival, Argentina. Brazilian Portuguese spoken in the south is much closer to Spanish in its pronunciation and is easier to understand by a Spanish speaker, but one should never assume that Brazilians speak Spanish or that they are Hispanic or Latino. Brazil is Lusophone, and its Portuguese heritage is evident in its laid-back attitude toward adaptation and accommodation.

While the different regions of Brazil enjoy their own cultural expressions and customs, Brazilian culture has many common expressions and taboos that are invaluable to know and incorporate when visiting any part of Brazil. Brazilians tend to be a warm and vibrant people who are proud of their nation and their culture. Brazilians view interpersonal relationships as the foundation of everything they do, so a foreigner traveling to Brazil should be prepared to invest the necessary time and energy to develop relationships. A sincere effort to develop a solid relationship with a Brazilian will be rewarded with a lasting friendship and partnership that will form a strong personal bond linking you to Brazil for life.

Brazilians are generally an intimate and friendly people, and hugs between friends are a common greeting regardless of gender. Women will lightly touch cheek to cheek or air-kiss both cheeks. Women will often greet male friends the same way. Personal space is considerably less among Brazilians than most North Americans are used to, and a casual touch on the arm or a pat on the back is an expected element of interpersonal communication, so to back away and distance oneself may be regarded as insensitive or unkind. Professional relationships often carry on outside of the workplace, so an invitation from a member of the opposite sex to a coffee or drink after work is more often an extension of the friendship and not necessarily a romantic overture.

Brazilians typically like to look nice—dress customs vary based on the activity and location, but it is always important to look your best. Business dress means a well-pressed suit for men and an elegant and professional dress for women. Women's business suits are appropriate, but Brazilian women pride themselves on their femininity and physical beauty, so any business suit should avoid looking overly masculine. Appearance remains important even out of the office, so when going out socially, men should be neat with their shirt and pants pressed and their shoes shined. Tennis shoes or sneakers are not commonly worn in social settings, but are reserved for the athletic activities for which they were designed. Similarly, T-shirts, shorts, and sandals are common among the younger generation and are absolutely appropriate for the beach or walking about town, but not for dance clubs or restaurants, and never the office. Beach attire for Brazilians generally means speedos for the men and skimpy bikinis for the women, but despite the Brazilian practice of wearing as little as possible on the beach, public nudity is frowned upon.

Meals in Brazil often run long, with lunches regularly taking up to two hours and dinners even longer. Many restaurants will serve typical regional fare buffet style, and Saturday is a great day to enjoy a *feijoada* (black bean stew with different meats) buffet. Brazilians almost never eat with their hands, so a knife and fork are standard at every meal and should be used at all times, as well as a napkin. Mealtime is reserved for friendly, casual conversation, so even a business lunch or dinner may not be accompanied by business conversation. It is best to avoid talk about business unless your host brings it up. This allows people to enjoy the opportunity to get to know their dining companions on a social level. Brazilians are always eager to discuss the beauty of their country, family, their national pastime, *futebol* (soccer), the progress of the economy, and even some politics, but extensive questioning about personal life may be unwelcome and cause embarrassment. In all situations, it is best to avoid any topic of discussion in which a negative opinion or unflattering observation may be interpreted as a criticism. Brazilians are well aware of the negative aspects of their country and culture and therefore do not like to be reminded of them or feel that they need to explain or justify them. The meal will continue until someone specifically asks the waiter for the check, which can be done by asking, *A conta, por favor*, and holding up your hand and miming the act of signing a check. Splitting the check is not common, so if a person invites his companions to join him for the meal, he should be prepared to pay for them. Even if the group has agreed to split the check ahead of time, the waiter should not be asked to split it for the group. One person in the party should be responsible for paying the entire bill and the rest of the party can discreetly pay him or her for their part of the meal.

When visiting Brazil, one should always remember that personal relationships are paramount. Business arrangements are best established when the agreeing parties have a strong personal connection, the establishment of which is often aided by a cultural liaison, known as a *despachante*, who introduces potential business partners and facilitates their personal connection before they begin any business consideration. Brazilians are just as dedicated to their professional success as their North American counterparts, but the laid-back culture allows for plenty of provision for tardiness in arriving at meetings or appointments and ample time for friendly chitchat to strengthen the personal relationship between the partners before tackling the more serious business matters. When bureaucracy or other impediments rise up in the way of an arrangement or agreement, Brazilians may turn to the *jeito*, a cultural work-around that allows them to simply skirt the challenge and arrive at the desired outcome. Foreigners should understand that the *jeito* is not a universal free pass that allows them to completely disregard established rules and regulations, especially institutional requirements. Rather a *jeito* operates on the mutual respect and trust between the two parties that ultimately desire to see each other succeed. The successful use of the *jeito* is a testament to the strength of the relationship between the two parties involved.

Scott R. Infanger

Further Reading

Eakin, Marshal. *Brazil: The Once and Future Country*. New York: St. Martin's Griffin, 1997.
Guillermoprieto, Alma. *Samba*. New York: Random House, 1990.
Ickes, Scott. *African-Brazilian Culture and Regional Identity in Bahia, Brazil*. Gainesville: University Press of Florida, 2013.
Vincent, Jon. *Culture and Customs of Brazil*. Westport, CT: Greenwood, 2003.

BULGARIA

Bulgaria is situated in the southeastern corner of Europe, surrounded by multiple countries with very different languages and cultures including Romania, Serbia, Macedonia, Greece, and Turkey. Bulgaria is also located in a very strategic area as it is the gateway to Europe from the East. Throughout history this beautiful country has been inhabited by many different cultures that have left their mark on present-day society. Thracians, Greeks, Romans, Ottomans, Russians, and others have occupied the territory that is current-day Bulgaria, and one does not have to be in Bulgaria long to experience some of these cultural nuances. The Bulgarian people have a long and interesting history filled with struggles, change, and victories that have helped develop a unique set of values, customs, and traditions.

In Bulgaria foreigners often become confused as soon as they ask a question, especially if the answer comes in the form of a shake or nod of the head. The reason for this is that for the majority of the world when someone answers yes to a question they nod their heads up and down. When they answer no to a question they shake their heads left to right and back again. However, in Bulgaria, this is the complete opposite. When Bulgarians choose to say yes to a question they shake their heads sideways, and when they answer no to a question they nod their heads up and down. For the foreigner this simple miscommunication can cause them to misinterpret directions, misunderstand if a shopkeeper has a certain item, or not understand if an establishment has a toilet.

The welcoming of spring begins on the first of March with a holiday called Martenitsa. Martenitsa is a holiday that has a deep-rooted tradition and is celebrated by nearly all Bulgarians. The symbol of this holiday is an ancient deity believed to be the "constant cycle of life." Martenitsa is widely celebrated by wearing bracelets and necklaces made of red and white yarn. During the month of March street vendors from all over sell the little trinkets for all ages. Bulgarians purchase the jewelry and when they see the first sign of spring in the vegetation of the city, they tie the red and white Martenitsas to a branch as a sign of health.

Many superstitions exist in Bulgaria and are followed extremely closely by some, including superstitions like not walking under a ladder, tossing salt over a shoulder, or believing that black cats crossing in front of someone will bring bad luck. Much like other countries in Eastern Europe, Bulgaria practices a tradition that involves odd and even numbers of flowers. For example, one would only want to give an even number of flowers to someone if that person has died, because an odd number is only for the living.

Bulgaria is rich with culture and beauty. With a very lengthy history, Bulgaria is continuing to not only strive to maintain its culture, but also showcase its culture to the world. Bulgaria has much to offer a travel enthusiast, not only including the four main mountain ranges, beautiful rivers, ancient ruins, and scenic landscape, but also a wealth of cultural and historical experiences. Anyone visiting Bulgaria will absolutely leave further enriched and wanting more.

Cameron Phillips

Further Reading

Barth, Linda, ed. *Frommer's: Eastern Europe*. Hoboken, NJ: Wiley, 2009.

Bokova, Irena, et al. *The Cultural Diversity of Bulgaria*. Plovdiv: Lettera, 2012.

Sachsenroeder, Agnes. *Culture Shock! Bulgaria*. Tarrytown, NY: Marshall Cavendish, 2011.

Stamatov, Prof. Dr. Sc. Atanas. *The Bulgarian Civilization*. Sofia: TanNakRa Publishing House, 2007.

C

CANADA

The discussion of common etiquette and taboo in Canada mirrors that of many Western nations. Euro-Canadian culture, which dominates the modern nation, evolved over the past four hundred years since the colonization of the land, first by the French and later the British. Many Canadian customs are drawn directly from their experience as colonists from these two European empires. However, Canadians also share many other customs more closely associated with various settler colonies including Australia, New Zealand, South Africa, and the United States of America. This is not to suggest, however, that Canada is devoid of its own unique etiquette or taboos. Canadians tend to relish their role as polite individuals and bristle at the mention of cultural similarities with the United States. This compilation of characteristics lends itself to the creation of a unique set of cultural customs that make Canada both familiar and difficult to grasp for foreigners.

In Canada it is difficult to claim any cultural custom is truly a national custom due to the nation's many divides. These divides occur between English Canadian and French Canadian, as well as those between Euro-Canadians, First Nations peoples, and recent immigrants from non-European nations. As with many other immigrant nations, the immigrant populations bring a constant wave of new ideas that mix into the cultural stew of accepted customs. Canada is also a regional nation, divided between the Maritimes; the Central Provinces, further divided by Ontario and Quebec; the Plains; and the West. However, at a national level many of Canada's rules of cultural etiquette resemble those found within the wider Anglophone world. This "world" consists of the many nations that the British settled over the course of their imperial expansion, and, for the most part, contemporary readers may recognize these nations as part of the British Commonwealth with the notable exception of Canada's closest neighbor, the United States. Although the United States was a settler colony of the British, it is not a member of the Commonwealth. This aside, it shares many cultural customs with these nations. In the case of Canada, these customs extend from personal and professional greetings, acceptable discussion in public, and proper manners.

In Canada, it is proper to greet an individual by the shaking of hands. This is particularly done when greeting an individual who may be higher than one's self in social status or leadership positions. Any other form of greeting towards an individual, like a boss or other social superior, may be mistaken for a lack of respect. Likewise, handshaking happens when greeting an individual who is generally unknown or a simple acquaintance. Along with the handshake, an introduction of oneself generally includes one's name and a short but relevant commentary on one's position, informing the individual of either employment or relation to a mutual friend or colleague. These are dependent on the situation. Canadians do embrace more intimately with close friends and relations. Generally this occurs with a less formal handshake or a hug. As a whole, Canadians have begun to embrace the soft cheek kisses within groups of close friends or family, following this common European trend. This type of greeting originated in Quebec, the largely French province within Canada that typically embraces European trends more quickly than the rest of English-speaking Canada.

In addition to the most common social greetings discussed above, Canadians typically observe a social taboo on the discussion of politics, sex, and religion. It is also taboo to discuss one's private life in public. An individual is expected to keep discussion of these topics to a minimum within the public sphere, unless required to by one's employment. Some of these jobs may include professions such as journalism where the reporting of news may include all of these listed subjects. In most public situations, and in many private moments as well, Canadians feel the discussion of these topics could lead to unnecessary hostility between individuals. This taboo is certainly one followed by many other Western nations to some extent and practiced with even more fervor in those nations with strong roots in Christianity. As with many cultural customs, these rules are not observed evenly by the entire nation, but rather represent accepted cultural norms.

Some of the etiquette and taboos listed above come directly from the style of Canadian upbringing, one that encourages both respect toward authority figures as well as friends and family. Canadian politeness, accommodation, understanding, peacefulness, and humble attitude are known globally and many within the country take great pride in these attributes as a marker of high civility. Due to this, popular media like movies and television portray Canadians as "aggressively friendly" in comparison to their American counterparts to the south. These forms of entertainment created outside of Canada that feature Canadians often highlight this tendency in their characters, along with the elongation of certain vowels and an overemphasis on the exclamation "eh," to allow the audience to instantly recognize a character as Canadian. This commonly accompanies the character's intense love of the nation, normally wearing a hockey jersey or shirts adorned with the Canadian maple leaf. In ironic fashion, one may hear Canadians refer to themselves as morally and culturally superior in comparison to their southern neighbors, the Americans, due to these attributes of politeness, understanding, and humility.

Other taboos in public discussion include those centered on the status of cultural minorities within Canada. Despite Canada's vast multiculturalism, trumpeted as a major positive of the nation, it is similar to other importing nations of the New World that welcomed millions of immigrants over the past two centuries. Like its cousin immigrant nations of the United States, Brazil, Argentina, Australia, New Zealand, and to a degree Mexico, Canada struggles with a degree of racism. Due to this, it is generally believed to be more taboo in Canada to discuss ethnic groups compared to its southern neighbor. Because of Canada's internal ethnic divide and competing nationalities, there exist varying degrees of social awkwardness when discussing the status of French Canadians or First Nations peoples in particular. Canada was first settled by the French and then came under the control of Great Britain after the French and Indian War, or Seven Years' War, in 1763. The defeat, and rule, of the French and First Nations peoples remains a consistently touchy subject. Quebec, the largely French province of Canada, has on three occasions attempted to break away from the federal government to create its own independent nation based on French culture and language in North America. This leads to a socially tricky situation for both everyday Canadians and those in national politics who attempt to recognize the rights of subcultures to exist in quasi-independence from the dominant culture.

Social discussion taboos do not stop with the topic of an independent Quebec, but include the nation's First Nations peoples. A large portion of these people in many cases feel removed from the nation-building process. Discussing the rights and status of these individuals as either Canadians or tribal members is considered a political topic to avoid in public. However, recent protests by First Nations tribes have brought the topic to the forefront of contemporary Canadian politics, at least forcing the nation to confront one of its taboos. Furthermore, the quasi-independence of Quebec creates a whole new set of cultural etiquette rules and taboos for this subset of Canadians. Without detailing all of these, in general, Quebecois, the people of Quebec, tend to closely align their social etiquette with French customs compared to typically English customs.

Perhaps the most interesting taboo in Canadian culture is the discussion of similarities between the United States and Canada. This taboo is interesting for several reasons. First, it is directed at foreigners in Canada. For a non-Canadian to tell a Canadian that the cultures of Canada and the United States are inseparable, or, at the very least, are very similar is considered highly rude and likely extremely insulting. Second, in terms of dominant language, development of the nation-state, major industries, food types, and even things like sports, the two nations are quite similar. Regardless, Canadians define themselves in opposition to Americans, and even to a lesser extent the British, although geographically anti-Americanism is far more important. A Canadian self-defines as a North American, but a different one from the Americans. The relationship between the two nations resembles something similar to sibling rivalry. Both nations come from the same lineage, originating as British, and to a lesser extent French, imperial colonies. Over time the United States outgrew Canada, becoming an economic and military powerhouse.

For Canadians their past is defined by opposition to the United States, beginning with the War of 1812 when the United States invaded then British Canada. As the United States expanded west, Canada quickly mirrored the United States, building its own transcontinental railroad in order to expand its hold over the western provinces and to prevent the United States from carving out Canadian territory. Even today Canadians remain on the defensive towards their neighbors in terms of independent culture. Markets in Canada are flooded with American-made products, brands, television shows, Hollywood movies, and music at such a high rate that domestic programming and production struggles to keep pace. To an individual visiting Canada, on the surface there appears to be little that separates the two nations. Both nations represent each other's largest trade partner and arguably closest ally. Additionally, many families that live near the border often have close relations on the other side, resulting in frequent visits by many border peoples to the opposite nation, creating a semifluid national boundary. Perhaps because of this long-standing fear of being overwhelmed by their dominating neighbor, and the reality of the near identical cultures, some Canadians have developed a non-hostile anti-Americanism. It is important to note that it is a nonhostile relationship. In order to define themselves, and thus differentiate from Americans, Canadians often point to things like socialized health care, parliamentary government, high standards of living, and a sense of cultural sophistication that Americans lack as what defines Canada. This is a critically important cultural marker and thus generates the taboo.

Marc Anthony Sanko

Further Reading

Cameron, Elspeth, ed. *Canadian Culture: An Introductory Reader*. Toronto: Canadian Scholars Press, 1997.

Mannani, Manijeh, and Veronica Thompson. *Selves and Subjectivities: Reflections on Canadian Arts and Culture*. Edmonton: Alberta University Press, 2012.

Mezei, Kathy. *Translation Effects: The Shaping of Modern Canadian Culture*. Montreal: McGill-Queen's University Press, 2014.

Vance, Jonathan F. *A History of Canadian Culture*. Oxford: Oxford University Press, 2009.

THE CARIBBEAN

The Caribbean is made up of multicultural tropical islands. There are diverse influences from settlers who came from Europe, Africa, Asia, South America, and the Middle East. The Caribbean islands each have different dialects, languages, and races. The first populations living in the Caribbean included Tainos, Arawaks, and Caribs. Later populations included African slaves who were brought to the region. These slaves mostly worked on sugar cane plantations until they fought for independence. Today, this history has resulted in an incredible mix of cultures, and with this came a variety of languages, religions, and taboos. The Caribbean is now a tourist, wedding, and honeymoon destination. Celebrating Carnival in different areas of the Caribbean is very popular. Religion is also very varied with Christianity the most popular religion, but with others including Hinduism and Islam.

In the Caribbean, behaviors and actions of persons greatly affect how they come across in society. Polite behaviors are appreciated in this society and certain actions outside the norm will be viewed differently. When visiting different islands in the Caribbean, eating practices, visiting friends or family in their homes, greetings, conversations, attire, and bathroom visits will all be different from other places around the world.

Creole food was introduced when African slaves came to the Caribbean. Stews and one-pot food items were adopted and localized. These items include macaroni pie, pelau (pilaf), and callaloo as well as various soups. Any meat or legume can be stewed, but favorites include chicken and red beans. This type of food can be eaten with a knife and fork or spoon. Fingers may be used depending on the piece of meat given: if the piece is a leg or wing, fingers can be used; if the piece is a breast or thigh, a knife is normally used.

East Indian food in Trinidad and Tobago includes those food items brought to the region from Indian indentured laborers. Curry is a loved spice. Roti and doubles are the two most common dishes of this cuisine. *Doubles* refers to a local dish that includes fried flour with curried chickpeas. These items are eaten by hand. Most people buy doubles and eat it on the spot, standing with the *bara* (fried bread) and *channa* (curried chickpeas) in their hands. Some may buy and take it away. Either is acceptable. There is also an abundance of Chinese restaurants that have an option to dine in or to take away.

Street cuisine includes coconut vendors or those who serve food such as doubles, gyros, snow cones, and oysters. A visitor can and should ask politely to see food badges of persons he or she is buying from as a precaution. Coconuts can be enjoyed on the spot since the vendor will cut it up in front of the customer. Bake and shark is a favorite dish at the popular beach called Maracas Bay in Trinidad and Tobago. It is made up of deep-fried shark placed in between fried bread called fried bake, together with an assortment of condiments. Eating with one's hands is allowed with this dish.

Barbados is a popular Caribbean island, known for its gorgeous beaches, flora, and fauna. When considering etiquette, due to the island's British influence, Bajans typically prefer more formal greetings when meeting people. This means that hand-shaking between both sexes is considered a norm, followed by a salutation such as "Good evening" or "Pleased to meet you." Hugging and kissing is generally used with friends and family only, which is also practiced in Trinidad and Tobago.

On introduction, or when referring to a Bajan, one should always use a title and surname, unless the person is a close acquaintance or family member. Using first names is considering too casual and even impolite. To exhibit proper etiquette, it is good to introduce oneself first to a Bajan, instead of waiting for them to intro-duce themselves or for someone else to make introductions.

English is the official language of the Bahamas and is widely spoken. Creole is commonly used among Haitian immigrants. Bahamians are very humorous and use humor often. Jokes often tend to be self-deprecating remarks. In general, Bahamians respect people who are modest and humble. They are very down-to-earth people. They can also tease others, intended as a harmless act to poke fun at each other.

Residents of the Virgin Islands are modest in their dress, although Carnival costumes are a different matter altogether. In public, one should not wear a bathing suit or revealing clothing unless at the beach. In general, though, dress is casual. When meeting other people, it is considered good manners to greet everyone you meet. It is acceptable to say "Good morning" or "Good afternoon." If this is not done, it will be considered rude. Greeting in the evening is "Good night" when you meet and when you leave.

In the Caribbean, certain taboos have been passed on from one generation to the next. Not everyone believes in the taboos, which generally suggest a person can bring bad luck to others. Some taboos are believed more than others. For instance, it is considered bad luck to walk under a ladder that is open, even if there is not an easy way to walk around it. Cactus plants also have a taboo attached to them. The cactus is a plant that is said to bring bad luck to people and their families. Negative changes are said to occur with these plants. This only applies if you have cactus growing anywhere in your house. Bathing in the sea on Good Friday is also a taboo. It is said that if someone bathes in the sea on Good Friday, he or she will turn into a fish.

There is a taboo about height and the crossing over of a person's legs in Trinidad and Tobago. If someone steps over another person's legs, it is said that his growth will be affected, and he will not be able to reach his potential height. Like elsewhere, it is considered bad luck to open an umbrella inside the house. Umbrellas are normally kept closed when in houses, but sometimes they are even kept outside to reduce the risk of incurring bad luck.

There are different types of marriages based on religion. Most people live by this quote: "A family that prays together, stays together." Some people may not accept marriages that have two different religions, but to others, it's a social norm. Sometimes, to honor both religions, the bride and groom get married twice in the two different religions.

The main types of rituals for the deceased are cremation and burial. This can also be looked at from a religious aspect. Hindus normally cremate, which involves burning the body and collecting the ashes to throw into the ocean or somewhere significant to the person. Muslims and Christians normally bury the body.

Candida Khan

Further Reading

Calder, Simon, and Gail Simmonds. "The Complete Guide to the Spanish Caribbean." 2006. http://www.independent.co.uk/travel/americas/the-complete-guide-to-the-spanish -caribbean-6109891.html. Accessed March 20, 2015.

French Caribbean International. "Welcome to the Islands of Your Dreams." 2013. http:// www.frenchcaribbean.com/. Accessed March 20, 2015.

IIWINC. "The Culture of the Caribbean." 2015. http://caribya.com/caribbean/culture/. Accessed March 20, 2015.

James, Roger. "Superstitions." 2015. http://www.tntisland.com/superstitions.html. Accessed March 9, 2015.

kwintessential. "The Bahamas—Language, Culture, Customs and Etiquette." 2014. http:// www.kwintessential.co.uk/resources/global-etiquette/bahamas.html. Accessed March 21, 2015.

Rose, Miranda. "Caribbean Culture Too Diverse to be Labelled—Prof Nettleford." 2008. http://www.stabroeknews.com/2008/archives/09/05/caribbean-culture-too-diverse -to-be-labelled-%E2%80%93-prof-nettleford/. Accessed March 20, 2015.

SVE/VARS. "English in the Caribbean." 2015. https://www.uni-due.de/SVE/VARS_Carib bean.htm. Accessed March 20, 2015.

TDC. "Trinidad and Tobago History." 2014. http://gotrinidadandtobago.com/trinidad-and -tobago/culture-in-trinidad-and-tobago.html. Accessed March 8, 2015.

TravelEtiquette. "Etiquette in Barbados." 2015. http://www.traveletiquette.co.uk/etiquette barbados.html. Accessed March 21, 2015.

TripAdvisor. "U.S. Virgin Islands: Tipping & Etiquette." 2015. http://www.tripadvisor.com /Travel-g147400-s606/U-S-Virgin-Islands:Caribbean:Tipping.And.Etiquette.html. Accessed March 21, 2015.

Wilson, Peter J. "Reputation and Respectability: A Suggestion for Caribbean Ethnology." *Man* 4, no. 1 (1969): 70–84.

CENTRAL AFRICA

Central Africa is a huge geographic area located in the heart of Africa, covered with savanna and rainforest. Often referred to as humanity's cradle due to its proximity to the Great Rift Valley where some of the earliest hominid fossils have been found, this subregion has generated Western fantasies and projections for centuries. The nine countries officially gathered are clearly distinguishable, from the giant territory of the Democratic Republic of Congo to the tiny islands of São Tomé and Principe, passing by Angola, Gabon, Cameroon, Chad, Equatorial Guinea, Central African Republic, and Republic of Congo. These countries do not always share a common language, religion, or history. However, their social and cultural practices can extend over state borders.

During the precolonial period, several kingdoms and chiefdoms characterized by oral traditions shared the territory. Among them, the powerful kingdom of Kongo gave its name to the river and the two countries. From 1482, contacts were established with the first Portuguese explorers leading to the king's conversion to Christianity. Evangelization was gradually established. During the eighteenth to the mid-nineteenth century, the region was ravaged by the transatlantic slave trade. This tragic episode of history is still alive in the collective memory. For example, many public monuments reflect a duty of memory.

In 1885, as a result of the Berlin Conference, Central Africa was divided between the different colonial imperial powers. Then came decades of colonialism by the Portuguese, Germans, British, French, and Belgians, marked among others by the establishment of Indigenous status for the African, considered as uncivilized and inferior. The creation of the borders of modern states has profoundly changed the ratio of populations to their territories and sometimes brutally inverted the status of foreigners and natives.

In Central Africa, the presence of substantial natural resources (oil, copper, diamonds, and gold) does not prevent the extreme poverty of a large part of the population. People are often subject to very unstable political situations. The wave of independence in the 1960s has not prevented multipronged and complex conflicts, such as the Chadian wars or the conflict in Central African Republic, which began in 2012. The crisis generated population movement between some countries. The residence status as migrants, refugees, or asylum seekers further complicates the identity construction process in the region. Despite regular tensions, international unions have been established, for example through the Economic Community of Central African States that tries to maintain economic stability.

There are stereotypes surrounding the populations in Central Africa. The stereotypes can be divided into two groups. According to the *optimistic* view, the region is considered as a land of solidarity, respect for elders, and connections preserved to nature and exotic wildlife. According to the *pessimistic* view, on the contrary, the region is considered as a land of repeated tribal wars, famine, disease, corruption, and brain drain. All these intellectual constructions need to be handled with care.

The respect for authenticity and ancestral customs has great importance for Central Africans. However, the traditions are not static but rather dynamic. That is to say, they are constantly transformed and reinvented to suit modern situations. Indeed, dialogues between the present and a mythologized past are very common. For example, a politician can adopt the attributes of traditional leaders in some situations.

One of the most operative and global etiquettes concerning the Central African population is the concept of resourcefulness. In the Democratic Republic of Congo, a popular expression reflects this concept: "Refer to the Article 15!" which means "Cope for yourself!" In 1960, the head of the breakaway state would have commented the 15th article of its new constitution by inviting his population to get for themselves. The term "Article 15" has been popularized to mean state deficiency in general. Most sectors (agriculture, health, schooling, culture) suffer from a lack of financial resources. This context generates many crafts, inventions, and informal solutions. For example, when garbage pickup is not organized in a neighborhood district, the habitants set up a labor division, in order to remove, recycle, and destroy the waste. When a cemetery is not maintained, then a small group of people organize an informal system, reselling coffins and burying the dead. Based on survival logics, the informal sectors reflect both the resourcefulness of people and the disengagement of state.

Solidarity and generosity are often praised by foreigners and claimed by the Central Africans themselves. These qualities take many forms such as helping with field work or taking care of another woman's baby. The poverty condition often explains this situation. The family is considered as a refuge and understood in a very broad sense. For example, a man is called "uncle" by a child without being his biological uncle.

The Bantu People

Many ethnic groups live in Central Africa, joined by the same culture, blood ties, or geographic belonging. *Bantu* is a general label profusely used to designate an immense human group, from several ethnic groups, living in Central Africa regions and beyond. The Bantu population is estimated at nearly 150 million people.

In the mid-twentieth century, a German named Wilhelm Bleek first use the term *Bantu* (plural of *Muntu*) to designate a population using common languages and living in sub-Saharan Africa. "Ba-ntu," meaning "the people" or "the humans," is akin to the terms *Inuit* and *Manush*, also universal terms. In the nineteenth century, physical and biological classifications refocused on linguistics. In the 1950s, a Bantu philosophy characterized by belief in vital forces was proclaimed. Thirty years later, the term was popularized by the foundation of the International Center of Bantu

Civilization. The mission of this interstate project is to retain, promote, and conserve Bantu cultural heritage. This political refocusing on Bantu identity is measurable by the desire to pacify and strengthen the union between people, whereas globalization is perceived as threatening. This general context explains the gathering around a primordial concept.

The general denomination *Bantu* creates questions about non-Bantu people, for example the Pygmies. In the Republic of Congo, the two groups live together, but the Pygmy population (nearly 2 percent of the global population) is endangered, according to the United Nations. The opposition between Bantus and Pygmies is based on multiple considerations (physical, cultural, societal) but also on the fundamental criterion of the priority of land use, which leads to political repercussions.

When failures, misfortunes, or accidents occur in Central Africa, it is often associated with an act of witchcraft or a curse, although the level of religiosity is not the same in all families. Among animists, it is often called witchcraft, and for Christians, it is more about curses. Not having respected certain religious taboos is a very common explanation for the occurrence of a problem.

Sexuality is surrounded by many taboos. For example, homosexuality is often considered in opposition to African traditions. In some societies, it is a part of certain initiation stages during adolescence, before becoming a man or woman, but must be strictly supervised. Any abuse is prohibited and can lead to prison. The first explorers and missionaries claimed that African sexual practices were depraved and that homosexuality did not exist at all on the continent. According to an old myth, homosexuality was introduced by Westerners. A lot of people still believe that homosexuality did not exist before the arrival of Europeans. This belief, associated with monotheism precepts, explains the negative perception of homosexuality and its categorization as a social taboo in Central Africa.

In these originally oral societies, words are very important and can become taboo. For example, if a child dies, people respect his or her name and no longer pronounce it. Only after the family's mourning is accomplished may a newborn be called the same name. Suicide is taboo. Even the word is taboo, not spoken but replaced by the word *accident*. Thus, it is very difficult to obtain official statistics on suicides, since people do not record the dead as such.

A great taboo in Central Africa is infertility, particularly of women. In this region, a woman who cannot bear a child is often rejected by society. However, numerous studies show that infertility is very common in Africa due to health care deficiencies, poor childbirth conditions, and clandestine abortions (another great taboo). Access to in-vitro fertilization for infertile patients is only available to very rich people. Most of the time, the concept of extended family comes to the aid of those women, who will help to take care of the family's children.

The wrapper is a basic element of the feminine Central African wardrobe. It is a colorful piece of cloth, knotted in different ways around the waist or above the chest. In everyday life, it can also securely wrap a child on the back of the mother at the same time. A similar, but smaller cloth can be used as a head scarf. During important ceremonies, such as weddings, funerals, or national holidays, the wrapper acts as a sign of social recognition.

The African wax is a type of wrapper. Made in cotton treated with colorful wax, its colors do not fade. The possible patterns are countless. In order to support a candidate during a political campaign, people wear wrappers showing the face of the politician and name of the party. The wax has emerged in the high fashion world, inspiring the greatest creators, such as French fashion designer Jean-Paul Gaultier.

"La Sape" is an abbreviation based on the phrase Congolese Society of Ambianceurs and Elegant Persons. It refers to a fashion movement born in the Republic of Congo and diffused in the Democratic Republic of Congo. Among the various branches that exist, "sapeurs" plead elegance under any circumstances, wearing designer suits and shoes with extravagant colors. They also distinguish themselves by a particular way of greeting each other: rubbing their foreheads. In Brazzaville, the sapeurs observe a certain sobriety by respecting the rule of "three colors only," whereas in Kinshasa any liberty concerning bright colors is taken. Perhaps this trend is pronounced today because it was prohibited during the reign of Mobutu, judged too Western and not authentic enough. For some people, la Sape symbolizes a futile display of overpriced clothing in poor countries, but for others it symbolizes a return to freedom and a label of African elegance.

In Central Africa, each country has its traditional meal, but also a wide variety of culinary preparations based on local habits. The food bases are essentially from the garden (manioc, eggplant, yams, sweet potatoes, peanuts), tropical fruit (banana,

Sapeurs strike a pose at Parc de Prince in Kinshasa, Democratic Republic of Congo. Sapeurs and "sapology" were outlawed during the reign of Mobutu Sese Seko (1965–1997), who considered them too Western. They have since enjoyed a resurgence in popularity. (Miguel Juarez/ Getty Images)

plantain, mango, pineapple, papaya), seafood (fish, shellfish), meat (beef, goat, veal), and bush-meat (porcupine, snake, antelope). For each ingredient, many preparations exist, such as fried manioc, cooked manioc leaves, or steamed manioc. The sauces accompanying these dishes are spicy. Cube broths are often used by the cooks for their convenience and their preservation.

Essentially always prepared by women, meals consist of large portions in order to be able to serve a "surprise" guest. They are high in calories because people often only have one meal a day. They mostly consist of a main dish, without starter or sweet. Sodas (Coke, Fanta, Sprite, etc.) are very appreciated. Sold in consigned bottles, they substitute for dessert. Moreover, sodas are called "sweets."

Many people are affected by drinking water problems. Therefore, in the cities, street vendors sell plastic bags of water for a few pennies. One bites the corner of the bag and is easily hydrated. People also drink local beer or palm wine in taverns. They will first take a small sip, and then pour a few drops on the floor to toast their ancestors.

Nora Greani

Further Reading

Ayimpan, Sylvie. *Economie de la Débrouille à Kinshasa. Informalité, commerce et réseaux sociaux* [Economy of resourcefulness in Kinshasa. Informality, trade and social networks]. Paris: Karthala, 2014.

Chrétien, Jean-Pierre. "Les Bantous, de la philologie allemande à l'authenticité africaine [The Bantous, from German philology to African authenticity]." *Vingtième Siècle. Revue d'histoire* 8, no. 8 (1985): 43–66.

Courade, Georges, ed. *L'Afrique des idées reçues* [Africa of received ideas]. Paris: Belin, 2006.

De Boek, Filip. *Cemetery State*, DRC, 72 min, FilmNatie BVBA. English/French, 2010.

Greani, Nora. "Art sous influences. Une approche anthropologique de la créativité contemporaine au Congo-Brazzaville [Art under influences. An anthropological approach to contemporary creativity in Congo-Brazzaville]." PhD diss., EHESS, Paris, 2013.

Hobsbawm, Eric, and Terence Ranger, eds. *The Invention of Tradition*. Cambridge: Cambridge University Press, 1983.

Pourtier, Roland. "Introduction thématique. L'Afrique centrale entre incertitudes et renouveau [Thematic introduction. Central Africa between uncertainties and revival]." *Afrique contemporaine*, no. 215 (2005): 21–27.

CENTRAL AMERICA

The geographical area of Central America is composed of seven independent and autonomous countries between Mexico and South America, beginning with the northernmost country, Guatemala, and continuing south to Belize, Honduras, El Salvador, Nicaragua, Costa Rica, and Panama.

Spanish is the dominant language spoken in all but Belize, which was a British colony until 1981 and where English predominates. For the remainder of the countries Spanish dominates because of the large influx of emigrants from Spain after Columbus's discovery of the "New World" in 1492. In the centuries that followed, thousands of these Spaniards flooded the area, plundering natural resources and building settlements that continue to flourish to this day. In most of the Spanish-dominant countries there also exist several indigenous groups, some of which are descendants of preexisting Aztec and Mayan cultures that were subjugated during the Spanish conquest. All of this intermingling of cultures resulted in a rich heritage of customs still enjoyed by nationals and visitors alike. The vast majority of Central Americans identify themselves as Christian. Though Roman Catholics are in the vast majority, many would be considered merely culturally Catholic, that is, Catholic by heritage rather than through regular religious practice. Most evangelicals groups are represented, with Pentecostals being in the majority. The varied ethnicity of Central American peoples means there are also a number of indigenous religious practices as well as traditional Western practices.

Due to this varied mixture of cultures and national identities, it is impossible to give specifics that would cover each Central American country in detail. Nevertheless, the following attempts to provide some generalizations will help the reader better understand the area.

When entering a room or a place with others, it is customary to give a general greeting such as "Buenos días" (Good day, or Good morning), "Buenas tardes" (Good afternoon), and "Buenas noches" (Good evening). Greetings are very important, and failure to greet can be seen as rude. The shaking of hands is also customary, and once a level of friendship is established it is not unusual for women to kiss each other on the cheek, for men to give each other a hug, or for good friends of the opposite sex to kiss each other on the cheek. Another important part of the greeting custom is to ask about the welfare of the individual, their family, and so on. This is especially true in business transactions, where failure to do so would be considered rude. An important part of "business" is following cultural practices and appropriate etiquette.

The year-round tropical climate in many of the cities of Central America means that formal wear does not include a jacket and tie for men. Instead dress slacks and a dress shirt are considered correct male formal attire. Men often wear the *guayabera*, a shirt with pockets on both sides of the front that is worn loose and not tucked into trousers. Short shorts, for men and women, are not common and should be reserved for the beach. Ostentatious dress should be avoided.

When invited to the home as a guest it is customary to bring a small gift of appreciation to the host. In most of Central America the sense of time is different than in the United States. Punctuality, cherished by North American standards, is not understood in the same way. The need for many to take public transportation and other unpredictable issues cause many people to be what North Americans would consider late. Those native to Central America do not expect precise arrival times. In fact, showing up exactly on time or early might be taken as rude. A starting time means different things in different countries, especially with regards to evening meals. Dinner is eaten much later than in the United States. Another aspect of dining etiquette in Central America expects men to remove their hats during a meal. Many find delight in the varied foods of Central America. Myriad combinations of rice and beans fill plates throughout the area, as well as a host of tropical fruits. Drinks made from fruits match the popularity of coffee, which is grown in many of the countries. A common assumption is to equate food in Central America with the Mexican-influenced American version (TexMex), but many of the countries do not share the North American desire for spicy food. Each country has its own national dishes and has much pride in them, so the guest should investigate ahead of time if spicy sauces are used before assuming their availability in every country. Visitors are encouraged to practice some Spanish when in Central America, especially basic greetings, but word-related problems can occur around subjects such as food. For instance, many English speakers visiting Central America will ask if food is "hot," meaning "spicy," and will use the word *caliente*, meaning hot temperature, instead of the correct word, *picante*. Another issue occurs when a host is serving the guest and the host asks "How much?" If the guest responds with the word *bastante*, which can mean "enough," thinking that the serving was plenty, the host will actually serve more and repeat the question. The problem is that *bastante* in this context actually means "more," so the host believes the guest is requesting more food.

Just as it is wrong to assume Central American food is akin to American-influenced TexMex, so it should be noted that some gestures used in North America do not have the same meaning in Central America. For instance, in Central America pointing with the index finger is to be avoided; rather people use the open hand to indicate. Also, some of the hand signals used in North America have a very different meaning in Central America and should not be used. When indicating the height of a person do not use a flat hand with the palm down, as this gesture is reserved for animals and inanimate objects. To indicate the height of a young child, it is polite to bend the hand so that the fingers are roughly at a 90 degree angle with the palm down and indicate the height.

Sometimes Central Americans show a tendency not to use the word "no." This would be best understood as a desire not to offend or displease a guest. For example, a North American may invite a Central American over for a meal, and receive an affirmative response. The Central American desire not to disappoint or lose face in the eyes of the guest might cause them to respond positively to the invitation, even though they know they cannot make the appointment. Similarly, Central Americans have a different sense of space and are more comfortable standing closer together in social gatherings than their North American neighbors. It is not unusual for a North American to feel somewhat uncomfortable in public gatherings when a Central American seems to "invade their sense of space" by coming close to converse with them.

Family is of great importance to life in Central America. Family rituals and celebrations are considered major events, and senior family members are treated very respectfully. Family relationships are considered more important than any other relationship, especially when doing business. For example, rather than call a traditional helpline, Central Americans consider it preferable to make contact through a family member who knows someone who can provide assistance. Education is very important and sacrifice for the family is common. Moreover, traditional male and female roles are clearly defined with the "macho" man acting authoritatively and dominating women while women are typically self-sacrificing and nurturing.

However, as is occurring in other cultures, some of these traditional gender roles are in transition.

Ed Steele

Further Reading

"Central American Etiquette." *Etiquette Scholar.* https://www.etiquettescholar.com/dining _etiquette/table-etiquette/central_america.html. Accessed February 8, 2016.
"How Culture Affects Work Practices in Latin America." *Knowledge @Wharton.* http:// knowledge.wharton.upenn.edu/article/how-culture-affects-work-practices-in-latin -america/. Accessed February 8, 2016.
McGoldrick, M., and J. Giordano. *Ethnicity and Family Therapy*, 3rd ed. New York: Guilford, 2005.

CHILE

Chile is a country in South America with a population of nearly 17 million people and an area of 291,930 square miles. It is situated south of Peru and west of Bolivia and Argentina, and fills a narrow 4,506-kilometer-long space between the Andes and the Pacific Ocean. The Andes mountain range constitutes one-third of Chile. At the southern tip of Chile's mainland is Punta Arenas, the southernmost city in the world, and beyond that lies the Strait of Magellan and Tierra del Fuego, an island divided between Chile and Argentina. The southernmost point of South America is Cape Horn, a 424-meter rock on Horn Island that belongs to Chile. The Atacama Desert in the north is one of the driest regions in the world. The center of the country has a Mediterranean climate, while the south is cooler. Spanish is the national language, a consequence of the Spanish conquest in the sixteenth century. The population of Chile is 95 percent white with small populations of Mestizos (white and Amerindians) and blacks. The Chilean people tend to have different customs and beliefs from the other peoples in South America; this may be because of their geographical position, of being separated by distance and the Andes Mountains from the rest of the world. Chileans tend to be a traditional and isolated people who, nevertheless, possess a wealth of knowledge about world issues. Chile is one of the most peaceful countries in South America. The country has a very low crime rate; there is little corruption and the police (*carabineros*) do not accept bribes. Interestingly for those from other countries, people who have tattoos on their bodies may be assumed to be criminals.

The etiquette of Chileans typically derives from habits formed in their childhood, and women are treated with courtesy and kindness. As children, most Chileans are taught to do everything in the traditional ways as everything new and unknown might be dangerous. They typically do not like uncertainty and need security in family life and work alike. Many Chileans like to have guidelines, rules, and formal policies. As a predominantly Catholic country, people in Chile often do not feel they need to take charge of their own destiny. They are predisposed to accept fatalism and do not believe that accepting personal responsibility for future outcomes is necessary on their part. Chileans' sense of fatalism also means that they tend not to take responsibility for their own actions. For example, if a person forgets to send money to somebody on time, Chileans are unlikely to admit it was their fault, preferring instead to make excuses and blame circumstances rather than take responsibility.

In Chile, connections are important in obtaining employment. An employee is thought to owe respect, discretion, and commitment to his or her employer. Often Chilean organizations are inefficient, unwilling to change their focus or strategies. This is partly because Chilean ways often support a hierarchical employment structure with inequality among workers, meaning that lower-level workers have to respect their superiors without questioning their actions. Chilean people tend to like a communal life and prefer to meet in person rather than to rely on telephones, social media, or e-mail. Within Chilean society there are always social and work circles; these involve family members and those that share an affinity with a social class, profession, or institution. Group members consider people that do not belong to circles of family or friends to be strangers, and might not feel any moral or ethical obligations to the "outsiders." The "outsiders" could also be considered undeserving and untrustworthy. If a person wishes to gain access to a specific circle then he or she must gain the personal trust of the people within the group through an introduction by an existing group member. When an employer is seeking the best qualified Chilean to fill a position, the applicant's background, social class, or loyalty to a group are taken into consideration. Personal relationships often take precedence over performance in Chilean organizations.

The collective moral force in Chilean society closely ties employees and companies together, blurring the lines between personal life and work obligations. For example, if a long-term employee in a Chilean firm experiences illness in the family, the company provides financial assistance to them. The work ethic is based on loyalty and mutual moral obligations.

Communication in Chile is twofold, through verbal and nonverbal means. Chilean people tend to be warm and friendly and supplement their spoken words with embraces, kisses, or energetic pats on the back. These physical gestures are additional aspects to the unspoken, subtle, silent language of Chileans that also includes the wearing of appropriate clothes, using appropriate facial expressions, educational titles and certificates, displaying family social affiliations, and displaying correct eating habits. For example, in professional situations men always wear suits and ties and behave in a warm but professional manner. Chilean men would never come to work wearing shorts or put their feet on the desk, as to do so would be seen as unprofessional. Women, meanwhile, dress modestly but with great care and attention to detail.

In Chilean culture the area of close personal space is of major importance. People stand very close to each other—often within inches. If the distance is greater than this then people might make an effort to stand closer together because they feel that if the distance is greater they will not be able to achieve any meaningful understanding of each other. Close personal space is courteous behavior for Chileans, and direct eye contact has to be maintained at all times. Chilean society tends to view time as cyclical and so people believe that if you put off doing something until later, there will always be another opportunity to do it. Similarly, professional meetings are very relaxed and may take a long time because many Chileans consider life to be too short to worry about keeping up with daily schedules. Chilean culture does not equate time to money, and Chileans' agendas are often filled with numerous and sometimes conflicting activities that are constantly being changed and/or erased. Meetings are often interrupted and important personal issues are always given priority in any workplace. People stress the enjoyment of life and often are unaware of the passage of time. If a visitor is supposed to meet a Chilean person at 10 a.m., he should not be too disappointed that she or he might turn up half an hour later and may soon have to cut the meeting short because of the impending lunch at midday. Similarly a host would expect a guest to turn up at least 15 to 30 minutes late for an invited dinner as they might be in the process of making the last-minute preparations or taking a shower. Chileans seem to be unaware, or unconcerned, that their attitude towards time and personal space can be irritating and disturbing to non-Chileans. Indeed, many Chileans feel it is not necessary for them to accommodate the niceties of other nationalities, instead believing that visitors should accept the ways of their host and earn their trust. Social traditions must be followed in Chile. Formal education is very important and people use all of the titles they have earned through their education. It is imperative to address people using the correct formal title of *Ingeniero* (Engineer), *Licenciado* (BA or BS), or *Doctor* (PhD). The more titles a Chilean has, the more respected she or he and the more entitled to formally, or informally, mentor younger people.

Chileans like to entertain their business counterparts in restaurants. There is always plenty of food and drink and lively social talk about family, football, world events, art, and music before the conversation turns to business transactions. In this way Chileans get to know someone in order to better understand the person with whom they are dealing. It is much more important than a strict, cold, businesslike environment for anyone looking for a successful outcome from the business trip to Chile. It is also important for non-Chileans wishing to do business in Chile to respect Chilean sensitivities to the political issues of their country and the country's problems, as well as the topics of religion and U.S. policies towards Chile. It is also better to avoid mentioning Argentina to Chileans because of the competition and turbulent history between the two neighbors. It is also wise to avoid mentioning the history of Araucanian Indians and the human rights violations against them. Another topic that would not be discussed freely concerns different religions and varied beliefs. Also, as Chileans are very patriotic, they do not feel comfortable discussing any negative aspect of their history. It is safe to talk about children, local culture, hobbies, and travel, however.

When a Chilean person invites a guest to dinner, she or he will normally pay for the meal, and table manners are seen as indicators of a person's breeding. When in the company of Chileans at a dinner table, a person should not speak when they have a mouthful of food nor put their elbows on the table. It pleases the host if the guest orders the same dish as he or she did. One of the most interesting taboos in Chile is that people will never use their hands to eat; they use cutlery even if pizza or French fries are served. Additionally, licking your fingers or using toothpicks is considered vulgar.

The majority of Chilean people will never criticize anybody openly as they are concerned about other people's feelings. They may ask guests openly about their private lives. This is a sign that they are interested and care about them. People in Chile are emotional, and logic is less appealing to them than expressing what they feel at a certain time and in general. At the same time trust, dignity, and honor are important values that help build social and business relationships with others. People in Chile are appreciative if you can communicate with them in Spanish. Although curious about different countries and cultures, Chileans are not prepared to give up their traditions, their manners, and their ways whether at home or abroad.

Anna Hamling

Further Reading

Erickson, Carol. "Chile's Information Transformation. Boils, Enzo Abbagliati." *American Libraries* 34 (2003): 51–52.
Jerrill, Eileen. "Wish You Were There." *American Libraries* 16 (1985): 602–4.
Roraff, Susan, and Laura Camacho. *CultureShock! Chile: A Survival Guide to Customs and Etiquette*. Tarrytown, NY: Marshall Cavendish, 2011.
Sabath, Ann Marie. *International Business Etiquette: Latin America*. Franklin Lakes, NJ : Career Press, 2000.

CHINA

China is a country with many new high-rise buildings and long-held cultural traditions. There are urban centers with millions of people and isolated villages in remote areas. As a result, there are a variety of cultures, and what is considered acceptable etiquette or taboos differs according to these settings. The concept of "face" means that a person goes to great lengths to avoid embarrassment. Understanding this concept enables a person not to offend their host. Showing respect for the culture and people of China contributes to good relationships. One should avoid acting or speaking in a way not considered appropriate by inhabitants of China.

Respect should be shown in greetings. In ancient times bowing was a way to show honor to another person. Today, a visitor would be wise to watch how a person to whom he is introduced responds, since customs vary in different settings. If they extend a hand to shake hands with the visitor, he should respond by offering his hand in return. If not, the visitor should not plan to shake hands. A nod may be used instead of shaking hands. Hugging would not be an acceptable greeting. Plan to stand when being introduced to others.

A typical greeting would be "How are you?" ideally spoken in the Chinese language of the person with whom the visitor is meeting. Visitors should be certain to use proper titles such as Dr., Mr., Mrs., and Miss, and not call someone by their first name when introduced. One greeting asking "Have you eaten?" is very similar to asking "How are you?"

When conducting business, the senior company person usually enters the room first, since the Chinese may enter a room based on seniority in the business. If one offers a business card to the host, he should offer it with both hands. The normal process is for the person in a lower position to be introduced first to a person in a higher position. A Chinese person will give their family name, or last name first and then their given name. One should listen carefully and try to remember how to pronounce a person's name properly. Courtesy should be shown by not talking when someone else is speaking, and avoiding too many direct yes-or-no questions. For instance, a person may not give a direct answer about a possible business deal, but will more often answer indirectly.

When entering an apartment or home, it is customary to take off one's shoes. The host may have slippers in various sizes just inside the door for guests to use while in the house. A recent variation would be to have covers that fit over shoes.

"Face" relates to living in an honor and shame culture. It includes helping a person have a sense of dignity and importance. One aspect related to "face" is to avoid embarrassing another person. This means treating the other person with honor and respect. In some cultures it may be acceptable to tease another person as a way to put them at ease, but what is considered teasing may seem offensive in Chinese culture. The host should determine what may be humorous. If the host jokes, one should avoid being sensitive and be able to laugh at oneself.

Treating people with respect gives "face" to them. In Chinese culture, displaying a lack of respect causes the disrespected person to lose "face," which in turn leads to embarrassment. This will impact relationships in employment. Similarly correcting a person for an error should be done in private because to be ridiculed publicly in front of co-workers causes one to lose face. Losing one's temper in public is also seen as a loss of face.

Traditional Chinese culture teaches that good family relationships are extremely important. The concept of respect for parents or filial piety means that parents have great impact on the life choices of their child. As parents age, they may also live with their adult children. Multigenerational households are quite common. Guests should show respect for the family structure, especially the older family members.

Appearance and dress should fit the social occasion. In large cities, a business-man will often dress in a suit with dress shirt and tie while businesswomen would dress in a conservative manner and avoid bright colors for meetings. It is important to avoid looking sloppy and seek to have a respectful personal appearance whether in a business or casual setting. Comfortable clothing that one would wear in the home, such as worn-out jeans or shirts, should not worn in public in China. In China, a guest whose appearance and dress is considered inappropriate might be seen as disrespecting both their host and Chinese society in general.

When invited to meet someone at a restaurant, the guest should be certain to be on time. When invited to a home for a meal, it is appropriate to bring a small gift to give to the host. A gift should be given with both hands. The host should indicate where guests should sit at the table and when it is time to begin eating. Guests should eat what is offered to them and be prepared to try foods that may be new to them, such as chicken feet. Chinese food is considered very tasty to those who acquire an appetite to enjoy it. Rice bowls may be held with the left hand close to one's mouth while eating from them, but chopsticks should be placed down when drinking or while pausing for conversation during the meal. Burping and belching may be seen as a sign that a meal is being enjoyed, and hosts will want to ensure that their guests are full. Leaving food on a plate or in a bowl is an acceptable way to indicate that additional food is not desired, and guests should not take the last piece of food on a serving dish.

In a restaurant, serving plates or dishes may be placed on a rotating circular glass in the middle of a table. One should allow the people seated next to them the opportunity to serve themselves first. One should pace oneself while eating and be sure to eat a variety of the foods offered, as otherwise the host may be offended. If toothpicks are avail-

A woman of the Yi ethnic group enjoys a bowl of rice, Laohuzui, China. According to traditional Chinese etiquette, the bowl of rice is held in the left hand, close to the mouth, and the rice is scooped into the mouth with chopsticks held in the right hand. (Nono07/iStockphoto.com)

able, one should wait until the end of a meal to use them and the mouth should be covered while using it. If someone wishes to pay for the meal, they should offer to do so more than once, as it is often the case that in China people may say "No" twice before agreeing to a request the third time. In some areas of China it is appropriate to say thank you to servers, while in southern China tapping your first two fingers on the table represents a way to thank waiting staff. There are a number of taboos surrounding food in China. For example, it is considered bad luck to knock over a container filled with rice. People also avoid putting chopsticks face-up in a rice bowl as this means you hope someone at the table will die. If asked to order food, one should be sensitive that some Chinese will not eat pork because of their religious background. Also, cutting a pear in two to share is not done because this action is associated with separation.

In China the distance between two persons engaged in conversation may be closer than that to which a visitor is accustomed. The host determines the distance between speakers, but one may adjust the distance if it seems uncomfortably close. The host should also be the person to start a conversation and control its flow. If the person being spoken to is a stranger, one should use shorter answers at the beginning of the conversation. Genuine interest in the other person should be shown. One should expect to be asked personal questions about such things as age, weight, income, or the value of one's home. However, a recent study notes a decrease in the use of such questions. One should, however, avoid sensitive topics that have political overtones. Visitors to China should also note that a laugh or grin might not mean a person thinks something is humorous, but may express embarrassment for not understanding what is being said.

As in conversation, personal space may also be limited in public situations. For instance, one may find very little personal space when using public transportation. Also in lines, or queues, one should be prepared that the notion of "waiting one's turn" is not the norm. Instead crowding in lines is to be expected.

In China some gestures are frowned upon. For example, one should not motion to people turning your palm up and motioning with your index finger. Instead, one should indicate to someone by using a sweeping motion with the palm down. The palm-down sweeping gesture is used to hail a cab. One should avoid pointing using with the index finger, but should use an open palm or hand instead. Snapping fingers or showing the soles of shoes should also be avoided.

A number of taboos are associated with the Chinese New Year. For instance, people should not sweep, have their hair cut, use certain words associated with death or ghosts, or break objects. Topics related to death should be avoided during festivals and during happy occasions like weddings. One should also avoid touching strangers, and people following Taoist beliefs will not place mirrors in bedrooms.

Gift-giving also has a number of associated taboos. For example, if more than one item is given as a gift, then an even number of items should be given and the gifting should not include four of any one item, since in some Chinese languages the number four sounds like the word for death. Gifts should not be wrapped in white paper since that color is associated with sorrow and poverty. For this reason white flowers should not be given either. Roses should not be given to a friend since roses carry connotations of romance. Other gifts that are taboo include books, since the word for book sounds like the word for fail, and fans, as the word for fan sounds similar to that used for separation. Green hats should not be given as gifts (or worn), as green hats are related to an ancient story about a woman who was not true to her husband. Clocks should not be given since the word sounds like a word associated with a funeral and, similarly, towels are associated with funerals too. Umbrellas are not given as gifts either since the giving of an umbrella implies the desire to end a friendship. When someone receives a gift it is customary for the receiver not to open the present in front of the person who has given it to them.

Philip A. Pinckard

Further Reading

Chin, Fuyu. "Taboos in China: To Be or Not to Be." *English Language Teaching* 5, no. 7 (July 2012). http://www.ccsenet.org/elt. Accessed March 24, 2015.

"International Dining Etiquette: China." http://www.etiquettescholar.com/dining_etiquette /table-etiquette/pacific_dinner_etiquette/chinese.html. Accessed March 20, 2015.

Lawrence, Anthony. *The Fragrant Chinese*. Hong Kong: Chinese University Press, 1993.

Mack, Lauren. "Chinese Culture: Chinese Gift Giving Etiquette." http://chineseculture. about.com/od/chinesefestivals/a/Chinese-Taboo.htm-. Accessed March 21, 2015.

Mack, Lauren. "Chinese Etiquette: Visiting a Chinese Home." http://chineseculture .about.com/od/businesseconomy/qt/Chinese-Etiquette-Visiting-A-Chinese-Home .htm. Accessed March 23, 2015.

"Top 7 Taboos in China (Beginner)." October 2012. http://www.echineselearning.com /blog/top-7-taboos-in-china-beginner. Accessed Feb. 24, 2015.

"Traditional Etiquette and Taboos." http://www.chinatravel.com/facts/traditional-etiquette -and-taboos.html. Accessed Feb, 24, 2015.

COLOMBIA

Beyond the larger culture of Colombia, located in northwestern South America, a mixture of subcultures exists due to the geographic divisions within the country. These social subcultures and their unique features can be seen in the different geographic regions as well as among the various indigenous groups. The indigenous groups vary so much, in fact, that generalizations fail to capture their richness and distinctiveness. While realizing this diversity of subcultures, a more general Colombian culture dominates most of the country's urban and rural settings.

The standard Spanish greetings used in Colombia include "Buenos días" (Good day or Good morning), "Buenas tardes" (Good afternoon), and "Buenas noches" (Good evening). These greetings are used commonly among acquaintances, but are also used when eye contact is made with others, for in Colombia eye contact is the key to knowing whether to express a greeting or not. Sometimes just "Buenas" or "Buenos" is used for quick greetings outside of family and friendship contexts, such as on the sidewalks and in commercial areas. For greetings between men, handshakes are normal. When among friends, the common greeting with women may include a light kiss on the cheek. Most often this is not an actual kiss but rather more of a touching of cheeks. But this is not required, with light handshakes being acceptable alternatives and the norm when not in a friendship or family group. As a general guide, the woman should initiate a kiss greeting, with a handshake taking place if she does not. Another important gesture to note is that when indicating the height of an animal, Colombians display their hand in a horizontal position with the palm facing down. When indicating the height of a person, however, the hand is held vertically, with the palm facing the person being addressed.

When expressing approval of something or some action, saying "Bueno" or "Muy bueno" is normal, although a regional greeting of "Chévere" (somewhat like "Cool" in English slang) is often used in the Cali region. "Gracias" (Thank you) is the normal way to express thanks, but can also signal a polite end to an encounter when used in reply to a sales pitch by a street or store vendor, with the implication being that you are thanking them for their time and are going to move on. In traffic, eye contact implies an obligation, whereas no eye contact implies no obligation to the other driver or street vendor. "De nada" ("It was nothing") is common in some parts of the country as a way to express that it was not a burden to have helped. Sales clerks often use it in stores, for example, to say that it was a pleasure to serve you.

For referring to people, *señor* is used for adult men, and *señora* for married women or *señorita* for unmarried women. A more formal term for older men would be *caballero*, which shows a higher level of respect. Last names are used in public forums and even in private unless a high level of friendship has been developed. For those in their twenties or younger, the terms *muchacho* or *muchacha* can be used (meaning respectively "young man" or "young lady"). Children are addressed as *niño* or *niña*. If a group is composed of a mixture of men and women, the masculine form is used for addressing the group with the exception of the initial greeting in formal settings. The formal setting would begin with *Señores y Señoras*, with the masculine plural form being used thereafter when referencing the group, as long as at least one man is part of the larger group.

Due to the differences in climate based on altitude, dress codes vary in different parts of the country, but they are modest overall, albeit with a trend to more casual attire. The colder climate in Bogotá and somewhat in Medellín support more formal attire in business settings, with a coat and tie not unusual, while in Cali more informal attire is acceptable. In the coastal areas like Barranquilla and Cartagena, less formal attire is seen more often (although some business settings still favor suits even in those contexts). With the exception of the beach, tourist settings, and sporting events, ladies generally do not wear shorts in public settings. It is not uncommon for youths and children to wear shorts, though.

An invitation to dine in someone's home is a major overture of friendship and cordiality, so the opportunity should not be taken lightly. Latin American culture holds dear certain values of honor and shame (*honor* and *vergüenza* in Spanish). Those hosting a dinner consider it a great honor and will treat guests with the best possible hospitality. Guests at dinner in a private home or restaurant should repay their host with compliments. Thank you notes are very appreciated, especially handwritten, after being invited into someone's home. Also, "Gracias" (Thank you) is a good way to end an encounter, thereby leaving on a positive note. When dining in restaurants, 10 percent is the usual rate for tipping, with more than that appreciated but not generally expected. When parking the car, one should always tip the person that watches the car—that likely will keep them from letting anything happen to it and so is well worth the small amount of the tip. Tipping also takes place in public restrooms, which vary in quality and availability. Sometimes there is an attendant at the entrance to the bathroom who both cleans the setting and provides toilet paper for those needing it. A tip is expected and sometimes even required for using the public toilets, and ideally should be given before entering.

Colombian society tends to be very expressive in both conversation and celebration, with festivals throughout the year as part of the Colombian culture. Loud voices, therefore, are not necessarily signs of anger or abrasive behavior, but rather may simply be showing good interaction and engagement. When in a public or group forum, negative statements about others within the conversation will likely foster a defensive response since such is seen as besmirching the honor of the other person and could be seen as shameful and dishonoring behavior.

Colombian food overall is not hot and spicy, but rather has a rich favor with such herbs as cilantro (coriander) flavoring it. Shared meals generally last for some time, with the meal eaten slowly. Conversation is considered part of the meal, so a two-hour meal is not unusual for business purposes. Do not discuss serious topics and business matters until after the meal, with a rapport and friendship having been established by way of the casual conversation during the meal itself.

As in so many parts of the world, family and marriage patterns are changing in Colombia. It is usual for youths to date informally as part of a group before private dating occurs, with the shift to private dating being considered a very serious stage of a relationship. A major event in the life of a young lady is her 15th birthday, which the family celebrates with a *quinceañera* (15th) celebration. The event normally lasts for several hours (or even most of the day) and includes a major celebration and dinner in honor of the daughter, who is dressed formally as a young lady. Historically this event would have been to announce that the daughter was of age for consideration of marriage, but today the celebration is more about arriving at the stage of being a young lady.

As for marriage, families are involved in any serious relationship matters, with the parents' permission being sought for marriage traditionally. Marriage itself is a very public ceremony for a first marriage, normally with a major celebration that takes place both at the church and afterwards at a house or other arranged setting. Colombian law recognizes both Catholic marriages and civil marriages, so in non-Catholic religious settings, a civil marriage takes place first, then the religious ceremony is held after that.

The dominant religious group in Colombia is the Roman Catholic Church, with a major Catholic church being the norm on the central town square. Protestant and Evangelical growth has led to numerous other types of churches throughout the country, with a more charismatic or Pentecostal emphasis being common. Discussions of religion, as with specifics about politics, are not normal in public conversations except in a topical fashion.

Bill Warren

Further Reading

Cathey, Kate. *Culture Smart! Colombia: The Essential Guide to Customs & Culture*. London: Kuperard, 2011.

Diran, Kevin. *How to Say It: Doing Business in Latin America: A Pocket Guide to the Culture, Customs and Etiquette*. New York: Prentice Hall, 2009.

DuBois, Jill, and Leslie Jermyn. *Cultures of the World: Colombia*. New York: Marshall Cavendish, 2006.

Guerrieri, Kevin, and Raymond Williams. *Culture and Customs of Colombia*. Cultures and Customs of the World Series. Westport, CT: Greenwood Press, 1999.

CUBA

Cuba, the largest of the Caribbean islands, is home to one of the most vibrant yet misunderstood cultures in the Americas. There are three major contributing factors to Cuban culture: the island's Spanish colonial heritage, the African slave culture, and the socialism/communism of Fidel Castro's regime. Perhaps the most immediately evident contributing factor to Cuba's culture is the communist/socialist political ideology of the Castro regime. In Cuba the influence of the Castro regime is evident in anti-American propaganda painted on walls and buildings, and in official government publications. This is part of the official discourse of the Revolution, which is ongoing since Castro's triumphant entry into Havana on January 1, 1959. Cuba, the only Marxist nation in the Western Hemisphere, was once a playground for North Americans, but shortly after the Revolution on January 1, 1959, and Castro's rise to power over the dictator Fulgencio Batista, the political and economic relationship between Cuba and the United States changed dramatically. Over the more than half a century since Castro took control, the primary sentiment between Cuba and the United States has been antagonistic. It must be remembered, however, that this ideological conflict is a projection of the attitudes of political figures in Havana and Washington, D.C., and does not, for the most part, reflect the general sentiment of the Cuban people, who in general are amicable, industrious, and eager to make new friends, no matter their nationality. There are significant Spanish and African influences on Cuban culture too. Cuba was the longest held territory in the Spanish empire in the Americas, being home to one of the oldest Spanish colonies (established in 1511) and among the last to gain independence from Spain, in 1898. The Cuban colonial economy became dependent on sugar, the production of which led to the importation of African slaves to the island. The Spanish element of Cuban culture is evident in the Spanish language that is the country's official language, the presence of Spanish guitars in Cuban music, and the Spanish architecture of the major cities of Havana (especially Old Havana), Santiago de Cuba, and the colonial towns like Trinidad, Cienfuegos, Baracoa, and Camagüey. Cuba participated in the Atlantic slave trade from the sixteenth century until 1867, and slavery remained legal in Cuba until 1886. During this time, over 1 million African slaves were brought to Cuba, and by the time slavery was abolished on the island, the Spanish landowners were a racial minority. Upon the abolition of slavery, Cuba faced the challenge of integrating the majority of its population into society. Today, despite the official position that Cuba is an egalitarian society, racism continues to be a significant social problem.

The traditional Spanish form of addressing a man as *señor* (Mr. or Sir) and a woman as *señora* (Mrs. or Ms.) has been replaced with the more egalitarian terms *compañero* and *compañera*, which translates to English literally as "comrade" but can be taken to have a meaning akin to buddy, friend, or colleague. The word symbolically unites all people together in the socialist/communist community. Cubans will readily shake hands in a greeting, but they will also hug friends, and the common kiss on the cheek can be expected when women meet or when women and men who are friends greet each other. Cubans will often call a friend *asere*, which is derived from an African term meaning "I salute you" that has become a common

Two Cuban men shake hands on a street in Trinidad, Cuba. Shaking hands, hugging, or a kiss on the cheek are common when Cubans greet each other. (MariaPavlova/iStockphoto.com)

term of endearment for a dear, close friend. Although this word is commonly used in Cuba, it may be considered vulgar when used in the presence of an older person, so it is best to reserve this term for close interpersonal relations with friends of a similar young age.

The tropical climate of Cuba combined with a weaker economy has led to an informal dress code. Children in elementary and secondary schools wear uniforms, but for everyday attire, casual clothing is common. Most Cubans will wear a short-sleeved, collared shirt with jeans or khakis. Cubans do not usually wear shorts, and most do not have access to athletic shoes, so if a visitor wants to blend in on the island, it is best to wear long pants and a simple leather loafer shoe. The *guayabera*, a buttoned shirt with four pockets on the front and pleats or designs sewn vertically on the front and back, is perhaps the most popular article of clothing for men and is appropriate almost any time and can be seen at any event. Jewelry is not commonly worn, except maybe a simple wristwatch and a wedding band. Tourists wearing eye-catching jewelry may find themselves the target of pickpockets.

Many Cubans in Havana are eager to assist tourists with their needs, and though the offer of assistance will be given in a sincere tone of friendship, sometimes the helpful person is really hoping to receive a tip or gratuity for their assistance. This practice, called *jineterismo*, is most common among younger people, but even middle-aged men and women will frequently be eager to help you locate a special souvenir if they feel they can profit from doing so. In some cases *jineterismo* does not stop with the innocent offer to assist you in finding goods, for in many cases *jineterismo* also includes procuring prostitutes. Not all offers of *jineterismo* or assistance are made with ulterior motives, but because most tourists will spend more in one day than the average Cuban citizen will earn in a month, a small tip can mean a significant improvement in someone's economic situation. For this reason, tipping for services is expected for almost everything.

Since the early 1990s, the Cuban government has allowed its citizens to have small private businesses. One of the most common businesses in Havana is the *paladar*, a small restaurant that is most frequently operated out of the front room of the proprietor's own home. The *paladar* provides the tourist with an intimate dining experience in a real Cuban home, and there are countless numbers of *paladares* ranging from small, one-table operations offering a menu limited to the food that the family may be eating that day to larger, multi-table establishments with professional chefs offering a varied menu. Tourists should always ask for bottled water or drink soft drinks when eating out, even though tap water may be considered safe for consumption. Though there will always be someone willing to take a visitor to "the best restaurant in Cuba," and may even promise certain dishes or prices, the visitor should be wary of these offers, because more often than not, the helpful person has prearranged a deal with the restaurant owner to receive a finder's fee for bringing them customers. Also, the *paladar* is most likely unwilling or unable to comply with the promises made to the tourist. If a visitor does find themselves ushered into an establishment where they feel uncomfortable or are not satisfied with the facility, they may excuse themselves without any obligation to buy. Visitors are not, however, permitted to change their mind and leave once they have been seated and have begun the ordering process.

First-time visitors to Cuba may be eager to inquire of the Cuban people about their political views and opinions about the relationship between the United States and the Castro regime. This is a topic that should be avoided, however. Close friends may be willing to share their opinion about the government in private conversation, but open discussion about the government, whether positive or negative, may be perceived as dissident thought and could lead to political and social problems for that person or their family. Tourists should also avoid photographing military installations or government buildings, as this could lead to suspicions that they are spying.

Scott Infanger

Further Reading

Chomsky, Aviva, Barry Carr, and Pamela Maria Smorkaloff, eds. *The Cuba Reader: History, Culture, Politics*. Durham, NC: Duke University Press, 2003.

De Ferari, Guillermina. *Community and Culture in Post-Soviet Cuba*. New York: Routledge. 2014.

Luis, William. *Culture and Customs of Cuba*. London: Greenwood, 2001.

E

EAST AFRICA (KENYA, TANZANIA, UGANDA)

Because of their shared histories and colonial experience, the cultural practices of the eastern African countries of Kenya, Tanzania, and Uganda can be examined together. The three countries occupy more than 1.7 million square miles, a little larger than the combined area of the United Kingdom, France, Germany, and Spain. The combined population of the three countries is more than 138 million originating from more than 200 different ethnic groups. The ethnic groups differ markedly in culture, social organization, and language. Despite the ethnic diversity in the region however, the peoples of Kenya, Tanzania, and Uganda tend to share cultural norms, etiquette, and, taboos.

In East Africa, a right-hand handshake is the most common form of greeting. Handshakes are typically exchanged at first encounter and also when parting. "Jambo?" (How are you?) is the most common verbal greeting in Swahili, a language spoken mostly in Kenya and Tanzania and some parts of Uganda. East Africans lower their eyes when greeting someone of a higher status or an older person. As a matter of fact, prolonged eye contact during handshakes can be interpreted as intimidating. Depending on their familiarity, the handshake may be followed by a hug among men or a hug and kiss on the cheek among women. Handshakes between men may comprise a solid, firm grip (Uganda and Kenya especially) while handshakes between men and women are more careful and light. In many rural areas, greetings between men and women are mostly verbal unless the woman offers her hand first. It is also common to see people holding the right forearm with the left hand while shaking hands as a show of respect to a superior. Most Muslim communities will hold a hand across their chest as a show of respect. Adults typically greet children verbally and, in some instances, an elder may place their right palm on a child's head. In many African cultures, status is often closely linked to age, socioeconomic class, and sometimes gender. This hierarchy sometimes determines the form of greeting. For example, among the coastal communities of Kenya and Tanzania, young children greet older people using the Swahili term "Shikamoo." The response is always "Marahaba." In some parts of Uganda, it is common to see women and children kneel upon arrival of guests as a cultural sign of respect.

Greetings among people with a personal relationship are more elaborate than many other cultures and may involve a longer conversation than just "How are you?" East Africans use the greeting opportunity to inquire about the other person's general well-being, family, and business in general—to the extent that an encounter between two people can constitute "small talk" that may last a few minutes. During the small talk, it is common to hear questions like "Habari ya jamii?" (How is your family?) and "Habari ya nyumbani?" (How is your home?). Rushing greetings or interrupting the questions can be considered impolite or rude.

During introductions, it is regarded as a sign of respect to refer to people by their last name and use appropriate titles that reference marriage status, academic achievements, or professional positions such as Dr., Mr., Mrs., Ms., Captain, Engineer, *Mwalimu* (Teacher/Professor), and so on. Only when a certain level of familiarity has been established can one refer to people by their first names. Because of the cultural diversity in the region, it is always wise to avoid topics on ethnicity, religion, politics, and gender. East Africans generally avoid overly critical and argumentative people. As a general rule, greeting everyone in a group is an expectation among adults.

The concept of time (meaning punctuality) as observed in business settings especially in big cities and formal institutions is similar to that in Western societies. Everyone is expected to arrive on time to scheduled formal events such as meetings. However, in many social settings such as weddings, merry-go-round meetings (informal fundraising events that revolve within group members), women's groups, and birthday parties, the concept of time is rather flexible and can frustrate outsiders. Among rural communities, for example, where attending a meeting can sometimes involve an hour's walk, it is unrealistic to frown at people who show up 30 minutes after the scheduled meeting time. Furthermore, informal social functions have no scheduled end time. It is not a surprise that informal meetings generally start 15 to 30 minutes after the scheduled meeting time.

East Africans tend to dress quite modestly and conservatively. While men wear trousers and a shirt or T-shirt, women will wear skirts or dresses and tops that generously cover the shoulders, back, and upper arms. In more urbanized areas, however, it is common to see women wearing shorts and trousers. When women wear shorts and trousers within the household, they may add a *kanga*, a cloth wrapped around the waist or shoulders. As a general rule, wearing torn or revealing clothing, especially among women, is frowned upon in most parts of East Africa. In fact, women in Muslim communities wear a *buibui*, a head-to-toe black veiled gown designed to prevent male scrutiny of their physical beauty. In business settings, a dark-colored coat and tie and well-shined shoes is an expectation for men, while trousers, a knee-length skirt, or a dress suit with low heels are expected for women. In more urbanized areas especially, dress and appearance among young adults and teenagers has been heavily influenced by hip-hop culture.

Hospitality is an important element of African cultures and is expressed in various forms. It is common to see women visiting other women in their homes or men meeting other men at public places. When invited to a home, a small gift, while not required, is always an expression of gratitude and friendship. While the occasion may dictate what kind of gift to bring, bread or snacks for children, fruits, and various forms of sweets are acceptable. Because gifts are opened in private or after guests have left, it is better to wrap or deliver gifts in a covered bag. Except among educated and more urbanized families, many African communities generally associate flowers with condolences and therefore they are not a preferred gift item. Helping the needy is an integral aspect of African hospitality that stems from the traditional communal (rather than individual) approach to life. Help comes in many forms such as hosting an event, building a house, tilling land, carrying luggage for women or older persons, or simply helping an older person push a bicycle uphill. Africans show great respect for the elderly and also pregnant or nursing women and will go out of their way to help accommodate their needs.

Although dining patterns vary from place to place, table manners in most African settings are similar. Aware of prevailing cultural differences, many hosts will typically explain dining procedures, but guests are also expected to watch and follow the lead of their host when in doubt. Except in business settings, there is usually no dining seating plan in most households. However, there may be a special place for the most honored guest and the head of the family. Guests are usually served first, followed by the head of the household, men, children, and then women, with slight variations. In some places, especially in reserved villages, children are not allowed to eat in the same room with highly regarded guests for the fear that they may display unacceptable behaviors. Because eating many East African dishes involves the use of hands, people always wash hands at the table before and after meals. As the kitchen is out of bounds for visitors and grown men, an empty washing basin is brought to the table. People at the table will hold their hands over the basin while someone pours warm water over. In most Christian households across East Africa, the host may lead a short prayer before a meal and say "Karibu mezani," Swahili for "Welcome to the table," meaning "You may eat." It is better to wait for the eldest man and guests to start eating before everyone else can begin to eat. If buffet is the serving style, people are expected to serve a small portion the first time and return for a second helping. While not mandatory, it is polite to finish all the food on one's plate. East Africans generally do not serve beverages with meals as many cultures consider it impolite to eat and drink at the same time. Beverages will be served at the end of the meal. On rare occasions where everyone eats from the same big plate or food tray (such as in Tanzania and Kenya), people are expected to eat food on their side of the plate. It is instilled to children from an early age not to use the left hand to eat. Smelling food in many African cultures is perceived to indicate that the food is bad—and can be seen as an insult to the cook or host and therefore is unacceptable. Whether prepared food is served at home, events, institutions, or restaurants, it is highly valued and wasting it can be frowned upon.

Sharing is a big part of African culture. It is common to see families share meager family resources with extended families and sometimes even with strangers. Despite the prevailing poverty in the region, East Africans still honor their guests with elaborate dishes that may involve a good deal of preparation, time, and money. It is therefore considered disrespectful for guests to turn down a meal offer, although a promise to eat the next time may be an acceptable excuse. Likewise, not to offer food to a guest can be seen as a disgraceful act. When it is time for guests to leave, the host and sometimes the entire family may escort guests out to the gate, car, or to the bus stop as a show of respect and appreciation.

Touching is common in East Africa, but there may be restrictions tied to social settings, religion, and sometimes personal relationships. It is common for men to shake hands or hug, and women to embrace and sometimes kiss on the cheek or hug, but excessive public show of affection is generally unwelcome. This restriction is more extreme for members of the same sex and can sometimes draw public outrage. Many East African communities observe the "left hand rule" with varying degrees. In some cultures, the left hand was traditionally considered unclean. It is therefore generally considered impolite to eat, take, or pass things with the left hand. Similarly, pointing at people with a finger may sometimes be interpreted as confrontational and therefore is avoided.

Most East Africans prefer nonconfrontational and polite communication styles. Conversations will revolve around people's general well-being and are accompanied by questions like "How is your family?", "How is your work?", "How is your home/place/town?", and so on. While these questions may appear repetitive and invasive to a non-African, they are actually a show of interest in another person's well-being. Most people will preserve peace at any cost. In fact, losing one's temper, acting angry, or shouting in public are considered rude. Sometimes people may remain polite even when frustrated.

For various reasons, personal space, as perceived in most Western settings, is almost a nonissue in Africa. First, there are too many crowded public spaces where expectations for personal space can be unrealistic—including *matatus* (in Kenya), *taxis* (in Uganda), and *dalla-dallas* in Tanzania. These are public buses and minibuses for fare-paying passengers that can at times ferry more people above their capacity. Second, public schools, through which most people have received education, are crowded themselves. Other crowded public spaces may include churches, banks, post offices, hospitals, bus stops, markets, and so on. In fact, being overly concerned about personal space may be interpreted as an unnecessary show of pride or snobbish. In such crowded places, young people are expected to volunteer their seats to the elderly and nursing or pregnant women as a show of respect.

With decreasing cost of communication technologies, there is a culture emerging in East Africa around the use of electronic media and devices. The mobile phone has become the most common form of electronic communication. Because it is cheaper to send a text message than to call, texting is more often utilized to send short informational items and photos, but occasionally a long conversation may be carried out using texting for cost purposes. For convenience, especially with busy professionals or more serious family matters, texting may be used to inquire about availability for a phone conversation. While mobile phone credit vendors may be found virtually everywhere in East Africa, most people cannot always afford it. The system of "flashing" is used where a caller without phone credit will make a call and let it ring once and then disconnect. When the receiver sees a missed call, they are expected to return the call or sometimes send phone credit to the caller, a method called *sambaza* in Swahili. As most people carry their mobile phones all the time, it is generally considered disrespectful to not respond to text messages. Social media and e-mail are also common forms of communication and social interaction either between individuals or groups. However, written letters, cards, and notes are still the preferred forms of conveying "very important information" such as wedding, fundraising, and other formal and informal invitations.

Regardless of the purpose for interaction through electronic media, politeness is expected, a factor that reinforces the nonconfrontational behavioral expectations across the region.

Taboos as traditionally observed in many African societies served many functions, including protecting the individual or group and sometimes protecting resources. In some cases, observing taboos created cohesion in a group, a sense of identity and belonging. Food customs in traditional Africa varied according to ethnic group and religious beliefs, and so were food taboos that dictated what may not be eaten. In the face of modernization and Westernization, some food taboos have lost meaning among educated and urbanized populations and may only be observed among rural communities. For example, among the Banyankole, Ankole, Baganda, Iteso, and Kigezi of Uganda, women above the age of six (with variations) were traditionally forbidden from consuming chicken, eggs, pork, and sometimes fish. It would be unrealistic to observe such taboos considering the nutritional value of fish, eggs, and chicken especially. The Baganda also believed that salt and hot food could burn an unborn child in the mother's womb and therefore were forbidden for pregnant women. Interestingly, many food taboos across East Africa affected mostly women and children.

Marriage taboos are common across East Africa but also vary from one ethnic group to another. Among groups organized in clans (blood relations such as cousins) such as the Kamba, Kikuyu, and Luo of Kenya and the Sukuma and Chagga of Tanzania to name a few, marrying within the clan is considered inbreeding and therefore strictly forbidden. Also across the East African region, a mother-in-law is especially revered among married men. Things that could cause a mother-in-law embarrassment or anger are greatly avoided. For example, among the Kamba of Kenya, it is considered a disgrace for a married man to see or be seen by a mother-in-law undressed. For that reason, married men prefer not to sleep in the same house as the mother-in-law to avoid that possibility altogether. Across the entire region, marriage is considered an association between one man and one or more women (with variations). Consequently, same-sex marriage is not tolerated.

There are many taboos related to death, but the most common one across the region is sexual abstention during the mourning period. Death in Africa is seen as a misfortune to a family. When a person has died, members of the immediate family may not engage in sex during the mourning period, typically until the body has been buried. As sex is directly associated with procreation, it is believed that engaging in such an activity while somebody is dead within the family would cause another misfortune. Among many communities, it is believed that children under a certain age may be traumatized by the sight of a dead body—and therefore are prohibited from body viewing at funerals.

In keeping with respectful and polite nature of conversations in East Africa, potentially embarrassing utterances especially within the household are frowned upon. For example, calling out certain body parts such as reproductive organs is prohibited. Similarly, no matter how upset children get, they may not hurl insults at parents as it is believed to cause them misfortunes in adulthood. The Kambas of Kenya, for example, believe that a person who fights their parent will be fought by their own child in old age. Whistling at night is forbidden among many communities as it is believed to invite reptiles. This taboo is especially common among communities that inhabit the open savanna grasslands where snakes roam freely.

This covers only a very small part of etiquette and taboos in East Africa. The account has been kept general enough to accommodate the cultural diversity in the region. Most of the attributes discussed, though not exhaustive, are also applicable to many other parts of the African continent.

Francis Koti

Further Reading

Department of Tourism and Hospitality Management, Saint Augustine University of Tanzania. "DO's and DON'Ts List of Tanzania." http://tourismsaut.ac.tz/department-projects /dos-and-donts-list-of-tanzania/. Accessed January 3, 2016.

"Kenya." http://www.kwintessential.co.uk/resources/global-etiquette/kenya.html. Accessed January 3, 2016.

"Kenya." Culture Crossing Guide: A Community Built Resource for Cross-Cultural Etiquette and Understanding. http://guide.culturecrossing.net/basics_business_student .php?id=107. Accessed January 3, 2016.

Meyer-Rochow, V. B. "Food Taboos: Their Origins and Purposes." *Journal of Ethnobiology and Ethnomedicine* 5, no. 18 (2009).

Stock, R. *Africa South of the Sahara: A Geographical Interpretation*. New York: Guilford, 2013.

"Tanzania." Culture Crossing Guide: A Community Built Resource for Cross-Cultural Etiquette and Understanding. http://guide.culturecrossing.net/basics_business_student .php?id=202. Accessed January 3, 2016.

"Uganda." Culture Crossing Guide: A Community Built Resource for Cross-Cultural Etiquette and Understanding. http://guide.culturecrossing.net/basics_business_student _details.php?Id=7&CID=212. Accessed January 3, 2016.

ECUADOR

Ecuador is a culturally and geographically diverse nation located on the Pacific coast of South America along the Equator, from which the country receives its name. Ecuador is populated by at least 12 indigenous nationalities that speak different languages, white-mestizos (mixed-race or mixed-culture population), and Afro-Ecuadorians. Having been colonized by Spain in the sixteenth century, Ecuador's official language is Spanish. Native languages are used in the areas inhabited by indigenous peoples. Given this marked cultural diversity, this entry will make reference to urban and rural culture when describing etiquette and taboos.

In urban Ecuador men typically shake hands or tap each other on the back when meeting, while the typical greeting between two women (or between a man and a woman) is a kiss on the cheek. It is customary to ask, "How are you? How have you been doing? How are the kids?" when greeting a relative, friend, or acquaintance. The extended family is important. Therefore, it is considered polite to ask about the family when approaching an individual, starting a phone call, or sending an e-mail. In rural Ecuador, it is polite to say "Good morning" or "Good afternoon" to passersby, even if the visitor is a stranger. "Imanalla" (How are you?)

or "Kawsankichu" (Are you still alive?) are common greetings among the Kichwa indigenous community. Elders or otherwise important people should be respectfully addressed as *tayta* (father) or *mama* (mother).

The middle classes of urban Ecuador tend to pay a great deal of attention to their appearance and are well groomed. People often dress neatly when they go out and also at home if they have visitors. Most women take care of their hair, nails, and makeup on a daily basis. On the other hand, clothing colors tend to be subdued, and styles tend to be classic. A visitor who goes out unkempt may be mistreated when shopping or dining, particularly if she is a woman. Tourists should not go out in Quito, the capital city, dressed as if they were going to a safari. In rural Ecuador, the Kichwa people dress in their colorful traditional outfits. Each community wears a distinctive hat and a particular color for the men's poncho. The color and style of pants and skirts worn by indigenous groups also vary between communities. A visitor to an indigenous community in the highlands should have warm clothing available for the evening when it gets cold. The visitor should wear comfortable shoes that can endure dust and mud. If invited to a ceremony such as a wedding or christening, the visitor should dress appropriately even if the hosts are very poor, to show respect to their hosts and acknowledge the importance of the ceremony.

Urban Ecuadorians are usually very hospitable. It is considered more fitting to invite a guest home than to take him or her to a restaurant. Table manners are elaborate. Women are served before men, with the oldest female guest served first. Similarly elders are served before youths, though small children may be fed first. Trays bearing food are offered so that guests may take as much food as they like. Guests should serve themselves smaller quantities and have seconds instead of serving themselves a large plate. Guests are served from their right side so that they can take the food from the tray comfortably. Contrastingly, empty plates must be removed from the left side of the guest. Even middle-class families have domestic staff that may serve guests. It is polite to greet serving staff when coming into the house and to thank and praise the cook (as well as the hosts) for the meal. In the urban highlands, soup is often the first course. Even if the guest does not care for soup, he or she should definitely try it in Ecuador. Soups are made of local ingredients such as varieties of potatoes that are native to the Andes and unknown elsewhere, organic dairy products, peanut sauce, quinoa, and other hearty ingredients. Soups are very elaborate and are decorated with avocados, lupin beans, strings of dry meat, fried plantain bits, and other delicacies. After the soup, a *seco* (dry dish) is served consisting of meat or fish accompanied by rice and vegetables. Traditional desserts are inspired by Spanish cuisine but modified with tropical ingredients. For example, bee honey is substituted with cane sugar syrup mixed with the pulp of tropical fruits such as mango. Lunch is eaten around 1 p.m. and is the main meal of the day. Many people in the highlands only have a light dinner because it is difficult to digest and then sleep well at high altitude. Dinner is served at around 8 p.m.

To the dismay of many visitors, a guest, particularly if white, typically will be seated in the main room of the house to eat alone in Kichwa Ecuador while the

Kichwa family eats separately in the kitchen. The meal will have several courses starting with a chicken broth that will contain a large piece of meat. Cutlery or napkins are not provided and the visitor must eat the piece of chicken with his or her hands. Another starter may be corn on the cob served with fresh cheese and fava beans grown on the host's land. The specialty dish of the Kichwa is the *cuy* or guinea pig. Guinea pig is served to important guests and on ritual occasions. It is a ceremonial food, and it is an honor to be served *cuy*. The guinea pig is seasoned with wild herbs and roasted in the fire before being cut in half or quartered for guests. The most important male guest will be served the head of the guinea pig. The lower legs are reserved for less important guests such as women. The guest must eat the guinea pig with their hands and is supposed to eat the whole piece. In the northern highlands, *cuy* is served with *mote* (hominy corn). In the southern highlands, *cuy* is served with boiled potatoes seasoned with peanut sauce. The amount of food served to guests is meant to be too much. Guests should not refuse food or leave it on a plate, but it is polite to ask for a plastic bag to take the leftovers home.

After the guests have eaten alone, the male host will come to the main room and offer *trago* (sugar cane alcohol) or *chicha* (corn or cassava beer). *Chicha* has had ceremonial functions since pre-Hispanic times and is a symbol of hospitality. Like food, *chicha* or *trago* should not be refused, but the guest needs to drink only a little. When drinking *trago* or *chicha*, everybody drinks from the same cup or glass. The first person to drink spills a bit of the liquid on the earth to be consumed by the ancestor spirits. If invited to a ceremony, a guest should bring alcoholic or nonalcoholic beverages, bread, food, candy for the children, or a gift. Instead of giving the drinks to the host, the guest is expected to distribute them among those present. Although the guest will be asked to stay and keep drinking for many hours, it is advisable to leave at a prudent time to avoid problems when hosts and their friends have drunk too much alcohol.

There are no food taboos in Ecuador, but some foods are not to be consumed at night because they are considered strong and difficult to digest in the high altitude. For instance, ceviche, a dish of marinated seafood, should be eaten only at lunch. Similarly, avocados and mangos are considered strong foods that should not be eaten at night.

People in urban and rural Ecuador tend to be very religious, though there is a tradition of liberal anticlericalism originating in the nineteenth century. In urban Ecuador women tend to be more religious than men. As a result of Spanish colonialism Catholicism is Ecuador's main religion. However, some native peoples practice Catholicism mixed with their own preconquest beliefs. In addition, since at least the mid-twentieth century, a considerable number of indigenous peoples have converted to evangelical Protestantism due to the work of missionaries. A number of indigenous people have, therefore, come to associate Protestantism with progress and literacy, while rejecting Catholicism as a colonial imposition. Furthermore, over the last few decades many urban, middle-class Ecuadorians have converted to Protestantism.

When a person dies in urban Ecuador, family, friends, and even acquaintances are expected to stop what they are doing in the middle of the workday and go to spend time with the family of the deceased. In the past, the body of the deceased was honored at home for at least one night before being buried the following day. The dead used to be buried in the ground, but more recently it has become common to cremate bodies. People used to dress in black for a funeral, but today it is considered appropriate to combine black with white or grey. Colors, except for dark navy, are considered inappropriate for a funeral. Urban people visit their dead and place flowers in tombs for years after the funeral. They also give masses dedicated to the deceased for years to come.

In rural Ecuador, death is a communal event. When a person dies, family members go to church and ring bells to let everyone know about the death. The family prepares the deceased for the trip to the afterlife by dressing the corpse in his or her best outfit and comfortable shoes, symbolic of the equipment needed for the long walk to the afterlife. The body of the deceased stays home for at least one night, and everybody in the community is invited to the deceased's home. Visitors are expected to bring with them something for the funeral: money, food, drink, cigarettes, and other items are welcomed. A complete meal is served to the relatives and friends of the dead, and to the community as a whole. A special person is put in charge of organizing relatives' prayers and laments. After eating and praying, mourners play a series of games that are intended to both entertain the visitors and help them forget the pain of losing a loved one. Anyone who loses the games is beaten or whipped to save the deceased some of the pain necessary to have his or her sins forgiven. The next day, the deceased is transported in a coffin to church for a mass and then on to the cemetery, where food and drink are again shared. In the past, the Catholic Church buried native people separately from whites. Today this kind of discrimination is uncommon, though it might still be practiced in some remote rural areas.

Like indigenous people, Afro-Ecuadorians consider death a communal issue. During the wake, men and women of the community often work together. Also during the wake it is thought appropriate to leave open windows and doors so as to allow the soul of the deceased to vacate his or her home. According to Afro-Ecuadorian popular belief the soul of the deceased will linger in the neighborhood for nine days until a second wake is enacted. During the nine days women sing entreaties to saints and sacred virgins in order to counteract any dangerous, supernatural powers that may be present. If people are still unsure about the whereabouts of the deceased's soul, they will enact another special ceremony to dismiss it.

Carmen Martínez Novo

Further Reading

De la Torre, Carlos, and Steve Striffler. *The Ecuador Reader: History, Culture, Politics*. Durham, NC: Duke University Press, 2008.

Hurtado, Osvaldo. *Portrait of a Nation: Culture and Progress in Ecuador*. Lanham, MD: Madison Books, 2010.

Ulcuango, Maria Carmen. "Los rituales funerarios de la comunidad de Zuleta." M.A. Thesis, Facultad Latinoamericana de Ciencias Sociales, Quito, 2013.

Whitten, Norman. "Emerald Freedom." In Carlos de la Torre and Steve Striffler (eds.), *The Ecuador Reader*. Durham, NC: Duke University Press, 2008.

EGYPT

Egypt is located in northeastern Africa and is the most populated country in the Middle East. Egyptians speak Arabic and have mixed African, Arab, European, and Ottoman ancestry. Home to the Nile River, the Great Pyramids, and holy sites for Jews, Christians, and Muslims, Egypt's religious heritage and remarkable role in world history are evident within modern Egyptian customs. The vast majority of Egyptians are Muslim, but Egypt also has a bustling Christian population. Both Islamic and Christian traditions are deeply woven into the country's social tapestry. Like its land and people, Egypt's customs are nuanced and diverse. Etiquette standards can vary greatly from region to region, and migrants from all over the country move to large urban areas for employment, making places like Cairo and Alexandria sprawling cultural hubs.

Greeting customs are heavily influenced by age, social class, and religion. Egyptians are widely regarded as friendly, outgoing people, and their greetings are reflective of this warmth and joviality. A very common greeting is "Ahlan w'sahlan," which is similar to saying "Welcome" or "Hello," but directly translated means "You are like family to me, so take it easy." This is not a religious greeting and is the salutation of choice when speaking to someone whose religion is unknown. Other popular greetings are "Izayak?" (How are you?) and "Akhbarik eh?" (What's new?). In more formal settings "Sabah al kheer" (Good morning) or "Masaa al kheer" (Good evening) are often used. Although "Salaamu alaikum" (Peace be with you) is the most significant greeting in Islam, most Egyptians only use the phrase when speaking to someone new or unfamiliar. For example, it would be unusual for friends gathering for dinner to greet each other this way.

Titles of respect are very important in Egyptian society. When speaking to someone older or of a higher social class, one must address the person as *hadretak* for a man or *hadreteek* for a woman. This term does not have a direct English equivalent as formal titles have generally fallen out of use in English-speaking societies, but roughly translates to "good sir" or "good madam." Although much less common than in the past, some Egyptian children still use these titles to address their parents. Other common terms of respect are *ya fandem*, *ya beh*, and *ya basha*. None have closely correspondent words in English, but all relate to the once formal social hierarchy established during Egypt's Ottoman Era (1517 CE to 1914 CE). Though service workers often refer to their customers with such titles, it is also normal for Egyptians of all social classes to use these terms as slang among friends— "Izayak ya basha?" is similar in English to saying "How are you, chief?"

While handshakes are typically reserved for people of the same sex in some other Muslim-majority countries, handshakes between men and women are quite common in Egypt. Since not all Egyptians are comfortable shaking hands with someone of the opposite sex, however, it is best for tourists and other visitors to follow the lead of the Egyptian they are greeting. It is also very common for Egyptians to greet by kissing both cheeks, though this is almost exclusively reserved for individuals of the same sex.

Generally speaking, Egyptians care a great deal about appearance. For adults, items like flip-flops, sweat pants, or tank tops are not typically worn in public as they are perceived as inappropriate and as belonging to the lower social classes. When doing something of importance, like going to an embassy or meeting prospective in-laws for the first time, men often wear suits. When visiting mosques, men wear clothing that covers their torso and legs to the knee and women cover their hair, torso, arms, and legs. Both men and women remove their shoes upon entering a mosque. One will find a wide range of clothing styles on any city street in Egypt. Fashions vary by region and social class, often making style of dress a strong indicator of a person's geographic and socioeconomic origin. Clothes worn by members of the urban middle and upper classes are very similar to those worn in American and European cities. However, female members of the fellahin (peasant) class, a distinction also implemented during Ottoman rule, typically wear black dresses and loosely draped black headscarves. Male peasants generally wear an *emama* (turban-like head wrap) and a *galabeya* (floor-length, wide-cut garment worn in a variety of colors). Though the fellahin are from rural areas, many travel to urban areas for jobs or to sell their produce and handicrafts.

The hijab (Islamic headscarf) is worn by many Egyptian women. Variations in hijab style and use are extensive and differ among countries. In Egypt, hijab is most commonly worn using a colorful piece of lightweight, oblong fabric wrapped under a woman's chin and pinned at the side of her head, covering her hair but revealing her face. This classic style can take on many iterations, including very artistic designs involving carefully plumed fabric and jeweled adornments. A bride's hijab, for example, is often custom made to match her wedding dress and styled intricately on her head by a professional. Most hijab-wearing Egyptian women in urban areas

Muslims attend evening prayers at a mosque in Aswan, Egypt. Shoes are removed before entering the mosque. (Robert Harding/Alamy Stock Photo)

pair their scarves with Western-style clothing like jeans and cardigan sweaters, while others wear long skirts or dresses. A small segment of Egyptian women wear the niqab (face veil). Clothing style is a matter of personal choice in Egypt, and some Muslim Egyptian women choose not to wear hijab or niqab. Female members of Egypt's Christian population generally do not cover their hair in public, though many wear headscarves in church. It is easy to find Egyptian women from all social classes, educational backgrounds, and professions who wear and do not wear hijab.

It is common for Egyptian men to be affectionate with each other as a sign of friendship. Egyptian women also show warm fondness for their friends, often walking together arm-in-arm. As a way of acknowledging something very humorous or clever, Egyptians clap palms with one another, similar to a high five. A commonly used gesture is an upturned hand with all fingers drawn together in a point as the hand slowly bounces up and down. This means "wait a second" and Egyptians use this signal frequently during conversations or while navigating the country's intense traffic.

Egyptians of all ages and backgrounds use social media to keep in touch with friends and relatives and to stay abreast of current events. Egyptians rely on social media to obtain most of their news and for political organizing. The significance of this was evident in January 2011, when Egyptians used the Internet to mobilize massive protests that led to the overthrow of then president Hosni Mubarak. Amid tremendous sociopolitical change and violence since 2011, many Egyptians frequently check social media and news Web sites for political updates. As such, it is not usually considered rude for a person to be focused on their phone while in the company of others.

Text messaging is referred to as "SMS" (short message service) in Egypt. Even in professional settings, Egyptians tend to utilize texting more than e-mails or phone calls. It is not viewed as unprofessional for supervisors and employees to text each about important work matters throughout the day and evening. Because the preference for texting is so great, very few Egyptians use voicemail, and personal and professional voicemail accounts are very rarely activated.

Like many others in the Middle East, Egyptians take hospitality very seriously and guests are treated with great respect and generosity. Egyptians do not generally remove their shoes upon entering homes. Guests usually bring chocolates or baked goods for the host and a small toy for children. In accordance with Islam, most Egyptians eat strictly with their right hands and do not drink alcohol or eat pork. Food is an important currency, and visitors are showered with large meals and a variety of desserts and drinks. Egyptian hosts will repeatedly try to feed guests, even if the guests insist they are full. Eventually the guests relent and eat more. Similarly, guests often tell their hosts they are ready to leave, only to have the hosts insist they stay longer. Rituals like these are a kind of game that allow guests and hosts to demonstrate their appreciation for one another. Unlike in some societies where it would be considered rude to force guests to eat when they are full or stay after they've expressed a desire to leave, in Egypt it is inhospitable not to do these things.

Marriage is the most important rite of passage in Egyptian society. Once someone reaches marital age (early to mid-twenties) their friends and family get very involved in the spouse selection process. Young people are set up on blind dates until the right match is made. Based on the strong roles both Islam and Christianity play in Egyptian culture, premarital sex and general physical affection outside of marriage are taboo. Instead of spending time together as boyfriend and girlfriend, men and women engage in a somewhat formal courting process before marriage.

Egyptian weddings are lavish events. Brides wear ornate white dresses and heavy makeup. Grooms wear suits or tuxedoes. Female wedding guests often have dresses especially made for the occasion. Weddings in Egypt are similar to what would be considered a wedding reception in the West. The religious ceremony takes place separately, and the wedding is normally held in the evening as a joyful dinner party. Gifts are not normally given at Egyptian weddings. Instead, friends and relatives visit the bride and groom in the days following the wedding and bring gifts for the new home. In Egyptian society marriage and a new home go hand-in-hand, and couples often delay marriage until they are able to purchase a house or condominium.

In Egypt it is not uncommon for cousins to marry each other. Though this practice is highly taboo in many parts of the world, it is viewed as quite normal in the Middle East. It would be offensive for tourists or other visitors to express disapproval or make jokes about cousin marriage. Pointing the bottom of the foot at someone is considered an insult. While sitting with others, it is important that the bottom of one's shoe does not face another person. Some Egyptians find it offensive when a person crosses their legs while sitting because the sole of their shoe may be visible. Parents are highly respected in Egyptian society. It is considered profoundly offensive to insult or joke about parents, especially mothers. It is also considered very disrespectful to make jokes about a man's wife or to tell a man his wife is attractive. It is less taboo for a woman to compliment or joke about someone else's husband. Additionally, inflammatory remarks or negative statements about religion and religious figures are highly taboo.

Although they strongly adhere to their own cultural norms, Egyptians are generally very accustomed to foreigners and are not easily offended by well-intended faux pas.

Emily R. Sutcliffe

Further Reading

Marsot, Afaf Lufti Al-Sayyid. *A History of Egypt: From the Arab Conquest to the Present.* New York: Cambridge University Press, 2007.

Osman, Tarek. *Egypt on the Brink: From the Rise of Nasser to the Fall of Mubarak.* New Haven, CT: Yale University Press, 2013.

Rodenbeck, Max. *Cairo, The City Victorious.* New York: Vintage Books, 1998.

Starrett, Gregory. *Putting Islam to Work: Education, Politics, and Religious Transformation in Egypt.* Oakland: University of California Press, 1998.

Thompson, Jason. *A History of Egypt: From Earliest Times to the Present.* New York: Random House, 2009.

F

FRANCE

The French refer metaphorically to France (pop. 66.8 million) as *L'Hexagone* (The Hexagon), because of its six-sided shape. It is a country of varied geography, from the beaches on the English Channel, the Atlantic Ocean, and the Mediterranean Sea to the Pyrenees Mountains on the border with Spain, the Cévènnes Mountains in the south, and the Alps on the border with Italy and Switzerland. Farmland, pastures, and vineyards (lots of vineyards) complete its topography.

The late-nineteenth and early-twentieth-century French poet Charles Péguy observed that people of differing persuasions can civilly coexist with a shared standard of etiquette. Perhaps his sentiment is why French politicians of opposing parties cite Péguy's influence. If one desires, therefore, to have a successful visit in France, one must master French etiquette. Proper etiquette is essential to establish and maintain civility among people of different cultures.

Etiquette in France begins with the greeting. In fact, before doing anything else or saying anything else, one should greet one's French counterpart. The classic French greetings are "Bonjour" (Good day), from morning until late afternoon or evening, about 6 p.m., after which the greeting is "Bonsoir" (Good evening). However, one should only say "Bonjour" and "Au revoir" (Goodbye) once to anyone. Eventually a "Re-bonjour" (Good day again) is permitted for subsequent greeting later in the day.

When formally greeting the French individually, they should be greeted without the last name, using only *Monsieur* for a man and *Madame* for a woman: "Bonjour, Monsieur" or "Bonjour, Madame." If the woman is unmarried and 18 years old or younger, she should be greeted with "Bonjour, Mademoiselle." If a group composed of men and women is greeted, they may be addressed with "Bonjour Messieurs dames" (Good day, Gentlemen and Ladies). If the group is of men only, greet them with "Bonjour, Messieurs" (Good day, Gentlemen), and if the group is of women, "Bonjour, Mesdames" (Good day, Ladies).

When addressing the French by their name, they should be addressed by the last name, unless they have indicated otherwise. For instance, they should be addressed as *Monsieur DuPont*, *Madame DuPont*, or *Mademoiselle DuPont*. Only friends and family members address each other by the first name. Professional colleagues may address each other by the first name in private, but by last name and an appropriate title in public. For students, they address each other by the first name.

When one is shopping or when one needs to request help or directions from a stranger in France, one should greet the stranger first with "Bonjour, Monsieur" before asking for help, and before parting should be sure to say "Au revoir,

Monsieur." The appropriate titles, usually *Monsieur* or *Madame*, should be used to address them formally. For an extra measure of deference, one should greet them and express one's regrets for bothering them: "Bonjour, Monsieur. Excusez-moi de vous déranger." The French shopkeeper or stranger might be more willing to help and not feel inconvenienced. The use of "S'il vous plaît" (Please), "Merci" (Thank you), and "Je vous en prie" (You are welcome) should not be spared.

In a formal setting such as a business meeting or a meeting with a university professor, the official should be greeted with "Bonjour," followed by a handshake. If multiple participants are present for the meeting, each one should be greeted, and everyone should shake after arriving at a meeting and before departing. Men can initiate the handshake with women.

Men and women who are on a first-name basis and family members usually greet each other with a kiss (*bisou*) on each cheek. The number of kisses varies from region to region. For example, in the southern region around the city of Montpellier, friends and family members greet each other with three kisses on alternating cheeks. The greeters do not actually place their lips on each other's cheeks. They softly touch cheeks and make a light kissing sound. Men who are friends typically shake hands with each other. Friends typically do not hug each other, as it is considered too forward.

Visitors should try to speak in French when in private groups. Friends and hosts can help visitors with how to say particular phrases and to learn new French vocabulary. Most French like to encourage foreigners who show a genuine interest in the language. Showing an interest in the French language is a means of being a gracious guest and winning the respect of the French.

Visitors should speak softly, keeping a low voice in public and adopting a reserved and gracious demeanor versus boisterous verbal mannerisms. One should not shout across a room at a friend or colleague, but should instead cross the room before addressing them, even just to say "Bonjour."

Body language is important in France. When seated, legs should be crossed at the knee. Do not spread your body out. The tendency of Americans is to spread out their arms and legs when seated. The French usually keep their arms close to their bodies and their legs crossed, not spread, when seated.

The French are incorrectly stereotyped as mean, because they do not continually wear a smile. Many French people view someone who is always smiling as insincere. To always smile is seen as an empty gesture. The French generally only smile when the occasion warrants this expression of pleasure and approval.

The personal bubble is smaller in France, but one should not stand or sit so closely that one touches the French counterpart. One should also not place one's hand on another person's arm, nor should one slap a friend on the back in an affirming manner. A simple "Féliciations" (Congratulations) will suffice.

In France, visitors should dress in at least business casual attire when in public. When attending a business meeting, one should dress initially more formally, such as wearing a business suit. Blazers with slacks may be worn later if appropriate. A dress or a skirt with a matching top are acceptable for women. French women do not wear pantyhose in the summer. Jeans or more casual attire are generally reserved for trendy professions, including fashion, advertising, or digital professions. The French are not averse to wearing the same outfit a couple of days in a row. They often prefer wearing a few quality outfits to wearing a different but cheaper outfit each day. Appropriate attire is a sign of respect for counterparts, from the post office worker to the grocery worker.

Food is to be enjoyed in France, but one eats a meal at a table, whether at a home, in a restaurant, or on a picnic. Eating and drinking while walking in public is frowned upon. Even though the French are doing this more than in the past, it is seen as being *mal élevé* or uncouth—also when chewing gum in public.

The typical courses in French meals are the appetizer, main dish, salad and/or cheese, and dessert. A cup of coffee may be served after the dessert and a digestive—a liqueur to help with digestion.

Diners should keep both hands exposed at all times at the table, but keep elbows off the table. Bread should be broken apart with the hands, and the bread should be kept on the table, rather than on a plate. The French handle the utensils Continental style, fork in the left hand and the knife in the right hand. They do not switch the utensils after cutting the food with the knife. They eat with the fork in the left hand. However, observing this little tradition is not critical.

Water will always be served as bottled water or tap water in a pitcher or carafe. Typical beverages include mineral water, a carbonated water, or a glass of wine with the meal. An *eau minérale* or *gazeuse* would be ideal. Coca Cola or a fruit juice is acceptable before the meal, with the aperitif, if an alcoholic beverage is not ordered or accepted, e.g., muscat, pastis, kir, or a whiskey. Coffee is served or may be ordered after the dessert. After the coffee a digestif may be ordered or accepted, e.g., cognac, Armagnac, or another brandy. The host will usually keep glasses filled, so guests should pace themselves by sipping the wine.

Cheese may be included as part of a menu at a restaurant or ordered à la carte. It is always served at the end of a home dinner party. When a guest is offered a cheese platter at someone's home, the guest should select two or three kinds of cheese. Each cheese has its own cut, and the shape in which it is served should be maintained when cutting a piece. When cheeses are served in precut wedges, such as brie, cut wedge cheeses vertically. Do not cut the point. If the cheese is round like a camembert or goat cheese, the guest should cut and serve himself a wedge.

A guest should taste everything that is served and clean his plate. In the case of an allergy, the guest should discreetly and kindly inform the hostess in advance of being seated at the table. The host should also be informed discreetly in advance and with regrets if alcoholic beverages are not preferred for health or religious reasons.

While business breakfasts and lunches are becoming more common, business should not be discussed during dinner. The French consider dinner to be a social event, where the time, food, drink, and conversation are enjoyed, and where spouses are included. Spouses are not invited to business lunches. Business partners should enjoy and comment on the quality of the food and drink at a meal. The goal of the meal is to build relationships and enjoy good conversation, to nourish the soul as much as the body. The one who arranges the business lunch discreetly pays for it.

When friends meet at a restaurant, the bill should not be divided with precise calculations (on the napkin or with a calculator). Each person should offer to pay the whole bill, unless overruled. One person can pick up the bill the next time the friends go out for dinner together. If the bill is shared by the members of the group, it should simply be divided by the number of members in the party. One should not be excessively frugal, nor should one request a to-go bag. Guests of honor, such as those celebrating a birthday, farewell, or homecoming, should be treated to the meal.

The tip will be included in the tab at about 15 percent of the bill. An additional 1 to 2 percent could be added for an additional expression of generosity and appreciation, but it should not be added to the credit card receipt, to ensure that the waiter gets the gratuity. He will appreciate the gesture, because the tip included in the tab usually goes to the restaurant owner, who does not always give the servers a share. Tips should also be given to porters, about 1 euro per bag, and to the waiter in a café for drinks. In a café let the waiter keep the change for his tip.

If invited to a home for dinner, one should bring a gift for the hostess, such as flowers or a live plant, but never chrysanthemums. They are only for funerals or to be placed on graves for All Saints Day.

Guests should not "make themselves at home" when invited to a French home. They should always act as a guest, waiting to be shown where to sit, not exploring the home and not following the host around, unless invited. One should not follow the hostess into the kitchen to help. The guest should wait for the host or hostess to request help, which will be a sign of the guest's relationship with him or her moving to a more familiar level. The French want to serve their guests, and the kitchen is one of the private spaces of the home. Guests should not expect a tour of the home, and should not ask for a tour of a home to which he is invited.

Public restrooms are scarce in France. Visitors may see a sign for the "Toilettes" or "W.C." They range from pay toilets on the sidewalks or parks to public toilets in cafés, restaurants, train stations, airports, and shopping centers. Visitors should never use the restrooms in a café or restaurant without purchasing at least a drink, as this comes across as being rude. The pay toilets are not consistently maintained, and the automated sanitation system may not always function properly. Other public restrooms may be maintained by a concierge who is visible and attends to sanitation and supplies. Toilet paper may be in a dispenser outside the stall, and one should collect what one will need before entering. The concierge may have a table or countertop at the entrance of the restroom with a small ceramic plate for a tip. One should leave a tip of a few euro cents before entering the restrooms or upon exiting.

Conversation is a final element of proper etiquette. In a conversation, it is taboo to ask someone for whom he or she voted, about his or her salary, children, psychiatrist, or religion. Topics that can be discussed include life in the guest's home country, personal experiences, international travels, sports, food, history, culture, the art tastes of a visitor's home country, and the performing arts. Visitors should be informed of current events and international events, as well as a little French history. Visitors can add to this knowledge by asking the French for clarification, additional details, and express gratitude for their help.

One should not discuss politics, unless one is truly interested in an explanation of political events in France—never to win the French to one's point of view. Guests should learn to discuss the differences in cultures and politics in a value-free manner. Differences should be acknowledged, but not evaluated. One should not insinuate that one's preferences are superior to the opinions of the French.

One should not be superlatively positive in expressions, instead using double-negatives to make a positive statement. An example of this is: "That is not a bad idea" rather than "That is a perfect idea." The French perceive optimism as arrogant or insincere. Nothing and no one is perfect. The French prefer honest, though pitiless, evaluations.

Visitors to France should not employ the "hard-sell" approach, and should not be overly self-confident. This personality could be interpreted as arrogant and rude. If in France on business or other professional reasons, one will want to build consensus or support for one's idea or product. This goal is better accomplished in a collegial atmosphere. A meal or business deal should not be rushed but instead the process should be appreciated and enjoyed by savoring the process.

Howard D. Owens

Further Reading

Asselin, Gilles, and Ruth Mastron. *Au Contraire! Figuring Out the French*, 2nd ed. London: Nicholas Brealey, 2010.

"France." eDiplomat. http://www.ediplomat.com/np/cultural_etiquette/ce_fr.htm. Accessed January 14, 2015.

"French Etiquette: How Not to Act Like Such a Tourist." French Culture Guide. http://www.pariscultureguide.com/french-etiquette.html. Accessed January 14, 2015.

Nadeau, Jean-Benoit. *Sixty Million Frenchmen Can't Be Wrong*. Naperville, IL: Sourcebooks, 2003.

Platt, Polly. *French or Foe?: Getting the Most Out of Visiting, Living and Working in France*. London: Culture Crossings, 2003.

Steele, Ross. *The French Way: The Keys to the Behavior, Attitudes, and Customs of the French*. New York: McGraw-Hill, 2006.

THE FULANI

Pastoral nomads generally known as Fulani are found in a narrow belt that stretches south of the Sahel, from Sudan to Cameroon. The Fulani are basically breeders of cattle and zebu, and Fulani life revolves around breeding. Nomads first, they gradually settled down and abandoned transhumance, except for some Bororo clans. Their dispersion in the Middle Ages from the Fouta-Toro along the Senegal River and their slow and intermittent migration to the east are known as well as the principal states they created over centuries: Fouta-Djalon, Macina, Sokoto, and Adamawa. These kingdoms, which are most often the result of a local victory of a nomadic Fulani group over sedentary groups, quickly became centers of attraction for the members of the community.

The process of migration and settlement of the Fulani in northern Cameroon was accelerated by the launch of Ousmanou Dan Fodio's jihad in 1804. In this vast sociocultural area, organized political entities and territorial hierarchies called *lamidat* were established by the Fulani under the authority of a *lamido* who solidifies his power through internal alliances (with others kingdoms surrounding Maroua) and external (relations between Maroua and the neighboring empires such as Wandala and Bornu), their relationships tending to be consolidated by Islamization. The "fulanization" of the Maroua Lamidat built on the ashes of the Marva village by the animists Guiziga is a permanent hegemonic influence in the political, economic, and social life of northern Cameroon.

One ethnic identity feature of the Fulani, apart from their language (Fulfulde), is the *pulaaku* that determines the behavior or the code of conduct of the Fulani: ethics, the importance of the community, jurisprudence, and religious principles. Therefore, the present study intends rather to apprehend the sociocultural factors affecting the attitude and behavior of the Fulani by putting their society at the civilization's crossroad.

Fulani society requires competence in performing greetings and communication while visiting and hosting guests. A lack of attention to these social customs may be perceived as selfish. Other than an always-acceptable inquiry about another person's health, the different Fulani greetings depend on the time of day. In the morning a visitor asks "Jam wali?" (How did you spend the night?); at midday "Jam gnalli?" (How are you spending your day?); and in the evening, "Jam hirti?" (How was your day?). The answers to all these questions may just be "Jam" (Peace) or "Jam ni" (Peaceful). The host may go through the same questioning of his visitor in return. Greetings are highly ritualized; failing to do so or looking straight in the eyes of the elders instead of at the ground is considered rude and impolite, *semtata* (rude person). Every time one meets a visitor, one asks several appropriate questions and handshake. It is normally the visitor who should begin the greetings. In other words, greetings are the mark of politeness themselves. Foreigners who customarily fail to greet are viewed as being very impolite.

The Fulani can be distinguished from other Cameroonian ethnic groups by their striking physical differences. Although dark-skinned, their anatomy is not negroid. They are usually tall and slender. The typical oval-shaped face has a straight, narrow nose quite distinctive from the broad Bantu nose. The Fulani appearance is characterized by the incidence of higher nonnegroid physical traits in pastoralists (nonsedentarized Fulani). The typical Fulani have a coppery complexion, little frizzy hair, a narrow nose, thin lips, and a thin but muscular body. Fulani were often viewed by other ethnic groups as lighter skinned and described as "whites." There is not a single Fulani type, but there are several types according to their geographical location. *Baban rigga* or *gandoura*—a long tunic—is one of their cultural dresses.

The Fulani woman's manner of walking is characterized by a slow pace and a slight swing of the buttocks and arms. During a conversation, a woman tilts her head down or sideways, so as not to look anyone in the eyes. She then looks out of the corner of her eyes or quickly in the eyes of the other person, before fixing another point in space. Unlike women, Fulani men walk fast (*pargal*) by making big steps (*taasaago*).

To sublimate their "natural" beauty, Fulani women use different kinds of cosmetics. While temporary tattooing of hands and feet is a fashionable Arab-Berber loan, the practice of definitive tattooing of the area around the mouth in black seems to be a native practice. The aim is to produce a contrast between the reddish skin, the black of the tattoo, and the white of the teeth when Fulani women smile: that is *guilawaku* (a well-educated woman) in the spirit of *Pulaaku*.

Etymologically, *Pulaaku* (Fulani way of life) is subdivided into two parts: the *Pul* root, which refers to the *peul*, and the suffix *Aaku*, which means way. So the Pulaaku is the way of being of the Fulani. *Pulaaku* is the code of politeness, the conduct of the Fulani man, which contains within it a number of great fundamental values. These are *hakkilo* (common sense, intelligence), *munyal* (reserve, patience, self-control, stoicism), and *semteende* (respect for modesty, shame). In addition to these values, *neddhaaku* (dignity, self-love) and *cuusal* (valor, bravery, lack of fear) are also important.

Among the Fulani women in Diamaré (northern Cameroon) the culinary aesthetic is based on the notion of taste. In the staging of the meal, the visual assessment of a dish is achieved by the color of the food and the shine of the container. The act of eating among the Fulani is codified according to social values, such as *semtede* (shame). Drinks and food consumption limit the private and public spheres: the meal is exclusively among family and obeys a sexual division. Milk (*kossam*), with millet (*gaouri*), is the basis of the traditional diet of the Fulani.

The Fulani have three meals a day. The meal is generically called *nyiiri*. Breakfast is called *kacitaari*; the meal of midday, *nyalawmaari nyüri nyalawma* (literally, "meal of the day"); dinner, *mangaribaari* or *nyiiri mangariba* (literally, "meal time prayer sunset"). The Fulani eat together around a platter and everybody takes from the food before him. Children are not allowed to take a piece of meat before the parents. A meal time is an opportunity for an initiation session in etiquette (*neidi*).

The Fulani culinary art is a specific means of expressing the group food taste and its particularities. A woman who does not master *kilanta* (the Fulani way of cooking) can be dishonored and sometimes divorced, for there is no Fulani without their culinary patrimony.

Among the Fulani, the control of speech is a criterion of decorum: the practice of *bandol* (talking by referring) and discretion are among the fundamental virtues of the *Pulaaku*, which refers to the way of being and behavior regarded as distinctive and ideal. For the Fulani, "Speech is like water: once thrown away, it cannot be picked up any more." They also considered language as "the wind: its source is full and its container is never filled."

The abandonment of *Pulaaku* is perceived as the worst danger for the Fulani's culture and collective personality. In particular the sedentary Fulani in northern Cameroon are seen as endangering Fulani traditions. First, it is believed that parents make no effort to teach their children respect for *Pulaaku*. They have almost stopped talking about Fulani culture with its proverbs, taboos, and body languages. Nowadays, few children can speak Fulfude correctly in comparison to their language skills and proficiency in French and English.

In northern Cameroon the most widespread opinion considers that Islam places women in an inferior position compared to men. So the Muslim woman is deemed to have no personality or activity, no independence or freedom. She has only duties, the right to keep silent and submit. The prevailing idea in northern Cameroon argues that the Muslim woman is the slave of her husband, father, or brother. These stereotypes and clichés result from the relationship between Islam and local culture that is dominated by the Fulani model. If abuses exist, no doubt this should not be seen as the fulfillment of any Islamic prescription. It is rather that local and ancestral practices are contrary to Islam. In reality, Islam has made the status of women much better than it was before Islamization.

The Koran clearly states that men and women are of the same spiritual and human nature. The holy book clearly states that the only basis is the superiority of piety and righteousness, not gender, race, color, or wealth. The Koran criticizes the attitude of some parents who tend to favor their son. Since Fulani society is patrimonial, their stereotypes (lack of education, early marriages, and marginalization) of girl children are sometimes portrayed as Islamic. That is completely against the teachings of the Prophet who advised Muslims to seek for knowledge even if they have to travel as far as China. The Koran insists on affection for the wife as the basis of the relation between the bride and the groom (Surah 30, verse 21). The wrong interpretation of holy scriptures by the Fulani lead sometimes to their failure to pay attention, kindness, and respect to their sisters in faith as recommended by the Prophet. This situation is radically changing nowadays. Islam admitted total financial independence of women and granted them codified rights.

In the Fulani family structure, the roles of the individuals are determined by sex and age. The men are the heads of households and the eldest man is usually the head of the extended family, which consists of two or more generations of individuals. Male roles include farming, rearing of animals, and other nondomestic activities. He also provides shelter and protection to the family. The male children are socialized to identify with these roles. The gender-based division of roles creates a situation in which the female children are closer to their mothers while the male children are closer to their fathers. Traditionally, the eldest child takes over the household and the cattle on behalf of the family after the death of the father. Women are socialized to assume domestic roles, and men are socialized to assume the roles of herding, especially if they reside in the rural areas. The women, on the other hand, are expected to exhibit the peculiar characteristics of *Pulaaku*. A woman is expected to have *gikku* (good character), which is demonstrated through faithfulness and obedience to her husband and elders. She should respect her husband's parents' senior kin and be capable of looking after the husband's property in his absence. Early marriages exist among Fulani for it is a dishonor for parents if their daughter gives birth outside of marriage. A *jalujo* (bastard) is completely rejected as extramarital sex is forbidden by Islam.

Fulani identity is not separable from Islam. However, they were not always Muslims. The Fulani conceived the world as populated by supernatural beings, so they were able to embrace the Islamic belief in jinn as a supernatural power capable of impacting one's life. Therefore, they combine complementary beliefs in Allah and their ancestral religion to create a new Islamic world. People they conquered would adopt the Fulani ways of life instead of adopting Arab ways. In fact, the Fulani were not fluent in Arabic. Thus, they only taught the basics of the Koran recitation to the people they newly converted alongside of Qadiriya, Tidjianiya, and tardiya practices. Moreover, the Kamite Islam the Fulani were practicing did not include any artistic influence of the Arab conquerors. The brotherhoods replaced secret societies and assigned an engineering role to the marabouts. These holy men (of *ribats* and monasteries) imposed themselves by the magical procedures that they used besides scholarship. The marabout manufactured talismans, made up of sheets of paper on which they inscribed some Koran verses, enclosed in a leather bag that is worn on the body or deposited in the house for protection and good fortune.

The Fulani are proud and do not fear death. Rather, they are afraid to die without leaving any child. If one lives up to the *Pulaaku* code and obeys Allah's laws, there will be rewards after death. The Fulani believe in material rewards after death.

Adama Ousmanou

Further Reading

Calame-Griaule, Geneviève. "Les voix de la parole." *Journal des Africanistes* 57, no. 1–2 (1987): 7–17.

Mohammadou, E. *Les royaumes foulbé du plateau de l'Adamaoua au XIX siécle.* Tokyo: Institute for the Study of Languages and Cultures of Asia and Africa, 1978.

Riesman, P. *Freedom in Fulani Social Life: An Introspective Ethnology.* Chicago: University of Chicago Press, 1998.

Schultz, E. A. "From Pagan to Pullo: Ethnic Identity Change in Northern Cameroon." *Africa* 54, no. 1 (1984): 46–54.

Tauxier, L. *Moeurs et histoire des Peuls.* Paris: Payot, 1937.

G

GERMANY, AUSTRIA, AND GERMAN-SPEAKING SWITZERLAND

The Federal Republic of Germany, commonly referred to as simply Germany, is a large European country bordered by Denmark, Poland, the Czech Republic, Austria, Switzerland, France, Luxembourg, Belgium, and the Netherlands. With a population of around 83 million people, Germany is the most populous member of the European Union. Germany has great historical, cultural, and linguistic ties with both Austria and Switzerland. Germany and Austria were united until 1866, and in 1918, after the end of World War I, Austria renamed itself the Republic of German-Austria in an attempt to unify with Germany (this move was prohibited ultimately by the Treaty of Saint-Germain-en-Laye in 1919). The German-speaking part of Switzerland makes up around 65 percent of the country, including north-western Switzerland, eastern Switzerland, central Switzerland, and most of the Swiss plateau as well as the majority of the Swiss Alps. The German spoken in Switzerland is known as Schweizerdeutsch (Swiss German). Schweizerdeutsch is also spoken in some Alpine areas of Italy.

Germans, Austrians, and German-speaking Swiss are typically very keen on shaking hands and so perform the gesture both when greeting and bidding farewell. Handshakes should be firm, and are not reserved merely for greetings and farewells between individuals but are also used in group situations—typically a

---

Culture Shock! ⊕

Schuhplattler

Schuhplattler (meaning shoe-slapping or slap-dancing) is a folk courtship dance that is popular in the Alpine regions of Germany and Austria. The name *Schuhplattler* probably derives from the fact that during the dance performers slap the soles of their shoes (*schuhe*) with flat (*platt*) hands. There are about 150 regional variations of *Schuhplattler*, but in general the dance sees men wearing lederhosen jump up and down and slap the soles of their shoes and various body parts (thighs, buttocks, knees, and cheeks) percussively to create a syncopated rhythm. Meanwhile, women twirl in circles around the dancing men. These boisterous movements mimic the mating rituals of the Bavarian black grouse.

Victoria Williams

person who is joining a group will shake hands with every single individual. Older or very formal German and Austrian men may on formal occasions bow to kiss a woman's hand as a gesture of greeting. This gesture, known as *Küss die Hand*, does not involve an actual kiss but rather the man will bow and hover his lips above the woman's hand. Meanwhile, the traditional German or Austrian heel click is no longer performed at social or civic events. In Austria kissing, hugging, and physical closeness in public are not often seen, and these actions are not normally used as greeting gestures apart from between good friends.

In these countries people tend to be extremely punctual, so arriving even a few minutes past an arranged meeting might cause offence. If one is running late for an event, it is important to telephone the host to explain that one will not be on time. For important appointments, it is correct to arrive around 5 to 10 minutes early. There is no such thing as being fashionably late in Germany, Austria, or the German-speaking parts of Switzerland.

Common greetings in Germany, Austria, and German-speaking Austria are "Guten Tag" (Good day), "Guten Morgen" (Good morning), and "Guten Abend" (Good evening). In southern Germany and Austria another common greeting is "Grüß Gott," which literally means "May God bless you" and is said to strangers, while in the German-influenced part of Switzerland a common greeting is "Grüezi" (Hello). This greeting is used when meeting friends, encountering strangers on the street or on hiking trails, and when striking up conversation with shop assistants. Also in this part of Switzerland this informal greeting is usually accompanied by a triple air-kiss that sees people kiss first the right cheek, then the left, then right again. This triple kiss normally takes place when women meet other women or when a man meets a woman. Men and boys living in this area of Switzerland will shake hands even in informal situations. When greeting people in Germany, Austria, or the German-speaking parts of Switzerland, it is typical to address men as *Herr* (Mr.) and women as *Frau* (Mrs.). If a person is a doctor, professor, or something similar, then they should be addressed as both Herr or Frau as well as their honorific title, such as Herr Doctor Schmidt. After the initial greeting the person's family name may be dropped: for example, at the second meeting Herr Doctor Schmidt would be addressed as simply Herr Doctor.

The term *Fraulein* (Miss) is the traditional title given to an unmarried woman, but this is seen increasingly as outdated by most German speakers and is used less often than once it was. The word was even banned from official use in West Germany in 1972. Therefore many modern etiquette guides suggest addressing all German women as *Frau* regardless of their marital status. That said, in certain circles of German society the term *Fraulein* is actually seeing a resurgence in usage, with some people considering it to be a buzzword or vogue term.

Germans, Austrians, and people living in the German-speaking part of Switzerland typically dress much the same as other Europeans. In business situations people often wear conservative, formal suits in somber colors with low-key accessories. However, the wearing of sneakers when not playing sports is frowned upon, and it is not acceptable for people to wear shorts when shopping or dining out in Austria. Indeed when dining in restaurants Austrians typically dress in business casual attire, meaning that they do not wear jeans or sandals. People living in more rural areas of Austria may wear traditional Austrian regional dress (*Trachten*) including lederhosen for men and dirndl skirts decorated with embroidered edelweiss for women. Both men and women may also wear a cropped jacket known as a loden.

Many people in Germany, Austria, and Switzerland take great pride in keeping their homes and the surrounding environment clean and tidy. Moreover the people in these areas of Europe tend to be extremely environmentally aware and keen on recycling. For this reason if a neighbor discovers that someone has thrown something that is recyclable into the regular trash, their relationship might become tense. Usually it is only close friends and family members who are invited into the home, which is seen as a private sanctuary and a place where individualism can come to the fore. Therefore it is important for guests to show their gratitude to a host if invited into a house. A typical gift for a host includes flowers, wine, or sweets. It is, however, important to only bring French or Italian wine as a gift, as bringing German wine to a German host can be seen as casting aspersions on the host's ability to choose good wine. Similarly any flowers brought as a gift should not include red roses, as these are associated with romance, or carnations, lilies, or chrysanthemums, as these are all associated with death.

In these parts of Europe people hold their cutlery Continental-style with the fork in the left hand and the knife held in the right. When finished eating, one should lay the knife and fork side by side together on the plate with the handles resting on the lower right rim of the plate and the tips of the utensils pointing to the center of the plate. It is considered rude to leave uneaten food on the plate, so one should not take more food than he is able to eat. Also in Austria it is never acceptable to cut a dumpling using a knife. Instead, the dumpling should be held with a knife, and then broken apart using the fork.

As in many other parts of Europe, in Germany, Austria, and Switzerland people do not typically eat with their hands, even when eating foods such as pizza in an informal setting. Eating with the hands is only truly acceptable if eating a hotdog or when eating at a barbecue. When eating in Germany, Austria, or Switzerland it is polite to wait for everybody to be seated and to have been served before anyone starts to eat or drink. In order to indicate that everyone may begin to enjoy the meal in unison, a host will normally say "Guten Appetit!" (Good appetite!).

Traditional German food includes lots of meat, with pork being the most popular meat to eat. In Germany meat is often served in the form of sausages while vegetables are often served in stews, with potatoes and cabbage being very popular. White asparagus is something of a delicacy in parts of Germany, with some restaurants serving entire menus based around the vegetable. Austrian cuisine is also meat heavy and particularly keen on sausages. Though pork is used widely in Austria, the traditional Wiener schnitzel is made from veal. The Swiss are famous for fondue, for which they like to stick to traditional cheeses such as Emmentaler, Gruyère, and Vacherin rather than including foreign cheese such as cheddar. It is also useful to note that the Swiss do not wash the fondue pot as soon as the fondue has been eaten, as the hard cheesy crust that forms at the bottom of the pot, the

Grossmutter (grandmother), is considered a delicacy. Also it is not acceptable in Switzerland to ask for chocolate fondue, as this is an American invention rather than a traditional Swiss dish. When eating fondue in Switzerland, wine, schnapps, or tea is usually offered as an accompaniment. It is not acceptable to drink beer with fondue as the Swiss believe that beer makes the fondue difficult to digest. Another part of fondue etiquette to bear in mind is that rather than delicately swirling the fondue fork in the cheese mixture, one should stir the fork around forcefully as soon as the fondue pot arrives in order to prevent the cheese mixture from burning when it sits upon the heater.

Most Germans rarely drink tap water, preferring instead to drink bottled water. Tea and coffee are also popular in this part of the world as are beer and wine. After dinner people will sometimes also drink brandy, cognac, grappa, or a herbal liqueur (*Kräuterlikör*) such as Jägermeister. When wine or beer is served at a meal, the host will usually propose a toast. The most common and simplest toast is "Prost!" (Cheers!) while "Zum Wohl!" (To your health!) is also used. At formal dinners, it is more usual to lift the glass by its stem and nod significantly to fellow diners rather than to exclaim a toast.

Despite their reputation for orderliness, the Swiss often do not practice forming lines. Instead, whether in a shop or while waiting for public transport, the Swiss will nudge each other while trying to be served. Even if the nudging is aggressive, it is not considered proper to show irritation. A person should instead say "Scho guet" (That's okay) to the person doing the nudging and move out of the way. The person nudging should then apologize by saying "Äxgüsi" (Excuse me).

Germans and Austrians are often very direct when speaking, leading to accusations that they are rude. Additionally Germans value their privacy and differentiate between their public and private lives. Since Germans and Austrians do not usually enter into friendly relations easily, outsiders often interpret this attitude as remoteness. However, this is not the case, for after a while, Germans and Austrians will let down their guard allowing relationships to evolve.

People in these countries also do not generally like to give or receive compliments. Compliments, especially from strangers, are regarded with suspicion. Similarly the Swiss can be reserved and hard to get to know intimately, resulting in others believing them to be unfriendly. The Swiss take friendships seriously and so show reticence when making friends.

While Austrians may enter into light conversation easily even ahead of business meetings, Germans tend to prefer speech to be brief and to the point, thus often avoiding small talk. In Germany it is considered rude for foreigners to assume that Germans speak English. Although Germans tend to speak excellent English, many Germans will be offended at any assumption that they speak English. Also Germans aged 55 years and above often do not feel as confident as younger people when it comes to speaking English, so do not address an older German in English. In contrast Swiss people tend to be excellent linguists and all generations will easily switch between speaking Schweizerdeutsch and English.

Germans, Austrians, and Schweizerdeutsch-speaking Swiss enjoy entering into conversation. Germans typically like to talk about philosophical matters and politics.

However, visitors should avoid any casual mention of Germany's Nazi past. It is also taboo to show any sympathy for Nazi Germany.

Victoria Williams

Further Reading

Goethe Welcome Centre. *Guide to German Culture, Customs and Etiquette.* June 3, 2014. https://www.uni-frankfurt.de/62886456/Guide-to-German-culture_-costums-and -etiquette-Aug-2016.pdf. Accessed January 16, 2017.

Lord, Richard. *CultureShock! Germany: A Survival Guide to Customs and Etiquette*, 6th ed. Tarrytown, NY: Marshall Cavendish, 2011.

McLean, Catherine. "Etiquette in Switzerland: Tips and Pitfalls." *The Local.* July 25, 2012. http://www.thelocal.ch/20120725/3726. Accessed January 16, 2017.

Roraff, Susan, and Julie Krejci. *CultureShock! Austria: A Survival Guide to Customs and Etiquette*, 3rd ed. Tarrytown, NY: Marshall Cavendish, 2011.

Rousset, Kerrin. "The Nun at the Bottom of the Pot." *My Kugelhopf.* 2008–2017. http://mykugelhopf.ch/2009/02/la-religieuse/. Accessed January 16, 2017.

GREAT BRITAIN

Great Britain is an island in the North Atlantic lying off the northwest coast of continental Europe. Great Britain is composed of England, Scotland, Northern Ireland, and Wales. The country has a population in excess of 60 million people, making it the third-most populous island in the world. A large number of nationalities, religions, and cultures make up the population of Great Britain with various forms of social etiquette being observed by the different communities. There is, however, a general sense of which types of behavior and modes of speech are considered acceptable by the majority of people. On the whole the British take etiquette extremely seriously, for value is placed on how a person acts in social situations. Some commentators suggest that the British adherence to social etiquette may be waning, yet the same critics complain that a rise in so-called political correctness is stifling free speech. Nevertheless the stereotype of the polite Briton exists still today, with etiquette and courteousness considered a very British, especially English, concern.

In Great Britain the rules of etiquette are generally unwritten but rather are passed down through generations. In the recent past it was common for young women from the upper classes to attend finishing school where they would learn the rules of social etiquette. Doing so was thought to ensure that their manners were perfected—something that was thought crucial to securing a good marriage. Moreover during the reign of Queen Victoria (1819–1901 CE) good etiquette was an important social weapon that could be used to advance socially. In recent years the rise in multiculturalism, changing economic circumstances, and the introduction of social and gender-specific equality laws have, in the main, occasioned the eradication of the strict British class system, with the result that an increasingly informal attitude to social etiquette has developed. Today, however, rules of etiquette do still apply in Great Britain and are enacted as a sign of respect for others.

The way in which British people typically greet each other depends on the situation in which they are meeting and their relationship with each other. Traditionally in Britain a firm handshake accompanied by direct eye contact is the common form of face-to-face greeting for most social situations and all business meetings. In Great Britain handshakes are always performed using the right hand and consist of two (or possibly three) pumps before the hands are unclasped. The British tend to feel that a great deal can be told about a person by their handshake, with a person who performs firm handshakes generally thought to be self-possessed and honest. Handshakes that are considered too strong are disliked, as are limp handshakes or ones involving sweaty palms. Though eye contact may be made when shaking hands, it is taboo to make eye contact with strangers on British public transport. This is also true of other confined spaces such as in elevators. Other etiquette rules applicable to public transport include giving up seats to older people, pregnant women, and the disabled, and not placing feet on seats. Despite the prevalence of handshaking, Britain is still a comparatively nontactile society. That said, the location of Great Britain—lying between continental Europe and North America—means that the British are subject to European and North American influences. This can be seen in modifications to British modes of greeting, for on the one hand some young men do not perform the traditional handshake but instead opt for American-style fist bumps or "man-hugs," while other younger Britons, especially women, perform Continental-style cheek kisses. The cheek kiss is, however, fraught with potential social awkwardness because, since the cheek kiss is not embedded within British culture, it does not come naturally to everyone. The cheek kiss also impinges on the traditional British desire to remain reserved and not infringe on personal space. The British typically do not enjoy overfamiliarity even among friends, so it is important for people to judge whether any deviation from the conventional handshake greeting is welcome.

In terms of oral greeting the rhetorical "How do you do?" is the traditional greeting said when two strangers meet. This is a salutation rather than a question, and so it does not require a response, though it is usual to return the gesture by saying "How do you do?" back. This question is not an actual enquiry as to someone's health, however, and should not be met with a true report of a state of well-being. In recent years "Pleased (or nice) to meet you" has started to be used in place of "How do you do?" This greeting is, however, scorned by the British upper classes who feel the greeting is an insincere Americanization, since it is impossible to be pleased to meet someone whom you have never met before. For the most part a quick "Hello" or "Hi" suffices as a greeting in informal situations. It is generally thought rude to address a stranger by their first name unless invited to do so. Older Britons in particular do not like to be addressed by their first name unless they have specified that doing so is acceptable. Instead a courtesy title such as Mr., Mrs., or Miss should be used. If a person is a doctor, professor, or similar then their professional title should be used instead. Contrastingly the British have a habit of using informal, affectionate words to address strangers and friends alike such as *love*, *darling*, *babe*, *honey*, and *mate*.

One of the most basic forms of British social etiquette is the saying of "Please" and "Thank you," often abbreviated colloquially as "minding your P's and Q's." It is considered extremely rude not to say "Please" when asking for something, while saying "Thank you" when you receive a service is considered especially important. It is also normal to leave a tip (gratuity) when service is received in a restaurant, hairdresser's, and the like. Another important British concern is punctuality. It is considered extremely discourteous to arrive late for a business meeting or formal social occasion such as a wedding or funeral. It is generally advisable to arrive up to 10 minutes early for a business meeting in order to appear professional and as a mark of respect to the host. On the other hand, it is considered inconsiderate to arrive too early for a dinner party. Similarly, it is thought impolite to call unannounced at someone's home. When attending a British dinner party it is usual for a guest to give a small present to the host such as a bottle of wine, flowers, or chocolates. Smoking is falling out of fashion in Great Britain and is banned in pubs, eateries, and many public spaces. For this reason a smoker should not smoke in someone's home unless invited to do so. The day after a party, it is normal for guests to send the host a thank you note or to telephone or e-mail to show gratitude for the hospitality. It is also traditional for a recipient to send a thank you note to the person that provided the gift—though a host that receives a gift from a guest will not be expected to send a note of thanks.

One of the most important aspects of British etiquette is the strict adherence to queuing (waiting in line). In Great Britain the queuing system is held sacrosanct so that, even if a queue has not formed, people will note who was waiting before them and allow them to be served first. It is strictly taboo to jump a queue or butt in, and anybody who does so can expect to be met with a level of scorn. For this reason, when in any doubt as to who is last in a queue or where the end of the queue lies, it is always correct to inquire so as not to accidently jump the queue. The British hatred of queue jumping is most likely connected to the cherished British concept of fair play. It is also considered courteous to hold a door open for someone following close behind through the same door. When entering a building it is traditional for a man to remove his hat, though if a man wishes to remove his jacket it is customary to ask permission of those present before removing the item.

The British generally consider good table manners to be very important, and it is socially unacceptable for someone to eat using their fingers rather than cutlery unless they are attending an event like a barbeque. The British hold their knife in their right hand with their fork in their left hand, with the prongs of the fork kept pointing downwards so that food can be pushed onto the fork's back. At formal dinners where numerous cutlery items may be placed at a table setting, it is usual for diners to start with the outermost utensils and work inwards with each course. At all forms of dinner or formal lunches it is considered impolite for someone to start eating before everyone else has been served. Once the meal is in progress it is considered rude to reach across somebody else's plate for something such as seasoning. Instead it is correct to ask the person sitting nearest to the item to pass it onwards. Other general rules of table etiquette include diners not leaning on their elbows while at the table, and not burping, breaking wind, slurping soup, or reading. It is also a no-no to talk with a full mouth or to chew open-mouthed. At banquets it is traditional for the meal to close with a toast to the monarch.

There are no truly fixed rules regarding dress and appearance in Great Britain. It is, however, necessary to follow any specified dress code when attending a social function. Men working in certain jobs (especially business related) are expected to wear a suit and tie, though the advent of so-called dress-down Fridays suggests this tradition may be on the wane. Dress-down Fridays are a new tradition in Great Britain and do not occur in the most traditional businesses in the City of London.

The advent of new technology has resulted in additional rules of social etiquette or so-called netiquette. British e-mails tend to be polite and grammatically correct with careful spelling. Moreover, writing in capital letters is avoided as this is seen as an electronic written form of shouting. Emoticons and Xs as kisses are not normally included (especially in business communications) and when e-mailing, the British tend to avoid sarcasm for fear that the recipient will not understand the British sense of humor. It is normal when e-mailing more than one recipient simultaneously to list recipients alphabetically or, in a business situation, according to hierarchy. Meanwhile blind copying is usually avoided, as it is regarded as somewhat dishonest to the e-mail's main recipient. It is thought courteous to reply to e-mails speedily and is considered rude to reply to nonelectric correspondence by e-mail (unless an e-mail address is provided as an RSVP option). The related area of social media requires its own netiquette. For example it is seen as impolite to bother someone on Facebook repeatedly or to send an inordinate number of tweets per day. Similarly cell phone usage is governed by etiquette too. In Great Britain phones should be switched off in a number of public venues including theaters, cinemas, and art galleries, and many restaurants ask diners to refrain from using their phones. On public transport loud cell phone conversations are normally avoided, especially in so-called quiet zones on trains.

The advent of social media has, arguably, fueled what some commentators refer to as "political correctness" leading to a number of taboo words and phrases. To this end it is no longer socially acceptable for the majority of Britons to use terms such as *nigger*, the exception being when black people use the term, and even then, the use of the word is still contentious. The British, particularly younger generations, are fairly relaxed about swearing. In September 2016 OFCOM (the government-approved regulator of the United Kingdom's broadcasting, telecommunications, and postal industries) released a report into British attitudes to offensive language and gestures that found the most offensive words were *cunt* (often referred to as "the C word"), *fuck* (often called the F word), and *motherfucker*. Of these three words *cunt* and *motherfucker* were deemed the most shocking by audiences.

On the whole the British consider racial insults to be taboo in polite society, as are religiously offensive phrases and terms to describe disabilities. It is also best to avoid conversational topics about money, politics, religion, weight, and age, though this is due to courtesy rather than political correctness. Indeed it is especially frowned upon to ask a mature woman her age. Certain politically incorrect actions such as wolf whistling are also scorned by some people.

Victoria Williams

Further Reading

Hanson, William. "Why Etiquette Is a Very British Problem." *The Telegraph*. August 8, 2015. http://www.telegraph.co.uk/news/features/11790437/Why-etiquette-is-a-Very -British-Problem.html. Accessed December 20, 2015.

IPSOS Mori. *Attitudes to Potentially Offensive Language and Gestures on TV and Radio*. September 2016. https://www.ofcom.org.uk/__data/assets/pdf_file/0023/91625/OfcomQRG -AOC.pdf. Accessed January 20, 2017.

Johnson, Ben. "British Etiquette." *Historic UK: History Magazine*. 2015. http://www.historic -uk.com/CultureUK/british-etiquette/. Accessed December 20, 2015.

Norbury, Paul. *Culture Smart! Britain: The Essential Guide to Customs & Culture*, 7th ed. London: Kuperard, 2010.

Tan, Terry. *CultureShock! Great Britain*. Tarrytown, NY: Marshal Cavendish, 2008.

Winterman, Denise. "Queuing: Is It Really The British Way?" *BBC News Magazine*. July 4, 2013. http://www.bbc.co.uk/news/magazine-23087024. Accessed December 23, 2015.

GREECE

In many ways Greek manners and social mores vary little from the rest of the world. However, conventional Greek traditions are still practiced, especially in areas of the country less frequented by tourists. Overall, Greeks are remarkably gracious and inquisitive, to a degree that can appear almost invasive. One should not be taken aback when a Greek poses private queries—especially right after a first meeting. Being a guest in a boisterous Greek household, typically filled with joy, prosperity, and a sense of being with an extended family, can be a wonderful experience. Getting invited into a Greek home certainly does not mean a guest must be punctual—30 minutes late is considered fashionably late—and guests are advised to bring a small gift, typically flowers or cakes from the neighborhood bakery. If one is asked out to a meal, one can propose to pay the bill, although doing so is often considered rude. In all likelihood the guest can leave his wallet at home and be treated to an exquisite night of food, drink, and dance.

The majority of Greeks dress formally to go out. Many monasteries and churches enforce a somewhat strict dress code for guests, allowing no shorts, and women are often expected to cover their arms and to wear skirts, although most Greek women visitors will be in pants. Modesty wraps are sometimes provided at tourist locations.

Body language can cause inadvertent offence. People should not hold their hand up, palm out, to anybody. Furthermore, one should not make the okay sign by forming a circle with the thumb and forefinger. This is a major taboo because in Greek culture this gesture is used in an insulting way toward an irritating or contemptible person. Additionally, nodding and shaking of the head for positive and negative answers is usually misunderstood. Greeks employ a small forward leaning of the head for yes as well as an added energetic backward bob for no. The Greek taboo related to marrying a non-Greek has become less important in recent decades given that immigration has created communities with different ethnicities living in proximity to each other.

With fixed prices most shops make it difficult for customers to bargain. Negotiating over rooms as well as car rentals, particularly outside of tourist season, can be effective. Tipping is not mandatory in Greek culture, though taxi drivers generally expect a tip and most service staff are very poorly paid. Restaurants usually add in a service charge, but rounding up the bill is typically sufficient.

Among the heaviest smokers in the world, Greeks officially disallow tobacco use in public places like bars, restaurants, and shopping malls. Most Greeks, however, disregard no-smoking laws and smoke freely in public places.

A decreasing part of traditional Greek celebrations is the folk custom of plate and glass smashing. In a contemporary context, plate and glass smashing is most characteristic of an outsider's stereotypical perspective of Greek culture. More specifically, plate smashing, in all probability, originated from an ancient rite of "killing" plates on sorrowful events, as a way of coping with defeat. Breaking plates could also have its roots in the practice of clear diminution, a show of one's affluence, as plates or glasses are tossed into a fireplace subsequent to a festivity as a replacement for washing and reusing. Georgios Papadopoulos, the leader of the military coup d'état that transpired in Greece on April 12, 1967, and organizer of the military rule that lead Greece from 1967 to 1974, outlawed plate smashing. Greeks as well as foreigners were upset. Although plate smashing is illegal in Greek clubs, it nevertheless occurs sporadically. For festivities like weddings, current Greeks might buy specially produced plaster plates, because they are cheaper and not as hazardous while being more easily breakable. An additional recent variant on plate smashing for patrons at Greek restaurants or watering holes is the purchasing of trays of flowers that can be tossed at musicians and other patrons.

Gerardo Del Guercio

Further Reading

Bliangas, Johnathan. "Greek Taboos." http://greekgateway.com/news/greek-taboos. Accessed on February 28, 2016.
Leontis, Artemis. *Culture and Customs of Greece*. Santa Barbara, CA: ABC-CLIO, 2009.
Pantahos, Eugenia. *Greek Life: Family, Culture, Food*. Sydney: Greek Lifestyle, 2014.
Rouvelas, Marilyn. *A Guide to Greek Traditions and Customs in America*. Bethesda, MD: Attica Press, 1993.

GUJARAT

Gujarat is a state in west India, most of which lies on the Kathiawar peninsula. The population is in excess of 60 million people. People and things from Gujarat are referred to as Gujarati. Gujarati is also the name of the language spoken by Gujarati people. Most Gujarati people are Hindu, although there are also many Gujarati Muslims, Jains, Parsees, Christians, Sikhs, and Buddhists. There is a very large Gujarati diaspora around the world, with Gujarati communities located in the United Kingdom, South Africa, East Africa, and the South Pacific.

Gujarati modes of greeting vary according to an individual's religion, caste, and level of education. In general, Gujarati Hindus greet each other by pressing the palms of their hands together as though to pray, in an action known as *añjali mudrā*, *hrdayanjali mudra*, or *praṇāmāsana*. As he or she does this, a Gujarati Hindu will usually say "Namaste," which translates as "I bow to the divine in you." A Hindu may also bow his or her head forward slightly while saying this. "Namaste" is said at any time of day. If a Gujarati wishes to say a greeting specific to a time of day, then he or she may say "Suprabatam" (Good morning) or "Shubh sandyaa" (Good evening). It is also correct, when meeting an acquaintance, to ask about the health of their family. When leaving a group of people, it is polite to say goodbye to each person individually, for example, by saying "Shubh raatri" (Good night). In group meetings, elders or group leaders are acknowledged first, using their appropriate title.

In urban areas, among educated and Westernized Gujaratis, people will also shake hands—this is especially true of Gujarati men. Traditionally, Indian women in general do not shake hands with men because bodily contact between men and women in public is not encouraged, particularly if a man and woman have not met previously. Westernized Gujarati women may, however, shake hands with other women. If in doubt, visitors should wait to see if a Gujarati woman initiates a handshake before reaching forward to touch her hand. If a Gujarati woman begins to shake a visitor's hand, then he or she should reciprocate the gesture.

In areas where traditional patriarchal values prevail, Gujarati women may seem reserved during introductions. If this is the case then the visitor should avoid making direct eye contact with the woman—this is especially true if the visitor is a man. In general, Gujarati men are allowed greater freedom than women. Gujarati women tend to have to act modestly and chastely as a woman's honor is inextricably linked to her family's reputation. Moreover, regardless of a family's wealth or class, women are expected to be devoted wives and mothers whose role it is to support their husbands, perform acts of religious devotion, run the household, and rear children.

In some conservative Hindu and Muslim Gujarati communities, women may be subject to purdah, a tradition that has women live in general seclusion and wear a type of veil called a *ghunghat*—often the long end of a sari (a *pallu*) or a long scarf called a *dupatta* is used as a *ghunghat*—which a wife holds across her face when in the presence of older male relatives such as her father-in-law. Under purdah women are largely restricted to staying at home. Communities that practice purdah consider it to be a sign of a family's social status and wealth, because purdah prevents a wife from having to perform housework with servants employed to perform menial duties. Though purdah may be a fairly alien concept to Westerners, it is important not to voice qualms about the practice when visiting a household. Though purdah is not especially common in Gujarat, married Gujarati women are expected to be devoted, obedient wives, and any suspicion of sexual impropriety is taboo for a woman as women who lose their husbands (whether through divorce or widowhood) are considered to have lost their value. There are also taboos surrounding menstruating women, who are seen as ritually polluting. In Gujarat, elderly relatives remain well respected even when their authority has waned, and they will be cared for by their family. Gujarati parents tend to spoil their children, with sons given more attention than daughters. Daughters may also be subjected to supervision by male relatives in order to protect the woman's much-valued chastity. In order to protect a woman's honor, Gujaratis do not tend to take part in Western-style dating. Instead marriages are normally arranged between families, with brides expected to be virgins. Once married, codes of sexual propriety mean that a married couple should not display affection publicly, especially when in the presence of other family members.

In India, clothing is considered an important indicator of social status. The diverse ethno-cultural groups of Gujarat wear a variety of clothing styles, but the overriding principles of Gujarati clothing are that clothes should display modesty (this is particularly true of women's clothes) and care should be taken when dressing as this indicates self-respect.

Gujarati women's outfits are nearly always very brightly colored and richly embroidered. The traditional garment worn by Indian women is the sari, a long rectangle of cloth that is wrapped and folded around the body. In Gujarat, the highly ornate, embroidered section of the sari known as the *pallu* is typically folded over the shoulder and across the chest, rather than across the woman's back as occurs in other areas of India. The sari is partnered by a blouse called a *choli*. Gujarati women also wear outfits known as *lehenga choli* (or *ghagra choli*) that has an open-backed *choli* paired with an ankle-length, billowing skirt. This outfit is typically accessorized with a long scarf called an *odhni* (or *dupatta*) and lots of jewelry. Another accessory traditionally sported by Gujarati women is a bunch of keys and a

Gujarati women in traditional dress, Ahmedabad, Gujarat, India. In some more conservative Gujarati communities, women wear veils in public. (Pisit Burana/iStockphoto.com)

Culture Shock! ⊕

Sindoor

During a Hindu wedding the groom parts his bride's hair and marks her hair parting with *sindoor*, the vermillion cosmetic made from cinnabar (a naturally occurring form of mercury sulfide), turmeric, and lime. The *sindoor* is the identifying mark of Hindu wives. The ritual marking of the *sindoor* is called *sumangali kriya*, meaning "auspicious ceremony." It is very important that a Hindu bride wears the *sindoor* as it marks the woman as being a wife. The *sindoor* mark is also thought to protect a bride from evil. Another part of a Hindu wedding ceremony sees the bride pray that her husband enjoys a long life before applying *chandan tilak* to his forehead. *Chandan tilak* is a mark made from sandalwood (*chandan*) paste, the ash of a sacred fire, turmeric, cow dung, clay, and charcoal or red lead. The mark is thought to convey good luck.

Victoria Williams

---

ring holder worn at the waist. Many Gujarati women also wear a red bindi (dot on the forehead) and/or *sindoor*. *Sindoor* is a red cosmetic powder that is applied in a line to the scalp along a woman's hair parting. A woman's bindi may also be made from *sindoor*.

Traditionally Gujarati men wear a dhoti. This is a piece of white cotton that is wrapped around the waist like a skirt. Men often wear a dhoti with a shirt, jacket, and turban. Many Gujarati men also wear Western-style trousers.

When in Gujarat, a visitor should realize that locals will likely judge their social status on what the visitor is wearing. Therefore it is best for visitors to wear clothes that are clean and conservative, as these will demonstrate respect for locals. Visitors should also avoid wearing clinging or revealing clothes and check what to wear if visiting a sacred site. Indeed when visiting a temple (or a person's home) it is correct to remove one's shoes. It is also important to ask before taking photographs or filming videos at holy sites in Gujarat. Furthermore it is good practice to ask permission before taking photographs of Gujarati people too.

Gujaratis will often invite people to eat at their homes. When visiting a Gujarati's home for dinner a guest should wear clean, modest clothes, and should be prepared to remove his or her shoes before entering the house. It is considered polite to bring a gift for the host, but this is not essential. If a guest does bring a gift then the gift should not be ostentatious but rather something small such as candy, flowers, or fruit as the gesture is more important than the actual gift. If the host is a Hindu or Jain, then a gift made from animal products (especially leather) is prohibited. Similarly a Muslim host will not accept anything made from pork or alcohol. When presenting the gift it must be given with either the right hand or with both hands together, as Gujaratis consider the left hand to be impure since it is associated with personal hygiene. Also when wrapping the gift a guest should not wrap the gift in white paper or fabric, as white is the color of mourning in Gujarat. Instead green, red, or yellow wrapping should be used.

In Gujarat, guests are always treated with the utmost respect and will be given the best available food and drink. However, dining customs vary according to a household's financial and class status and a host's religion. In general before any meal in Gujarat guests should wash their hands as meals are usually eaten with the fingers rather than with cutlery. A host will usually direct guests to their seats and guests will typically be served according to their social standing, with guests served first, followed by all the men present, then any women and, lastly, children. In traditional communities, especially in rural areas, women will cook and serve the food, meaning that they will dine after everyone else. Alternatively a guest will dine while his or her host watches on. Then again at some dinner parties everyone will eat simultaneously.

Food in Gujarat is usually served in big communal bowls, from which everybody takes their share using a large spoon with which they transfer food to their plate. Alternatively a host may spoon food on to a guest's plate. Once the food is on a plate it should be eaten using the right hand or bread (usually in the form of roti) may be used to scoop up food. It is expected that a guest should leave a small amount of food on his or her own plate in order to demonstrate that they have eaten their fill. This is because the etiquette of Gujarati dining commands that any empty plate should be refilled with extra food. After a meal it is important that a guest express how much they have enjoyed their food.

Hindus and Jains believe in nonviolence, and this greatly influences the dietary habits of Gujaratis, who are mainly vegetarian. While beef features prominently in a lot of Indian dishes, Hindus consider cows to be sacred and so do not eat beef. Non-Hindu Gujaratis may eat beef, however. Whether or not a visitor to Gujarat is Hindu, it is important that he or she is respectful of any cows they encounter for cows roam freely in both urban and rural areas of Gujarat. Gujarati food is known for its use of sweet, salty, and aromatic flavors, with meals consisting of vegetables, beans, lentils, and cereals. Most Gujarati dinners are typically served on a *thali*. This is a tray containing small servings of lots of different dishes usually including rice, and bread in the form of roti or chapatti, beans or lentils served as dal, pickles, curries, chutneys, and yoghurt. A yoghurt-based drink called *chaas*, tea (*chai*), and coffee are the most common drinks to serve with a *thali*. If ordering something to drink in Gujarat it is important to remember that public water sources are not normally safe to drink and so visitors should order drinks without ice. Only bottled water bearing a safety seal or boiled public water should be consumed. The sale and drinking of alcohol is generally forbidden in Gujarat. Foreign visitors may, however, buy a permit allowing them to consume alcohol in their hotel rooms, or they may visit a hotel's alcohol shop. Foreigners must not drink the alcohol in public though, as Gujarat prohibition laws are enforced rigorously. Smoking is also banned in public places in Gujarat.

As Indians in general traditionally eat with their hands, many Gujarati restaurants do not provide cutlery for diners. It is therefore expected that diners will wash their hands before and after eating. In most Gujarati restaurants the process for ordering food is similar to that in restaurants in the West. Gujarati restaurants tend to serve vegetarian food with meat dishes unavailable in most eateries. In particular, beef and pork are hardly ever served in Gujarati restaurants as both meats are subject to religious restrictions. Therefore diners should not try to order these meats, as to do so is considered highly disrespectful. The tipping rate for serving staff in middle or upscale restaurants is around 5–10 percent of the bill, although a service charge may already be included in the bill with a tip being optional. If dining out in Gujarat it is usual for the person who arranged the meal to pay for it. Splitting the bill is an alien concept to Gujaratis and indeed, to Indians in general. Bathroom facilities will vary between restaurants. The more expensive a restaurant the more likely it is to have a flushable sit-down toilet; most other eateries will have traditional squat toilets.

When shopping in Gujarat, shoppers should carry low denomination notes for use with independent traders. Otherwise it may be necessary to overpay for items. Gujarati street traders can be very persistent, especially when they see a foreigner. If a foreign visitor does not wish to buy from a persistent street trader, then the visitor should make it clear in a polite manner that they do not wish to buy anything.

In general it is common for Indian people to move their heads in a side-to-side manner (as though shaking their head in disagreement) when listening to someone with whom they are in conversation. Though in the West this gesture indicates disagreement, in Gujarat (and the rest of India) this is simply a sign that someone is listening and does not reveal whether they agree or disagree with what is being said. Other important aspects of Gujarati body language include the fact that it is considered very disrespectful to point your feet towards a sacred image or at another person. Similarly, when sitting it is important that people keep the soles of

Culture Shock! ⊕

Indian Children Paid to Use Indoor Bathrooms

Around 1.1 billion people worldwide practice open defecation with an estimated 590 million people practicing open defecation in India. This poses a major health risk to Indian children with hundreds of thousands of Indian children dying annually from diseases spread through human excrement. Moreover, fecally transmitted infections are a primary reason for almost half of all Indian children aged under five years being underdeveloped physically. In some Indian communities the practice of open defecation is so entrenched that many people opt to defecate openly even when facilities are provided, because people fear that witches live inside the lavatories, that children might be abducted if they enter the cubicles, or that women will be raped if they go to a public toilet alone. In response to this situation the state council of the Gujarati city of Ahmedabad has implemented a scheme that sees children being paid to use public lavatories with rewards of money and chocolate.

Victoria Williams

their feet flat on the ground so that the soles of the feet are not visible. Also it is thought rude to point with the finger—instead the entire right hand (never the left) should be used to point towards something. Many Gujarati people also dislike being touched on the head, as this is considered discourteous. Public displays of affection are often frowned upon in Gujarat as well. Although physical contact between people of different sexes is considered unacceptable on the whole, it is usual for Gujarati friends of the same sex to touch each other when speaking, with gestures including pats on the back and hand-holding.

Gujarat's telecommunications network is more developed than that in many areas of India. The telephone service (both landline and cell networks) is available in almost all of Gujarat. As of 2007, 1 in 5 Gujaratis owned a cell phone, including many lower caste people. Therefore in an emergency it is possible to borrow a cell phone to make an emergency call.

Driving in Gujarat can be a hair-raising experience. Although roads in urban areas are usually in fairly good condition, traffic accidents are a frequent occurrence because Gujarati people tend to drive aggressively and take risks when driving. Furthermore traffic laws are typically ignored or not enforced. When visiting Gujarat it may be best for visitors to hire a local driver rather than attempt to drive themselves, as locals are accustomed to local driving habits. If a driver is involved in a road accident while driving in Gujarat, it is best policy to leave the scene of the accident as soon as possible and find help at a police station before an irate crowd has time to form. This is particularly true if a driver hits a pedestrian or cow with their vehicle. Accidents involving cows are particularly likely to anger Gujaratis, as cows are considered sacred by Hindus.

Victoria Williams

Further Reading

Kolanad, Gitanjali. *CultureShock! India: A Survival Guide to Customs and Etiquette*, 7th ed. Tarrytown, NY: Marshall Cavendish, 2012.

Minahan, James B. *Ethnic Groups of South Asia and the Pacific: An Encyclopedia*. Santa Barbara, CA: ABC-CLIO, 2012.

Technology Integration Division. *Gujarati Cultural Orientation*. April 2009. http://field support.dliflc.edu/products/gujarati/gw_co/gujarati.pdf. Accessed January 11, 2017.

H

HMONG

No one knows exactly how many Hmong people there are in the world today. Scholars estimate that there are at least 3–4 million. The majority lives in China, where Hmong is one of the 55 ethnic minorities lumped under the classification *Miao*. A Hmong is a *Miao*, but not all *Miao* are Hmong. The identity of who is Hmong, wherever they live, is complicated by politics, history, language, and culture. Outside of China, people take offense to being called *Miao* or *Meo*, terms whose meanings include "savages" and "barbarians."

The Hmong history is a complex story that is constantly being revised with new findings and discoveries. Genetic studies indicate that Hmong people lived in China as early as 4,600–6,400 years before the present. In fact, they might have been one of the first peoples to cultivate rice. The domestication of this plant marked the beginning of agriculture and enabled the rise of complex human civilizations. Clues attesting to the centrality of rice to Hmong lives can be found in their language and daily life. The Hmong phrase for "to eat" is *noj mov*, which literally means "to eat rice." In Hmong American homes, plain white rice is served at every meal of the day.

To escape conflicts in China in the 1800s, thousands of Hmong migrated to Southeast Asia. Vietnam, Laos, and Thailand are home to the descendants of these immigrants. During World War II, Hmong in Southeast Asia sided with the Americans and French. After the war, the United States viewed communism as a major threat to its interests at home and abroad. This fear led the United States to intensify its military involvements in Southeast Asia, sending CIA agents into Laos in 1959 and troops to South Vietnam shortly thereafter. In Laos, Hmong soldiers were recruited, equipped, and trained by the CIA to fight in a 15-year-long secret war, carrying out objectives crucial to the broader war efforts in Vietnam. In 1975, when the United States withdrew from Southeast Asia, hundreds of thousands of Hmong became war refugees. All of them ended up in refugee camps across northern Thailand. The majority of these have resettled in the West. Today, Hmong are contributing citizens of Argentina, Australia, Canada, France, Germany, and the United States.

The United States is home to 270,000 Hmong Americans. After 40 years of resettlement, every aspect of Hmong culture has changed, as Hmong Americans have picked up new ideas from others in this multicultural nation. Following are select examples of etiquette and taboos that continue to be observed by Hmong Americans.

In Hmong culture, people use different terms of address to refer to relatives on their father and mother's side of the family. In everyday conversations, a Hmong

American will address a paternal grandmother as *puj*, but a maternal grandmother as *tais*. The same term *yawm* applies to both paternal and maternal grandfathers. All maternal uncles (mother's brothers) are referred to as *txiv dlaab* and their wives as *nam dlaab*. A paternal uncle (father's brother) is either called *laug*, "older uncle," or *txiv ntxawm*, "younger uncle." The wife of an older uncle is addressed as *puj laug* (elder mother) and that of a younger uncle as *nam ntxawm* (younger mother). A paternal aunt (father's sister) is *puj nyaaj*. Her husband is *txiv kwj*. The sons of brothers and sisters (or sons of sisters if they marry into different clans) refer to each other as *npawg*, "cross-cousin."

Each term of address indicates how a person is related to others. More important, it informs them of his or her manner and decorum as they engage in conversation. When two Hmong Americans, let us call them Jack and John, meet for the first time, a good starting point in their conversation is to ask each other their names and then clan names. This is the first step to establishing a social tie between them.

If Jack and John share the same clan name, then they are *kwv tij*, fictive kin related by blood. They will want to know more precisely the depth of their relationship. Jack and John will throw out the names of well-known individuals in their lineage to see if they can find a common link. If there is a name that is familiar to both, then the next step is to determine how each is connected to that individual. How does Jack or John address that person? This fact is important because it will help them to determine what generation they each belong to. If they both refer to this common individual as uncle, *laug* or *txiv ntxawm*, then they know that they occupy the same generational rung in the web of their clan hierarchy. If so, they are to view each other as brothers. The younger person will defer to the older one as *tij laug*, "older brother." The older person will refer to the younger one as *kwv*, "younger brother." If Jack refers to this common individual as *laug* or *txiv ntxawm*, but John calls him *yawm*, then Jack is an uncle to John. John is to address him as such, even if Jack is many years younger.

If Jack and John are from different clans, then their focus turns to marriage relationships between their extended families. Through the women in their lives, they are related to each other as *neej tsaa*. Once they have identified an individual as the common link, they will work out the term of address that is most appropriate for their situation. I will underscore three possibilities: *npawg*, *txiv kwj*, or *txiv dlaab*. *Npawg* is used if Jack and John are related as cross-cousins. This term is also preferred when no precise relationship can be worked out. *Npawg* are social equals. *Txiv kwj* or *txiv dlaab* indicates that the relationship is not equal, with Jack and John occupying different rungs on the generational ladder. Jack is a *txiv kwj*, to John if one of John's paternal aunts or *puj nyaaj* is married to Jack's male relatives. Jack is a *txiv dlaab* to John if John's uncles are married to Jack's sisters or distant cousins. The wives of these uncles are John's *puj laug* or *nam ntxawm*. In both cases, John is a nephew to Jack. Marriage relationships are a significant influence on how Hmong people relate to and interact with one another.

As seen across cultures, when visiting friends and relatives, Hmong Americans do observe cultural protocols. Before entering the doorway of the host, it is proper for a visitor to ask, *Mej tsi caiv puaj*? Loosely translated, this phrase means "Are you restricting guests from your home?" *Caiv* is a period of religious observance, lasting from several days to several weeks. *Caiv* is usually observed in the midst of a major illness. It can take place at any time during the year. The length of *caiv* is usually determined by a *txiv neeb* (shaman). During this time period, a family is prohibited from entertaining guests. With the exception of immediate family members, no one else is allowed to enter the home. A *caiv* does serve a practical purpose. It minimizes the burden placed on a family as it copes with an illness. It is important for a visitor to make sure that he is not intruding.

The word "taboo" is derived from the Tongan root *tabu*, meaning "to set apart, forbidden." By definition, a taboo is a custom that is prohibited or restricted. Taboos exist in every culture, but they differ greatly across cultures. Handed down across generations as cultural traditions, taboos play important roles in regulating social behaviors in family and community life. In Hmong culture, there are taboos that are specific to clans or subclans. The following are examples from the Her, Lee, and Yang clans.

Many taboos are religious in origin, linked to ritual mishaps in the past. Their relevance to the lives of people in the present is often a source of intense debate. Some lineages in the Yang clan (*xeem Yaaj*) are prohibited from eating or using any part of the heart (*plawv*) in their food preparations. Likewise, certain lineages in the Lee clan (*xeem Lis*) are careful not to eat or include the spleen (*po*) in their ritual meals. What are the consequences for not observing these taboos? Will there be sickness? Is there a lineage-wide calamity waiting to occur? Short on facts, explanations are crammed with no more than just cautions and warnings. Ensuring the solidarity of the community is one of the functions of taboos. People observe them primarily as a matter of tradition, not necessarily because they fear some looming misfortune. The Lee and Yang have the help of others in the community to maintain these lineage-specific taboos. People who are related to them through marriage will take steps to not include these organs in their food preparations.

In contrast to what we have seen in the Yang and Lee clans, there is a different taboo that is well known and continues to be respected by certain lineages of the Her clan. A father is prohibited from entering the bedroom of his son and daughter-in-law. Likewise, a daughter-in-law is not allowed to go into the bedroom of her father and mother-in-law. The reasons for this taboo are not very explicit. As all taboos are cultural strategies to address social concerns, one interpretation of this custom is that it was put in place to thwart illicit behaviors. Were such conducts the origin of this taboo? No one knows for sure, leaving many to speculate about its intent and purpose.

Hmong culture has a history that stretches back at least five thousand years. Many of its customs and traditions have no doubt changed in response to internal and external pressures. Highlighted in this essay are a few examples of the ideas and practices that continue to influence the lives of modern Hmong Americans. These cultural traditions are not outdated. Their wisdom and teaching hold as much relevance today as they once did in decades or centuries past.

Vincent K. Her

Further Reading

Cooper, Robert. *Hmong: A Guide to Traditional Lifestyles*. Singapore: Times Edition, 1998.

Her, Vincent K., and Mary Louise Buley-Meissner. *Hmong and American: From Refugees to Citizens*. St. Paul: Minnesota Historical Society Press, 2012.

Symonds, Patricia. *Calling in the Soul: Gender and the Cycle of Life in a Hmong Village*. Seattle: University of Washington Press, 2004.

Yang, Kao Kalia. *The Latehomecomer: A Hmong Family Memoir*. Minneapolis: Coffeehouse Press, 2008.

HORN OF AFRICA (DJIBOUTI, ERITREA, ETHIOPIA, SOMALIA)

The Horn of Africa is a peninsula of northeastern Africa that juts out into the Arabian Sea with a coast along the southern side of the Gulf of Aden. The Horn of Africa covers some 770,000 square miles and has a population of 115 million people. The majority of these people live in Ethiopia, with the rest living in Djibouti, Eritrea, and Somalia. The people living in the Horn of Africa tend to be Muslim, Christian, or Jewish, though some people also follow traditional, indigenous religions.

When greeting someone in Somalia it is usual to start a conversation with "Sidee tahay?" or "Nabad myah?" (How are you?). Another common Somali greeting is "Soo maal." This greeting refers to milking an animal because it is traditional for Somalis to offer a guest the chance to milk an animal and thereby get a drink. Additionally "Soo maal" recalls the traditional Somali greeting gesture of offering someone a milky tea to drink. Somalis also greet each other by saying "Maalin wanaagsan" (Good day). Much of Somalia's etiquette derives from Islamic traditions so it is also the case that another greeting often said in Somalia is "Salam alechem" (God bless you). When bidding someone farewell a commonly used phrase is "Nabad gelyo" (Goodbye).

When making introductions, men from the same clan-family will typically greet one another by enjoying a prolonged handshake. Somali women greet each other in an informal manner, usually by hugging or kissing each other on the cheek. When people from different clan-families meet they do not perform handshakes. Somali society pays great respect to community elders, whom people address as "aunt" or "uncle" whether or not they are related to them. At work Somalis do not usually use last names to address people. Instead Somalis call each other by their first name or by the first of their three given names. That said, most Somalis have a nickname that they use frequently, even when completing official documents.

In Ethiopia handshakes are the preeminent greeting gesture. Another typical Ethiopian greeting gesture sees people kiss each other multiple times upon the cheek while exchanging pleasant small talk. If during an introduction somebody tries to act superior, that person will be treated with contempt. In Ethiopia, as in Somalia, elders are treated with great respect, and when an elder enters a room everybody else will stand to greet them. Showing respect is an important aspect of Ethiopian verbal greetings. For this reason it is important to enquire of someone "How are you?" when meeting as well as to ask after the health of their children.

Another way in which Ethiopians show respect to each other when meeting is by employing titles including *Woizero* (Mrs.), *Ato* (Mr.), Doctor, or Engineer.

In Eritrea people will typically greet each other by saying "Selam," which translates as "Peace," but is the equivalent of saying "Hello" in English. The correct response is to repeat the word back to the person who first said it. When greeting each other informally Eritreans will often call each other *Ati* (sister), *Ade* (mother), *Ata* (brother), or *Abo* (father) depending on the age and gender of the person they are greeting.

Somali people take pride in their appearance and welcome compliments on their clothes. Traditional Somali attire for women includes the *dirac*, an elegant, full-length loose dress that is worn over another garment called a *gorgorad*. Another traditional Somali garment for women is the *boubou*, which is very similar to a *dirac* except where the *dirac* has close-fitting armholes the *boubou* has open armholes. During day-to-day activities, Somali women often wear a long length of fabric tied at the shoulder and draped round the waist called a *guntiino*. When at work women may wear loose-fitting trousers, together with a loose-fitting top that is not revealing. Women should also ensure that their head is covered as women are not supposed to display their hair in public in Somalia. Somali boys and men tend to wear fairly loose shirts with trousers.

Most women in Ethiopia wear Western-style clothes. However, traditional Ethiopian garments are still worn on special occasions. These garments include the *shemma*, which is a long length of cotton fabric that is used to make *habesha kemis*, a floor-length dress. Many Ethiopian women also wear a large shawl called a *netela* (or *gabi*) over their *habesha kemis*. The *netela*, which is also worn by Eritrean women, is usually made from very delicate woven cotton and is typically white in color with a brightly colored border. Ethiopian women belonging to the Tigray and Amhara groups often wear their hair in a style of braid known as *sheruba*. Ethiopian and Eritrean men tend to wear knee-length shirts with trousers. In work situations Ethiopian men usually wear trousers with long-sleeved shirts or T-shirts with sleeves that reach to the elbow.

The overriding characteristic of Somali cuisine is that it consists of halal foods, that is, food that is permitted by Islam. Therefore any meat eaten by Somalis must be halal in that the animal from which the meat derives must have been slaughtered in a special way as Muslim prayers were recited. If one is invited to a Somali house for a meal it is important to remember to wash hands before eating. This is because Somalis typically use their hands to eat from a communal dish. Also people will use their hands to take a share of *injera* (unleavened bread) though etiquette demands that people only take the portion of bread that sits directly in front of where they are sitting. When eating at home women will usually present food to the men before eating with their children once the men are full. In rural areas of Somalia some people eat by scooping food from a bowl using just the first three fingers of their right hand, or by using a spoon or rolled-up banana leaf. As is the case in other Islamic and African countries, the left hand is not used to eat with, as this hand is considered unclean.

Meals in the Horn of Africa typically begin once a guest has started to eat, with empty plates replenished quickly. Conversation throughout a meal is cordial and prolonged as it is thought very rude for diners to give their full attention to their meal and not to speak to each other. Under the rules of Islam the drinking of alcohol is prohibited, as is smoking.

Drinks commonly enjoyed in the Horn of Africa include milk, tea, and coffee. Somali men are often nomadic herdsmen and drink milk from camels, goats, and cows. Indeed, during the rainy season young Somali nomads tending camels may drink up to ten quarts of milk per day. The nomads will also slaughter older camels and eat their meat, with the fatty meat of the camel's hump considered a delicacy. Somalis also eat goat meat and lamb. *Durra* (a type of sorghum), honey, dates, and rice are also commonly eaten in areas with nomadic populations. Farmers living in the south of Somalia grow corn, beans, sorghum, millet, squash, and various fruits and vegetables. The people also eat millet and rice, though the rice has been imported. The most popular bread in Somalia is *muufo,* a flatbread made with corn flour. In the south of Somalia pasta (especially served with marinara sauce) is a favorite food— this is a result of the fact that much of Somalia was once Italian Somaliland, a colony of Italy (1889–1936 CE). Arab food is also popular in Somalia. Major Somali cities usually have quite a few restaurants, though only recently (since the late 1990s) have women started to eat out with men. The restaurants in major Somali cities tend to serve Arab, Chinese, European, and American foods. This is especially true of restaurants in the Somali capital city, Mogadishu. When eating in restaurants some people will use cutlery while others prefer to eat with their hands.

In Ethiopia the most commonly eaten food is *injera*, a type of bread that is present at every meal. All foods in Ethiopia are eaten with the hands; even liquid-rich

Men eat a meal at a home in Wutafa, Tigray, Ethiopia. Ethiopians traditionally use their hands when eating, rather than utensils. (Sean Sprague/Alamy Stock Photo)

foods such as stews will not be eaten using cutlery. Instead bite-sized pieces of *injera* will be dipped into the stews, which typically consist of vegetables such as carrots, cabbage, spinach, and potatoes, as well as lentils. In Ethiopia many people belonging to the Ethiopian Orthodox Church observe food taboos originating in the Old Testament. Therefore the people will not eat the flesh of animals with un-cloven hooves and that do not chew the cud. These animals are not eaten as they are considered impure and unclean. Pork is almost never eaten or sold. Any animals slaughtered for food must be killed in line with religious practice. For example, animals whose meat will be eaten by Christians will have their throats slit as their head is kept turned towards the east and the slaughterer says, "In the name of the Father, the Son, and the Holy Ghost." If the slaughterer is a Muslim then he will say "In the name of Allah the Merciful."

Another facet of Ethiopian dining etiquette is the popular coffee ceremony. Coffee drinking is a very social event in Ethiopia. To start the ceremony a host will summon all his neighbors, for failing to do so is considered exceptionally rude. It is also at this time that the host introduces his guests to his neighbors. The person preparing the coffee lights a fire over which green coffee beans are roasted while incense is burnt. Once the beans are roasted, they are ground with a mortar and pestle, before being put in a traditional black pot called a *jebena* to which water is added.

There are three stages to the coffee ceremony. The first round of coffee (*abol*) sees everyone given a cup of coffee that is then returned to the person who is brewing the coffee. Additional water is mixed with the coffee that is then returned to the fire for the second round (*tonna*) to take place. During *tonna*, more incense is burnt. The third round, *baraka*, includes a blessing of the coffee. Any guest or neighbor who enters the place where the coffee is being brewed during this stage is considered blessed too. It is considered rude to drink the coffee made during *abol* and then leave the ceremony. However, it is also thought impolite to linger over a cup of coffee to such an extent that the coffee is tepid when drunk, as Ethiopians feel coffee must be enjoyed very hot. After everyone has drunk their coffee it is customary to proclaim thanks to the host by saying "Yabaraka yasesay bet yarigaw," which translates as "May He make the house blessed and prosperous."

Another very popular drink in both Ethiopia and Eritrea is a particularly alcoholic honey wine called *tej*. This wine is enjoyed both on special occasions and at *tej* houses. *Tej* consists of honey and water flavored with *gesho* (*Rhamnus prenoides*) twigs and leaves. The wine is drunk from special tube-shaped flasks. Another notable feature of hospitality in the Horn of Africa is the consumption of qat (or khat as well as many variant spellings). This is a lightly narcotic leaf, native to the area, the consumption of which causes loss of appetite and euphoria. Nearly all men living in the Horn of Africa and on the Arabian Peninsula (especially in Djibouti, Ethiopia, Somalia, and Yemen) consume qat recreationally and legally, usually after lunch. Qat is also used in religious rituals.

People living in the Horn of Africa tend to be very sociable and like to talk a lot. Somalis typically enjoy talking about food, world culture, and family matters. Many Somalis also like to joke. Moreover Somalis are inquisitive by nature and will typically ask a stranger what their occupation is, where they come from, how many siblings they have, and whether they are married or have children. However, many Somalis are said to be suspicious of foreigners, particularly aid workers, since from the Somali point of view the aid workers take many photographs and ask lots of questions about the community before leaving, never to be heard from again. Very few topics of conversation are taboo in Somalia, but there are certain subjects that may be best avoided. These include criticism of Islam, or of cultural practices enacted in Somalia including polygamy and female genital cutting.

In general, in Ethiopia people like to converse about work and family matters. That said, most Ethiopians do not tend to discuss personal matters outside of their family group. For this reason it is best to avoid discussing family matters unless advice is sought, thereby meaning that the family becomes a conversational topic. When Ethiopians do discuss their families, relatives are always spoken of in a respectful manner. When in conversation in Ethiopia it is preferable to avoid asking "Where are you from?" as this question can be interpreted as asking about a person's ethnicity, which in turn is seen as a divisive, negative line of interrogation. Other taboo areas of conversation in Ethiopia include religion, sex and sexuality, and regional politics.

Eritreans do not tend to discuss personal matters or subjects such as religion, politics, and marriage. A particularly taboo area of conversation is the Eritrean–Ethiopian War that lasted from May 1998 until June 2000. This war is an especially sensitive area and it is easy to cause offense when discussing it. Moreover the political climate of Eritrea may make open discussion of the conflict unwise.

Body language varies in Somalia depending on the sex of the people speaking. For instance if an unmarried Somali man is talking to an unmarried Somali woman, then the two will not stand close together (about three paces apart) and will avoid touching each other. Also in general women will avoid making direct eye contact with men, as this is considered disrespectful. Conversely if two men are in conversation the men will stand close together, may touch each other when speaking, and will make direct eye contact. As Somali culture is Muslim, people do not engage in any kind of intimate activity with the opposite sex if they are not married to each other. Indeed, Somali culture is so modest that even if a husband and wife were to show affection in public, this would occur in a very discreet way. Such is the desire for modesty and reserve that Somalis will also not display anger or joy in public. Instead any high emotion will only be displayed in private.

In Ethiopia people greet each other warmly and employ open, positive body language including smiles and other signs of cheerfulness when talking. Ethiopians also show respect for other people in that they will often give guests priority, for example, by allowing guests to be seated first. Ethiopians tend to stand quite far apart when talking but at the same time do not shy away from making eye contact with each other. Indeed avoiding eye contact may be interpreted as a sign of duplicity. Many Ethiopians think nothing of touching someone of the same sex on the shoulder or arm while in conversation. Conversely, physical contact in public between people of the opposite sex is frowned upon, and couples do not usually express affection in public. Another taboo physical gesture is pointing fingers at

Culture Shock! ⊕

Female Genital Cutting

Female genital cutting (FGC), also known as female circumcision, is the collective name for ancient, yet highly controversial, rituals that see the partial or complete removal of a female's external genitalia. FGC is known to occur in 28 African countries, particularly in the Horn of Africa where an estimated 80 percent of women living in Somalia, Djibouti, Sudan, and Eritrea have experienced FGC. Muslims, Christians, Ethiopian Jews, and animists all perform FGC. There are many reasons why certain societies practice FGC: the clitoris may be considered an aggressive organ that threatens the supremacy of the penis, could hurt fetuses during birth, or will grow to the size of a penis if it is not removed. The excision of the clitoris is also thought to tame female sexuality, thereby preserving female chastity. Indeed the physical scars of FGC are often taken as proof of female virginity, which is a precondition of marriage in many cultures.

Victoria Williams

other people, as this is considered very discourteous. Similarly, it is thought very rude in Ethiopia for someone to display anger through gesticulations or a raised voice.

Victoria Williams

Further Reading

Akou, Heather Marie. *The Politics of Dress in Somali Culture*. Bloomington: Indiana University Press, 2011.

Allman, Jean, ed. *Fashioning Africa: Power and the Politics of Dress*. Bloomington: Indiana University Press, 2004.

Bahiru, Bekele, Tetenike Mehari, and Mogessie Ashenaf. "Chemical and Nutritional Properties of '*Tej*,' An Indigenous Ethiopian Honey Wine: Variations Within and Between Production Units." *Journal of Food Technology in Africa* 6, no. 3 (July–Sept. 2001): 104–8.

Beckerleg, Susan. *Ethnic Identity and Development: Khat and Social Change in Africa*. Basingstoke, UK: Palgrave Macmillan, 2010.

Davila, Florangela. "Food and Fasting in Somali Culture." *EthnoMed*. June 1, 2001. https://ethnomed.org/clinical/nutrition/food-and-fasting-in-somali-culture. Accessed January 15, 2017.

Getahun, Solomon Addis, and Wudu Tafete Kassu. *Culture and Customs of Ethiopia*. Santa Barbara, CA: Greenwood, 2014.

Global Affairs Canada. "Cultural Information—Eritrea." November 13, 2014. https://www.international.gc.ca/cil-cai/country_insights-apercus_pays/ci-ic_er.aspx?lang=eng. Accessed March 1, 2017.

Global Affairs Canada. "Cultural Information—Ethiopia." November 17, 2014. https://www.international.gc.ca/cil-cai/country_insights-apercus_pays/ci-ic_et.aspx?lang=eng. Accessed March 1, 2017.

Global Affairs Canada. "Cultural Information—Somalia." November 13, 2014. https://www
    .international.gc.ca/cil-cai/country_insights-apercus_pays/ci-ic_so.aspx?lang=eng. Ac-
    cessed January 15, 2017.
Lewis, Toby. "Somali Cultural Profile." *EthnoMed.* 1995–2017. https://ethnomed.org
    /culture/somali/somali-cultural-profile. Accessed January 15, 2017.
Mohr, Adam. "Ethiopia." *Countries and Their Cultures.* 2017. http://www.everyculture.com
    /Cr-Ga/Ethiopia.html. Accessed January 15, 2017.
Shurgin, Ann H. "Somalia." *Countries and Their Cultures.* 2017. http://www.everyculture
    .com/Sa-Th/Somalia.html. Accessed January 15, 2017.

HUI

The Hui people are China's most widely distributed ethnic minority. There are around 9.8 million Hui people living in China, with the majority of the group living in the Ningxia Hui Autonomous Region and the Zhongyuan, but there are also Hui communities located in Beijing, Inner Mongolia, Hebei, Hainan, and Yunnan. The Hui are also found on the frontier between China and Myanmar and in the Central Asian nations of Kazakhstan, Uzbekistan, and Kyrgyzstan. The name *Hui* is the abbreviated form of *Huihui*, the generic name given to China's Muslims during the Ming and Qing Dynasties. Today nearly all Hui people are Muslim. The Hui living in China are descended from Persian, Central Asian, and Arab traders who travelled the ancient Silk Route trade network and who intermarried with local Chinese women. The Hui are known by other names outside of China. For instance, in Russia and Central Asia the Hui are termed *Dungan*, which is the name given to the descendants of Chinese Muslims who emigrated to the Russian Empire (nowadays Kyrgyzstan and Kazakhstan) in the 1870s and 1880s.

Some people postulate that the Hui are virtually indistinguishable from China's Han majority, while others suggest that it is difficult to make generalizations about the Hui as they are geographically diverse, have slightly different historical backgrounds, and experience life differently depending on where they live. It is for these reasons that some academics suggest that the Hui should not be seen as a single, unified ethnic group. That having been said, it is possible to describe certain Hui social conventions and taboos, much of which have been greatly influenced by Islam.

Many Hui men wear traditional hats, which are small, brimless, and usually colored white, though some men wear black hats. Other Hui men wear pentagonal, hexagonal, or octagonal hats. Alternatively, Hui men may not wear a hat but rather wrap their heads in white towels or lengths of fabric. This variation in headwear reflects the various branches of Islam to which the men adhere. Hui men tend to wear double-breasted white shirts, which some sport together with white trousers and socks. Hui women normally wear white hats with rounded brims and veils. Young Hui girls wear green veils trimmed with golden thread and embroidered with floral patterns. Once a Hui woman has married, she traditionally wears a black veil that covers her head and shoulders. Elderly Hui women wear white veils that hide their heads and backs. Hui women usually wear side-opening clothes. Those worn by young Hui girls and married women are decorated with threads and embroidered flowers.

Hui cuisine varies from location to location. Hui people living in the Ningxia Hui Autonomous Region typically eat food made from flour, while in Gansu and Qinghai the Hui prefer foods based on cereals and potatoes. The Hui people tend to be very particular about what they drink. For example, they will drink only flowing water or water from a clean source. Similarly the Hui will not bathe, wash clothes, or pour dirty water near sources of drinking water. Also before and after every meal, the Hui will wash their hands in running water. One of the most well-known treats the Hui present to guests is Gaiwan tea (tea served in lidded cups). Drinking Gaiwan tea is a Hui cultural practice that can be traced back to the Tang Dynasty (618–907 CE). The Hui make their Gaiwan tea using jasmine tea mixed with ingredients including longan, dried persimmon, medlar, and jujube, as well as sesame and sugar candy. These ingredients are then added to melted snow or spring water. When serving the tea to a guest the Hui host first fills the guest's cup with boiled water to show the guest that the tea is fresh rather than tea left by someone else. The Hui host then pours the water from the cup, places the dry tea ingredients in the cup and then pours boiling water into the cup on top of the dry ingredients. The Hui host will use two hands to give the cup to the guest, as this is a sign of respect. The guest will then drink the tea, leaving the lid on the cup but leaving a small gap so that they are able to drink. It is often the case that when welcoming a guest to their home, a Hui host will serve the guest Gaiwan tea as well as homemade cakes and candy accompanied by fruit. Most Hui have a sweet tooth, with their preference for sweet foods likely related to the Hui's Arab heritage. When a guest visits a Hui home it is customary for all the host's family members to come welcome the guest, and, if the guest has travelled from afar, once the visit is completed he or she will be escorted out of the Hui village/town.

The Hui eat beef and mutton but consider the eating of some other meat to be taboo. For instance the Hui consider pigeons to be sacred and do not eat them except under certain circumstances. For example, if pigeon is included in medicine then it may be fed to someone who is ill as long as an imam (leader of worship at a mosque) has blessed the medicine. In general the Hui also consider it taboo to eat dog, horsemeat, donkey, mule, animals that kill their prey, and blood. The Hui also do not eat any animal that has been killed by non-Hui people or that has died naturally. Moreover the Hui tend to only eat meat from animals that have been killed by a Hui cook or by an imam. It should be noted, however, that though the Hui are greatly influenced by Islam and are referred to as Chinese Muslims, and areas in which the Hui live tend to have many mosques, it does not necessarily follow that all Hui are practicing Muslims. Indeed some Hui living along China's south coast eat pork (which is forbidden in Islam), and many Hui people do not fast during the Muslim holy month of Ramadan. This being said, Hui people are often offended if asked whether they believe in a Hui religion, because Hui people take great pride in belonging to the world religion of Islam even if they do not adhere to every facet of Islamic life.

The influence of Islam on Hui society is evident in the three major festivals enjoyed by most Hui people: Hari Raya Puasa, Eid Al-Adha, and Mawlid an-Nabi. The three-day Hari Raya Puasa (Fast Ending Festival) is widely celebrated among Chinese Islamic communities during Ramadan. On the festival's first day, families get up early to clean the mosques and courtyards, thereby creating an atmosphere of cleanliness and comfort. All the participating Hui people then dress in their best clothes and hang up colorful lanterns. Eid al-Adha, the feast of sacrifice, fidelity, and filial piety, is usually celebrated 70 days after Hari Raya Puasa. To mark the occasion the Hui sacrifice strong animals and divide the resultant meat into three lots. One lot is presented to close family members; the second is given to relatives, friends, and neighbors; and the final portion is given to the poor. Hui elders boil the meat and then children bury the bones underground, covering them with soil. Many Hui families also feel it is correct at this time to invite imams into their houses to recite the Koran and partake of food. The third festival, Mawlid an-Nabi, which takes place on the 12th day of the third month of the Islamic calendar, commemorates the birthday and death anniversary of Prophet Muhammad. On this day, Muslims visit the mosque to recite the Koran, sending blessings to Prophet Muhammad and his family, and attend lectures on the life of Muhammad given by imams. The Hui also donate cereal, oil, meat, and money to the local mosque. The Hui also consider it right to perform voluntary work and charitable deeds on this day.

The Hui typically follow a fairly puritanical lifestyle and tend not to tell jokes (especially jokes about food), smoke, drink alcohol, gamble, or take part in fortune-telling activities. Also young Hui people are not allowed to socialize with older group members—Hui elders sit in special seats while children and younger people sit on the edge of seats or on benches. Other proscribed behavior includes sitting or stepping on thresholds because, according to Muslim lore, Prophet Muhammad used the threshold as his pillow. It is also taboo in Hui society to employ certain foods as similes. For example, a Hui person would not say that the reddish skin of a chili was as red as blood.

The Hui tend to discourage their people from marrying outside of their ethnic group. If, for example, a Hui man wants to marry a girl from another ethnic group such as the Han, then it is made clear to the girl that she must gain an understanding of Hui culture and convert to Islam. The marriage will not be allowed to go ahead if the girl does not fulfill these criteria. At a marriage feast, the couple is served 8 or 12 dishes. The number of dishes served must be even because this symbolizes that the new couple will be paired together forever. Hui funerals do not involve many rituals or customs. One of the few Hui funeral taboos is that mourners must not wail, as this is viewed as showing contempt for the dead.

The Hui's heritage means that in some areas the Hui speak Mandarin that also includes Arabic, Turkish, Central Asian, and Persian vocabulary. The resultant way of speaking, known as Hui speech (*Huihui bua*) is not a language as such but is a distinct mode of expression of both Hui ethnicity and religion. The Hui living in areas bordering regions of China often use the dialects of other local ethnic minorities. Although Hui speech includes elements of Arabic, this does not mean that the

Hui necessarily speak or understand Arabic. Indeed many Hui recite Islamic scriptures in Koranic Arabic as they cannot read or write Arabic.

Victoria Williams

Further Reading

Dillon, Michael. *China's Muslim Hui Community: Migration, Settlement and Sects.* Richmond, UK: Curzon, 1999.

Gladney, Dru C. *Muslim Chinese: Ethnic Nationalism in the People's Republic.* Harvard East Asian Monographs 149. Cambridge, MA: Harvard University Press for the Council of East Asian Studies at Harvard University, 1996.

Gladney, Dru C. "Muslim Tombs and Ethnic Folklore: Charters for Hui Identity." *Journal of Asian Studies* 46, no. 3 (1987): 495–532. www.jstor.org/stable/2056897.

Travel China Guide. "Hui Nationality." *Travel China Guide.* 1998–2017. https://www.travelchinaguide.com/intro/nationality/hui/. Accessed January 3, 2017.

Zhou, Ruru. "Hui Minority." *China Highlights.* December 14, 2015. http://www.chinahighlights.com/travelguide/nationality/hui.htm. Accessed January 3, 2017.

HUNGARY

Hungary is a landlocked Central European country bordered by Austria, Croatia, Romania, Serbia and Montenegro, Slovakia, Slovenia, and Ukraine. Hungary has a rich cultural history due to its successive habitation by various ethnic groups and tribes including the Celts, Romans, Slavs, Gepids, and Avars. Hungary was founded during the late ninth century and converted to Christianity around 1000 CE. During the sixteenth and seventeenth centuries Hungary was part of the Ottoman Empire and later became part of the Austro-Hungarian Empire together with Austria. Hungary's borders were established in 1920 after the end of World War I; after World War II Hungary became a satellite state of the Soviet Union. This in turn led Hungary to be ruled by a communist dictatorship (1947–1989). Today Hungary is a democratic nation that is a member of the European Union, NATO, and the United Nations. The nation's population of around 10 million enjoys a very high standard of living, with the concept of the family considered central to modern Hungarian lifestyles. To this end it is common for several generations of a family to live together with older relatives helping to raise children.

When greeting in Hungary, it is typical for both men and women to shake hands, though if a man and woman meet then the man should wait for the woman to extend her hand first. It is not uncommon for older Hungarian men to greet women by bowing or by kissing a lady's hand. If two people meeting are close friends, then the couple may greet each other by kissing one another on the cheek starting by first kissing the left cheek.

In work situations it is safest to address people by their titles and surnames when meeting them for the first time. Work colleagues may address each other by their first name, but for strangers to use first names would be considered impolite. Once a cordial business relationship has become established, one may be invited to use a person's first name. Most Hungarian people have long and short forms of their names, but these must be used only when they invite you to do so. It is usual for Hungarians to go by their formal name in business situations with the shorter form of their name used by friends and relatives. Common examples of Hungarian long/short names include Laszlo–Laci, Sandor–Sani, and Zoltan–Zoli for men and Zsofia–Zsofi, Zsuzsa–Zsu or Zsuzsi, and Monika–Moni for women.

As a people Hungarians are generally quite informal, but they tend to dress more formally and conservatively at work. Hungarians tend to wear suits if they work in offices. People who do not work in offices might wear jeans and a top to work. In cities, especially in the Hungarian capital Budapest, people dress more ostentatiously. Hungarians take great pride in their appearance. Arriving at work wearing dirty or unironed clothes is utterly frowned upon.

Hungarians often go to great lengths when providing hospitality to guests. When visiting a Hungarian's home for dinner it is important to arrive on time or at least no more than five minutes late. The host will then invite the guest into the house ahead of him- or herself. It may be expected that a guest should remove their shoes before entering the house. Once inside the house a guest should not ask to be shown around. It is not necessary for a guest to bring a gift for the host, but if the guest wanted to, chocolates, bunches of flowers, and Western alcohol make the most welcome gifts. Any flowers brought to a home should not include lilies or chrysanthemums, as these flowers are associated with funerals. Also it is not a good idea to give foreign wine to a Hungarian, as Hungarians are immensely proud of the wine produced by Hungarian vineyards.

In Hungary people eat Continental-style with the fork held in the left hand and the knife held in the right hand while eating. When not eating, people should keep their elbows from resting on the table and should make sure that their hands are visible at all times. At the start of each course, the host will wish all the guests a healthy appetite, but it is important that guests do not start eating until the host has started to eat. As a host will measure how successful his or her hospitality has been by how much guests eat, it is therefore polite for guests to try all the food served to them. To indicate that a guest has eaten his fill, he should lay his knife and fork parallel across the right side of his plate. Similarly a host will refill any glass as soon as it is empty, so if a guest does not wish to drink any more, the guest should leave their glass half full.

The guest of honor is responsible for proposing the first toast, which should include best wishes for the health of everybody present. When everyone has finished eating, a guest should make a toast thanking the host for their hospitality. When visiting Hungary it is important to be sensitive to the fact that Hungary has seen great economic upheaval fairly recently, and as a result of this most Hungarians (including professionals such as doctors, teachers, and professors) are poorly paid and might be unable to afford the same level of entertainment as foreign visitors. Therefore, while a foreigner may be able to afford to eat at upscale restaurants, locals most likely will not have the income to do so.

Hungarians' body language depends on the backgrounds and heritage of individuals. Typically a Hungarian man will walk on the left-hand side of a woman. This is because in times past men kept their swords to their left side with the swords intended ostensibly to protect women. It is quite usual for Hungarians to make physical contact with each other when talking, especially touching each other's hands, arms, and shoulders. This is less true for men than it is for women, though. When in conversation, however, Hungarians will stand at arm's length from one another if they are acquainted or further away if they are strangers.

Hungarians tend to stand close to each other when travelling on public transport and in shops. In isolated rural areas, villagers will normally stare at strangers out of curiosity. Hungarians value eye contact in that while it is not essential to maintain steady eye contact when talking, the refusal to make eye contact at all is seen as rude and thought to indicate that someone is dishonest. Public displays of affection are not uncommon in Hungary, though older generations may disapprove of overly affectionate behavior in public.

Hungarians are known for being forthright speakers who do not hide their true feelings or opinions. That said, while Hungarians can become emotional when discussing art, music, and so on, Hungarians consider public displays of anger to be impolite.

Safe topics of conversation in Hungary include the weather, sports, and family life. Hungarians also like to hear about life in other countries. Hungarians have a very dry sense of humor and like to be told jokes while also telling jokes about bureaucracy, which they see as a remnant of Hungary's communist past. Hungarians also enjoy talking to foreigners about Hungarian food and wine, of which Hungarians are very proud. It is best not to discuss politics with Hungarians. Many Hungarians still feel upset about the Treaty of Trianon that was signed after World War I and which many Hungarians feel was a bad deal for their country, as the treaty resulted in Hungary's borders being redrawn with more than 3 million Hungarians given over to Slovakia, Ukraine, Romania, and Yugoslavia. This subject is taboo to discuss in Hungary, especially with foreigners. Another political subject that is best not discussed when in Hungary is Hungarian nationalism. Similarly, many Hungarians view foreign involvement (particularly American investment) in

---

Culture Shock! ⊕

The Treaty of Trianon

The Treaty of Trianon was a treaty concluding World War I signed by representatives of both Hungary and the Allied Powers. The treaty was signed on June 4, 1920, at Trianon Palace at Versailles, near Paris. The treaty's terms meant that Hungary lost around two-thirds of its former territory as well as two-thirds of its population. Hungarian land was given to Czechoslovakia; Austria; the Kingdom of Serbs, Croats, and Slovenes (later known as Yugoslavia); Romania; and Italy. The terms of the treaty caused much resentment and ethnic tension, with many Hungarians complaining that the treaty violated Hungary's historical character while displacing ethnic Hungarians.

Victoria Williams

their country with suspicion. For this reason, it is better not to suggest that foreign investment has benefitted Hungary's economy or infrastructure.

Victoria Williams

Further Reading

Buranbaeva, Oksana, and Vanja Mladineo. *Culture and Customs of Hungary*. Santa Barbara, CA: ABC-CLIO, 2011.

Commisceo Global Consultancy Ltd. "Hungary Guide." 2016. http://www.commisceo-global .com/country-guides/hungary-guide. Accessed December 18, 2016.

Esbenshade, Richard S. *Cultures of the World: Hungary*, 2nd ed. Tarrytown, NY: Benchmark Books, 2005.

Global Affairs Canada. "Cultural Information—Hungary." November 17, 2014. https://www .international.gc.ca/cil-cai/country_insights-apercus_pays/ci-ic_hu.aspx?lang=eng. Accessed January 13, 2017.

HUTU AND TUTSI

The Hutus and Tutsis are peoples living in the Great Lakes region of Africa that includes Burundi, the Democratic Republic of Congo, Kenya, Rwanda, Tanzania, and Uganda. The Hutus live mainly in Rwanda, Burundi, and the east of the Democratic Republic of the Congo, where they form one of the main population divisions alongside the Tutsis. Tutsis reside primarily in Rwanda and Burundi, but also have sizeable populations in Uganda, the Democratic Republic of the Congo, and Tanzania. In 1994 the Hutus and Tutsis were involved in what has become known as the Rwandan Genocide. Today in an attempt to promote unity, the Rwandan government has outlawed any discussion of ethnicity. The population of Rwanda is thought to be 85–90 percent Hutu and 10–15 percent Tutsi, with the remaining 1 percent consisting of the Twa people. The demography of Burundi is much the same as that of Rwanda. Burundi is one of the poorest nations on Earth with 67 percent of the population living below the poverty line, and in 2016 Burundi was ranked as the world's least happy country in the World Happiness Report. This entry will concentrate on Rwanda and Burundi.

In Rwanda proper greetings are a major element of social etiquette. Rwandans have an intricate greeting system that varies depending on whether someone is greeting another person of the same social status, a relative, or a friend. In rural areas of Rwanda it is usual to greet everybody that is met. Common Rwandan greetings are "Mwaramutse" (used in the morning), "Mwiriwe" (an afternoon greeting), "Muraho" (meaning "Good day") and "Amakuru" (which means "How are you?"). Rwandan people shake hands using their right hands. A particularly friendly greeting sees people lay a hand on each other's hip while placing their right hand on the other person's shoulder. Friends might also hold each other's hand as a sign of their closeness. Holding hands between people of the same sex is a sign of friendship. Very close friends and people of the same social status will also hug as a greeting. This hug is different from Western-style hugs, however, as it involves people holding each other by the shoulders and brushing together their heads first

Culture Shock! ⊕

The World Happiness Report

The World Happiness Report is an assessment of happiness in United Nations member nations published by the UN Sustainable Development Solutions Network. The report aims to help member nations shape their public policies. The first World Happiness Report was released in 2012 and outlined the state of world happiness, causes of happiness and misery, and the correlations between policy and case studies. The reports include input from leading experts in fields such as economics, psychology, and national statistics who consider areas including mental illness, the benefits of happiness, the importance of ethics, and so on. The World Happiness Report uses data from the Gallup World Poll and is available to the public via the World Happiness Report Web site. Thus far Bhutan is the only country to have officially adopted gross national happiness as their main development indicator rather than gross domestic product.

Victoria Williams

on one side and then on the other side. Men also often touch the sides of their foreheads when meeting someone, beginning with the right-hand side of the forehead and then touching the left side. A greeting intended to signal respect sees Rwandans hold their right forearm with their left hand while shaking hands with someone. When two Rwandans of the opposite sex meet, they will not normally make any physical contact. If they do touch, then it will be in the form of a handshake that must be initiated by the woman.

Handshakes are extremely important in Burundi. When Burundians greet they usually shake hands using their right hand, though a variations on this sees a person place their left hand on the other person's elbow. Burundians who have greeted each other by shaking hands will continue to shake hands for several minutes after the initial introduction, all the while standing close together and talking. When meeting each other Burundians will typically greet each other by wishing each other a large cattle herd. Furthermore greetings will also usually involve symbolic references to cattle. In Burundi, friends will usually air-kiss three times or hug by grasping each other's shoulders when greeting each other. As in Rwanda Burundians will hold their right forearm with their left hand while shaking hands with someone they respect and close friends of the same sex will hold hands. Also, as in Rwanda, when a man meets a woman he will wait to see if she initiates a handshake before reaching forward to shake her hand.

In Rwanda people typically wear European-style clothes. The clothes are usually secondhand as the people often cannot afford to buy new clothes. Nonetheless Rwandan people take appearance seriously and like to look their best. Typically men wear long trousers because the wearing of shorts is associated with children and boys who are still at school. In rural Rwanda, women wear long garments that cover their legs. The traditional Rwandan dress for women is a silk garment called an *umushanana*. Traditionally the *umushanana* was worn by older women and consisted of a wrap skirt that was gathered at the hips with a sash that was worn draped over one shoulder. Today the *umushanana* is worn as a one-piece outfit that resembles an Indian sari and is usually worn on formal occasions.

In Burundi people typically ensure that their clothing and shoes are always in good condition despite having very low incomes, and place great significance on looking good. The traditional Burundi garment is a fabric wrap called a *pagne* that is worn by girls, women, and older men living in the rural parts of the country. The *pagne* is worn over dresses, blouses, and shirts. Burundian women also wear scarves in order to cover their heads. As in Rwanda, men always wear long trousers since boys wear shorts.

Rwandan society is hierarchical with great emphasis placed on social etiquette that demonstrates respect and social rank. At family get-togethers seats are traditionally reserved for men, with other family members made to sit on mats laid on the floor. Men also get to eat first, followed by any women and children present. If guests are present then the guests will also be given chairs as well as the best food and drinks available. The Rwandan diet is rich in starches but low in protein and fat, with the most commonly eaten foods being bananas, potatoes, and beans. Rwandans sometimes eat fish but eat meat infrequently. If meat is eaten then it will most likely be goat, unless it is a special occasion in which case a bull or cow will be sacrificed and the resultant beef will be eaten. Rwandans view cattle as both status symbols and producers of milk. When providing hospitality Rwandans may not always offer guests food but will always serve drinks. Indeed in Rwanda it is considered an insult not to provide someone with a drink when others are partaking of liquid. The usual drinks enjoyed by Rwandans are tea and coffee, and Rwandans tend to frown upon women drinking alcohol.

Burundians are often very outgoing and enjoy meeting up with their friends. It is also quite usual for Burundians to drop in on each other unannounced. In Burundi it is usually the case that if somebody has some money to spend, then they will invite their friends out to drink beer. Those who are invited are not expected to pay for any of the drinks. Instead the person who issued the invitation is expected to pay for everyone else's drinks. As in Rwanda it is generally socially unacceptable for a woman to drink alcohol. In Burundi all social gatherings feature food and drink, most especially beer. It is considered rude for any guest to refuse any food or drink that they are offered. Both Rwandans and Burundians take a fairly flexible approach to time and tend not to be punctual when attending social events. This is not true for business meetings, however, as potential business partners are expected to be punctual to meetings.

Rwandan people tend to make indirect eye contact when talking together. Moreover, women and children will usually look downwards or look away from the person that they are talking to in order to convey respect. Rwandans perform certain gestures when they wish to point or call to people. For example, if a Rwandan wishes to point to someone, they will hold out their arm with the palm open and facing upwards, because in Rwanda it is considered extremely discourteous to point at another person using the index finger.

Burundians also tend to avoid direct eye contact, and during a conversation women and children might glance towards the ground or away in order to demonstrate respect. Burundians beckon to other people by extending an arm with the palm facing downwards and bringing the fingers inwards as though scratching an imaginary object. Burundians also have a specific way of giving and receiving gifts. When a Burundian receives a gift they will customarily take the object using both hands in order to demonstrate respect for the gift-giver. This action is learned during childhood, for children are expected to perform this gesture when receiving a gift from an adult.

Since in Rwanda people can be put on trial for discussing ethnicity, it is important not to ask a Rwandan about their ethnic heritage. Indeed it is not just considered bad manners for a Rwandan to discuss ethnicity but can actually lead to a Rwandan being charged with the offence of divisionism. The Rwandan government insists that just as ethnic difference can be learned, so people can be educated not to believe in ethnicity. Rwanda has an ingrained culture of conformity and of obeying authority, and many foreign commentators have noted that modern-day Rwandans have quickly learned to follow their government's policy of nonethnicity. It is also best not to ask Rwandans about the Rwandan Civil War (1990–1993) or the Rwandan Genocide, as memories of these traumatic events are still vivid and recalling the events can be very upsetting for Rwandans. In both Rwanda and Burundi acceptable topics of conversation include food, soccer, and geography. Rwandans also enjoy jokes, but foreigners should avoid sarcasm in case sarcastic jokes do not translate well.

Both Rwanda and Burundi have social taboos. In Burundi it is taboo to boil milk as Burundians believe this interferes with cows' ability to produce milk. In Rwanda taboos also relate to cattle for it is traditionally taboo for someone to smoke while milking a cow, or to allow cattle to return home without lighting a fire to welcome them back. These taboos reflect that Rwandans consider cattle to be almost sacred animals. Another Rwandan taboo, known as *gutsinda*, reflects women's place in society, for according to tradition a wife should not refer to her parents-in-law by their name. Traditionally women are also not permitted to whistle, build fences, close gates, or milk cows. It also used to be illegal for women to cut firewood or tend cattle. If a woman was unmarried or had no male offspring, she would have to ask a neighbor to perform these tasks.

Victoria Williams

Further Reading

Falola, Toyin, and Daniel Jean-Jacques, eds. *Africa: An Encyclopedia of Culture and Society.* Santa Barbara, CA: ABC-CLIO, 2016.

Great Lakes Agency for Peace and Development International. "Rwanda—Culture and Customs." https://glapd.com/about/where-we-are-from/rwanda-culture-and-customs/. Accessed January 10, 2017.

Lacey, Marc. "A Decade After Massacres, Rwanda Outlaws Ethnicity." *New York Times.* April 9, 2004. http://www.nytimes.com/2004/04/09/world/a-decade-after-massacres-rwanda -outlaws-ethnicity.html?_r=1. Accessed January 10, 2017.

Rugina, Silvia. "Changing Face of Umushanana, the Rwandan Traditional Dress." *The East African.* October 18, 2013. http://www.theeastafrican.co.ke/Rwanda/Lifestyle /Changing-face-of-umushanana-Rwandan-traditional-dress/1433242–2038426 -t9yr9s/index.html. Accessed January 10, 2017.

INDIA

In order to appreciate the intricacies of India and its people, one must look into this region's history. India was originally part of the Indus Valley Civilization in the northwest Indian subcontinent (including present-day Pakistan and some regions in northeast Afghanistan). It is one of the world's oldest civilizations along with Ancient Egypt and Mesopotamia; it was one of three early civilizations and the most widespread among them, covering an area of 1.25 million km^2. Around 1500 BCE, Aryan tribes infiltrated the Indian subcontinent and merged with earlier Dravidian inhabitants and thus created the classical Indian culture. The Maurya Empire of the fourth and third centuries BCE united much of South Asia under the patronage of the Indian emperor Ashoka the Great. This was followed by over 200 years of the Gupta Dynasty; this was the classical period in India, with leaps made in the arts, science, and mathematics. This time period also saw many foreigners come to India and early versions of assimilation from the visitors. India then saw a rise in Islam from the seventh and eighth centuries, which led to the Mughal Empire being established during the early fifteenth century, lasting for around 200 years.

Early and late modern history of India is mostly composed of European explorers and ultimately with Britain colonizing India in 1612 up until 1947. It is important to note that before the East India Company was set up in 1600, Britain was producing 1.7 percent of the world's GDP, whereas India was producing 13 times that in the same period. By the time Britain left India, India had become one of the poorest nations in the world, its literacy rates were below 15 percent, life expectancy was below 30, and millions died in avoidable famines and genocides carried out by the British. This was a time of great hardship for India, with little leaps made through modernization, and of immense profit for Britain through trade companies such as the East India Company.

Foreign policy at the time was to divide and rule or *divide et impera*. Partition of India left over a million dead and had the largest number of people displaced in a single event in human history—13 million. These events are still fresh in the collective memory of Indians and some Indians feel that the British owe some form of reparations for their actions.

India's culture is among the world's oldest, while Hinduism is the oldest religion in the world. Hindus are highly religious and tend to observe all auspicious days of the Hindu calendar with great vigor. The longevity of a core popular religion such as Hinduism gave rise and staying power to strict social hierarchy in all facets of life. Social hierarchy is the root to understanding Indian etiquette and taboos, and to a large degree dictates an Indian person's experience. Other popular religions (Islam, Sikhism, Buddhism, and Jainism) divide the Hindu culture to some extent. However, a far more powerful division is the caste system, which is in effect even today, though mostly in rural India.

India's official languages are English and Hindi, though many prefer using Hindi greetings such as "Namaste" or the more formal "Namaskar" when greeting both family/friends and strangers, which mean literally, "I bow to the divine in you." More Westernized Indian men and women generally shake hands or hug (if they have an existing relationship) and ask about a person's heath, family, and business, work, or academic success.

Traditionally, people bring their palms together, in front of the chest or face. Similar gestures are seen when Indians pray or meditate. The gesture holds the meaning and can be used without any utterance of words as the gesture itself symbolizes great honor.

With various ethnicities, customs, and traditions, most states have their own rendition of a sari (a single-piece female garment usually worn over a petticoat and consisting of a drape) or a *shalwar kameez*. The *shalwar* are loose trousers, resembling pajamas with the legs wide at the top and narrow at the ankle. The *kameez* is a long shirt or tunic, with a collar. Both men and women wear the *shalwar kameez*, which have countless designs and colors to suit every occasion. Women cover their heads with a *dupatta* (a colorful embroidered scarf that can either match the clothes or contrast).

Indians believe that staying well groomed and dressing respectably vastly improves one's impression among people. Traditionally and culturally, Indians are conservative about their appearance. Both men and women are expected to dress modestly, with legs and shoulders covered. However, younger generations and modernized Indians do not usually subscribe to this in their daily lives.

Social hierarchy is also observed during dining as guests are served first, followed by the elders and then children, while women typically serve the men and eat later. People are urged to take second and third helpings, and saying "I'm full" is usually taken as a courteous gesture and not accepted at face value. Indians always offer second and third helpings; it is rude to outright say "No," so instead leaving a small amount of food on the plate indicates that the guest is satisfied, whereas finishing all the food on the plate means that the guest is still hungry.

India has twice as many vegetarians than anywhere else in the world and the fewest meat consumers. Most local food is eaten with one's fingers, and only with the right hand. In India, as across Asia, the left hand is used for unclean or unsavory practices such as toileting, cleaning feet, or putting on shoes, while the right hand is for eating, shaking hands, and so on. Children are taught from an early age to not eat, pass food, point at anyone, or wipe their mouth with the left hand. This rule is fundamental as Indians most often only accept things given to them using the right hand, or using both hands (a sign of respect).

People in India are also particular about contamination of food or *jootha* (not to be confused with *juta* [shoes] or *jhoota* [liar]. There is no direct word for *jootha* in

Office workers eat street food for lunch in Kolkata, India. Hindu religion prohibits the consumption of beef, so meals are often vegetarian. (Max Ferrero/Dreamstime.com)

English, but it is something like already-tasted food that is sullied: for instance, double-dipping a chip in a dip would be considered *jootha*. Any food contaminated with saliva is considered *jootha*; for instance, when sharing a bottle of water, it should be poured directly into the mouth instead of touching the lips. It should also be noted that Hindus do not consume beef or products derived from beef. Similarly, Muslims do not consume pork or any affiliated products, nor do they drink alcohol.

Indian use of the English language can be very formal and even ceremonious, frequently using words such as "Sir" or "Madam," even "Good lady" or "Kind sir." It is not appropriate to address someone by their first name if they are older in age or of higher status: they are always termed as "Uncle" or "Auntie."

Indians typically use body language to communicate feelings without speech, which is mostly done by facial cues or hand gestures. Common gestures such as a loose side-to-side head nod or head movement in a figure eight mean "yes" or "understood/in agreement." Indians frequently interpret the Western side-to-side hand wave for "Hello" as "No" or "Go away." Indians also avoid direct eye contact; it is a sign of respect to look away from someone's face. Similarly, any pointing of the finger during a greeting should be avoided because of its accusatory connotation. Rather, Indians beckon with their hand and point with the chin, whole hand, or thumb but not a finger.

India utilizes a polychronic time system, which is a continuous, free-flowing concept of time. Hinduism's underlying belief of the cyclical nature of time has influenced this concept, which could be attributed to the concept of reincarnation whereby a living being begins the life cycle again in a different physical body or form after death. Most people living in India therefore have been raised using this concept of polychronic time, meaning that they are much more willing to do multiple things at a time and do not have a strict schedule (monochronicity is doing one thing at a time). Essentially, polychronic people do not see the need to separate work and personal life; Indian culture is more focused on relationships.

Note there are various taboos across India, many of which are specific to a region or culture. The following are some that are observed all over India.

India is a country proud of its conservatism and traditionalism. However, this is quickly changing through the mass media (such as Bollywood), which regularly have racy or controversial scenes in movies and magazines. Nevertheless, a majority of Indians disapprove of kissing, embracing, or hugging between the opposite sexes in public. It is common to see men hold hands as a sign of friendship, but it is looked down upon if an unmarried man and woman hold hands. This is because Indians hold the sanctity of marriage with the utmost fervor and often restrict young people from dating or "seeing someone." For most Indians, there has always been a fascination with romance, especially when talking about marriage. Younger, more modern Indians tend to opt for romantic marriages, but this is hard to do because marriage is still tightly bound by traditions and to a certain extent religion and the caste system. Most Indian families will often arrange marriages. This is usually due to cultural and religious sensitivities but also for economic reasons; for instance, marrying into the "right" caste, that of equal or better status, would help secure their children's future.

There are more Hindus in India than anywhere else in the world, as 98 percent of all Hindus live in South Asia. India has had a steady proliferation of various religions for hundreds of years, with none more popular than Islam. Other religions such as Christianity, Sikhism, Buddhism, Jainism, and some forms of indigenous ethnic religions also had a foothold on the subcontinent. Most Hindus love talking about Hinduism and enjoy discussing Vedic philosophies and their experiences of prayers.

Indians do not wear any shoes or sandals when inside their homes (guests are urged to do the same) as they are considered unclean and also because all houses have a religious shrine or room where prayer takes place. It is also rude to point the soles of one's feet at anyone, at the altar, or at Hindu gods. Hindus generally do not touch anything they deem important with their feet. Avoid topics or materials such as leather (as cows are sacred), alcohol, pigskin, or dogs, as it could be insulting.

Talking about death or someone dying is a cultural taboo, as many Indians believe in curses and are extremely superstitious. Indians generally avoid such topics in all cases, and will be quick to change topics and only hope or wish for the best.

Indians can be very vocal on many topics, from religion to politics. However, this is in many regards a strictly "Indian privilege," as they believe that outsiders are not part of their culture and hence should not bad-mouth or openly criticize the ways of Indian people. Indians value knowledge and it is sacred to them: children are taught not to step on books or money and to treat educational materials as a gift from God. Sexual topics are also avoided, especially by women who present themselves as rather demure outside of the home, but not necessarily among their family.

Dinesh Asudo Punjabi

Further Reading

Bayly, C. A. *Rulers, Townsmen, and Bazaars: North Indian Society in the Age of British Expansion, 1770–1870.* Cambridge: Cambridge University Press, 1988.
Cohen, R. *Negotiating Across Cultures: International Communication in an Interdependent World* (rev. ed.). Washington, D.C.: United States Institute of Peace, 2004.
Grihault, N. *Culture Smart! India: A Quick Guide to Customs and Etiquette.* Portland, OR: Graphic Arts Centre Publishing Company, 2004.
Keay, J. *India: A History.* New York: HarperCollins, 2013.
Nandy, A. "The Changing Popular Culture of Indian Food." *South Asia Research* 24 (2004): 9–19.
Nilekani, N. *Imagining India: The Idea of a Renewed Nation.* New York: Penguin, 2009.
Wright, R. P. *The Ancient Indus: Urbanism, Economy, and Society.* Cambridge: Cambridge University Press, 2009.

INDONESIA

Indonesia is a nation consisting of over 17,000 islands. The archipelago forms one of the most diverse nations on the planet, having a population of approximately 250 million that speaks more than 700 languages. Located in the Asia-Pacific region, Indonesia is the world's largest Muslim country. Islam and indigenous traditions add an extra layer to the country's cultural richness and incredible diversity. The range of languages, ethnicities, and religions within the country creates an environment where each village can have its own customs, and therefore, its own system of etiquette and taboos. However, because Indonesia shares more than 500 years of colonial experience, followed by independence due to a popular nationalist movement, a set of authoritarian regimes, and a transition to a centrally controlled democracy, a generalized sense exists of what is appropriate and inappropriate behavior. Indonesian etiquette has evolved from the country's behavioral norms. Each person must demonstrate respect, honor, and loyalty to fellow members of society. Thus, good etiquette is about being polite, considerate, and tolerant in every situation and social encounter. To do otherwise would lead to a tarnished reputation, loss of face, and difficulties maneuvering within mainstream society.

Indonesians typically value honor, respect, and loyalty to extended family, friends, and the community. The importance of acting respectfully toward and within these groups is woven into the country's social fabric. There is value placed on a person's actions, especially in social situations. Therefore, how a person behaves in social settings, particularly in how one maneuvers in face-to-face encounters, is of utmost importance. Having good etiquette revolves around acting on an even keel in both speech and gesture. In fact, one of the tricks to practicing good etiquette is to do everything with a smile. All first-time encounters with new people begin with a similar set of questions. The first question is usually "Where are you from?" From there, the rest of the series unfolds. For these conversations, the scripting will deviate only slightly depending on the given answers, and each set of questions may start to feel like a game of 20 questions. For non-Indonesians, these questions may seem invasive and personal. In reality, they are actually part of the ritualized small talk of getting to know someone. The best recourse is to respond politely to the questions with short answers and a smile. If these questions become annoying, it is important not to express frustration or unwillingness to participate. If there is time and interest, asking the same question set to the original interviewer expedites the process of getting to know that person.

Handshakes are common greetings, especially in more formal interactions. The correct form is to extend a limp hand that shakes the other with minimal pressure. A firm handshake should be avoided because it sends a message of being domineering and aggressive, which are unattractive traits in Indonesian society. Men only shake women's hands if the woman extends her hand first. Even in this case, a man who has gone on the hajj, the pilgrimage to Mecca, will refuse the gesture from a woman on religious grounds. With the exception of handshakes, men avoid touching women in public. Public displays of affection do occur, especially in larger cities, but are far from being socially acceptable behavior. In some places, such displays can lead to ostracization. After the handshake, it is common for men and women to take their palm and touch it to their heart. This gesture comes from an Islamic tradition, but because it shows reverence and respect, it is not restricted to Muslims. Most Indonesians use touch to communicate sentiments and social cues in ways that do not cross the gender barrier. However, they never pat people on the head and never give slaps on the back.

Clothing is an area where etiquette plays a strong role. Men and women should wear conservative clothes when leaving the home. Local men tend not to wear shorts or tank-style shirts unless they are at home, though this is island dependent. Men commonly wear shorts on Bali. In the same vein, women also dress conservatively. A safe outfit covers everything from neck to ankle, though it is permissible to wear skirts hemmed below the knee. Pants are acceptable to wear except in Aceh, where local law prohibits women from wearing trousers. Women's tops that expose the shoulders or even show too much skin on the arm are not appropriate. Technically, bikinis and swimming suits that reveal navels are illegal, though this policy is not always enforced. Women should be cautious with clothing choices because certain amounts of skin exposure violate the country's controversial anti-pornography law passed in 2008. The general rule is to dress conservatively.

Following the rules of etiquette can lead to great gains in social integration. Private social events and parties are staples of Indonesian culture. It is an honor to receive an invitation to dine at someone's home, and a delicate matter to turn down such an invitation. When invited to someone's home, it is important to bring a small but ethnically considerate gift. For example, alcohol and pork are taboo for a Muslim family. Sharp objects, such as scissors or knives, are inappropriate for ethnic Chinese hosts, as these instruments symbolically sever a relationship. Wrapping will depend on the relationship with the host and the formality of the event, though when in doubt, always wrap. With wrapped gifts, good hosts will not open them during the event. Event etiquette has its own norms. For private gatherings, most Indonesians arrive around 30 minutes after the indicated start time. This delayed start often is true for plans to meet publically, though it would never apply to a business event. Upon arrival at a home, it is common to remove shoes before entering. If in doubt, one should consult the host before stepping through the door. Removing shoes at other locations is unlikely, though there are restaurants and shops such as certain *warnets*, or Internet cafés, in southern Kalimantan where entrance is prohibited if shoes are not first removed.

Food constitutes an important aspect of an Indonesian social engagement. In parts of the country or for specific types of food, it is traditional to use the hands as utensils. In a restaurant or dinner party, typical utensils are a fork and spoon. The spoon is for the right hand and the fork is for the left, with the fork used to push food onto the spoon. The fork allows the diner to prepare all of the grains of rice for consumption by sliding them onto the spoon. Many Indonesians believe that a person has not eaten a meal if it did not include rice. Appropriate use of the fork allows one to eat the rice more easily. When finished, the fork is placed horizontally across the plate, with the tines pointed left and the handle pointed right. The tines usually face downward. After placing the fork, the spoon either rests on top of it or crossed over it. Leaving the utensils on the plate in this manner indicates to wait staff and other diners that the meal has concluded and not to bring or offer additional food. Food taboos are common across the country, though many of these taboos pertain specifically to pregnant women.

Food taboos vary by region. In parts of Sulawesi, food falls into the categories of hot or cold. For example, vegetables (e.g., tubers and beans) are cold foods, whereas meat and fish are hot. Women primarily eat hot foods after birthing to restore proper blood flow to the womb. In other parts of the country, pregnant women do not drink carbonated beverages. The concept of hot and cold foods exists in Indonesian traditional and holistic medicines, which means the system can apply to other ailments and conditions that are not limited to women. For example, Indonesia has a thriving herbal remedies market that includes *jamu*, a traditional tonic, and ginger tea to cure multiple illnesses.

Smoking is common across the country. By law, many public buildings, including malls, offices, hospitals, and universities, ban smoking in public areas. The law is usually enforced. However, enforcement is more common in urban areas and less likely to occur in rural environments. Many restaurants still have smoking sections, so it is advisable to request the smoking or nonsmoking sections when being seated if the establishment has a hosting station. Restaurants with outdoor seating may permit smoking without restrictions.

Personal space does not exist as it does in some Western societies. It is normal to stand close to someone when speaking, and even closer if two friends are having a serious conversation. There are also many public spaces, such as when riding the bus, where adding space between bodies is impossible. Maintaining a personal bubble of space around one's self, as is common in Western societies, creates unnecessary social distance. Locals may view extra personal space as being disinterested or

---

Culture Shock! 🌐

Jamu Medicine and Massage

Jamu is a traditional form of indigenous herbal medicine and healing prevalent in Indonesia as well as Malaysia, Singapore, and Brunei. *Jamu* incorporates roots, flowers, seeds, bark, fruit, and leaves with remedies taken as pills, powders, capsules, and ointments as well as other preparations. Traditionally *jamu* medicines are created at home, usually by women known as "*jamu* women," who seek out the correct herbs, prepare the medicine, and take their wares to villages, towns, and cities. There is some interest in pregnancy massage using *jamu* products in the United Kingdom and Australia. However, unlike Indian Ayurvedic medicine and Chinese herbal medicine, *jamu* is generally failing to take off in the West as *jamu* products often fail to conform to international manufacturing standards. Additionally, some critics consider *jamu* medicine to be linked to white magic.

Victoria Williams

---

even *sumbung*, prideful and snobbish, both of which can lead to a loss of respect and social standing. The lack of personal space can be discomforting at times. However, it is important not to step back from known acquaintances to create extra space, as the gesture sends a negative message. In addition, it is important to avoid the label *sumbung* because a poor reputation can make the process of acculturation difficult. Along with regular conversation, body language communicates a lot about how a person complies with Indonesian social norms. Touching can be common among Indonesians, but there are gender and relational restrictions (i.e., acceptable behavior between siblings or close friends) that often govern how acceptable certain actions are. Handholding between same-sex friends is common, while male-female contact is extremely limited. The most important rule of body language etiquette is not to use the left hand when interacting with other people. The left hand is considered to be the unclean hand. Passing an object to or taking an object from another person with the left hand is an insult. Non-Indonesians who are left-hand dominant should make an effort to limit the use of their left hand when the action involves a native person.

In Indonesia, there is an additional facet of etiquette, that of behavior pertaining to the use of electronic devices in social situations. Mobile phones are the primary means of electronic communication. The cost of sending a SMS, or text message, is cheaper than the per minute charge of a live phone conversation, making it common to send short messages to send invitations, share news, and even as segments of a longer conversation. In general, the courtesy given to text messages is to respond immediately. Most people carry their phones constantly so that they can respond to friends, family, and business interests quickly. When using the phone to make a call, most often the caller allows the recipient's phone to ring once so that the phone displays a missed call message. Once that missed call notification appears on a phone, it then becomes the original recipient's turn to call back until the original caller responds. In the past, spoken telephone conversations were only for important topics that were not possible to have via text. However, as more people opt to use monthly plans with minute allowances, this practice is changing slowly.

Etiquette on the Internet reinforces Indonesia's social expectations. Whether in a one-to-one communication, such as e-mail, or a one-to-many exchange such as a newsgroup or forum, it is important to demonstrate respect. Communications should not include controversial themes, such as overt racism or intolerance. They should refrain from an extensive use of capital letters or use provocative language. To avoid misinterpretation, many Indonesians rely on the use of emoji, or pictures that convey emotion such as smileys for happiness and frowns for sadness, in online postings. Though there are individuals who break the rules of netiquette, in general the principle of maintaining harmony is just as important online as it is in other social interactions.

Laura Steckman

Further Reading

Expat Web Association Jakarta, Indonesia. "Indonesian Cultural Habits and Idiosyncrasies: Tips for Cross-cultural Interaction." http://www.expat.or.id/info/culturalhabits-idio syncrasies.html. Accessed December 2014.

International Protocol Institute of California. "Indonesia." http://mbjprotocol.com/wp -content/uploads/2012/03/CE-Indonesia.pdf. Accessed March 2015.

Kompasiana. "Pentingnya Kesadaran Akan Netiket Saat Berinternet." http://teknologi .kompasiana.com/internet/2014/11/02/pentingnya-kesadaran-akan-netiket-saa -tberinternet-684263.html. Accessed January 2015.

Widihapsari, M. A. "Cyber Space, Cyber Culture." http://komunikasi.us/index.php /course/15-komunikasi-teknologi-dan-masyarakat/2678-cyber-spacecyber-culture. Accessed January 2015.

IRAN AND CENTRAL ASIA

Iran has had a strong influence over the culture of Central Asia, although the majority of Iranian citizens are Persian speakers and the majority of Central Asian citizens are Turkic. This is the result of the interpenetration of Persian and Turkish/ Mongolian population groups over more than a millennium. Greater Persia extended far into Central Asia for many centuries and left its mark on Central Asian civilization in terms of language and customs. One example is the widespread observance of the ancient Persian New Year at the Spring Equinox on March 21. This holiday is the actual start of the Iranian calendar year, but is also observed throughout Central Asia. Many Central Asians have no idea of the Iranian origin of this major celebration.

Throughout the Iranian and Central Asian regions the universal greeting is "Salaam aleikum," with some local variations in pronunciation, an Islamic-influenced Arabic greeting meaning "Peace be upon you." The universal response is "(Wa) Aleikum sa-laam" (And upon you, peace). This can be shortened to a simple "Salaam." Variations in local languages such as "Ruz ba xeir" ("Day be good," or "Good day" in Persian) are used often by non-Muslim minorities as an alternative. In Afghanistan one might be greeted with "Xub hastid? Chetour hastid?" (Are you good? How are you?). In Uzbekistan one might hear "Xush kelibsiz," in Kazakh "Xosh keldiñiz," and in Kyrgiz "Xos kelingiz," all meaning "Welcome" (literally "You come happily").

In general the person who is lower in status must initiate the greeting. Because there is a strong virtue in Iran and Central Asia to show humility toward others, people may vie for giving the "first" greeting. For intimate friends and family, men and women will shake hands with those of the same sex and often kiss them on both cheeks. For conservative Muslims, men and women do not make physical contact.

Following greetings, a polite inquiry into the health of the other person and all the members of his or her family is proper. In general, men should not make a pointed inquiry about the spouse of the other man, unless they are intimate friends. An oblique inquiry into the health of the "family" or to the "house" is proper.

In Iran and Central Asia standards of modest dress as prescribed in Islam are required. Although standards of modesty vary, in today's world women are expected to have a head covering and clothing that does not reveal the contours of the body. Men are more relaxed, but do not wear shorts or tight clothing. Formerly only long-sleeved shirts were considered proper, but today, short-sleeved shirts are also seen.

Hospitality in Iran and Central Asia is a social obligation. Guests are eagerly sought, and are considered to be a "gift of God." For outsiders, hospitality can be

A man greets a traditionally dressed *mullah* with a kiss at the door of his ceramic workshop in Iran. Hospitality and politeness are highly valued in Iranian culture. (Guenter Guni/ iStockphoto.com)

almost overwhelming at times. Not providing hospitality to guests is a mark of shame, as much as generous hospitality is a mark of honor for a family and its leaders.

Iran has a unique system of etiquette, hospitality, and verbal communication known as *ta'ārof*. *Ta'ārof* is a nearly untranslatable concept encompassing a broad complex of behaviors in Iranian life that mark and underscore differences in social status, which might be defined as the active, ritualized realization of differential status in interaction. It underscores and preserves the integrity of culturally defined status roles as it is carried out in the life of every Iranian every day in thousands of different ways. Iranian youth cry in despair at its pervasiveness, but they are powerless against it, and practice it themselves even while complaining about it.

Ta'ārof has both a linguistic and a social behavioral component. Linguistic *ta'ārof* involves two kinds of language phenomena. One aspect has to do with word choice. Iran is a hierarchical society, and social hierarchy is marked linguistically by using vocabulary that emphasizes the higher status of the other person, while denigrating one's own status. Many common Persian verbs have corresponding "other-raising" and "self-lowering" forms.

The verb "to give" provides a good example of the functioning of the system:

Neutral Form	*dādan*
Other-raising (describing one's own action toward the other)	*taqdim kardan* (lit. "to offer")
Self-lowering (describing the other's action toward one's self)	*marhamat kardan* (lit. "to do a mercy") *mohabbat kardan* (lit. "to do a kindness")

More deference can be shown by substituting the verb *farmudan* (lit. "to command") for *kardan* (lit. "to do") in the self-lowering forms.

Pronouns are similarly marked for status.

Pronoun Description	**First Person**	**Second Person**
Neutral form	*man*	*to* (intimate)
		shomā (formal)
Self-lowering	*bandeh, nokar, chāker*	
Other-raising		*jenāb-e āli* (lit. "excellency")
		sar kār (used mainly in addressing women, lit. "head of affairs")
		hazerat-e āli (lit. "highness")

The second linguistic dimension of discourse has to do with "polite" and deferential general discourse. Iranian discourse routinely uses phrases that emphasize the low, dependent, or even servile status of the speaker, and the exalted status of the addressee, such as *qorbān-e shomā* (lit. "your self-sacrificer"), used as a routine departure phrase, or closing to a letter. There is no exhaustive list of these expressions. They are limited only by the imagination of the speaker. Some people are extremely skilled at this kind of discourse, and provide *ta'ārof* that rings true and sincere. Indeed, there are definitely people to whom this kind of language is due, such as revered teachers, parents, intellectuals, and leaders. Others are clearly using this language to flatter or deceive. The ambiguity in this language is part of its charm, contributing a distinct flavor to Iranian interaction.

The second area of *ta'ārof* has to do with social gestures that provide courtesy and hospitality to others. A simple gesture such as allowing another person to go first through a doorway, or seating someone in a place of honor are simple examples of everyday *ta'ārof*. However, *ta'ārof* can be much more elaborate. Extravagant offers of service or hospitality are labeled as *ta'ārof* in everyday discourse. Similarly refusing hospitality or favors is labeled as *ta'ārof*. When a generous gesture is offered and the recipient demurs, he or she is often told "Please don't *ta'ārof*." Since hospitality and generosity are deeply ingrained in Iranian society, it is often difficult to discern genuine from insincere offers. Sometimes it is a win-win situation. If the recipient accepts, the giver feels pride. If the recipient succeeds in refusing, the giver feels happy that he or she made the gesture. *Ta'ārof* can verge on aggressive behavior as participants try to outdo each other in their generosity. Needless to say, *ta'ārof* is an important social lubricant in Iran, and when everyone is practicing it, social life can be pleasant and discord can be suppressed under a veil of politesse.

These actions are universal in Iranian culture, whatever the religious, ethnic, or linguistic community of the participants. This extends to the Iranian and Tajik-speaking Jewish community in Uzbekistan. This applies equally to Zoroastrian and Christian communities. Azerbaijanis, Kurds, Baluchis, and tribal peoples are equally famous for their hospitality and practice *ta'ārof* in their own languages, though they may lack the elaborate vocabulary for "other-raising" and "self-lowering" found in Persian. This is also true in Turkic areas of Central Asia.

The dynamics of deferential language and polite behavior embodied in *ta'ārof* are widespread in the cultures of the world. If Iran and Central Asia are to be differentiated from other regions where politeness is highly elaborate, it is in the extensive use of *Ta'ārof* for strategic dealing in Iran. While much *ta'ārof* is utterly sincere, it is possible by "getting the lower hand" as a behavioral and rhetorical strategy to compel others to acquiesce to one's wishes. Essentially, one uses this strategy to invoke "noblesse oblige" in the other person, making it difficult for them to refuse requests.

On entering a home shoes are generally removed. Guests may be seated in a variety of manners. They may be seated on the floor around a dinner cloth that is spread for that purpose or at a table. For larger meals, guests may be invited to a buffet. In more traditional households men and women may be entertained in separate spaces. Plates, cups, and eating utensils (if used) will be placed before the guests, followed by plates of food. It is common in the Middle East for the food to be parceled in several dishes and spread around the table. To usher people to the table from another space the host will say "Befarma'id!" (Command [us]!) for Persian speakers, with several equivalents in Central Asian Turkic languages.

People proceed to the meal in order of prominence. It is customary for people to show deference by avoiding being the first to proceed to the space for eating, so there may be a polite "struggle" to avoid being the first to be seated, or the first to proceed to a buffet. When being seated, the most prominent persons will be seated furthest from the entrance to a room.

Occasionally a ewer of water and basin will be brought to each guest, and water poured to clean the hands before eating. The meal commences with "Bismilla ar-rahman ar-rahim" (In the name of God, the merciful, the compassionate), sometimes shortened to "Bismilla." In some areas food is eaten by hand, or with a fork and spoon. The fork is used to scoop food into the spoon, which is then taken to the mouth. One never eats or takes food with the left hand. When seated on the floor, one never turns the soles of one's feet toward others. Burping is not considered impolite.

In Central Asia Russian influence often prevails in the course of a large meal with many guests. Food is distributed on the table or dinner cloth, and vodka is then poured for everyone in small glasses. One person acts as a kind of toastmaster, who then asks individuals at the table to propose toasts in turn. After each toast everyone drinks. As their glasses are emptied, they are refilled. The process continues until everyone present has offered a toast.

The main meal is often followed by tea, and if the hands have been used to eat, an ewer and basin is again brought to wash the hands. At the end of the meal diners perform a small gesture of raising both hands to their faces and with a single downward stroke reminiscent of washing their faces, end the meal.

Most taboos in Iran and Central Asia revolve around Islamic laws and principles of behavior. Muslims in Iran avoid alcohol, pork, and shellfish. Non-Muslims are exempt from these prohibitions. Meat and poultry should be butchered according to halal practice. Aside from following dietary laws, Iranians and citizens of Central Asia also may have dietary practices that conform to "humoral medicine" dating perhaps back to Greek medical practice. The most common observation of this practice is to divide food into categories of "hot" and "cold." Hot foods are avoided in the summer, and cold foods in the winter. Consuming two cold foods together, such as watermelon and yoghurt, is seen as dangerous by many people.

Arranged marriages are still very popular in Iran and Central Asia, and in particular cousin marriage is still widely practiced, patrilineal parallel cousin marriage being the most prevalent. Weddings are extremely elaborate, involving whole neighborhoods or villages as guests. The bride and groom are separated from the bulk of the guests on a dais while innumerable toasts and immense amounts of food are consumed by the guests. Cash gifts to the bride and groom are frequent. The bride brings a dowry to the wedding, and in some areas the groom pays "milk money" to the family of the bride ostensibly to pay the family for raising her (providing milk to her as a baby). Women are expected to avoid social contact with men who are not related to them. This applies to wives, daughters, and sisters.

According to Islamic principles, persons are buried as soon as possible after death. Their bodies are washed and wrapped in a white shroud before burial. In strict Islamic practice, burial takes place in an unmarked grave, but in Iran and in

Central Asia graves are marked with tombstones, which may even include images of the deceased. Mourning ceremonies take place for a three-day period. In Shi'a communities, commemoration is also held after 40 days.

In general there are no strictly taboo words or expressions in Persian or Turkic expression in Iran and Central Asia, except for those that violate canons of politeness and decorum, which is a matter of relative social relations. Elders and distinguished persons are to be respected, and the use of rude or insulting terms in their presence to be avoided. There is a clear distinction between language found in intimate situations and that found in more public situations. Intimate language can be very rough-and-tumble between friends and close family members. The same individuals in public will use much more respectful and formal language towards each other to preserve "face" for themselves and the other.

William O. Beeman

Further Reading

Archer, W. K., and F. Minou Archer. "Some Observations Concerning Stylistics Amongst the Persians." In *Current Trends in Stylistics*, ed. Braj B. Kachru and Herbert Stahlke. Edmonton: Linguistic Research, 1972.

Beeman, William O. *Language, Status and Power in Iran*. Bloomington: Indiana University Press, 1986.

Beeman, William O. "Status, Style and Strategy in Iranian Interaction." *Anthropological Linguistics* 18, no. 7 (1976): 305–22.

Chotaeva, C. "Islam in the Social-Political Context of Kyrgyzstan." *Central Asia and the Caucasus* 6, no. 24 (2003).

Foster, D. *The Global Etiquette Guide to Asia: Everything You Need to Know*. New York: John Wiley and Sons, 2000.

Sprachman, Paul. *Language and Culture in Persian*. Bibliotheca Iranica: Literature Series, no. 6. Los Angeles: Mazda Publishers, 2002.

IRELAND

Ireland, officially the Republic of Ireland, occupies an island to the west of Great Britain. The island of Ireland is composed of the Republic of Ireland, a sovereign state as of 1922, and Northern Ireland, which consists of the six predominantly Protestant counties that voted to remain part of Great Britain. Tensions between these territories resulted in ongoing violence beginning in the 1960s, in what is commonly referred to as "The Troubles." The Good Friday Agreement in 1998 brought an end to this conflict. The population of the entire island of Ireland is 6.4 million, with 4.6 million residents in the Republic of Ireland and 1.8 million residents in Northern Ireland. Although Ireland's economy was negatively affected by the 2008 global financial crisis, today it is poised for growth. A 2005 report by *The Economist* ranked quality of life in Ireland as the highest in the world. Ireland also continues to be a major tourist destination with over 6 million visitors in 2012. Major tourist destinations in Ireland include the Cliffs of Moher along the coast of western Ireland, the scenic tourist route of the Ring of Kerry, and Dublin, the capital and largest city in the Republic of Ireland.

Shaking hands is the preferred method of greeting people in Ireland. Although the kiss on the cheek is becoming more common, it is traditionally reserved for close friends and relatives, and it is thus best for visitors to avoid kissing on the cheek particularly when meeting for the first time. Men generally wait for a woman to extend her hand before offering a handshake. Business travelers should ensure they are on time, although people in Ireland might have a fairly relaxed view of punctuality. Eye contact should be maintained throughout a conversation. Shaking hands at the end of a meeting is also expected. Personal space between participants in a conversation can be closer than in other areas of Europe, and it is not uncommon for people in conversation to touch each other on the arm.

It is helpful for a traveler to Ireland to learn a few key phrases in Gaelic, the language historically spoken in Ireland. Irish people are generally approachable. Visitors will find that a common topic of conversation is the weather, while sports, travel destinations, and Irish literature are all welcome topics to discuss. Poetic language and storytelling are common components of Irish conversation. This is because poetry is a valued form of art and the spoken word has been culturally important throughout Ireland's history. In Ireland it is, however, generally best to avoid discussing politics or religion in conversation. As in the United States, if a passing stranger says "Hello" or "Good day," it is simply a polite gesture and not an attempt to begin a conversation. Gentle teasing is common and is meant in a good-natured way.

Irish people generally avoid ostentatious clothing and prefer to dress modestly and avoid displays of wealth. Subdued colors and patterns are most common. Visitors to churches are expected to be quiet and reverent, but no special clothing is necessary. Rainfall in Ireland is unpredictable, and most people in Ireland carry a raincoat or umbrella. Dressing in layers is also common and a way to accommodate shifting weather.

Consuming alcohol in Ireland, particularly in local pubs, is common. Customers in pubs will often know each other and frequent the same pub often, but are generally welcoming of visitors. Even if a pub has table seating, table service is not customary. Rather, drinks and food are ordered and paid for at the bar and then taken to a table. Smoking is not permitted in restaurants, bars, or other indoor public places. When in a pub with a group of people, it is customary to take turns buying a "round" of drinks for everyone in the group. Each person is expected to take a turn buying a round, and it is considered rude to refuse your turn. While it is considered impolite to refuse a drink if offered, soft drinks are also commonly served in pubs if one does not wish to drink alcohol.

Table manners are generally fairly relaxed depending on the occasion, but visitors should avoid putting their elbows on the table. Hands should remain visible, however. It is not common for a woman to dine in a restaurant alone. When dining in someone's home, visitors are expected to eat everything that is served. Foods in Ireland are traditionally slow cooked, and soups and stews are common. The potato was introduced to Ireland in the late 1500s, and since then has figured prominently in Irish cuisine. A small plate is often placed on a table setting specifically for placing potato peelings while eating. Owing to its traditional Roman Catholic heritage, many people in Ireland abstain from meat and alcohol on Good Friday, the first Friday before Easter Sunday. Some people also abstain from meat every Friday, a more traditional Roman Catholic practice, and instead generally eat fish. The most notable food taboo in Ireland is horsemeat. While horsemeat is not illegal in Ireland, it is widely considered to be taboo and can be difficult to find. In 2013, a horsemeat scandal arose when Irish investigators found horsemeat in supermarket beef patties. Reindeer meat is similarly considered to be taboo, likely owing to its connection to Christmas mythology.

The family is critically important in Ireland, and extended families are often close-knit. Children are generally given a great deal of freedom. Although divorce rates were historically very low in Ireland, they have risen in recent years. Even still, Ireland has one of the lowest divorce rates in Europe. Since 2015 same-sex marriage has been legal in Ireland. Family is also an important factor when an Irish person dies. When a death occurs in Ireland a traditional Irish wake is usually held during which a family member or close friend stays by the body at all times until it is buried, it having been cleaned and dressed in white. A reception follows the funeral, and food and drinks are served as the deceased is honored. The body is traditionally buried in a coffin. Cremations were taboo in the Roman Catholic Church as the practice was viewed as contrary to belief in the resurrection of the human body. The Roman Catholic Church has relaxed its position on cremations, however, and while they are still rare in Ireland, they have been becoming more common. Euthanasia and assisted suicide are illegal, though this is generally viewed by the public as less taboo than in the past.

Other taboos in Ireland are also related to religion. For instance, in general it is taboo to openly discuss religion in Ireland, particularly for visitors, owing to the long conflict between Protestants and Catholics in the region. Although Ireland is historically Catholic, many people in Ireland are leaving the Roman Catholic Church, particularly as a result of the abuse scandal in the early twenty-first century. Catholicism is still influential in the realm of social laws, including marriage and abortion. Abortion is illegal in Ireland unless it is performed to save the life of the mother. Visitors should also avoid referring to Irish stereotypes, such as the leprechaun, as well as discussing politics. The word *begorrah*, which equates to "By God," or the greeting "Top of the morning to you!" should also be avoided. Though many Americans believe these phrases are widely used in Ireland, in actuality, few people in Ireland ever say them. Visitors should also refrain from attempting to speak with an Irish accent, which is generally considered offensive. Although the "F word" is generally considered to be a serious curse word in American English, it is commonly used in Ireland and not considered taboo. "Feck" is even more commonly used and can often even be seen on advertisements. The peace sign with the palm facing inward is considered to be an insulting gesture sometimes called a V sign. When signifying the number two, visitors should be sure to face their palm outwards. Visitors should also avoid referring to people from Ireland as English or British.

Caitlin C. Finlayson

Further Reading

Central Intelligence Agency. "Ireland." *The World Factbook.* 2014. https://www.cia.gov /library/publications/the-world-factbook/geos/ei.html. Accessed December 15, 2014.

Davenport, Fionn, Josephine Quintero, Neil Wilson, Catherine Le Nevez, and Ryan Ver Berkmoes. *Lonely Planet: Ireland.* Oakland: Lonely Planet, 2014.

Gerard-Sharp, Lisa, and Tim Perry. *Eyewitness Travel: Ireland.* London: Dorling Kindersley Limited, 2014.

Scotney, John. *Culture Smart! Ireland: The Essential Guide to Customs & Culture.* London: Kuperard, 2008.

Tourism Ireland. 2014. http://www.ireland.com/en-us. Accessed June 22, 2017.

ISRAEL

Israel is a state in the Middle East bordered by Egypt, Lebanon, Syria, Palestine, the Mediterranean Sea, and the Red Sea. The financial capital of Israel is located in Tel Aviv, and the country claims its capital city as Jerusalem. However, there is significant disagreement over Israel's authority over (and claim to) Jerusalem. The population of Israel is estimated to number around 8.5 million people, of which roughly 6.5 million people are Jewish. This makes Israel the only Jewish-majority state in the world. Israel's second-largest population consists of Arabs including the East Jerusalem Arabs and the Druze (an Arabic-speaking religious and ethnic minority whose beliefs developed from Ismaili Islam). Most of Israel's Arab population are Sunni Muslims or have Bedouin heritage. The rest of Israel's citizens are Christians, Arameans (a Semitic people), Assyrians, Samaritans, Armenians, Dom people (an Indo-Aryan ethnic group), Maronites (a Uniate religious group), and Vietnamese.

By far the most common greeting used in Israel is the word *Shalom*, meaning "Peace." This word is also used to say farewell to someone. In both work and leisure situations a handshake is considered an appropriate physical gesture of introduction. In the most conservative Jewish communities men and women will not shake hands, however. This is because, according to Jewish law, any Jewish man (by which is meant a boy aged over 13 years and thus accountable for his actions) is forbidden to touch any woman except his wife. Likewise, a Jewish woman must not touch a man who is not her husband. Therefore visitors to Israel should wait to see if a person initiates a handshake before shaking someone's hand. Israelis who are not especially religious may kiss close friends as a greeting. This gesture sees the person touch the arm or shoulder of their friend and then kiss them on both cheeks. This gesture is mostly performed by women. In Hebrew there is no formal form of "you." This is indicative of the fact that many Israelis quickly overcome formal reserve when talking to each other for the first time. If during introductions an Israeli notices somebody is feeling uncomfortable, they will often tell a joke to ease tension, thereby encouraging a sense of camaraderie. Similarly, although it is polite to address people by their formal title followed by their family name when greeting them, formalities will soon fall away with first names being used fairly soon after introductions have been completed.

While many Israelis wear Western-style clothing, different Jewish groups and Arab communities hold to various clothing etiquette rules and customs. For example, in extremely conservative, Ultra-Orthodox Jewish areas of Jerusalem such as Mea Shearim, women wear floor-length skirts, long sleeves, and high necks while men are expected to wear long trousers and shirts with full sleeves. Many Orthodox Jewish men will wear a *kippah* (brimless cloth cap or skullcap) to cover their heads. Some men also cover their *kippah* with black hats or with a fur hat called a *shtreimel*, though this is most usually worn by married men. Strictly Orthodox men often sport black suits. A number of Orthodox men also wear a fringed religious garment called a *tzitzit*.

Muslim women in Israel typically wear garments that cover their legs, arms, and heads when in public, while men are not supposed to wear shorts. When visiting holy sites in Israel visitors (especially women) should ensure that they are dressed modestly and that their shoulders are covered. Some sites that are frequented by tourists provide cloaks for people whom they consider to be inappropriately dressed. When entering a mosque it is necessary for visitors to take off their shoes, while men might have to put on a paper *kippah* when visiting a synagogue or an important Jewish sacred site such as the Western Wall.

When invited to an Israeli home for a meal, a guest is likely to be greeted with a great deal of food. Israeli food comprises dishes enjoyed by people native to Israel and foods brought to Israel by the Jews who helped found the state of Israel in 1948. Since the late 1970s, an Israeli Jewish fusion cuisine has evolved that has seen Israeli cuisine adopt and adapt elements of Mizrahi, Sephardic, and Ashkenazi Jewish cooking while also incorporating traditional Levantine, Middle Eastern, and Mediterranean dishes such as falafel, hummus, *msabbha* (a type of hummus made with whole chickpeas), *shakshouka* (eggs cooked in a spiced tomato sauce), *me'orav yerushalmi* (a mixed grill of various meats), and couscous. Other foods popular in Israel include fish, fruits and vegetables, and dairy products. Most food served in Israel is kosher, by which is meant foods that may be consumed according to Jewish law (*halakha*). According to the Torah (the first part of the Jewish Bible), Jewish people may eat meat from animals that have cloven hooves and chew the cud. Kosher animals include cows, bulls, sheep, and goats, so Jews may eat beef, lamb, and goat meat among some other kinds of meat. If an animal fulfills only one of the conditions of kosher, then Jews may not consume the animal's meat. For example, Jewish people are forbidden to eat pork because while pigs have split hooves they do not chew cud.

All animals considered kosher must be slaughtered by a ritual slaughterer known as a *schochet*. Jewish law forbids Jews from causing pain to animals, so the ritual slaughter of animals must be completed in a way that results in an animal's immediate loss of consciousness and death. Another aspect of kosher cuisine forbids milk and meat products from being combined. This means that not only may the two foods not be cooked together, but they must also not be served together on the same table or consumed simultaneously. This etiquette is adhered to scrupulously in strict Jewish households, to the extent that cooking and serving utensils will be kept separate and labeled *fleishig* (meat) or *milchig* (dairy).

There is also food etiquette specific to the Shabbat (Jewish Sabbath) and the foods customarily served at the various Jewish holidays. These foods include challah (braided bread served during Shabbat), *jachnun* (pastry served on the morning of the Shabbat), gefilte fish (often served at Shabbat or at holidays such as Passover), *hamin* (a stew served for lunch on Shabbat), and *sufganiyot* (jelly doughnuts served at Hanukkah).

After the meal, an Israeli host will serve his or her guests roasted nuts and salted sunflower and pumpkin seeds that people will typically crack open using their teeth before spitting out the shells into a container. In Hebrew these snacks are referred to as *pitzuchim*.

When invited for a meal in an Israeli home it is polite to bring a small gift such as a box of chocolates, to give to the host. It is also acceptable to offer to make part of the meal such as a salad or the pudding. If, however, a guest is invited to eat at an Israeli home during a major Jewish holiday, then he should bring a substantial gift as well as preparing a dish that will feed all the people present.

Many Israelis are not very punctual when it comes to social occasions. Israelis will typically turn up 30 minutes late to weddings with an actual ceremony starting 60 minutes after the scheduled arrival time stated on the invitation. Conversely, people are expected to be punctual to business meetings in Israel.

Smoking is banned in bars and restaurants in Israel, though the *nargila*, also known as a hubble-bubble, hookah, or *shisha*, is a ubiquitous sight throughout the country. A *nargila* is a water pipe used to smoke flavored tobacco and is popular in Israel, Turkey, India, throughout the Middle East in general, as well as in the West. Smoking the *nargila* is an age-old custom in Israel despite the fact that in 2005 the World Health Organization stated that one water pipe session, lasting between 20 and 80 minutes, was the equivalent to smoking 100 cigarettes. Smoking a communal *nargila* can also lead to the spread of herpes and hepatitis.

As in many other countries, in Israel it is considered rude to point at someone or something using the middle finger. Indeed in Israel this gesture is considered obscene. When hailing a bus, one should stand facing the bus and then use the index finger to point down the street. Another common Israeli hand gesture is when a person opens their fingers and points their hand upwards before twisting the wrist backwards and forwards. This gesture is used to ask "What do you think you are you doing?" Meanwhile when asking someone to be patient an Israeli might put their hands together and point the fingers upwards, forming a cone. The person will then move his or her arm up and down, from the elbow. When shopping at local markets Israelis rush around, pushing and shoving other people without apologizing. This is especially true on Friday afternoons just before Shabbat begins. Many Israelis drive in much the same way as they shop, with many drivers behaving impatiently, with frequent recourse to hooting, shouting, gesticulating, and overtaking. Another facet of Israeli driving etiquette means that in Ultra-Orthodox areas driving on the Shabbat (Friday evening to Saturday sunset) is disapproved of, and some roads may be closed to traffic. Touching in public is taboo in Arab areas of Israel with the exception of some places in Sinai. This taboo extends to public displays of affection between couples including romantic hand-holding.

Israelis are known to speak quickly and directly—something that leads to accusations that they are impolite and aggressive. Israelis also tend to speak loudly when in quiet, confined spaces, which may irritate non-Israelis. However, this loud speech should not be interpreted as anger. Unlike in some other countries, it is quite usual to strike up a conversation with a stranger when waiting at a bus stop or when using public transport in Israel. Very few topics are taboo when in conversation with an Israeli. Outside of the country's major cities, conversations tend to be more relaxed especially in the north of the country and on kibbutzim (centers of collective community enterprise).

In Israel road signs may be written in Hebrew, Arabic, and English with most people able to speak some English. This is especially true in areas frequented by tourists. In Israel photographing bridges or any kind of military instillation is forbidden.

Victoria Williams

Further Reading

Anglo-list.com. "Typical Israeli & Jewish Customs, Etiquette & Behavior." *Anglo-list*. November 1, 2016. http://www.anglo-list.com/general-3/about-israel/israeli-customs -behavior-etiquette#tipping. Accessed January 13, 2017.

Dorling Kindersley. *DK Eyewitness Travel Guide Jerusalem, Israel, Petra & Sinai*. London: Dorling Kindersley, 2014.

Galdi, David Sarna. "Word of the Day Nargila." *Haaretz Daily Newspaper*. June 4, 2013. http://www.haaretz.com/jewish/features/word-of-the-day-nargila.premium-1.527015. Accessed January 13, 2017.

Global Affairs Canada. "Cultural Information—Israel." November 17, 2014. https://www .international.gc.ca/cil-cai/country_insights-apercus_pays/ci-ic_il.aspx?lang=eng. Accessed January 14, 2017.

KIR. "What Does Kosher Mean?" *Kosher Certification*. http://www.koshercertification.org .uk/whatdoe.html. Accessed January 14, 2017.

Long, Lucy M., ed. *Ethnic American Food Today: A Cultural Encyclopedia*. Lanham, MD: Rowman & Littlefield, 2015.

ITALY

Located in southern Europe, Italy shares land borders with France, Switzerland, Austria, Slovenia, San Marino, and Vatican City. Italian etiquette and cultural taboos fall in line with much of the Mediterranean and Catholic world system. Although the rise of a more secular culture, influenced heavily by consumerism and modernity, has impacted the traditional beliefs of Italian culture, the importance of the region's Catholic roots still shines through particularly in the nation's many taboos. Much of Italian etiquette and cultural taboos echo that of other parts of Europe like Spain, southern France, and Portugal. Furthermore, Italian taboos and rules of etiquette are often rooted in the widely diverse Italian national divide between north and south. This type of regionalist divide, though present in other forms in different nations, is extremely important in understanding the national Italian culture. Etiquette and taboos that do materialize on a national level often arise from issues such as proper dress and food. The issue of food is important in much of Italian culture, owing to the closeness of family and the importance of meal times to the average Italian individual.

To understand Italian culture requires, at the basic level, an understanding of the national divide that drives Italian life. Italy as a nation is a relatively young state. Historically the peninsula that now represents the modern nation-state of Italy had been a mixture of city-states and loose regional associations. The unification of Italy in the late nineteenth century produced a mixture of results at best in terms of national perception. Many Italians are still keen to promote the idea of cultural divide between north and south, while others continue to doubt the Italian nation-state will remain intact. The northern regions in Italy, dominated by Milan, Turin, and Venice, represent states that were previously wealthy and industrialized prior to unification. Southern regions dominated by Sicily and Naples represent the more rural, agricultural, and poorer portion of the nation. Many ills of the modern nation, particularly organized crime and corrupt governance, are blamed on the cultural divide between northern industrial peoples and southern agricultural communities. This then translates to different etiquette and taboos that at times tend to dominate in particular regions, though a handful of cultural traits exist across the nation. Therefore, Italian culture as a national force faces a major obstacle in terms of identifying major and national taboos or etiquette.

In terms of etiquette and greetings, in Italy friends often greet one another with a soft cheek kiss. Some individuals will kiss friends only twice and reserve a third kiss for family only, moving first to the left and then to the right, followed back to the left for family. This is generally accompanied with the exclamation of "Ciao," used in this fashion as a colloquial hello and goodbye. However, strangers should not engage in this type of greeting; rather, they should use more formal language as well as a simple handshake. This type of formal greeting applies as well for official situations, for example an employee greeting a boss or higher-ranking official. Southern Italians can sometimes be construed as overly friendly in their greeting of individuals, tending to be more demonstrative than their northern counterparts.

In terms of appearance and dress, Italian culture bends, paradoxically, towards both the influences of the fashion industry and the Catholic Church. Milan in northern Italy represents one of the greatest fashion centers in the Western world, thus Italians have gained a reputation as fashionable individuals in terms of dress and appearance. Italian suits and dresses are almost always deemed to be the leading edge of "modern" fashion and both men and women strive to achieve a fashionable look in everyday situations. This translates to both work dress and leisurewear. However, following fashion trends closely is largely an urban preoccupation as more rural populations tend to dress modestly. This has shown evidence of changing in the past few decades, however, as mass consumerism creeps into every facet of Italian life. The root of this traditionally modest dress code stems from the Catholic Church. In Italy it is considered a major taboo to enter a church, even for sightseeing, without covering one's shoulders and knees. Therefore, revealing shorts and tops are considered poor choices to wear when visiting churches.

Italian hospitality is built on the virtues of welcoming individuals into one's home. In exchange for a meal within a home of an Italian, a small gift is considered appropriate in return. This is not uncommon among other Western nations where guests either ask the host what to bring or simply bring a small token of appreciation for the hosting of a meal. These small gifts in Italy can range from chocolate to fruit, wine, or flowers, depending on one's relationship to the host family. Unless one is familiar with the region and the host family, flowers could potentially break a minor taboo as certain flowers in different parts of Italy are used to represent grieving and are presented at funerals rather than at joyous occasions.

When eating a meal, it is often suggested that an individual not share food from their plate with others. Furthermore, particularly in the south of Italy but also found to a degree across the nation, it is polite to refuse an offer to eat at one's home. This deference is explained in Italian as *fare i complimenti* (meaning "to make compliments"). *Fare i complimenti* is a tricky concept to explain, but works on the basis that one would be rude to accept immediately an invitation to someone's home for a meal, or even the meal itself, when at the person's home. By politely declining an offer of food the invited person shows respect for the host, considering both the time, trouble, and food the host would need to provide to cater for a guest. The would-be host should invite the person for a second time, as this subsequent invitation signifies that the host finds it no trouble and truly wants the guest for a meal. Once at the host's home, the guest should enjoy the meal. Afterwards it is customary to enjoy a cup of coffee, generally an espresso, with the host. Refusing the largely ceremonial cup of espresso may be construed as rude and would signal that the guest is an unsociable individual. While meals include a large degree of socialization, conversation blossoms after a meal has concluded and individuals converse over a postmeal drink. Another major food taboo is the drinking of cappuccino after noon, as the drink is considered a breakfast drink. After noon, the expected drink to order is an espresso.

Italians are known, perhaps unfairly, for their use of hand gestures when in conversation. It is true, however, that Italians employ many hand gestures as a way of damning an individual or dismissing them. These gestures often involve a flick of the wrist and some combination of finger waving, perhaps originating from around the individual's nose. Italians, like many other Europeans, do not operate under the same belief in the need for personal space that is common in the United States. To Americans, who tend to keep a sizable distance from one another, Italians may seem to stand or sit too close to others when in conversation. This is, however, incredibly common in Italy and an expected form of body language, and is thought of as comfortable for two people engaged in conversation.

With regards to the family unit, Italian culture has changed drastically in the last half century much like in other Western nations. Women are now more empowered to join the workforce and carry out a life of their own, separate from the responsibilities of family. However, in Italy the family unit is still a very important social aspect. The family continues to rely on the strength of the Italian mother, who dominates the structure of the family through work that often seems strenuous, particularly for those who also hold a job outside of the home. Many Italians still live in proximity to their family members, thus providing care and keeping in close contact with their elderly parents or grandparents in return for the care provided to them as young children. In terms of marriage, many traditional rules of etiquette have slowly disappeared, but one that continues to exist is the gifting of Jordan almonds coated in white sugar. These almonds represent marriage and are always given in odd numbers to guests. An even number of almonds could potentially represent something divisible by two, therefore representing the potential breakdown of a marriage. An odd number is therefore indivisible, much like the expected wishes for the newlywed couple.

Finally, Italian etiquette and taboos continually receive influence from the Catholic Church despite the increasing secularization of the nation. Much of Italy's secular culture is built upon the foundations of the Catholic Church. To a lesser extent the remnants of fascism and the influence of the Communist Party continue to surface in various traditions. In terms of honoring the dead, it is considered proper to comfort the grieving and bring them food and flowers. Death seems to be less of a taboo subject than in Protestant nations, and this is seen by the way in which Italians treat cemeteries and the remains of the dead. Cemeteries are generally well kept, in some way resembling gardens, and seen as holy places. Due to their proximity to villages, many rural people feel it is proper to visit the graveside of a relative so that they can have regular spiritual talks with their dead relatives. Additionally, for those that can afford it, Italian cemeteries often feature a lit candle or lamp over the gravesite along with a picture of the deceased. There are many taboos focused on the living, many of which reveal the influence of the Catholic Church. The most important of these taboos is the discussion of sexual activity while eating a meal with family. This type of discussion is considered in poor taste, although the subject could potentially be discussed outside of mealtime or with individuals of a similar age group.

Overall, Italy is a country rooted in customs and traditions, many of which stretch back before the creation of Italy as a nation-state. While the north of the nation has secularized and modernized much faster than the south, the north retains many rules of etiquette and taboos that are evident in the south. However, the far more traditional south of Italy still clings tightly to its numerous modes of culturally acceptable modes of behavior and taboos, many of which are influenced by religion.

Marc Anthony Sanko

Further Reading

Allen, Beverly, and Mary Russo, eds. *Revisioning Italy: National Identity and Global Culture.* Minneapolis: University of Minnesota Press, 1997.

Baranski, Zygmunt G., and Rebecca J. West, eds. *The Cambridge Companion to Modern Italian Culture.* Cambridge: Cambridge University Press, 2001.

Cuilleanáin, Cormac Ó., Corinna Salvadori, and John Scattergood, eds. *Italian Culture: Interactions, Transpositions, Translations.* Dublin: Four Courts, 2006.

Forgacs, David, and Robert Lumley, eds. *Italian Cultural Studies: An Introduction.* Oxford: Oxford University Press, 1996.

JAMAICA

The island of Jamaica is the third largest in the Caribbean, with a population of 2.7 million. It was made world famous through the reggae music of the legendary Bob Marley, who also introduced the Rastafarian religion to the globe. Jamaica has its own unique rules of social etiquette and cultural beliefs that are practiced today. These stem from the eighteenth-century whispering of old wives' tales to the supernatural world of superstition and the occult.

Many business people meet and greet using the universal business standard—the shaking of hands accompanied by an appropriate salutation for the time of day such as "Good morning," "Good afternoon," or "Good evening." Formal titles are used to address each other such as Mr. and Ms. or Sir and Madame. When trying to seek the attention of someone they don't know, Jamaicans will almost always say "Excuse me Sir/Miss" before speaking.

All of that changes, however, when things become informal. People will bump knuckles together, or stand elbow to elbow or even shoulder to shoulder. The words will no longer have their origins in Standard English but come from local dialect, such as "Whaapun?" (What's happening?) or "Whaa gwaan?" (What's going on?). These phrases are most common among Jamaicans when greeting each other.

Many Jamaicans, especially in the capital city of Kingston, do tend to wear Western-style clothing in the form of business attire. As Kingston is the hub of the financial sector, it demands a shirt and tie whereas those in the service industry wear uniforms. Fridays are when the work force dress up, as they hang out after work. Further afield, there is a fusion of fashion and colors. Most Jamaicans are of African descent, but intermarriage has led to a diverse appearance. The island of Jamaica is divided up into several areas, and residents' appearance and dress depends on where you visit. With no seasonal change in the weather, the dress code remains constant throughout the year. Rastafarians wear clothing made from natural fiber with some in long, shirt-like outfits. Their most distinguishable trait is there matted hair, or dreadlocks.

Inherently friendly, the people of Jamaica are warm and accommodating. Tourists are especially taken care of with interesting historical anecdotes and welcoming interactive conversation. Bear in mind that courtesy yields courtesy. Good table manners are practiced in Jamaica, everything from holding the fork in the left hand to not starting your meal until the host states so. Generally, there is an informal air at food time, and drinking is mostly done on a social level.

Speech can be very animated with hand gestures, head shaking, and even a whole body motion, particularly in anger when arm waving and finger pointing is not uncommon. Getting someone's attention other than saying, "Excuse me" can be heard by the clap of hands or by saying "Psst" loudly. Friends can be seen bumping fists or shoulders together when in agreement. Some of the negative body behaviors are similar to those identified worldwide, such as the folding of the arms, forcing a smile, frequently checking the time, and not looking directly at the person speaking.

Many taboos regarding food involve children originating from old wives' tales, myths, and superstition. Though some may raise eyebrows, there are those which are still believed in today. It is said that if a child drinks from a bottle, they will grow up to be a drunk. If a child eats liver, they will have a heavy tongue. Many of these taboos have been handed down from generation to generation and adhered to without question.

Religion is fundamental to Jamaican life; it is an island that is reputed to have the highest number of churches per capita in the world. Most Jamaicans are Christians, with the largest denominations being Anglican. That said, it is the Rastafarian sect that is Jamaica's most famous Afro-Caribbean religion. It was founded in 1930 by wandering Jamaican preachers who were inspired by the teachings of Marcus Garvey. It has its own taboos, such as that the use of salt in food and the eating of pork is strictly forbidden.

Jamaica has strong Christian values and any talk about HIV/AIDS is taboo and homosexuality is not tolerated and considered an abomination of God. Prostitution, pornography, rape, incest, and sexual habits are also taboo to discuss. Men wearing earrings are viewed as effeminate. In a country where abortion is illegal and very much a taboo subject, many pregnant women in rural areas smoke marijuana to assist and alleviate the onset of nausea. Obeah or witchcraft, which once thrived in the days of slavery, is practiced in the rural areas, but it is the pharmacies in the city that provide the goods needed for potions or "medicine," and most everyone disassociates themselves from this taboo topic.

Death is also seen as a taboo subject as the deceased is believed to have superpowers associated with spirits. For this reason, Jamaicans take part in a ceremony known as a "Set Up" that involves staying up for a number of nights out of respect and affection until the early morning. This typically continues for the duration of nine nights in which family and friends take part in a traditional ceremony called "Nine Night." Mourners gather to eat and sing as if to bid farewell to the spirit, which they believe finally leaves the earth.

Jamaica's social etiquette and taboo beliefs are embedded in everyday life. This can be seen through its salutations, attire, and speech, which help to form Jamaica's cultural identity. Its rich history supports the existence of taboos, the most common of which are tied to sexual habits and spiritual beliefs entwined with death. Respect and love for the family and religion have remained a constant among Jamaicans, creating a great sense of community and belonging.

Nadia Ali

Further Reading

Chang, Kevin O'Brien. *Jamaica Fi Real! Beauty, Vibes and Culture*. Kingston: Ian Randle Publishers, 2010.

Davis, Nick. *Culture Smart! Jamaica: The Essential Guide to Customs & Culture*. London: Kuperard, 2011.

Mason, Peter. *Jamaica: A Guide to the People, Politics, and Culture*. London: Latin America Bureau, 2000.

Mordecai, Martin, and Pamela Mordecai. *Culture and Customs of Jamaica*. Westport, CT: Greenwood, 2000.

Sheehan, Sean. *Jamaica*. New York: Cavendish Square Publishing, 2004.

JAPAN

Japan, an island country lying to the east of China, South Korea, and Russia, is home to approximately 126,00,000 people. Japanese people are known for their rules of etiquette, particularly in relation to other people. They are often thought of as well mannered, considerate, reserved, and polite. This includes considering the interests of others, often above their own, within a group of people or society when making a decision. For example, Japanese people who are infected with the influenza virus or the common cold may consider wearing a face mask in order to prevent spreading the infection to others. Out of respect to other passengers, people on public transport are supposed to switch off their mobile phones or change them to silent mode; talking over the phone on public transport is considered inappropriate. This culture of consideration was influenced by Confucianism, a philosophy that promotes harmony between humans, nature, and heaven. In addition, Shinto, a major religion practiced by many Japanese, includes the belief that people's moral good deeds contribute to the wholeness of the body, mind, and spirit.

Japanese people are typically very punctual; arriving late to a meeting is considered very rude. In greeting each other, Japanese people tend to avoid bodily contact, including embracing, kissing, and shaking hands. For this reason a small nod is appropriate when greeting friends or people of a lower position in age or status while a light bow is suitable when greeting people of an equal position. A deeper bow is normally reserved for more respected people. The exchange of business cards is considered an important part of business relationships. Business cards should be given and received by both hands. In all documents, the family name usually goes first, followed by the person's given name. All electronic messages should be written in a polite and respectful way.

In business environments, a business suit is the most appropriate attire for both genders, though women should wear long business skirts rather than pants, as pants are considered offensive in this context. Japanese society places great emphasis on modesty and a natural look, so wearing short skirts, excessive makeup, perfume, and a lot of accessories is considered inappropriate. Instead a neat appearance, including a well-ironed suit and well-polished shoes, are a must to make a good impression. In a casual environment, many Japanese people follow Western fashions, and this has grown more acceptable over the years—except for formal and business occasions or when greeting those respected individuals to whom deference must be shown. The kimono, a robe-like traditional Japanese garment that comes as a set of separate pieces, is generally worn only on special occasions and at events such as tea

A woman whisks *matcha* during a traditional Japanese tea ceremony. The tea ceremony requires adherence to elaborate rules of etiquette. (Oluolu3/ iStockphoto.com)

ceremonies, weddings, and festivals. Kimonos come in different colors, fabrics, lengths, and designs, thereby reflecting the wearer's gender, marital status, wealth, and kinship, while also highlighting the nature of the event.

Ceremonies, such as tea ceremonies, are significant occasions in Japan, and it is necessary to follow the correct etiquette at such events. Tea ceremonies are conducted in a relaxing environment; guests observe and enjoy the process of utensil purification, tea preparation, gratitude, and cleaning. Many houses have a special room or a section allocated specifically for conducting tea ceremonies. The owners are responsible for the seasonal room decoration and masterful selection of tea bowls and table utensils in order to impress their guests. Guests' places are allocated according to their status; the most senior people usually sit close to the tea preparation place. A tea ceremony is a performance art, and takes many years of practice to become masterful. When a meal is served, Japanese people make a gesture of gratitude for the food preparation by joining their hands together.

There are some dining-related taboos; for example, chopsticks should never be left stuck in the food since this causes the chopsticks to resemble incense sticks used at funeral ceremonies. Soy sauce should be added in small amounts to the side of the dish and never be poured directly in white rice. Burping and blowing your nose while dining, and more generally in public, is considered rude, although, conversely, the tactful slurping of a soup dish shows diners' gratitude to hosts. It is considered inappropriate and disrespectful to eat outside or while walking. However, with the widespread opening of fast food outlets, this rule of etiquette is being eroded gradually, particularly among the younger generation.

Japanese people followed patriarchal traditions for a long period of time. All roles in traditional families were strictly divided in accordance with gender. A man was the main earner and was considered head of the family. In modern Japan, with increasing educational and employment opportunities for women, couples share family roles. In the past, families were responsible for arranging marriages. Nowadays, young people decide themselves when and whom to marry. The average marital age has extended from the mid-twenties to the late twenties. Marriage ceremonies are conducted in accordance with the couple's religious beliefs or their preferences. Christian wedding ceremonies in Japan are similar to ceremonies in Western countries. Shinto ceremonies take place privately in a sacred place located in a wedding hall, and guests are usually invited to attend a reception. In Japanese tradition, guests are expected to give and to receive wedding presents. Each guest usually gives a small personal gift to the couple before the wedding, and a sum of money is placed in a special wedding envelope at the reception. Foreign people invited to a ceremony should consider discussing their gift with other people who attend the ceremony. At the time of marriage ceremonies people should avoid saying the words *imi kotoba*, translated as "repeat," which according to Japanese belief may facilitate a future divorce and another marriage.

There are some precautions and taboos related to pregnancy, birth, and the postpartum period. For example, pregnant women are not supposed to eat vegetables and fruits of dark color, which are considered cold types of food that may cause a miscarriage. In late pregnancy, women abstain from tiring work and usually move to their mother's house, where they stay until birth. Japanese culture is a culture of care: postpartum women are required to stay in a hospital for a week, where they and their infants receive full care. After birth, women traditionally abstain from bathing and washing their hair for seven days. After a week of hospital care, women return to their mother's home and stay there for up to two months. The mother of a postpartum woman provides care for the newborn and teaches her daughter the basics of care. There is also a degree of taboo surrounding pregnant and postpartum women, for some Japanese people consider them unclean. This is because according to Shinto beliefs, maintaining purity and avoiding pollution are of the utmost importance. Furthermore Shinto considers pollution to be present in two forms: red pollution that is related to blood in general (including menstrual blood), and white pollution that is associated with death and funerals. Therefore people who come into contact with blood including the blood of childbirth or the bodies of dead must undertake a purification ritual.

In Japan older people are treated with great respect and are encouraged to participate in all aspects of family and societal life. Japanese people view aging and death as parts of the life cycle. Older people may believe in immortality and feel that their accomplishments in life are a way of leaving something good before death. Also, a large proportion of people in contemporary Japan do not affiliate themselves with any religion, but most funeral ceremonies are held according with Buddhist practices. These practices include the washing and dressing of the corpse by family members, as well as maintaining a vigil around the body, reading Buddhist religious chants by monks, cremation, burial, and celebrating anniversaries. It is considered appropriate for people to visit the mourning family at any time to express their condolence and offer flowers, cards, fruits, and cakes. People invited to funerals are expected to offer some money in a specially designed envelope, which is then presented to people at a funeral reception desk. According to

Japanese tradition black and white are the colors associated with mourning, so anyone attending a funeral ceremony is expected to wear black suits or dresses. Talking about death in public, particularly when children are around, is considered taboo. Additionally, pregnant women should abstain from attending funerals, because people traditionally believe that a spirit of the deceased may possess the spirit of the fetus.

Japanese people typically believe in lucky and unlucky numbers. The number 4 is considered unlucky because the pronunciation of the word for four in Japanese is similar to the pronunciation of the word for death. For this reason a room that should be numbered 4 in hospitals and hotels is usually designated room F. Some combinations of numbers may also be considered unlucky. This is true particularly of the number 33 when it is a woman's age in years—the male equivalent is 42 years. Both 33 and 42 years are considered unlucky because their pronunciation is similar to the pronunciation of the Japanese words for terrible and death.

Victoria Team

Further Reading

Bardsley, Jan, and Laura Miller. *Manners and Mischief: Gender, Power, and Etiquette in Japan.* Berkeley: University of California Press, 2011.

Brown, Ju, and John Brown. *China, Japan, Korea: Culture and Customs.* North Charleston: BookSurge, 2006.

de Leeuw, Paul, and Aidan Rankin. *The Essence of Shinto: Japan's Spiritual Heart.* New York: Kodansha International, 2006.

De Mente, Boye Lafayette. *Etiquette Guide to Japan: Know the Rules that Make the Difference!* 3rd ed. Singapore: Tuttle Publishing, 2011.

Kaneko, Anne. *Japanese for All Occasions: The Right Word at the Right Time.* Singapore: Tuttle Publishing, 2015.

Surak, Kristin. *Making Tea, Making Japan: Cultural Nationalism in Practice.* Stanford, CA: Stanford University Press, 2012.

Suzuki, Hikaru, ed. *Death and Dying in Contemporary Japan.* New York: Routledge, 2013.

K

KARENS

The Karens are a group of southeast Asian indigenous people populating the Myanmar–Thailand border area. A greater proportion of Karen people live in Karen State, located southeast of Myanmar. Many Karens have fled as refugees to Thailand and other neighboring countries, as well as to Western countries, due to ongoing oppression from militarized governments. The original religion of Karen people was animism. Nowadays, however, many Karens practice Buddhism, and some have turned to Christianity. Karen people are generally reserved and tend to avoid open confrontation.

Simple verbal exchanges, such as "Good morning" and "Good day," comprise the traditional Karen greeting practice. Bodily contact, including hugging and kissing, is avoided, particularly among people of different genders. Handshaking is considered an acceptable greeting practice, though the greeter should not extend their hand first. Similar to other Southeast Asian cultures, some practices, such as touching someone's head and pointing at someone with a foot, are considered rude and insulting. Rice is the main staple of Karen people, who are famous for their utilization of the dry method of growing rice on hillsides. The central importance of rice as their staple food is reflected in the Karens' main greeting phrase "Have you eaten rice?" being the equivalent to "How are you?" The main rule of Karen table etiquette is to not consume food until invited to do so. Well-mannered people usually wait to be invited to eat by their host a few times before starting to dine.

Nowadays, most adult Karen people choose their marriage partners themselves, although arranged marriages may still occur even in the diasporic groups. Homosexual relationships are considered an unspeakable taboo. Premarital sex, particularly among young girls, is a taboo. Sex education prior to marriage is discouraged, and sex during menstruation is a taboo because menstruating women are considered unclean. Traditional families may prefer having many children, and since children are considered a gift from God, some Karen women may refuse to use any contraceptives. Pregnant women have a lot of food-related taboos and are required to follow several precautions.

Elderly people are well respected in Karen society, and it is considered correct to follow behind elderly people rather than walking side-by-side with them. Karen burial practices can be quite complicated, and consist of many rituals performed to prevent the newly released spirit of the deceased from returning to their house or the village, bringing with them bad luck. These burial practices may include removing the deceased person's belongings from their house, building physical structures on the way from the cemetery to the house, and singing songs to help the released spirit reach its destination. Pregnant women are prohibited from attending funeral ceremonies.

Victoria Team

Further Reading

Centers for Disease Control and Prevention. *Promoting Cultural Sensitivity: A Practical Guide for Tuberculosis Programs that Provide Services to Karen Persons from Burma*. Atlanta: U.S. Department of Health and Human Service, 2010.

Marshall, Harry Ignatius. *The Karen People of Burma: A Study in Anthropology and Ethnology*. A Project Gutenberg of Australia eBook, 2008 [1922]. Available online at: http://gutenberg.net.au/ebooks08/0800061h.html.

Thawnghmung, Ardeth Maung. *The "Other" Karen in Myanmar: Ethnic Minorities and the Struggle without Arms*. New York: Lexington Books, 2012.

Ussher, Jane M., Michelle Rhyder-Obid, Janette Perz, Merelyn Rae, Tim W. K. Wong, and Paul Newman. "Purity, Privacy and Procreation: Constructions and Experiences of Sexual and Reproductive Health in Assyrian and Karen Women Living in Australia." *Sexuality & Culture* 16 (2012):467–85.

KHMER

The Khmer are the largest ethnic group living in Cambodia. Smaller communities of Khmer people live in neighboring Thailand and Vietnam. Khmer diasporic communities were also established in some Western countries when people fled Cambodia around the time of the Cambodian civil war (1967–1975). The majority of Khmer people practice Theravada Buddhism, which influences their etiquette and imposes some taboos. Khmer people are considered cheerful, welcoming, and kind. They tend to avoid open arguments, disagreements, and correcting mistakes in public that may cause social embarrassment or, as they say, the "loss of face."

Culture Shock! ⊕

Theravada Buddhism

Theravada Buddhism, sometimes called Southern Buddhism, translates as "the doctrine of the elders" with the term "elders" referring to senior Buddhist monks. Theravada Buddhism maintains that it is the form of Buddhism closest to the original teachings of the Buddha. However, Theravada Buddhism does not stress the Buddha's teachings in a fundamentalist manner—rather, these teachings are tools to help people understand knowledge and truth. Theravada Buddhism stresses the need to attain self-knowledge and enlightenment through one's actions, meditation, and concentration. Moreover Theravada Buddhism sees dedication to monastic life as the ultimate way to enlightenment. A person who achieves liberation through the teachings of Theravada Buddhism is known as an *Arhat* or *Arahat*, meaning worthy person.

Victoria Williams

The traditional way of greeting is *sampeah*, which involves putting one's palms together and slightly bowing one's head. According to Khmer etiquette, people should make the same gesture in return. While Khmer women practice the traditional way of greeting, men usually greet each other by shaking hands. Shaking hands between people of the opposite sex is acceptable in business settings, but a man should wait for a woman to extend her hand first. The most significant communication-related taboo is that people of the opposite sex should not touch each other in public. Other taboos include touching a person's head and pointing towards someone with a foot.

Most Khmer people dress modestly. The traditional outfit for women is a top and a wraparound skirt, which is called *sampot*. Men, particularly in rural areas, may also wear *sampot*. Wearing revealing short skirts, shorts, and tops was once considered taboo. Nowadays, however, younger people living in urban areas usually wear Western-style clothing.

Guests are expected to remove their shoes prior to entering a house, and when invited to dine, guests should wait for the owner of the house to show them their place at the table. People sit around the table according to their age and status. Older and well-respected people are served first. Other people should wait for the elders to start eating. Table etiquette dictates that people never touch their own plates with the serving spoon, and never stick their chopsticks in food since this gesture both imitates incense sticks used at funeral ceremonies and symbolizes bad luck. In Khmer culture blowing one's nose at the table is considered bad manners.

Sex-related taboos dictate that Khmer people do not practice oral sex or masturbation. Premarital sex, particularly for girls, is considered taboo traditionally, though men were permitted to have premarital sex and extramarital affairs, as well as to visit brothels. In recent years prostitution, fake marriages, visa marriages, human trafficking, and sex slavery have become extremely common. In the past, marriage was usually arranged by parents, or could be initiated by the groom. Nowadays, many young people choose their future partners themselves, and young couples decide when to marry. Intergenerational marriages between young Cambodian women and older foreign men are common. The modern wedding ceremony usually lasts for one day. Wedding guests are expected to bring with them an envelope with money and a wedding gift, which should be recorded in the wedding hall. Men usually wear formal costumes to weddings, with ladies wearing their most beautiful clothes and heavy makeup.

Pregnant women are expected to follow food-related precautions. It is considered taboo for pregnant women to eat garlic, eggplant, and chilies because Khmer people believe that these types of food may cause a miscarriage. Pregnant women should also avoid standing or sitting in doorways, as this is viewed as contributing to obstructive labor. Breastfeeding of a newborn baby may not be initiated immediately after birth because Khmer women view colostrum (first milk) feeding as taboo.

Traditional families may include three generations living in one household. However, due to increased urbanization, young couples may live separately. Traditional families may have many children, but modern families may have only one or two children. In Khmer culture it is considered rude to yell at children and to punish them in public. Children and younger people are expected to treat elderly people with respect. Respect to the elderly is shown through greetings, obedient behavior, and choosing to sit in a place that is lower than the place where elders sit. For example, if the elderly person sits on a chair, then a younger person should sit on a mattress; if an elderly person sits on the mattress, then the youngster should sit on a rug. Adult children are expected to look after their elderly parents as a matter of respect and reciprocity of care.

Death is considered a passage to a new life, with corpses usually cremated in the belief that cremation helps separate the soul from the dead body. Prior to cremation, family members take care of the body, which may be kept at home from three to seven days. Monks visit the home of the mourners and perform evening prayers to meditate and control the spirits of the dead. Family members and close relatives of the deceased may shave their head as a sign of mourning. People attending funerals are expected to wear white clothes.

Khmer people believe in reincarnation, that is, acquiring a new body for the soul after death. They also believe in karma, in which a person, in their current life, is either getting a reward for or experiencing punishment for their deeds in a past life. Religious practices include visiting temples, praying for ancestors' souls, providing food and clothes to monks, and abstaining from religious taboos. For example, a statue of the Buddha is considered sacred and should never be touched. Additionally people should not sit with their feet pointing at the image of the Buddha. Some other important religious taboos include wearing revealing clothes and keeping shoes on in a temple. Women should avoid any physical contact with monks, including passing objects hand-to-hand. Instead women should place the object close to the monk.

Victoria Team

Further Reading

Davis, Eric W. "Weaving Life out of Death: The Craft of the Rag Robe in Cambodian Funerary Ritual." In *Buddhist Funeral Cultures of Southeast Asia and China*, edited by Paul Williams and Patrice Ladwig. Cambridge: Cambridge University Press, 2012.

Hill, David. *Dos and Don'ts in Cambodia*. Bangkok: Book Promotion and Service, 2005.

Hoefinger, Heidi. *Sex, Love and Money in Cambodia: Professional Girlfriends and Transactional Relationships*. New York: Routledge, 2013.

North, Peter. *CultureShock! Cambodia: A Survival Guide to Customs and Etiquette*. Singapore: Marshall Cavendish Editions, 2008.

Saunders, Graham. *Culture Smart! Cambodia: The Essential Guide to Customs & Culture*. London: Kuperard, 2010.

Smith-Hefner, Nancy J. *Khmer American: Identity and Moral Education in a Diasporic Community*. Berkeley: University of California Press, 1999.

Townsend, Kimberley, and Pranee Liamputtong Rice. "A Baby Is Born in Site 2 Camp: Pregnancy, Birth and Confinement Among Cambodian Refugee Women." In *Maternity and Reproductive Health in Asian Societies*, edited by Pranee Liamputtong Rice and Lenore Manderson. Amsterdam: Harwood Academic, 1996.

L

LIBYA

Resting on the periphery of three worlds, Arab, African, and Mediterranean, Libya is a land that has been conquered, occupied, and administered by outsiders for centuries. Beginning in the seventh century CE, successive waves of Arab invaders arrived in Libya, imposing political domination together with the Islamic religion and the Arabic language. The spread of Islam was generally complete by around 1300, but the substitution of Arabic for Berber dialects proceeded much more slowly. Even today, communities in certain regions of Libya still speak Tamazight, the Berber language. The discovery of oil in 1959 led to rapid urbanization and industrialization, introducing unprecedented economic and social change in Libya. The culture and customs of modern-day Libya reflect the history and traditions of its location at the center of three worlds, together with the more recent influence of urbanization and globalization, notably the development of information and communication technologies.

Beginning with the first Arab invasion, Islam began to penetrate Libya, and over the next 12 centuries, Libya assumed a distinct Arab-Islamic character. The 1951 Constitution of Libya, adopted at independence, declared Islam to be the religion of the state, and all subsequent constitutional proclamations and charters have recognized Islam as the official religion. Almost all Libyans belong to the Sunni branch of Islam and adhere to the Maliki school of Islamic law. Religious proselytism of the Muslim community, drug use, and the consumption of alcohol are taboo in this conservative Arab-Islamic society.

In the early nineteenth century, Muhammad bin Ali al-Sanusi (c. 1787–1859) founded the Sanusi Order, an Islamic revival movement that blended orthodox Islamic teachings with Sufism, a branch of Islam noted for its contemplative and ritual practices. Centered in eastern Libya, the Sanusi Order spread to the southern part of the country but never achieved a widespread following in western Libya. The minority Berber community mostly belongs to the Ibadi sect, a distinct sect of Islam that grew out of a seventh-century sect known as the Khawarjj and is neither Sunni nor Shiite. A smaller group of Tuareg nomads, scattered in the southwestern desert, adhere to a form of Islam that incorporates nonorthodox magical elements. A few thousand Tebu also live in small, isolated groups in southern Libya. Converted to Islam by the Sanusi Order, they retain earlier beliefs and practices.

In the closing years of the Italian occupation (1911–1943), the small Jewish population suffered discrimination and persecution, but as World War II drew to an end, a deceptive state of euphoria in Jewish–Muslim relations developed. This false sense of normalcy was destroyed at the end of 1945 when anti-Jewish riots broke out throughout the country, resulting in the death of 130 Jews and one Muslim. After 1948, Libyan Jews migrated to Israel in growing numbers, and today, no more than a handful remain in Libya. The resident Christian community, numbering 50,000 or more before the February 17 Revolution in 2011, mostly consists of expatriates working in the oil and gas industries. Coptic Christians, Roman Catholics, and Anglicans are the major Christian denominations found in Libya.

Oil wealth, urban migration, and social change have eroded traditional forms of dress. Today, most men and women in urban areas favor Western styles of clothing, although older men and women can still be seen in traditional dress, especially during festivals. In the countryside, the primary function of clothing is to protect the wearer from the intense heat. In the summer, it is common to find men wearing loose cotton shirts and trousers, sometimes covered by a long, white gown, and in winter months, men often wear a black or brown wool *barracan* (gown) that resembles a Roman toga. Women also wear loose-fitting gowns that cover their body and head in keeping with Islamic tradition. Men often complete their dress with a flat, brimless hat, and women often cover their heads with a hijab (head scarf) or shawl.

One of the first things to remember is not to pass items, especially food, with the left hand, although this taboo is less strict in Libya than in other Arab societies. When invited into a Libyan home, one should check if shoes should be removed at the door, show respect for elders by greeting them first, and eat only with the right hand. It is also important to dress appropriately, especially in the case of women, avoiding skimpy or revealing outfits that might offend conservative Libyans. As a general rule, arms, shoulders, and legs should be covered, especially in the case of women. Head scarves normally are not required but have become more popular in recent years, and women should carry a light shawl in anticipation of unexpected situations requiring further modesty. Non-Muslims are welcome in Libyan mosques, except perhaps at noon prayers on Friday, as long as they remove their shoes and dress modestly, which means no shorts above the knees for men and no shorts, tight pants, or shirts that are not tucked in for women. When invited to a Libyan home, a small gift is not required but is appreciated, and a guest should avoid refusing offers of food or drink, as that is considered rude.

Libyan cuisine reflects the history and geography of the region with typical dishes reflecting Arab, Mediterranean, and Turkish influences. Meals normally are eaten at home, and they are an important part of family life, a time when the entire family gathers to converse and share. While urbanization and globalization have opened Libya to the food cultures of the world, dates, grains, milk, and olives remain staples in the Libyan diet. In western Libya, Italian pasta dishes and other foodstuffs with a Mediterranean flavor are popular. In the east, residents look to Egypt for culinary inspiration. Lamb and chicken are favorites throughout the country, and beef is also widely eaten. Islam has strict dietary laws, and certain consumables, including dogs and pigs, are taboo. Typical dishes include *sharba*, a thick broth containing lamb, spices, onions, vegetables, lemon, and tomatoes; couscous, steamed semolina served with a spicy stew; *börek*, a family of baked

Turkish pastries made from phyllo and often stuffed with minced meat and spinach; and falafel, a deep-fried patty made from chickpeas, fava beans, or both.

In Libya, the extended family is the basic unit of social, economic, and political life. Social life traditionally has centered on the family, and the individual's commitment to the family overrides any and all other social obligations. The extended family is also central to economic life with opportunities for employment in business, education, or government often dependent on family, clan, and tribal connections. Kinship is patrilineal (through the male members of the family), and the honor and dignity of individual members of a kinship unit is tied to the good repute of the kinship group, especially to that of its female members. The idealized Libyan household consists of a man, his wife, single sons and maybe married sons with families, his unmarried daughters, and possibly other relatives, like his parents or sisters. With family life in Libya extremely important, all men and women are expected to marry when they reach an appropriate age. Traditionally, adult status is bestowed only on married men and often only on fathers.

Marriage in Libya is more a family than a personal affair and more a social contract than a sacrament. In the past, taboos restricting interaction between young males and females resulted in little social contact among the sexes, and even today, younger men and women often enjoy limited acquaintance with members of the opposite sex. At the same time, the widespread use of cell phones and social media like Facebook and Twitter is increasing communication and interaction among the sexes. Marriage between members of different tribes is not as unusual as it once was, but there is still some preference for marriages within the extended family, often between the children of brothers. Otherwise, unions most often occur between people of similar social standing. Under current law, couples must consent to a union, but in practice, they may play little part in the preliminaries with marriages commonly arranged by the parents either through friends or a professional matchmaker. Young men may express a preference for a future partner, but the contract will establish the terms of the marriage as well as the recourse if they are violated. Islamic and secular law in Libya both allow for divorce, but the practice is frowned upon, and the rate of divorce is low. Traditionally, marriage in Libya is between a man and a woman, and gay, lesbian, bisexual, and transsexual relationships are discouraged if not taboo. Sexual relations outside marriage are also taboo in Libya.

Weddings celebrate both the union of two people and the union of two families, clans, and even communities. On the day of the wedding, the family of the groom presents the bride with gifts, including traditional items like gold, incense, and henna that is applied to the bride's hands and feet in traditional designs. In earlier times, wedding celebrations lasted for a week, but nowadays, three days is more typical. Weddings are often held in someone's home, and a tent may be erected to house the festivities. The wedding celebration is a time for eating, with evening meals often including rice pilaf, side dishes, and a sweet drink made from almond milk.

Birth control is legal in Libya, and women increasingly have the education necessary to take advantage of modern birth control methods. Consequently, Libyan women today are having fewer children than in the past, although they still tend to have more than their counterparts in the West. No special celebration marks the birth of a child, but when a boy is circumcised, the event is often the occasion for a small party and an exchange of presents.

When someone dies, the deceased's body is washed, clothed in clean white linen, and normally buried within 24 hours with the right side facing Mecca. Women wash female corpses, and men wash male corpses. Once the body is washed and wrapped, it is taken to a place where funeral prayers are said with an imam (religious leader) leading others in prayer facing Mecca. The body then is taken to the cemetery and buried without a coffin. Traditionally, only men attend the funeral, with women left to express their grief at the home of the deceased or to visit the cemetery after the burial.

Ronald Bruce St John

Further Reading

Falola, Toyin, Jason Morgan, and Bukola Adeyemi Oyeniyi. *Culture and Customs of Libya.* Santa Barbara, CA: Greenwood, 2012.

Joffé, George. "Minorities in the New Libya." In *Multiculturalism and Democracy in North Africa: Aftermath of the Arab Spring*, edited by Moha Ennaji, 293–309. London: Routledge, 2014.

Jones, Roger. *Culture Smart! Libya: The Essential Guide to Customs & Culture*. London: Kuperard, 2008.

Obeidi, Amal. *Political Culture in Libya*. Richmond, UK: Curzon, 2001.

St John, Ronald Bruce. *Historical Dictionary of Libya*, 5th ed. Lanham, MD: Rowman & Littlefield, 2014.

St John, Ronald Bruce. "Multiculturalism and Democracy in Post-Qaddafi Libya." In *Multiculturalism and Democracy in North Africa: Aftermath of the Arab Spring*, edited by Moha Ennaji, 277–92. London: Routledge, 2014.

St John, Ronald Bruce. *Libya: Continuity and Change*, 2nd ed. London: Routledge, 2015.

M

MADAGASCAR

The island nation of Madagascar, which lies off the coast of southeast Africa in the Indian Ocean, was one of the last large places to be inhabited by humans. People from Borneo, after stopping first in coastal Africa, brought their Austronesian language, Malagasy, to the island a mere 2,000 years ago. While some people conclude that Madagascar must be an isolated country, cut off from much of the world, the opposite happens to be the case. Much of Malagasy etiquette derives from contact with other peoples and cultures. Their taboos, known as *fady* in their language and seemingly shrouded in exoticism, have drawn outsiders to the island over the last 300 years in an attempt to understand them. In both etiquette and taboos, Malagasy people reinforce their regard for hierarchy that favors the old over the young.

In a Malagasy dictionary one finds the word "etiquette" meaning respectful customs of good and successful people. Complete strangers typically meet and greet each other with the utmost respect, referring to the other with the terms for *lord* or *master* with no gender designations. Greeting with a "Hi/Bye" is not the norm in Madagascar. After accepting a greeting, a conversation ensues, often with polite references to the welfare of people known to both parties in the dialogue. Much of this speech behavior is built into the language. Malagasy grammar takes the spotlight off the speaker and moves it onto a more ambiguous, and therefore more powerful, canvas. True meanings and feelings are hidden within the conversation indirectly. For speakers of other languages who pride themselves on direct speech—with active verbs and clear identifications of the doers of the action—and on providing clarity with as little effort for the listener or reader as possible, the Malagasy way of demanding an effort on the other's part can be disconcerting.

In appearance and dress, much has changed since the islanders came into contact with Europeans. Merina royalty who sought to unify the entire island, beginning with King Andrianampoinimerina in the late 1780s and ending with Queen Ranavalona-Manjaka in the early 1860s, borrowed liberally from the fashion of English and French royalty with whom their emissaries had visited. Missionaries campaigned against people wearing fetishes and relics of ancestors, and confiscated and burned objects that distracted Malagasy from God. With French colonization, more European styles of casual dress—short-sleeved shirts and shorts—were adopted by the population. Many coastal people, however, continue to enjoy the east African or Swahili *kanga*, the long wrap cinched at the waist with colorful patterns and interesting word phrases called *lambahoany*.

Netiquette among Malagasy speakers, at least among the majority of expatriates writing in the Malagasy language about political matters, tends to subvert the cultural politeness they exhibit towards one another when they are together in person. Personal identity is often masked on the Web but not their feelings towards political positions. They are often quite brutal with one another as they discuss politics back home. It is as if the virtual space of the Web has unveiled their true feelings for one another that their culture, when they are home on the island, shrouds behind the etiquette of verbal communication.

While scholars of Madagascar have given considerable attention to the workings of taboos on the island nation, their efforts can only approximate the lived experiences that Malagasy people have with *fady*. Thinking and writing about taboos is not the same as living with them. Outsiders' understandings of Malagasy *fady* have evolved over time, from being rules that act like sediment, which move or change very little, to seeing them as moral stories that are negotiated and renegotiated every time they are called upon to make sense of people's lives.

Missionaries from the London Missionary Society (LMS) regarded Malagasy devotion to their taboos as an inroad to their Christianization. While Malagasy taboos may be quite exotic and localized, such as a taboo affecting some families to not have fire out of doors, the missionaries recognized that the fear to break a rule laid down by an ancestor paved the way for the LMS message to fear a single God. Fear of forgetting to not light a match outside in one's natal village, of angering the ancestor who guards jealously this *fady*, worked in the favor of missionaries spreading the Word of the Lord.

Scholarship on Malagasy taboos flourished during the French colonial period (1895–1960). Natural historians, such as Alfred Grandidier, incorporated taboos into their descriptions of cultural life amid the grandeur of nature. The links between taboos and rare endemic species of plants and animals was made known to a wider world audience. Even theoreticians of sociological concepts, such as Arnold Van Gennep, drew from Malagasy taboos to form the basis of structural theories of human organization. Van Gennep's work on taboos formed the basis of his influential book *Rites of Passage*, in which the in-between phase of the passage of a person from one stage of personhood to another involved the transfer to the initiate of special knowledge about the connection between taboos and their consequences. Jørgen Ruud followed in Van Gennep's footsteps and saw in taboos various instantiations of Emile Durkheim's theories of rule-following behavior. He made lengthy ethnographic descriptions of the variety of forbidden behaviors in his book *Taboos*. Ruud assembled *fady* in categories within a structural-functional model that highlighted the cohesion of culture through following the rules handed down as taboos.

Following independence in 1960, cultural anthropologists investigated how taboos widened the social and historical world of their followers. Michael Lambek explored the ways taboos worked to engage the living with dead spirits. Gillian Feeley-Harnik brought out how taboos help people historicize places and ancestors by placing ancestors in a social map of lived experiences.

Recently, the conservation sector has become interested in Malagasy taboos. They see in them the chance to connect strict rules about Malagasy conceptions of the sacred with the environment. In short, they understand taboos, or those they consider most significant, as being an indigenous conservation ethic. Many conservationists, under pressure to save some of the rarest biodiversity on the planet, equate or conflate taboos to do the work of conservation within a vernacular mode of expression.

Conservation organizations working in Madagascar consider the biodiversity—much of it endemic to the island and found nowhere else in the world in its natural state—as belonging to everybody as part of a "global heritage." Madagascar's forests contain rich deposits of biodiversity, such as lemurs, chameleons, orchids, and tree species. Many Malagasy designate as sacred the places, such as trees and forest patches, in which their ancestors are buried or their spirits reside as *doany*—spirits capable of possessing the living as punishment for transgressing an ancestral taboo. Community rules (*dina*) and *fady* that keep humans away from parts of the forest have become appropriated or folded into conservation rules. Conservationists tend not to take seriously the rationale behind the local institutions that protect the forest. What they are interested in is transferring local rules and taboos that happen to protect the forest into an indigenous conservation ethic. Moving vernacular rules into a global discourse then justifies conservationists' demands that they behave as global conservationists. It is believed that trees collect *fady* by housing ancestor spirits. Thus trees help Malagasy gather knowledge about the past, the present, and the future.

Rather than considering taboos as cookie cutter rules, as ones that never change no matter who performs them, helping a society to not fall apart, it is more fruitful to see them as exchanges. Humans are able to create value out of making exchanges between themselves and with built places and events they infuse with meaning and capacity for innovation.

Malagasy are quite creative in their use of *fady* to create exchanges between the sacred and the lived-in world. Exchanges are ways of making value, by turning one thing into another through exchange. Malagasy form relationships with their ancestors by performing, or sometimes by not performing, certain behaviors. This creates a space for identities to be clearly marked off: ancestors have an identity (giver of the *fady*) and their descendants have a different identity (follower of the *fady*). People follow *fady* and perform with their bodies, even with the words they say, to get something back. They can receive the blessings of the ancestors, receive a favor, recognition, and identity formation. In all of these they are creating value by subscribing to not do certain behaviors proscribed as unfit, and to do certain behaviors prescribed as proper rule-following behavior.

Likewise, *fady* influence Malagasy notions of agency, of the motivation, energy, and power behind actions. For many Malagasy, there are agents in the world that are nonhuman—at least not the kind of human that one meets every day—and that reach into people's lives. For Malagasy, there are powers beyond one's individual autonomy that affect how one lives. Some people accept the demands that ancestors place on them, some do not. Some people never want to test the efficacy of a *fady*, some do. Some people transgress a taboo only in extraordinary circumstances, paying for the transgression in goods sacrificed to the offended ancestor.

There are a wide range of responses to *fady* rather than a single monolithic one. Though we might translate *fady* to mean "forbidden behavior," the responses may only approximate, and fall short of, the expected behavior. *Fady* leave open the possibility to those who try to accommodate them in their daily lives—in their dealings with relatives and strangers, and in their relationships with their ancestors—that they not be fulfilled but transgressed. Transgressing a taboo can reinforce or renegotiate the importance of the forbidden action and of the ancestor to whom it is associated.

Malagasy *fady* are moral stories that distinguish proper behavior from improper in relation to an event in the past. They connect the past with the present and the future. They each have a story (or multiple stories) of their origin. A tortoise showed an ancestor the way to water; henceforth his descendants have not harmed that species in fear of tragedy befalling their families. Or, an ancestral hamlet was surrounded by trees with lemurs, and one night the arboreal lemurs sounded alarm calls that alerted the residents to approaching murderous thieves, who were scared away. The residents remember that event and respect the ancestor who reciprocated by circumscribing that that species of lemur was off limits.

Malagasy live by *fady* that make sense of things that happen. Their sensemaking becomes a performance of the body. When hail wipes out a village's crops, the thatched roofs on the houses, or the fruit hanging in trees that was ripe and ready to be harvested, an elder consults a soothsayer, only to learn that a family has been cooking with garlic, which an ancestor spirit made *fady* to the inhabitants of the place. The ancestor is understood as having sent hail as punishment for the transgression. Righting the wrong will cost the transgressors, and the rest of the village will put pressure on them to make the sacrifice to the ancestor. The family will not question the taboo again. Malagasy taboos give explanations for an event, which is a function that religion in general has for people. The hail came because of a transgression. An ancestor spirit who resides nearby but in another dimension, who is there in some sense among them, invisible for the most part, was able to touch people's lives.

Jeffrey C. Kaufmann

Further Reading

Lambek, Michael. "Taboo as Cultural Practice among Malagasy Speakers." *Man* 27 (1992): 245–66.

Randrianja, Solofo, and Stephen Ellis. *Madagascar: A Short History*. London: Hurst, 2009.

Ruud, Jørgen. *Taboo: A Study of Malagasy Customs and Beliefs*. Oslo: Oslo University Press, 1960.

Van Gennep, Arnold. *The Rites of Passage*. London: Routledge, 2013.

MAORI

The Maori people originated from settlers to the New Zealand islands from eastern Polynesia between 1250 and 1300 CE. Said to have arrived via a series of canoe voyages, these settlers became known as the indigenous natives of New Zealand and went on to develop their own unique customs and cultural practices, many of which are still celebrated today. These practices included the creation of their own language, mythologies, and traditional customs and ceremonies. As well as these customs, the early Maori settlers formed various tribal groups. These early Maori groups were based around eastern Polynesian social customs and organization, and were inclusive of a distinctive "warrior" culture unique to the Maori people. While now a people highly integrated into both mainstream New Zealand and greater Oceanic society, the Maori people still hold strong to their historical and cultural customs. Maori people represent a major and influential dimension within New Zealand's society and culture, adding a unique flavor to the life of the nation through art, sport, and cultural life. Indeed, throughout the world the long-held cultural and traditional customs of the Maori people are synonymous with New Zealand's culture and identity.

After European settlement occurred in New Zealand during the eighteenth and nineteenth centuries many changes were thrust upon the Maori way of life. Significantly, after the signing of the Treaty of Waitangi in 1840, as well as the resultant colonization of the state that took place thereafter, the Maori people were integrated slowly into mainstream European society. The resultant changes were dramatic, and included the insertion of the English language into society, new technologies, as well as the introduction of the Christian faith by British missionaries. Traditional Maori religious beliefs have their origins in Polynesian culture, with many fabled stories from Maori mythology consistent with other mythical stories across the Pacific Ocean. Historically, Polynesian concepts such as what makes something sacred (*tapu*), what is nonsacred (*noa*), as well as the spirit (*wairua*) governed everyday Maori living. These practices remained strong until the arrival of Europeans, when much of the Maori religion and traditional mythology was displaced by Christian beliefs. Today the dominant religion in Maori culture is that of Presbyterianism as well as Mormonism, with Catholic, Anglican, and Methodist groups, as well as Maori-specific Christian denominations, such as Ratana, also prevalent. It is clear then that over the years the Maori people gradually adopted many aspects of European society and culture; however, to this day Maori cultural customs and historical practices remain strong. Indeed, in an effort to preserve Maori culture, New Zealand schools now offer Maori culture and language as a study option. A number of state-funded television stations that are broadcast partly in Maori now also exist, although it is worth noting that such endeavors were partly influenced by a desire to right past social injustices against the Maori people.

In relation to modern-day social customs, Maori people are noted as being friendly and welcoming, and continue to place great value on hospitality as per their tribal traditions. Notably music and song play a key role in the celebrations and social interactions of the Maori people, with a range of traditional dance routines and warrior-type orchestrations used during social and celebratory occasions. During such ceremonies, the traditional Maori greeting consists of a gesture known as a *hongi*, whereby one presses one's nose and forehead to another's. *Hongi* is still a popular greeting method used by the Maori people when interacting with each other in day-to-day life, but during interactions with strangers in contemporary society, hugs and handshakes are also common.

Clothing is an important part of Maori culture and identity. Primarily, Maori dress is now very much in line with mainstream New Zealand society; however, Maori jewelry remains prominent, as does traditional Maori dress during important social occasions. Traditionally the Maori people tended to make their clothes and adornments from native plants and bird and animal skins. These are still used to make Maori costumes in the twenty-first century. These costumes usually consist of a body piece (generally red and black in color); a headpiece, which is typically made of feathers; and necklaces and bracelets, which are traditionally made from animal teeth or carved wood.

The major taboos that exist in contemporary Maori culture center largely on food and dining customs. Sitting, or placing an object considered unclean (such as one's hat), on a dining table is strongly frowned upon. Such acts are considered offensive partly because they are unhygienic, but also due to the Maori notion of *tapu* (sacred) and its ties with food being revered. It is also considered highly offensive to eat or drink when inside a *wharenui* (meeting house). This is because the *wharenui* is an extremely important area in the *marae* (a fenced-off building that belongs to a particular Maori tribe) and again is considered sacred.

New Zealand and Western manners also apply to Maori etiquette, with swearing, as well as offensive language and gestures, all considered to be distasteful. Traditional Maori dining ceremonies generally follow a *powhiri*—a formal welcome that takes place on a *marae*. Here the visitors will be asked into the dining room, a separate building to the initial meeting room, to sit and eat. Guests are not permitted to eat until the food has been blessed or an elder of the home has said an official acknowledgment, with such a practice also applying in most Maori dining situations. Traditional Maori dishes would typically be served at such events, centering on a mix of cultivated, hunted, and gathered foods, as was the custom during early settlement life. Of these the *hangi* (a meal prepared by placing meat and vegetables on heated rocks buried in a pit oven) remains perhaps the most famous Maori culinary tradition, with it being readily available throughout the country. In the twenty-first century many traditional ingredients and preparation techniques remain an important component to Maori cuisine, ensuring it continues to be enjoyed by many people in New Zealand and across the globe.

The Maori people place a great deal of importance on the concept of ceremony, and have distinct protocols regarding how visitors should be welcomed and bade farewell. During formal ceremonies, traditional welcoming protocols may consist of *powhiri*. Such a ceremony will typically commence by calling the visitors onto the area in front of the traditional meetinghouse, whereby visitors should walk as a group in complete silence, except if they have designated one of their party to call out a reply to the person who called out the cry to proceed to the meeting house. A *powhiri* dictates where people sit and who speaks. The welcoming speeches are given by the agreed speakers of the home people and always end with the most revered speaker or elder. Speeches are given in the Maori language and are generally accompanied by a song.

Ceremony also surrounds the way in which Maori people treat death. Conventional Maori beliefs surrounding death center on the idea that the spirit continues to exist after death and that the deceased will always be a part of the *marae*. The customs that take place postdeath can differ depending on the tribal group with whom the deceased identifies. That said, a ritual called *tuku wairua* (release of the spirit) is commonly practiced in order to free the spirit from the body of the deceased. In this instance the body will typically be dressed in fine clothes (often traditional Maori garments) and the hair of the deceased is oiled. Once this is accomplished the body is transported to the *marae*. Once at the *marae*, people pay their respects to the dead ahead of the burial that takes place the following day. The night before the burial friends and family gather to sing songs to celebrate the life of the dead, and then a funeral takes place followed by the burial, whereby the body is said to return to *Papatuanuku* (mother earth).

Ashley Humphrey

Further Reading

King, Michael. *Maori: A Photographic and Social History*. Auckland: Raupo Publishing, 1997.

Macmillan Brown, John. *Maori and Polynesian, Their Origin, History, and Culture*. London: Forgotten Books, 2015.

New Zealand Trade and Enterprise. "Culture and Etiquette." https://www.nzte.govt.nz/en /export/international-marketing-and-communication-toolkit/culture-and-etiquette/. Accessed December 2015.

Patterson, John. *Exploring Maori Values*. Auckland: Dunmore Press, 1992.

White, John. *The Ancient History of the Maori, His Mythology and Traditions*. New York: Cambridge University Press, 2011.

MASAI

The Masai are an African tribe found in the East African countries of Kenya and Tanzania. Some spell the name Maasai. No one is certain where they came from, but it is believed that they migrated from somewhere north along the Nile River. Some believe they are Jewish, a long lost tribe of Israel. Unlike many other tribes around them, they have maintained their traditional type of dress and customs. The Masai speak a Neolithic language. The name *Masai* means "speaker of the language Maa." There are two distinct groups of people speaking Maa—the Masai and the Samburu. Their customs, like their language, are very similar. It is believed that in their southern migration the Samburu stopped in northern Kenya. The Masai consider them to be their poor cousins because they do not have as many cattle. The Samburu herd camels as well as cattle, goats, sheep, and donkeys.

Masai men typically greet each other with the word *Supa*, with the reply being *Ipa* or *Supa oleng*. When a woman or child greet a man, they lower their heads and the man touches them softly on the top of their head. There are various greetings depending on the age of the person the man is greeting. Masai men use a variance of the Western handshake. They lightly touch hands rather than grasping each other's hand.

Masai men tend to be tall and slender. Because of their diet and the fact that they walk miles, very few of them are overweight. When they are quite young, boys

In the traditional manner of greeting children in Masai culture, the hand is placed gently on the child's head. Men sometimes greet women in the same way. (Britta Kasholm-Tengve/iStockphoto.com)

traditionally pierce their ears and gradually stretch them until they hang down several inches, wearing ornaments in them. They typically wear leather sandals that look much like the sandals worn by Roman soldiers. Masai boys also carry short swords shaped like those carried by the Romans, as well as a stick made from a tree root called a *rungu*. Men and women both wear brightly colored cloths called *shukas*. Generally, one is wrapped around the waist like a towel, and another is draped from the shoulder diagonally to the waist. Women shave their heads and wear beadwork jewelry. Married women wear a bronze ankle bracelet that shows they are faithful to their husband. When young boys are going from the boyhood to the warrior stage, they wear red ocher in their hair. They live in specially prepared sites until the rite of *moranhood*, or the warrior stage of life is entered.

The main diet of the Masai is meat and milk. They do eat vegetables, which they buy or trade for at markets. They do not generally farm. Masai drink a fermented milk that is kept in gourd containers. When they eat, men sit by themselves and are served first. Women and children get what is left of the meal. A favorite part of the meat is the fat, which is always given to guests. The Masai do not eat game meat as some of the other tribes do. They typically use twigs from trees as toothbrushes and take care to keep their teeth clean.

Masai marriages are traditionally arranged. Their custom for marriage is much like the conservative Jewish custom. A member of the prospective groom's family, usually the father, an uncle, or older brother, approaches the father of the prospective bride. A payment of sugar, an animal, or other valuable is made in order to start the proceedings. After an agreement is made, the couple is considered engaged until the wedding date. Another payment is made on the wedding date. It is not unusual for negotiations to continue to the wedding day.

The Masai have many taboos. One example has to do with eating eggs or the meat of chicken, which they believe will make them weak. Another taboo has to do with death. If a person is close to death, they are removed from the house and brought outside. The Masai believe that if a person dies in a house, the house will be haunted by the ghost of that person. The house then has to be destroyed. However, Masai do not believe in an afterlife. They believe that when a person dies, they cease to exist. As they do not practice burial rituals, the Masai will leave a body out in the wild for animals to scavenge.

The Masai have a religion based upon beliefs similar to the Jews. They practice animal sacrifice as a way to obtain forgiveness for their sins. Natural disasters such as droughts are thought to be the result of sin in their lives. They go to the *laibon*, or witch doctor, and pay him to offer a sacrifice to gain forgiveness for their sins.

The Masai are facing increasing problems because of their refusal to change. They were accustomed to having group ranches or lands where everyone ran their cattle, goats, sheep, and donkeys together. In recent years the government has forced them to divide the land up into individual plots. Many Masai have sold or leased their land to farmers but continue to try and keep their animals. This has caused problems with those leasing their land and with others whose land they attempt to use. They are a proud people, but face many challenges in the twenty-first century.

Herb Cady

Further Reading

McQuail, Lisa. *The Masai of Africa*. Minneapolis: Lerner Publications Company, 2002.
Saitoti, Tepilit Ole. *The Worlds of a Maasai Warrior: An Autobiography*. Berkeley: University of California Press, 1988.

MEXICO

Mexico will mark the 500th anniversary of the arrival of Europeans in 2019. As conquerors and colonizers the Spanish introduced European culture, society, and religion, creating a "New World." Mexico was the first of the newly formed American societies and is still in its infancy compared to the antiquity of the "Old World."

The Spanish introduced a rigid and highly structured society with social conventions called *costumbres* (customs). These customs and standards of behavior developed over hundreds of years based on medieval society adopted from Roman and other ancient Old World cultures. Importantly, these customs are largely governed by more than 2,000 years of Judeo-Christian thought combined with 800 years of Muslim culture. Hebrew and Islamic thought mixed with Christian and enjoyed hundreds of years of assimilation in Spain. The result was the customs, traditions, and norms exported to Mexico in the fourteenth century. The norms governing how people should or could interact with one another in polite society were imposed on the rigid racial class system established in Mexico.

The arrival of Europeans in Mexico and their genetic mixing with the indigenous populations rapidly led to the creation of a new people called mestizos, "mixed people." This newly formed mestizo culture was highly varied due to the great diversity of native cultures in Mexico. The spectacular culture resulting from the mixture of ethnicity and race is the dominant culture in Mexico today. Customs in Mexico are predicated upon the dominant features of the class system and the required behaviors at each level. These customs, some of which will be discussed below, are strictly observed and form the basis of Mexican traditional society.

Many of the original native cultures of Mexico continue to thrive today, maintaining their identifying customs that are quite distinct from mestizo culture and customs but mixed with them. These differences have created dividing lines in Mexico, in general between Indians, mestizos, and Europeans. The rigid divisions in Mexico are not simply cultural; they are also the living basis of social class.

Indigenous peoples are referred to as *Indios*, which is a derisive and pejorative label describing the lowest level of social class in Mexican society. In Mexico today there remain small enclaves of Spaniards and Spanish descendants who maintain a unique European-like lifestyle at the top of the social class system. Additionally, contemporary Mexico demonstrates multiple levels of *mestizaje* (being mixed), producing an intriguing array of social classes and resulting in a diverse blend of *costumbres* and accompanying taboos. All classes and norms of behavior are played out and can be identified in Mexico daily.

In Mexico, Spanish and mestizo customs establish a cultural etiquette and pattern of social norm that are of the utmost importance for class placement and function. Almost all other social actions and resulting placement are driven from one's real or imagined class position in Mexican society. Very little social or class mobility is possible in Mexico, and appropriate behavior is absolutely required if one is to be accepted and function at one's assigned level. Violation of class norms and taboos leads to social rejection and the inability to participate in educational, employment, and social activities.

Etiquette is a French word literally meaning "a ticket," and in Mexico it is the ticket to social placement. One's etiquette is used to describe proper social behavior and the discernment of how a person is said to have been raised (*criado*). If raised well, placement in society may supersede the lack of wealth, but only to a point: it cannot, in a general sense, overcome social position. However, if social grace is lacking, one is not considered well raised but rather *mal criado* or poorly raised. Poor and unacceptable behavior is considered taboo and will lead to lower social class placement. How one behaves in social situations, that is, one's *costumbres*, is the societal gateway to limited upward class mobility and ensuing success in Mexico. Mexican novels and movies perpetually romanticize the forbidden and unattainable relationship between a man and a woman of vastly different class and culture. This forbidden pairing may be realized on screen but only rarely in reality.

All social situations are defined as any time a person encounters others in a public scenario that requires a greeting. In Mexico, Indians, mestizos, and Spaniards are separated by real as well as perceived status, and status dictates when and how people may speak to one another. For example, *Indios* are not expected to speak unless addressed by a person of a higher social class. Indians pay respect to those of a perceived higher social class status by removing their hat if male and lowering their gaze, never looking the person of a higher class in the eyes or face unless asked to raise their head. In many traditional native societies the landowners are revered as benefactors, and respect for them is shown by the kissing of their hand. In Indian society women are relegated to an even lower status and are virtually invisible. The Spanish masters considered all Indian men and women to be property, but they were not slaves. An Indian rarely has the occasion or need to address a member of the upper classes.

Greetings among mestizos, on the other hand, are marked by a combination of a handshake and/or an embrace (*abrazo*), depending upon their familiarity. Greetings are especially warm: if the two people addressing one another are related by ritual kinship called *compadrazgo*, that is, they are *compadres*, their greeting ritual is much more personal. Almost all aspects of society in Mexico are related to one another. Society, church, government, politics, source of wealth, and educational attainment are all related and dictate a person's social and class placement. Social position or status in Mexico dictates where and how one lives, beginning with one's childhood friends who are most likely lifelong friends.

In Mexico language is meaningful and formal. Distinct conventions of language are required in every social situation. If a person being addressed is perceived to be of a higher social class, they are automatically addressed by the formal *usted* and not by the more familiar *tu*. People of authority are automatically attributed a formal honorific title adopted from the Spanish, *Don* (Sir) or *Doña* (Ma'am), a reference to a title of nobility in Spain.

Social status determines one's residential neighborhood and one's speech pattern, vocabulary, and diction as well as behaviors toward parents, siblings, friends of equal status and other statuses, and especially toward gender differences. Social status determines educational and work opportunities and eventually one's possibilities in the selection of a spouse and life chances. For all practical purposes class status follows through life and is virtually impossible to alter. Violation of cultural norms and standards are seen as taboo behaviors and are not accepted. For example, inappropriately addressing women and girls is considered taboo in Mexican society.

Mexican clothing traditions are mostly associated with ethnicity and class. The numerous tribal affiliations have their unique dress styles ascribed by age and gender. Among the mestizo and European descent groups, clothing is also ascribed but distinct. Traditionally men wear some sort of head covering, a hat or sombrero, while women wear a type of shawl or *rebozo*. Many mestizo men will also wear a sarape or poncho. The most typically distinctive clothing style in Mexico is the cultural requirement that women wear black upon the death of a close family member, demonstrating mourning. In traditional Mexico, mourning is a perpetual state and is continued throughout life. Widows rarely remarry.

In Mexican society it is expected that whenever possible the evening meal be attended by the entire family, led by the male head of household. Breakfast and a midday meal are much less formal since the family is generally dispersed early in the morning. It is around the evening meal that children are expected to answer any questions their father may have and especially to discuss what they learned at school that day or important events occurring both locally and nationally.

In Mexican culture, the learning of proper etiquette or *costumbres* typically begins early in childhood and is based upon respect for one's mother and father. Children are expected to be respectful of all adults including those noticeably below their social status. They are also expected to be particularly respectful of the elderly, including not only elderly family members but all elderly, such as those employed in their respective households. To treat an employee rudely is considered taboo. This custom of respect for the elderly demonstrates a person is sympathetic of other classes and the elderly. This *costumbre* is derived from the teachings of the Roman Catholic Church, a dominant feature of Mexico society. Historically, the Church determined acceptable behaviors as well as those considered sins and, therefore, taboo.

Children learn from their earliest experiences how they are expected to interact with adults at all levels of society, from the highest levels to street beggars and Indians. In the presence of visitors to the home, especially if the visitors are family or friends, children are expected to properly greet their guests, no matter where they might be in the house or what they may be doing. While visitors are in the home, children are not expected to speak unless spoken to. That is to say, to present themselves to the guests displaying proper posture, respectfully greeting guests and pronouncing their name clearly including their surname, while making a pleasant remark of welcome or other complimentary statement. If the visitors are well known to the children, such as family or *compadres* (godparents) of the family, the children are expected to greet them with an *abrazo*, always over the left shoulder, while giving a ceremonial air-kiss: *beso y abrazo*, a kiss and a hug. From a very early age boys learn to stand in the presence of a female no matter what her age. Boys rise when females, young or old, enter or leave a room or the table.

Children, boys and especially girls, are never left alone to play, both inside their home compound and at a playground or park, without a responsible adult or caretaker present overseeing their activities and safety at all times. Usually there is a family household worker assigned to this duty. It is not uncommon for a revered household worker to rear multiple generations of the same family and to be treated as a full family member with all rights and privileges.

Young girls are expected to remain seated and to rise only if approached by a close friend or relative or as their parents introduce them. In a formal situation, parents may introduce their daughters but in general, young daughters are not introduced formally to people until it is their time to be formally presented to society around age 15. It is considered taboo for a stranger and especially a man to approach a girl or young woman who is unaccompanied by a chaperone. At their 15th birthday and coming-out party, daughters are now considered young women and must always be dressed and made up when socially presented, especially when a young man or potential suitor is present. Parents begin make marriage matches at any time during a young girl's life, and this is especially true after the young woman has been introduced to polite society. After they have come out, they are eligible to receive suitors and proposals of marriage.

Marriage arrangements are always made by parents in order to unite families, wealth, and social status. Marrying up is one of the only ways that a family may improve its overall social position. Marrying well is important for everyone in the family, both daughters and sons. The arrangement of marriages and family unions is common at all levels of Mexican society. In order for inheritance to be expected, both young men and women must adhere to the wishes of their parents who are interested in perpetuating social status, prestige, wealth, and land ownership. In Mexico marriages between second cousins is common in order to guarantee the purity of the bloodline, family wealth, and land ownership. Skin color is also considered and regarded as a mark of social class, the lighter the complexion the more desirable. Darker skin color is associated with the lower classes and Indians and is undesirable.

The Spanish custom governing the inheritance of land is still applied in Mexico but is ultimately determined by the wishes of the patriarch. The most commonly accepted custom is for the eldest son to inherit the estate or business and the position of family leader. Second and subsequent-born sons have the option of participating in the family business but are subservient to the eldest. Second and subsequent sons also have the option of joining a religious order, entering the military, or developing a political or government career. They remain important members of the family.

From the moment of the birth of daughters, families typically begin the arrangement of a good marriage, ensuring their social status in society. Daughters who are not successfully married have the option of entering the convent, becoming teachers, or choosing government service, all considerable honorable. If the eldest daughter is a spinster, she is expected to live in her parent's home, not to marry, and to care for them until their death. It is considered taboo for the sons and daughters of Mexican families to take up professions not sanctioned by the level of society to which they are ascribed.

The father of the household tends to be totally responsible for the financial support and maintenance of the household. He usually departs daily from home to work on a farm or ranch, but if his responsibilities are abroad, he may be absent for extended periods at a time. Fathers are typically expected to be a properly educated professional man who is also a pillar of the Catholic Church, a member of a men's club or organization, as well as a supportive, loving husband and father.

Mexican society views men who frequent bars to meet unmarried women as extremely inappropriate, eventually damaging the family's social status and reputation. However, fathers may belong to social or political clubs exclusively for men where drinking and smoking are permitted along with spirited social, religious, and political discussions. It is at these *cofradias* or confraternities that men are selected by their peers to become the political candidates of these cabals while the other members become helpful supporters of political, social, and religious campaigns.

In Mexico, at almost all tiers of society, households typically maintain at least one domestic worker to assist with child care, cooking, and cleaning. Depending upon financial status many homes have multiple household workers, usually women and girls from nearby peasant families. Male workers are also needed for the maintenance and upkeep of the grounds and animals such as horses, cattle, and sheep. Since many large family farms and ranches include small settlements and even towns on their property, the people who live on the land are offered employment opportunities. This is an appropriate form of the support of the community as well as a holdover from the days of the haciendas, when the Indians and peasants who lived on the hacienda were considered property. It is not unusual for well-to-do families to take on a peasant child who works in the household and is reared as one of the children.

The mother of the household, the *Doña*, is expected to be properly dressed at all times in order to receive guests, manage the household, and to support her husband. Often the husband's mother is present in the household, in which case she is the ranking female above the wife. The mother oversees the work of her staff in keeping the household clean, preparing food, and caring for the children. Additionally, the mother of the household is expected to be classically educated in the humanities and the arts and, therefore, responsible for the education and religious upbringing of her children. At the highest levels of Mexican society children are schooled in music and the arts, classical literature, as well as family and national history and are often boarded in the cities away from their homes for years at a time. More elite families send their children to Europe or the United States to be educated.

Mexican society is dominated by its faith in and following of the Roman Catholic religion. Most aspects of society and family are governed by religious tenets. The mother is the religious head of the household, and any divergence from this normal behavior is considered taboo. As the spiritual head of the family, the mother maintains the family chapel or altar, leads the family in prayer, and is responsible for the propitiation of the saints for the good intentions of the family. Lifespan rites of passage are the basis of Roman Catholicism, so beginning with Baptism a child is linked to the family and local society through ritual kinship where *compadres* or formal witnesses are selected. The child becomes the *ajado* or godchild while their godparents are *padrinos* or godparents. A child is expected to learn the necessary religious doctrine leading up to the First Holy Communion and Confirmation around age nine. These rituals provide the young person with a religious and spiritual basis for life and are common in traditional Mexico at every level of society. At all levels, from Indian to European, membership and participation in religious organizations connect people and families to the church and society. These organizations are called confraternities and exist for both men and women. Social position is often determined by one's participation and position in these groups. Status in a *cofradia* will determine political candidacy and prestige in local and even regional society. Beginning with Indian society and continuing through the highest levels, membership in religio-social groups produces status and opportunity for the family. Families rise through the levels of society over the course of generations, ascending while awaiting for their opportunity to sponsor or patronize the celebration of the town's patron saint, thus becoming important benefactors of the church.

Because boys and girls are raised as polar opposites in Mexico, boys more often than not tend to be dominant while the girls are socialized to be submissive but supportive. While this separation of genders functioned and was fully accepted in past centuries, it is not a rigidly enforced scenario today. Mexico today requires major adjustments in modern child-rearing practices. For example, in contemporary Mexican society, women are often equal partners in businesses with their husbands, and constant communication between husband and wife is essential for a successful relationship.

Properly raised and educated men are never vulgar or use profanities in public or show untoward emotion or anger, especially not toward those beneath their social class or where women are present. Vulgar language and behavior are not socially acceptable and are considered inappropriate. When a man of social status is in public, he is repeatedly acknowledged by those he meets by the calling of his name with the term of respect, *Don*. Additionally, a gentleman is expected to show respect for the poor by having coins in his pocket ready to distribute. A man who openly shows disgust or disdain for the poor is judged to be vulgar and, thus, poorly raised.

A gentleman may greet or acknowledge a woman he passes on the street by saying hello but must never stop to talk to her, as this shows disrespect and is a taboo act. Conversely, if a woman must leave the protection of her home, she must always lower her glance so as not to make any inappropriate eye contact with a stranger. Therefore, most errands are performed by household workers requiring them to leave the safety of the home. When a gentleman walks or strolls with his wife on the street or through a park, he always keeps her safely on the inside in order to protect her from assault or from a person walking on or cleaning the street. When driving in a car with her husband, a woman may sit in the front passenger seat. However, if any other man, such as a chauffeur, is driving, the woman always sits in the back seat.

Etiquette or *costumbres* in Mexico are based upon European customs and are generally conservative. North American customs were very similar to Mexico through the eighteenth and nineteenth centuries but were liberalized in the twentieth century as American society changed. This was especially true after World War II. Mexico on the other hand has maintained traditional customs and etiquette into the twenty-first century.

Mexico is predominately conservative and a person must follow a strict social code of conduct in order to be considered acceptable by polite society. The violation of accepted norms may lead to the questioning of one's social status and be harmful to the family's reputation. Family reputation both good and bad can run across generations.

Women, especially wives, are expected to be pious conduits through which religion and moral behavior enters and maintains a familial foundation of an acceptable level. All social institutions operate by the same set of rules discussed above. Any variation from the acceptable or required behaviors places a stigma on the person and the entire family, who may then be rejected by polite society.

The death of a family member follows a prescribed process beginning with the expectation of visitation to the home of the deceased where the remains are laid out for viewing. Members of the extended family and friends visit the family of the deceased, bringing an offering of food. All of the female members of the family of the deceased are dressed in black and sit around the parlor waiting for visitors to arrive and greet them expressing sorrow for the loss of a loved one. In very traditional families professional mourners are hired to cry and wail, which shows the family's grief. While the professional criers are generally subtle, at times their activity may reach a crescendo. Candles surround the deceased and the room where the corpse is displayed. This tradition is called a *velorio*, or display of candles. While the female relatives receive mourners the men generally gather outside reminiscing and recounting stories about the deceased. When the priest or his surrogate arrives a Holy Rosary or *Rosario* is recited. The *velorio* continues all night. The following morning the deceased is removed to the local parish church where a mass is celebrated, followed by burial in the adjoining church graveyard. In very traditional Mexico there is usually a boneyard or *huesero* to the rear of the church. Since the official church graveyard has only limited space, commoners are allowed to be buried there for only a certain number of years before their remains are exhumed to make room for a newly departed parishioner. The bones of the former are then very unceremoniously deposited in the *huesero* or bone yard. The social elite and especially the major benefactors of the church are often buried in or under the church in space reserved for the most important individuals, including clergy.

It is important to note that many of the mannerisms described here are for a Mexico of the past. Modern Mexico maintains many of these customs but is much more liberal today than in the past.

Antonio N. Zavaleta

Further Reading

Cope, R. Douglas. *The Limits of Racial Domination: Plebeian Society in Colonial Mexico City 1160–1720*. Madison: University of Wisconsin Press, 1994.

Hartley, Cecil B. *The Gentleman's Book of Etiquette and Manual of Politeness*. Ann Arbor: University of Michigan Library, 2005.

Merchasin Carol M. *This Is Mexico: Tales of Culture and Other Complications*. Tempe, AZ: She Writes Press, 2015.

Vargas, Gaby. *El Arte de Convivir y la Cortesia Social*. Mexico DF: Aguilar, 2005.

MONGOLIA

The name *Mongol* is first mentioned in Chinese literature dating from the ninth century CE. Mongolia, known as the "land of nomads," was first unified in the twelfth century CE under the leadership of Genghis Khan (1162–1227). The country, located between China and Russia, has a distinctive cultural etiquette and set of taboos that have been handed down over the centuries that help to define and shed light on the unique Mongolian culture, worldview, and modern way of life.

Most Mongolian greetings with strangers are informal, so a nod and a smile, with the greeting "Sain bain uu?" (Are you well?) typical. The proper response to this greeting is "Sain" (Well), even if a person is not feeling his or her best that day. Depending on context and social occasion, the Mongolian meeting and greeting customs can include many different ways to greet one another. The terms used to greet people also differ depending on the activities of the host family, the time of the year, and the age of the person being greeted. In general, younger people reach out to the Mongolian elders (or older people) with their two hands under the elder's elbow and in turn the elder people may kiss the younger people on the cheek. Mongolian children are expected to show respect to their parents and elders and so should not say improper or rude words or get angry towards them. Another facet of Mongolian greeting is that a husband and wife are considered to be one person and therefore they do not greet each other during the Lunar New Year that the Mongolians call *Tsagaan Sar*.

Most Mongolian men and a small number of women possess a *khuurug*, a small, semiprecious stone bottle that contains snuff or smokeless tobacco, and they exchange their snuff bottles when they greet one another. The snuff bottle typically takes the form of an elaborately crafted, carved perfume bottle made from precious stone that, usually, is embedded with jewels. The cap of the snuff bottle is also of great importance in the Mongolian culture and is typically made of coral. Elders use snuff on a regular basis, but younger people and women tend to use snuff only during the Mongolian holidays. Mongolian snuff culture is an important part of Mongolian life and etiquette.

The Mongolian people have 29 different ethnicities and over 400 different styles of hats and as many different costumes that they still proudly wear. Herders and elders typically wear Mongolian costumes on a daily basis. In urban settings people wear Western clothing. When they meet it is proper etiquette for people to take off their hats or sunglasses to show their respect for one another. The national costume of Mongolia is called the *deel*. Men should always wear a belt when wearing a *deel*, for Mongolian people believe that a man's belt and hat are imbued with his soul. For this reason it is taboo to touch a Mongolian man's hat, head, and shoulders since these are considered sacred. Wives and children are very careful with the belts and hats of their male family members and place them on the most enshrined places of the home.

Mongolian families traditionally live in a circular, tent-like dwelling called a *ger* or a yurt. Even in Mongolian cities the *ger* is the common form of dwelling. According to Mongolian tradition a family should not assemble a *ger* on the exact same location of a different family's previous *ger*. In the countryside when guests arrive at the *ger* they shout out "Nokhoi khori" meaning "Get the dog" or "Hold your dog." Dogs are used to guard property and are not seen as pets in Mongolian culture. For this reason guests should not pet the dog belonging to their host as

Culture Shock! ⊕

Bökh: Mongolian Folk Wrestling

Bökh is an ancient form of wrestling enjoyed by Mongolian men that is an integral part of Mongolian culture. The sport is an element of *ovoo* worship ceremonies and part of the Mongolian national Naadam festival. *Bökh* is also one of the traditional Three Manly Skills of the Mongols (wrestling, archery, and horsemanship) that are venerated by Mongolians and closely associated with the pastoral nomadic traditions of people living in the Central Asian steppes region. *Bökh* differs from Western-style wrestling as it does not include weight categories or (usually) time limits—until recently bouts could last as long as three hours. Also, *Bökh* takes place outside on grass while wearing traditional dress. *Bökh* participants also perform a dance before wrestling.

Victoria Williams

this could result in the guest being attacked by the dog. Guests are always welcome in Mongolian homes even without prior notice or without an invitation. When guests enter the *ger* they should not sit on the left side of the *ger* where the kitchen and all other belongings of the women are placed.

The wife of the home should always offer tea and other food to the guests respectfully with two hands and never put her fingertips on the rim of the bowl. A guest should never reject any tea or food they may be offered; rather the guest, out of respect and honor for the host and hostess, should always taste the food or drink before he or she places the food or drink down on the dining area in the *ger*. When accepting food or a drink only the right hand should be used. The left hand can be used to support the right hand from underneath. A person should never hold the cup by its rim; instead a person should hold a cup from the bottom. When a person passes a knife during a meal he or she should never point the knife blade towards other people, but rather the handle of the knife should be extended to the other person. When using a knife to cut meat one should always cut the meat drawing the blade of the knife back to himself or herself and not in the direction of other people seated in the *ger*.

The ancient Mongolian religion known as Tengrism that included practices of shamanism, animism, totemism, polytheism, monotheism, and ancestor worship influences meal-time etiquette, when a wife will offer a small amount of the tea and milk to the "Eternal Blue Sky" with best wishes for the whole world, country, family, and relatives before giving a meal first to her husband and then to his male guests. Mongolian people see their country as the "Land of Eternal Blue Sky" and offer prayers and offerings to the "Eternal Blue Sky" during meals, even though many of the people are Buddhists. It is taboo or offensive if a person does not pray to the "Eternal Blue Sky." Often in a Mongolian *ger* a statue of the Buddha occupies a place of honor. It is taboo if a guest to the *ger* does not honor the family shrine with the statue of the Buddha. Mongolian food taboos include the belief that it is wrong to consume small, baby animals like lamb, cattle, or a foal for food. Additionally Mongolians regard water as a pure spirit, thus it is taboo to wash dirty things or women's clothing in rivers. Similarly many Mongolians also worship fire as a deity, believing it drives away evil. Therefore it is taboo to dry one's feet or shoes over the fire or throw trash into the fire in a *ger*.

There are several aspects to Mongolian body language. For example, Mongolians tend to have different sitting positions for men, women, and children. The guests as well as the hosts should never stretch their legs out while sitting, except for children. It is taboo to show the bottom of one's shoe or foot as it is thought to be disrespectful. When sitting a man should stay cross-legged; however, a woman should not cross her legs. People should not count on their fingers in Mongolia as each finger connotes a different meaning. The thumb pointed up is a good sign; however, the pinkie finger should not be used as it is a sign of disapproval.

In verbal communication Mongolians typically prefer positive communication when speaking and they do not speak ill of their neighbors. Mongolians tend to avoid talking about subjects that they consider taboo including death, sickness, the devil, or other topics they view as negative topics in general. A conversation should always be positive and begin with an inquiry about the wellness of the family, the livestock, or the condition of the pasture and grazing lands. Then one may discuss other matters.

A number of Mongolia's taboos stem from people's belief in the devil. For example, many Mongolians believe in the devil and that the devil can inflict harm or bring illness upon their families, especially their children. A baby boy's hair must not be cut until he is two, while for girls this prohibition extends to three years. The practice of not cutting the hair of young children is to protect toddlers from the devil and possibly confuse the devil as to the gender of Mongolian babies. Mongolians do not prepare for the arrival of a baby in advance as it is believed by some that this would give the devil an opportunity to know about the coming of the child and potentially harm the child. It is taboo to ever call a baby beautiful, but instead a person should call a child ugly to protect the infant from the devil who desires beautiful children.

Mongolians have very intricate procedures of funeral etiquette in accordance with Buddhist and other Mongolian traditions. Mongolians, in general, do not say the name of the dead because they deem that doing so may prevent the deceased from resting in peace. According to Mongolian tradition, one should refrain from visiting the dead or even entering into a room where a corpse is present. If a person enters a room where a corpse is present, he or she must turn his or her hat back and fold his or her lapel and sleeves inversely. In Buddhist Mongolian families a Buddhist priest will be called upon to pray for the spirit of the deceased. The priest will also pray that no harm or sickness befalls the surviving family. In some parts of Mongolia a practice known as "sky burial" is practiced in which a corpse is placed on a mountaintop and left to the elements and birds of prey.

David H. Campbell

Further Reading

Bawden, C. R. *The Modern History of Mongolia*. London: Kegan Paul International Limited, 1989.

Bolingbroke-Kent, Ants. "A Guide to Mongolian Yurt Etiquette." http://www.adventure -journal.com/2012/07/declination-a-guide-to-mongolian-yurt-etiquette. Accessed June 9, 2015.

May, Timothy. *Culture and Customs of Mongolia*. Westport, CT: Greenwood, 2009.

Wallace, Vanessa A. *Buddhism in Mongolian History, Culture, and Society*. New York: Oxford University Press, 2015.

MOROCCO

Morocco is an extremely diverse country, and its social and cultural customs reflect the influence of many different communities over time. Situated in the northwestern corner of Africa, Morocco is geographically part of the greater Maghreb (Arabic for "west") that includes Libya, Tunisia, Algeria, and Mauritania. Morocco stands at a crossroads between Arab, African, and European cultures. Historically, Morocco was a very important center for intellectual and economic trade and exchange, and the country has been home to many cultures and civilizations. Indigenous Berber (*Amazigh*; a self-referential term) communities have inhabited the region for thousands of years. The Roman Empire controlled the region for several centuries, beginning in the first century BCE. Arab Muslims arrived and settled during the period of Islamic expansion in the seventh and eighth centuries, and today the majority of Moroccans identify as Sunni, rather than Shiite, Muslims. France and Spain both established a colonial presence in Morocco during the nineteenth and twentieth centuries.

The presence of these and other peoples in Morocco creates a diverse ethnic, linguistic, and social context. The vast majority of Moroccans are of Arab or Berber descent, though there are minorities of Sub-Saharan African, European, and Jewish populations. Arabic dialects, Amazigh dialects, and French are all spoken across Morocco, and Spanish and English are also understood in several areas. Morocco is a Muslim majority country, with a small, though historically important, Jewish community and an even smaller Christian community. Morocco is also a large and geographically diverse country. This geographical diversity has led to the development of different cultural and social customs in different parts of the country. Due to these factors, speaking of general social and cultural customs in Morocco can be difficult. The practices of certain Amazigh tribes of the High Atlas mountains might differ from those of French-speaking families in Casablanca or those of religious scholars and students in Fes. Despite this, there are several elements of etiquette and taboos that are acknowledged and useful across Morocco.

Greeting etiquette is dictated by respect for social boundaries. It is common to greet someone, male or female, with "as-Salaamu alaykum" (Arabic for "Peace be upon you"), a traditional Islamic greeting that is widely used in all parts of the country and social circles. This greeting is not restricted to Muslims. When meeting members of the same sex, it is common to shake hands and exchange between two to four alternating kisses on the cheek, beginning from the left cheek. For strangers, a simple handshake is most common. As a sign of special respect, some people may touch their hearts or kiss their hand afterwards. When meeting someone of the opposite sex, it is not appropriate to extend your hand or offer an embrace. It is best, when greeting members of the opposite sex, to allow them to decide the boundaries of exchange. If they do not extend their hand, it is appropriate to bow slightly or nod out of respect. Moroccan culture harbors great respect for elders and the elderly. It is common to kiss the right hand of respected elders of the same sex and, sometimes, of the opposite sex. This is common for respected elders, religious scholars, or elderly patriarchs and matriarchs of the community.

Standards of appearance and dress vary across Morocco. For both men and women, this ranges from more traditional and Islamic clothing such as the djellaba (a hooded robe commonly worn in Morocco) to traditional Amazigh clothes, headwear, and apparel to T-shirts, skirts, and jeans. In larger cities, such as Casablanca or Marrakesh, where there is a larger remnant of European cultural influence and larger foreigner communities, it is not uncommon to see men adorned in the latest European fashions and women with makeup and without headscarves. In more rural societies, a more conservative and traditional dress code among men and women is commonly observed. Moroccans are generally welcoming and understanding of foreign visitors, though sensitivity to local dress customs is always appreciated. In general, conservative attire is particularly important among conservative or religious communities. It is not appropriate, for men or women, to wear clothes that reveal the legs and shoulders. It is generally expected that women will cover their hair. Conservative attire is necessary when entering a house of worship or sacred place in Morocco. For women, it is generally not appropriate to appear unveiled in front of a male who is not a family member. Tight clothing for females is also considered inappropriate.

Moroccans are very friendly, hospitable, and welcoming in their relationships with family, friends, and strangers. It is not uncommon to be invited over to someone's home for a meal or tea and conversation. Visitors might be initially startled by the amount of hospitality they are offered by hosts and strangers, but this is a deeply rooted element of Moroccan culture, which highly values time spent communally. Gift-giving is a common practice in Morocco, especially if invited to someone's home, a family gathering, or a wedding. It is common to bring sweets, sugar, fruit, or milk as a gift, and gifts are generally not opened in front of the giver. Moroccan culture also focuses on the preservation of personal, familial, and communal honor and dignity.

A common cultural concept in Morocco is that of *hashuma* (shame that occurs from inappropriate social behavior), and is a term used when someone has broken these boundaries of dignity and respect. When entering someone's home, it is appropriate to remove one's shoes upon entry unless otherwise instructed. It is considered *hashuma* to step over people, put feet in the air, and step over sacred objects such as the Koran. People often sit communally, either in chairs or on the floor, sharing a communal meal. Punctuality is not a predominant aspect of Moroccan cultural etiquette, and it is common for appointments and meetings to be late, delayed, or extended. Public displays of affection are also generally regarded as *hashuma* for both men and women and should be avoided.

Rules of cleanliness and purity, rooted in Islamic law and culture, apply to Moroccan culinary culture. Pork and alcohol are generally taboo, as in most Islamic societies. Generally, it is not appropriate to gift or request pork or alcohol. Most food found in Morocco is considered *halal* (lawful in Islamic law), as it conforms to Islamic slaughtering and dietary restrictions. Restaurants and cafés are plentiful across Morocco. There is a strong café culture in Morocco, and the café is often a meeting place and social space for older men. These spaces, especially outside of larger cities, are not often frequented by women.

Eating etiquette is also important among Moroccans. Moroccans generally eat, drink, and accept food and drink with their right hands. It is common to eat and share a dish communally either by hand or with bread or utensils. It is considered *hashuma* to eat with your left hand or to take a portion of the communal dish that requires stretching and reaching over the food. Things are commonly passed to the right, and people begin eating by saying "Bismillah" (meaning "In the name of God") over the food. Ramadan, the Islamic month of fasting from sunrise to sunset, is observed across Morocco. During this time, it is difficult to find many restaurants or cafés open. It can be considered *hashuma* to eat or drink in public during Ramadan, especially in front of those who are fasting.

Family relations and marriage are essential social institutions in Moroccan culture. Extended family networks are often closely connected, and weddings are times of great celebration. Social boundaries and customs especially regulate the interactions of nonfamily members of different sexes. In more conservative and rural communities, having a boyfriend or girlfriend is a very taboo topic, and there is *hashuma* in speaking or interacting with someone of the opposite sex in public. It is also inappropriate to make extended eye contact with a member of the opposite sex. In general, having an intimate or sexual relationship outside of marriage is considered taboo. Despite this, discreet dating cultures exist in Morocco, primarily in urban areas.

Marriages often celebrate the union of two families and initiate a time of extended celebration. Respect accorded to elder family members and having children is greatly encouraged. There are extended family networks, and it is not uncommon for several generations to live together in the same house or apartment.

Many of Morocco's customs are rooted in Islamic culture, practice, and identity with the Muslim call to prayer sounded five times per day across the country. Morocco also has a rich and deep history of Sufism (Islamic spirituality and/or mysticism), and the practice of visiting the tombs of famous and important *awliya Allah* (Muslim saints) for *baraka* (blessing) is an accepted cultural practice. Morocco's Jewish community also has a practice of venerating *tzedikim* (Jewish saints) at their tombs during an annual gathering known as the *hilloula*. When entering a *zawiya* (Sufi lodge), the shrines of *awliya*, or mosques, it is common for men and women to dress in conservative clothing and to take off one's shoes upon entering, maintaining silence and decorum. It is disrespectful to walk in front of or interrupt someone who is praying. Many mosques have separate spaces for men and women and,

Culture Shock! ⊕

Origins of Imilchil Moussem, the Berber Marriage Festival

Imilchil Moussem, or the Berber Marriage Festival, is an annual marriage festival and wedding fair held at Imilchil in Morocco's Atlas Mountains. The event draws around 30,000 participants from several Berber tribes as well as many tourists. The festival is said to have begun when a young man named Isli (meaning "groom" in the Berber language) fell in love with a young woman, Tislit (meaning "bride"), but were denied permission to marry by their warring families. Consumed by sadness at being denied permission to wed, the lovers cried themselves to death with their tears combining to form a lake. Today two lakes at Imilchil are named after the lovers—though a mountain divides the lakes so that even in death the lovers remain apart. The families of Isli and Tislit are said to have been distraught at the youngsters' deaths so they vowed to forevermore allow the young to choose their own spouses, hence the Imilchil marriage festival sees young people select their own life partners.

Victoria Williams

unless specifically invited, non-Muslims are generally not allowed in Muslim houses of worship in Morocco. It is taboo to openly profess atheism or to openly profess doubts about God or religion. Missionary activity is strictly controlled in Morocco.

As in all countries and cultures, several political topics remain controversial and taboo in Morocco and are best avoided in conversation. Homosexuality and the LGBTQ movement are considered very taboo topics. In addition, the king of Morocco receives widespread, though not universal, respect and admiration across the country. Open criticism of the king can create social and political tension. The situation in the Western Sahara (known as the Saharan Provinces throughout Morocco) remains an unresolved political issue, though it is one about which many Moroccans feel passionately. Arguing about the Saharan Provinces with Moroccans can lead to social and political trouble. It is best to avoid these topics in conversation and discussion.

Peter J. Dziedzic

Further Reading

Abun-Nasr, Jamil M. *A History of the Maghreb in the Islamic Period*. Cambridge: Cambridge University Press, 1993.

Crawford, David, and Rachel Newcomb. *Encountering Morocco: Fieldwork and Cultural Understanding*. Bloomington: Indiana University Press, 2013.

Hoffman, Katherine. *We Share Walls: Language, Land, and Gender in Berber Morocco*. Oxford: Blackwell, 2008.

Miller, Susan Gilson. *A History of Modern Morocco*. Cambridge: Cambridge University Press. 2013.

Schaefer-Davis, Susan. *Patience and Power: Women's Lives in a Moroccan Village*. Cambridge, MA: Schenkman, 1983.

MYANMAR

Myanmar is an Asian country located between India and China, with a largely Buddhist population. Images of the Buddha, Buddhist monks, and Buddhists are revered. The people of Myanmar are generally friendly and informal. Most Myanmar households consist of extended families. Young parents have to work and need their own parents' assistance in the rearing of their children. Uncles, aunts, and cousins may also live in the same house. That being said, throughout Myanmar society men and women tend to segregate themselves. Men will usually talk with their male friends and women likewise with their female friends. Similarly, for outings, single females may prefer to go about with other single females. In work situations males and females work together but still may eat their lunch in segregated groups. Males and females, even husbands and wives, are seldom seen in public in intimate contact. In large religious ceremonies, men and women are usually seated separately on two sides of an aisle. Where monks are present, monks will be seated on raised platforms and the lay congregation must sit at floor level on carpets or mats.

Myanmar is well known for its meditation masters who are usually monks; there are strict rules to be followed at each monastery. When offering donations to monks, a person should give the donation in an envelope to the accompanying layperson or put it on a side table if he is in the monastery. If offering from the side of the road, cash may be put into alms bowls carried by the monks who go on alms-rounds in the early morning. Freshly cooked food cannot be offered after noon to monks, but medicines and preserved foods may be offered anytime.

Though people do shake hands in Myanmar, friendly nods and smiles can suffice as a greeting. Generally, introductions are not that important, but the exchange of business or name cards is acceptable. Males should not kiss or hug females of any age, even if they have known the females for some time. Touching between the sexes is taboo in most cases, so exercise great restraint regarding this practice.

"Mingala bar," meaning "Auspiciousness/blessings be upon you," is the standard greeting, though locals do not use the expression that much except for school children when they greet their teacher at the beginning of a school session. Locals ask their friends, "How are you?", "Where are you going?", "Have you had breakfast/lunch/dinner?" and similar questions that do not need a specific answer. "Hello" can be understood by everyone and is also used to answer phones. *Saya* (teacher, master, boss) is a term that can be widely used without offence for males. The feminine *Sayama*, though, should be used mainly for those in the teaching, medical, or nursing professions. *Sayalay* and *Sayagyi* are used for young Buddhist nuns and elderly Buddhist nuns respectively. *Uncle* and *Aunty* can be used for those who are not blood relations but are within the age range of one's own uncles and aunts. The very old may be addressed as *Po* and *Pwa* (also spelled *Hpo* and *Hpwa* or *Pho* and *Phwa*) meaning grandfather and grandmother; simply calling elders by their whole names may also be acceptable. Respect for elders (in age, rank, education, social status, and income) such as teachers, doctors, and elderly family members and friends, is shown by deference to them and avoiding having an argument with them or otherwise causing them to lose face.

It is important to dress appropriately in Myanmar, especially when visiting a temple. Shoes and socks should be removed before going up the steps when entering a pagoda or temple grounds. Females should wear sleeved and modest upper garments, or bare shoulders can be covered with a shawl or scarf. Long or medium-length skirts are best when entering temples and monasteries. Demeanor should be appropriate in temples and pagodas. One should not step onto or over images of the Buddha or take inappropriate photos around Buddha images. One can be fined for inappropriate actions in and around the pagodas. Encounters with monks are inevitable in Myanmar, so proper clothing etiquette is required.

At funerals, people wear somber colors but black is not compulsory. In the larger cities and towns, funerals may take place within 24 hours of death, but in the villages, there may be a wake held for a few nights because of the commonly held belief that the soul lingers around the house and that doors must be kept open. There is a special meal and other offerings, such as cash, medicines, monks' robes, and food provisions, offered to monks on the seventh day after death to make merit for the deceased. Such meals and offerings for departed loved ones may be offered at other times as well. The sharing of merits occurs at the end of the offering ceremony when those present should say "Sadhu, sadhu, sadhu" (Well done!); it is believed that by saying these words one can gain merits from the good deeds done earlier.

During meals, all the dishes are placed on the table at once rather than being served in courses, and it is expected that everyone should try all of the dishes on the table. There is no need to finish all of the rice or oil if it is more than a guest can eat. Lunch and dinner typically consist of rice, a meat dish, a vegetable dish, and a soup, accompanied usually by a side of fermented fish dip or tomato dip eaten with various boiled vegetables. Vegetarian dishes are usually available too. In the dry regions in the middle of the country where beans and pulses are abundant, bean or lentil dishes may be more common than meat dishes. The national dish is *mo-hin-ga*, a dish of thin rice noodles in a thick, fish-based soup. Snacks and desserts are usually made from rice flour, coconut, palm sugar, sesame, and fruit. Desserts are served at the end of the meal after the dishes have been cleared away. In Myanmar, breakfast usually consists of leftover rice, fried with eggs or boiled beans, and meat or shrimp. Boiled rice is also eaten with fried dried fish. Western-style breakfasts may also be eaten, especially in urban areas. Beverages at meals will often be water, with or without ice, and Chinese or Burmese tea.

When serving dishes, an age-based hierarchy exists, so the eldest person present must be served first. If an older person is expected after the meal begins, small portions of the dishes will be placed on an empty plate for them. Seating at the dining table is not fixed, however, except for the head of the household who sits at the head of the table. In villages and monasteries, low circular tables may be used and one must sit on small stools or on mats on the floor. At wedding receptions in hotels, seating is usually Western style at round tables seating 10 persons each, and guests are seated according to a seating plan. Notable people and very important persons are seated at the head tables nearest to the stage where the bridal couple sits. The bridal couple and parents wait at the entrance towards the end of the

A family takes their midday meal in the outdoor dining area of their house in rural Myanmar. Family members are served in order by age, with the eldest served first. (Julian Nieman/Alamy Stock Photo)

reception to thank guests as they leave. In villages, marriages may be celebrated with a feast at the local monastery where the whole village might come for breakfast or lunch.

Business matters are seldom discussed at business meals, which are for the parties concerned to get to know each other. Business will usually be discussed in the office and then a meal may be served there or in another venue. There are no strict rules on tipping. Salaries are generally low for blue-collar workers and tips and other small gifts can help to make their lives easier. At most meals rolls of tissue, rather than napkins or towels, will be placed on the table so that diners may wipe their hands and mouth. Silverware will usually be a fork and spoon, along with a soup spoon. For dishes such as soupy rice noodles or wheat noodles, a soup spoon and chopsticks may be provided.

It should be noted that though foreigners may visit local homes, they are not allowed to stay overnight. As a sign of respect shoes must be removed at the door before entering local homes. In addition, when visiting homes, gifts of flowers, food, or other useful items are appreciated though not requisite.

Respect for elders is apparent in people's body language. For instance, it is taboo to pass objects over the heads of elders or to talk to them with arms on hips or crossed arms, as these gestures may be interpreted as indicating a superior attitude when a humble attitude is preferred. Among peers, it is not necessary to be very formal. In work situations, there may be camaraderie, jokes, and antics if the members of the group have known each other for some time. It is important not to put feet up on a desk, however, especially if sharing workspace with Myanmar people. Similarly, a person should not touch the head and hair of locals when communicating with them or when trying to get their attention, nor should one use the feet or legs to point at or to move objects. Similarly in homes, beds are usually aligned so that the foot of the bed does not point towards the altar or shrine where the image of the Buddha is placed. Smiles are viewed ambiguously in Myanmar and can mean anything from genuine delight to embarrassment. A smile may also occur from lack of understanding or from being unsure about a situation. Keen observation helps with discerning the reason for the smile.

In verbal communication common English words such as hello, thank you, sorry, please, excuse me, the names of the days of the week, months, and numbers are all well understood by most Myanmar people. The indirect communication style of Myanmar people may confuse visitors and it may take a while to understand what is actually meant. It is not necessary to learn the Myanmar language, but it is always a great advantage to be able to say words like the names of the numbers and days of the week, and how to phrase simple questions. Loudness in speech and harsh actions are discouraged and can be interpreted as disrespectful, especially if there are elders present.

Certain topics of conversation are taboo in Myanmar, with political and religious topics best avoided. Locals can be sensitive to criticism, and living in a militarily controlled country with no tolerance for protest or criticism for many decades means that locals fear informers. One should not be offended if locals ask about age, marital status, or salary. This is the way locals have friendly conversations, and one is not required to give a detailed reply.

Saw Myat Yin

Further Reading

Khng, Pauline. *Countries of the World: Myanmar*. Singapore: Gareth Stevens, 2000.
Saw Myat Yin. *CultureShock! Myanmar: A Survival Guide to Customs and Etiquette*. Singapore: Marshall Cavendish, 2013.
Saw Myat Yin. *Cultures of the World: Myanmar*. Singapore: Marshall Cavendish, 2011.
Win Pe. *Dos and Don'ts in Myanmar*. Bangkok: i Press, 1996.

N

NATIVE AMERICANS, PLAINS INDIANS

The Plains Indians culture area of North America consists of a geographic setting in which discrete tribal groups share similar natural environments and cultural characteristics. These societies are best known historically for their use of tipi structures, dependence on the horse for nomadic mobilization and bison hunting, elaborate beadwork and vivid material culture, and their resistance to non-Indian encroachment through warfare. Hollywood films have portrayed these people as noble savages or fierce warriors, which consequently has led many to believe they no longer exist in our modern world. Interestingly, Indians of the Plains remain one of the most well-studied Native American groups in North America. Their cultural traditions have fascinated professional and amateur enthusiasts alike.

The contemporary scene in Indian Country for Plains Indians is a reflection of the numerous historical events that have led to their current social and geographic state. Amid broken treaties and assimilation policies by the U.S. government, Plains tribes continue to maintain their cultural identity and employ many traditional aspects of life known to their Native predecessors. Indian people in general are reluctant to open up to outsiders. Even those who have dedicated their careers to studying the cultural aspects of Indian people have a difficult time researching their social domain. This is partly a trust issue, and the result of historical oppression by non-Indians, but it can also be attributed to Native societies' dependence on ethnic compartmentalization and kinship ties.

Kinship structures remain one of the most important aspects among the Plains Indians. The extended family forms the basic social unit, and behaviors toward certain people are based on the functionality of that system. When an Indian person references or addresses a kin member, it is preferable for them to use a kin term such as "elder sister" or "younger brother" rather than the person's given name. Plains Indians also use fictitious kinship expressions towards people who are not related by blood. Designations such as "brother" or "cousin" allow the speaker to situate their level of closeness to the addressee on their own terms. Other social situations require Indian people to avoid conversations altogether. For example, traditionally, a Crow Indian male never spoke to his wife's mother. He used an intermediary, most likely his wife, to deliver messages to his mother-in-law. Research suggests this taboo was not a result of unfriendliness toward his mother-in-law but in fact an awesome display of respect toward her. Likewise, other Plains tribes such as the Arapaho frowned upon a wife speaking or even looking at her husband's father. There are many instances in which the continuation of these practices, in various degrees, is evident in contemporary Plains tribal societies.

Plains Indians are particularly known for their fascinating socio-religious systems. These activities include many taboos in various contexts. When influential anthropologist Robert H. Lowie took Yellow Mule, a Crow Indian, to a restaurant while conducting research on the reservation, Yellow Mule hesitated to eat cake because it may have contained eggs. It was told that the eagle medicine he had received from Yellow Crane, a Crow medicine man, prohibited him from consuming eggs. Comanche medicine men and women kept their medicine bundles where they could not be opened and polluted by the presence of menstruating women. Plains tribes considered menstrual blood as a physical manifestation of the woman's power. This power inevitably clashed with the power of men (even medicine men). For the Plains Cree, a girl at puberty had to be secluded for four nights in a small tipi or menstrual lodge under the supervision of an elderly woman. Most girls were encouraged to seek a vision for the four-day seclusion period while an older woman mentored her in the ways of her people. It was perceived that women did not have control over this power or the signs they produced. The Arapaho believed if a menstruating woman entered the room of a sick person, the power could kill the sick individual. Even the odor from the blood flow could contaminate the power of traditional ceremonial objects. Contemporary research among Oglalas indicates that it is still believed that menstruating women diminish the power of sacred things and if they should come in contact with them, the objects must be taken into a sweat lodge and be prayed and sung over by the medicine man to restore their power. Even at Southern Plains powwows it is common to hear announcements asking menstruating women to avoid the dance area.

A Plains Indian boy transitioned into manhood by gaining special recognition (or status) in warfare, and later in life for his ability to negotiate peace. An ideal man was a great provider and protector of his family—a sentiment that continues in modern Indian males. Men were raised to use their own forms of communication (greetings, commands, and questions) among one another and oftentimes they strongly avoided female speech patterns. Although there was no official puberty ceremony for boys, it was expected that they would eventually seek a vision. Visions were, and continue to be in particular contexts, very important to Plains Indians groups. This is a process of personal solitude in which the seeker (a man or woman but more commonly males) fasts for a special number of days and petitions the spirits to take pity on him. Some tribes, such as the Crow, would cut off a finger joint on the left hand as a way of stirring the supernatural realm. Sometimes flesh would be cut from the arms as a means of sacrifice. This special gift of flesh and blood would in turn establish an ongoing relationship with the seeker and the spirit. The personal maintenance of the vision seeker and the spirit's revelations to him were laden with taboos. In addition to revealing sacred songs, offering instructions concerning battle dress, or indicating whether he was called to be a medicine man, the spirits would instruct the seeker to adhere to rigorous dietary restrictions or social behaviors. If the seeker deviated from these specific instructions, he risked the loss of the spirit's protection or even personal devastation.

A return to vision quests was initiated with the American Indian Movement in the 1960s. Influential voices such as Indian activist Russell Means revived the vision quest and other traditional spiritual offerings such as the Sun Dance among Plains Indian people. Means was adopted by Chief Frank Fools Crow, a Lakota holy man and quintessential vision seeker. Fools Crow once stated: "Our children are us in the tomorrow of life. In them we remain here, and so it will be with their children's children—if the world survives." Although the vision quest was primarily an interaction between the individual and the spirit world, the revelations of the quest extended into the person's familial and social world. Since Plains Indian life is and always has been infused with elements of the supernatural, it only seems a logical progression that the vision quest be a key vehicle for cultural renewal. Young Plains Indian men are participating in these rituals as ways of connecting to their traditional past.

T. Eric Bates

Further Reading

Mails, Thomas E. (In Dialogue with the Great Sioux Holy Man, Fools Crow. *Fools Crow Wisdom and Power*. San Francisco: Council Oak Books, 2001.

NATIVE AMERICANS, SOUTHWEST

Every Native American tribe has its own etiquette and taboos, as is the case among the Native American Indians of the U.S. Southwest. The tribes that make up the American Indian population of the Southwest include the following: Apache, Comanche, Havasupai, Hopi, Jemez, Kiowa, Kiowa Apache, Lipan, Maricopa, Mohave, Navajo, Paiute, Papago, Panamint, Pecos, Pima, Pueblo, Shoshoni, Sobaipuri, Tewa, Ute, Walapai, Yavapai, Yuma, and Zuni.

Cultural etiquette in meeting and greeting among Southwestern tribes varies from tribe to tribe. Many groups, such as Apache, Yavapai, and Navajo, will simply greet each other with a handshake. In some cases an Apache man may throw his hands and arms up toward the sky as a greeting. When two Navajo women meet, they may hug each other. Sometimes a greeting may involve weeping for joy between two Navajo women who have not seen each other for a long time. In Native American hospitality guests are always fed. The normal greeting for guests is not "Hello" or "How are you doing?" but rather "Have you eaten?" Hospitality etiquette for Native American families is to do their best to keep a pot of food, such as mutton stew, always ready to eat for any guest who comes to the Navajo hogan (round, log house) or the wickiup (brush hut) of the Apache or Yavapai. The duties of the host in the Native American home are always to compliment guests, lend help to elders with entering or leaving the home, never sit while any guests stand, offer guests the places of honor in the home and the best food available, and protect guests as members of the family or clan. The duties of a guest are to accept any food offered, be grateful for any and all offers from the host, give honor and respect to the woman of the home, always compliment the host, and present the host with a gift.

Traditionally most Indians (Apache, Navajo, Mohave, Yavapai) wore clothes made from buckskin. Men wore Indian breechcloths and leggings, and women wore skirts and tunic-like shirts. For shoes, the Yavapai people wore moccasins, but others wore sandals made of yucca fiber. The Yuma (also called the Quechan people) did not wear much clothing at all. Yuma men typically wore breechcloths. The Yuma women wore dresses made of willow bark strips. In the winter season, the Yuma Indians wore rabbit-skin robes at night.

Native American tribes have a number of taboos, many of which center on food. The taboos vary from tribe to tribe; however, in some cases there are some cultural overlaps among the specific taboos in the Indian cultures of the Southwest. By observing the taboos related to their world, many Native Americans believe they can avoid sickness and even an untimely death. Among Native American tribes of the Southwest, gluttony is considered taboo. At a meal, a person should always make sure to leave enough food so that all the other clan members can have a portion of the meal that is served. Eating burned bread in the Navajo culture is taboo. Native Americans typically do not drink milk. Among the Apache and Navajo tribes, one should not eat snake, bear, reptiles, or fish meat. In many tribes, the owl is considered a messenger of bad news or even death, so eating owl meat is taboo. The Navajo and Yavapai tribes also do not eat fish.

Body language is very important to Native Americans. For instance, proper body posture is expected in the Navajo tribe. Navajos believe it is unattractive if a person slouches or gives any appearance of being lazy. A Navajo person should always sit in a position of readiness with a straight upper back and uplifted shoulders in order to communicate that he or she is ready to help and serve as needed in the home as well as in the tribe. In verbal communication, it is proper etiquette to listen more than one talks. This is especially true between a younger person and an older person or an elder in Indian society. During a conversation, a person should not speak until he or she is sure the other person has finished speaking. One should expect many pauses in a conversation. A person should not speak too fast or too much. When a person speaks, he or she should speak softly and deliberately. In general, a person should not speak of tribal politics, the dead, religion and religious ceremonies, witchcraft, or other sensitive cultural issues.

Traditionally, marriage was typically arranged in Native American tribes. In some cases, a bride and groom did not meet until their wedding day. In the Hopi culture, the engagement was signaled to the tribe when a man and a woman brushed each other's hair. In practically all the tribes, it was forbidden to marry within one's own clan down to the first and second cousins. Marriages were informal among the Ute, and once premarital intercourse occurred at the home of a young woman, she was considered married. In many Native American tribes, divorce was as simple as the wife putting her husband's belongings outside of the hogan or hut. The man was then forced to return to his own clan to live with his mother and father. The children stayed with their mother.

Most Native American tribes are matrilineal in their social structures, including the Apache, Navajo, Pima, Pueblo, Maricopa, Shoshoni, and Zuni. In such tribes, it is proper etiquette that when a couple marries, the husband will go to live with the bride's mother and her family. In most tribes of the Southwest, monogamy is observed (Navajo, Hopi, Pueblo, Zuni). Before the 1900s the Comanche Indians practiced polygyny and levirate (a widow would marry her late husband's brother) while sororate (a man marries his late wife's sister) marriage practices were not uncommon among the Apache, Comanche, and the Lipan. In Navajo cultures, a mother is very important to the social fabric and well-being of the family and the larger Navajo culture. A mother has certain responsibilities that she is obligated to fulfill. She is in charge of the hogan. The Navajo home is considered sacred, and the mother is to guard the home. She is responsible for the care of the home and its contents, the care of the children, and the tending of the sheep. The Navajo man's role is to provide for his family and for all the things that will keep the home operating. He must haul wood to warm the home, maintain the family's livestock, and hunt for wild game. The role of children and young men and women is to show respect to their parents and tribal elders and to do chores around the home. Since the role of mothers is so important to Native Americans, there are many taboos for when a woman is pregnant. For instance, it is believed that a pregnant woman should not tie knots when expecting or she may have a hard time giving birth; she should not try to count the stars or she will have too many children; she should not eat a lot of sweet foods because the baby will not be strong; she should not look at a wild animal or her baby will look wild; and she must not look at a dead person or a dead animal while pregnant because it is bad luck and her baby might be born sick (Navajo). In Zuni culture, the Indians believed that if a husband killed a snake when his wife was pregnant, the baby would be born spotted like a snake and die.

There are also taboos surrounding death, some of the strongest taboos in Native American cultures. In general among Native American cultures the subject of death or any discussions about the dead are taboo topics. Among many Native tribes, it is taboo to touch the body of a corpse. Even today it is taboo to mention the name of the deceased in most cases. If a dead person is named, the name is always mentioned using a past tense verb. Southwestern tribes, especially the Apache and Navajo, fear the ghosts of the deceased. For this reason the Apache and Navajo ensure that those who have died do not return by burying a deceased person's possessions with the body. A Navajo man's horse was sometimes killed and buried with him along with the man's saddle. A dead person's home was often burned to keep his or her spirit from returning to the home. In some tribes, such as the Shoshoni and the Yavapai, the dead were cremated along with all their possessions. It is taboo to wear a dead person's clothing or jewelry, so the clothing and jewelry are also burned along with the corpse.

The religion of Native Americans is directly linked to nature. Many Native Americans worship and pray to the earth (also called Mother Earth), the sky (also called Father Sky), the sun, and moon, as well as to what they call "the four winds," from the north, south, east, and west. The goal of Native American religions is to maintain balance and harmony between human beings, nature, and the spiritual realm. In the Native American worldview, everything has a spirit: rocks, trees, rivers, animals, the sun, the moon, stars, and people. Religious taboos for Native Americans involve anything that disrupts or disturbs this balance and harmony.

David H. Campbell

Further Reading

Collins, John James. *Native American Religions: A Geographical Survey*. Lewiston, NY: Edwin Mellen, 1991.

Spicer, Edward H. *The American Indians: Dimensions of Ethnicity*. Cambridge, MA: Belknap Press of Harvard University Press, 1980.

Trimble, Stephen. *The People: Indians of the American Southwest*. Santa Fe, NM: School of American Research Press, 1993.

Yazzie-Parsons, Evangeline, and Margaret Speas. *Diné Bizaad Bínáhoóaah: Rediscovering the Navajo Language: An Introduction to the Navajo Language*. Flagstaff, AZ: Salina Bookshelf, 2007.

THE NETHERLANDS

The Netherlands is the main constituent country of the Kingdom of the Netherlands. The Netherlands is a very densely populated nation located in Western Europe that also has three island territories in the Caribbean—Bonaire, Sint Eustatius, and Saba—that are sometimes referred to as the Caribbean Netherlands. The European Netherlands is bordered by Germany, Belgium, and the North Sea. The Netherlands also shares maritime borders with Belgium, the United Kingdom, and Germany. The name *Holland* is used to refer informally to the whole of the Netherlands. People and things that are identified as coming from the Netherlands are referred to as Dutch.

Much of Dutch etiquette resembles the etiquette of other Western countries. However there are some distinguishing elements to expected codes of behavior in the Netherlands. For example, the typical Dutch gesture of greeting is the handshake, which is performed by men, women, and children. Moreover the Dutch shake hands when they meet and depart. Women and men who know each other very well may also air-kiss three times on the cheek starting with the left cheek. A

Culture Shock! ⊕

Windmill Communication Etiquette

Windmills are an iconic symbol of the Netherlands. When windmills are not working their sails can be used to communicate news. When seen from the front, the sails of a windmill always turn counterclockwise so starting with the uppermost sail the sails of a windmill always move from right to left. If a miller wishes to announce joyful news, such as a birth, he makes the uppermost sail stop just before it reaches the vertical position and fixes the sail in place. This is known as the "coming" position. The opposite of the coming position is the "going" position, which is used to signal mourning. This position sees the uppermost sail fixed in place once it has passed through the vertical and is symbolic of death as it shows that the upper sail has travelled past the concluding point of its journey from top to bottom.

Victoria Williams

standard greeting is a simple "Hello." Indeed, visitors to the Netherlands should not be surprised if they greet a person in Dutch only to be answered in English. The Dutch are very capable linguists and easily pick up foreign languages.

The Netherlands has a very liberal, egalitarian society that pays increasingly little attention to people's age, status, and gender and as a result of this the use of the formal "you" (*U*) to address someone is used less and less, whereas the informal "you" (*jij*) is used increasingly frequently as a sign of the Dutch people's commitment to equality in all things. Although the Dutch are generally liberal this does not mean that they disapprove of formality. Indeed it is considered rude to address someone by his or her first name before invited to do so. This is especially true in work situations. It is usual to exchange business cards at meetings in the Netherlands that should include educational qualifications. Another thing to bear in mind when greeting people in the Netherlands is that the Dutch tend to be extremely punctual and expect people to arrive for events on time. The Dutch are also usually very keen on keeping to schedules, and it is not unknown for people to invite their friends to dinner six weeks in advance. Indeed, the Dutch live by their diaries and all schedules are adhered to very strictly. The Dutch rarely pop round to each other's homes on the spur of the moment, as any visit must be agreed upon in advance and scheduled into a diary. If a person is invited to a Dutch home, it is usual to bring a gift for the hostess. Common gifts include a potted plant or flowers (though not white lilies or chrysanthemums, as these are associated with funerals), a book, or chocolates. Wine is not usually given as a gift to the hostess as the Dutch usually choose the wine to accompany the meal beforehand.

The Netherlands does not have a distinct culinary culture, with food viewed as a utilitarian necessity. Traditional Dutch dishes include *snert* (pea soup), *pannenkoeken* (large pancakes), white asparagus, raw herrings, and a thick stew known as *hutspot*. The Dutch usually eat sandwiches with cheese, peanut butter, or chocolate for breakfast, while lunch (which usually lasts only about 30 minutes) consists of sandwiches, cold meats, and side salads. Dinner takes place between 5 p.m. and 7 p.m. and is typically a three-course meal beginning with a soup. The main dish usually features potatoes with vegetables served with meat or fish. The dinner is ended with dessert. Chinese–Indonesian, Surinamese, and Italian cuisine all feature in the Dutch diet.

The Dutch rarely invite people whom they do not know well to dinner. Instead, the Dutch prefer to invite people for coffee. Neighbors also often invite each other to their homes for a cup of coffee that is usually served with one cookie. Coffee drinking lies at the heart of a sense of cozy conviviality and general togetherness that is summed up by the Dutch word *gezelligheid*. This Dutch word is untranslatable into English, a rather abstract sensation of collective, shared well-being and positivity that is central to Dutch society. In workplaces the morning coffee break is enshrined as an essential daily event, and when it is someone's birthday they are expected to bring cakes to coffee break so that all their colleagues may enjoy the happy occasion. Furthermore, most Dutch homes have a birthday calendar hanging from the bathroom door that notes all relevant birthdays. In the Netherlands, forgetting a birthday is a major social faux pas.

A family gathers for brunch in the Netherlands. Convivial get-togethers are central to the Dutch concept of *gezelligheid*, the term describing an abstract feeling of well-being experienced during periods of time spent in the company of others. (middelveld/iStockphoto.com)

Dutch people are very open and direct, leading outsiders to sometimes label the Dutch as rude. The Dutch merely feel that they are being truthful and straightforward. Similarly the Dutch maintain direct eye contact when talking and their speech is also very to the point. The Dutch do not mind criticism and tend not to be easily offended by critical comments. The Dutch are also very direct when driving, something that leads to accusations that the Dutch are aggressive, impatient drivers who change lanes without warning. It is common to come across Dutch drivers gesticulating, hooting, and swearing at each other.

On the whole the Dutch are a very tolerant nation. One thing that is frowned upon, however, is being seen to spend large amounts of money, for this behavior is deemed vulgar and ostentatious. Similarly it is considered impolite to ask a Dutch person how much they earn.

Victoria Williams

Further Reading

Hunt, Janin, and Ria van Eii. *CultureShock! Netherlands: A Survival Guide to Customs and Etiquette*. Tarrytown, NY: Marshall Cavendish, 2009.

Jan, M. "The Dutch Culture." *Netherlands Tourism*. 2017. http://www.netherlands-tourism.com/dutch-culture/. Accessed January 9, 2017.

Mares, Dennis, and Antonius C.G.M. Robben. "The Netherlands." *Countries and Their Cultures*. http://www.everyculture.com/Ma-Ni/The-Netherlands.html. Accessed January 9, 2017.

NEW ZEALAND

New Zealand is an island nation comprising two major landmasses—that of the north and south islands—as well as a number of smaller islands scattered around its coastline. Located in the southwestern Pacific Ocean, the islands were initially settled by Polynesians somewhere between 1250 and 1300 CE, and resultantly harbored a distinctive Maori culture until European settlement began to occur in the early 1800s. This influx of European natives culminated in the signing of the Treaty of Waitangi in 1840, making New Zealand a British colony. Reflective of this, New Zealand's population of 4.5 million is today made up largely of European descent, with the indigenous Maori making up the largest minority, followed by people of Asian descent, and then Pacific Islanders. Despite this European dominance, Maori traditions still permeate throughout New Zealand society, making for a very rich and diverse cultural landscape. New Zealand, a First World nation, possesses a developed market economy built on farming, agriculture, and tourism. These exports contribute to New Zealand's classification as a high-income economy, noted as providing high standards of health care, education, economic freedom, and overall quality of life. Given the nation's colonial roots, New Zealand's principal values are largely consistent with mainstream British customs, with English serving as the dominant language used throughout New Zealand. Maori is also a recognized language of New Zealand, with around 4 percent of the population able to speak Maori dialect at a conversational level. Maori is a Polynesian language similar to the languages of other Pacific Island cultures, such as Hawaiian, Tongan, and Samoan. In an effort to preserve the Maori dialect, the state funds multiple television stations that are broadcast partly in Maori.

New Zealand's history as well as the nation's geographic location have made for a unique milieu in regards to popular etiquette, religions, and value systems. Indeed these customs have their origins in British, Oceanic, and European backgrounds, as well as the traditional Maori and Polynesian practices inherent to the land. This entry focuses on the dominant European aspects of such cultures and values in New Zealand, with those native to this element of the nation's culture noted as being friendly, outgoing, and hospitable. The dominant greeting method within the nation is that of a handshake, as is the case in most Western cultures. The influence of Western culture extends to modern fashion and appearance also, with dominant European dress and style prevalent among the nation. Typically Maori dress is also very much in line with mainstream New Zealand society; however, Maori jewelry is still prominent throughout all sectors of society, as is traditional Maori dress during important social occasions.

When it comes to cuisine New Zealand's most popular dishes are very multicultural, with a particular European influence present. As such table manners are very Continental, with European dining customs such as holding one's fork in the left hand and knife in the right while eating. Similarly, one would typically indicate they have finished their meal by placing their eating utensils together in a parallel position on the center of their plate. When it comes to dining out, there is an emerging café culture in New Zealand, with such spaces commonly used for socialization among friends and family, as well as business meetings. Along with this café culture, trendy eateries and fine dining restaurants reflective of the nation's affinity with good food and fresh produce are also prevalent throughout both the north and south islands.

Smoking tobacco in New Zealand is highly regulated in public spaces, with the country among the first in the world to make all indoor workplaces smoke free during the early 2000s. To break this code would be considered very taboo. Interestingly, the first building in the world to have a smoke-free policy was the Old Government Building in Wellington (the nation's capital) in 1876.

New Zealand etiquette has evolved from the nation's unique backdrop of native and European influence, as well as the resultantly developed behavioral customs such a context has fostered. Ultimately, as within any Western nation, good manners revolve around a politeness, ethics of reciprocity, tolerance, and equality in all social encounters. New Zealand is noted as placing a strong emphasis on basic Western courtesies, with phrases like "Please" and "Thank you" highly encouraged in day-to-day interactions. From time to time people may be heard swearing in public, but most New Zealanders view this as offensive, and such language is considered highly taboo throughout society. Such etiquette carries over to electronic communication, with these basic social norms also applying when using the Internet and cellular phones to communicate, as is the case in most Western societies.

Ashley Humphrey

Further Reading

Butler, Sue. *Culture Smart! New Zealand: The Essential Guide to Customs & Culture*. London: Kuperard, 2010.

King, Michael. *Penguin History of New Zealand*. Auckland: Penguin, 2004.

Kwintessentials. "New Zealand—Culture, Etiquette and Customs." http://www.kwintessential.co.uk/resources/global-etiquette/new-zealand.html. Accessed December 2015.

New Zealand Trade and Enterprise. "Culture and Etiquette." https://www.nzte.govt.nz/en/export/international-marketing-and-communication-toolkit/culture-and-etiquette/. Accessed December 2015.

NIGERIA

Nigeria is a West African country bordered by Benin, Chad, Niger, and Cameroon and with a coastline on the Gulf of Guinea. The population of Nigeria numbers around 184 million people, making Nigeria the most populous country in Africa and the seventh-most populous nation on Earth. Nigeria's population consists of over 250 ethnic groups including the Hausa-Fulani, Yoruba, Igbo (or Ibo), Ijaw, Kanuri, Ibibio, and Tiv peoples. The tribes with the largest populations are the Yoruba, Igbo, and Hausa-Fulani. Nigeria's ethnic mix means that over 500 languages are spoken in Nigeria, though English is the country's official language—English was chosen because the British colonized Nigeria during the nineteenth century.

In Nigeria, greetings tend to be warm and welcoming. Many Nigerians greet each other by shaking hands while smiling, though Muslim Nigerians may not shake hands with someone of the opposite sex. Handshakes are also used at fare-wells. It is important not to use the left hand during a handshake, as the left hand can be regarded as impure by some Nigerians, as it is associated with bodily functions and personal hygiene.

Nigerian introductions tend to be meandering and lengthy, with inquiries made as to a person's health and family. Failing to ask about such things is thought very rude. Most greetings are spoken in English with a "Hello" or "You are welcome" sufficient for informal greetings. A nod of acknowledgement is also an acceptable informal greeting. "Good morning," "Good afternoon," and "Good evening" are used in more formal situations. It is essential in Nigeria to employ the correct form of address—Nigerians address individuals by their academic, professional, or honorific titles followed by their surname. Using an incorrect greeting or wrong form of address can be seen as a sign of disrespect, and it is not acceptable to use first names in a business situation unless one has been invited to do so. When greeting people it is important to try to greet every person in a group individually, starting with the most senior (in age or status). Older people are respected because in a country with an average life expectancy that is fairly low, people who live into old age are considered to have earned respect. This admiration is true for both men and women.

In general, Nigerians dress conservatively. Women cover their arms and legs and some also cover their heads. Nigerian women tend to only wear shorts when participating in sport, though pants are being seen increasingly. Clinging and revealing clothes for women are frowned upon. Men often wear fairly casual clothes such as trousers with a short- or long-sleeved shirt. For business meetings people either wear formal suits or national dress. Just as there are many varied ethnic groups in Nigeria, so too are there many forms of traditional national dress that hark back to both Nigeria's ancient history and the colonial influence of the British, Portuguese, and French who colonized Nigeria during the nineteenth and twentieth centuries.

Though today many Nigerians wear modern, Western-style clothes, even more Nigerians sport some type of traditional, national clothing. For instance, the Yoruba wear very bright clothes, especially to special events such as weddings and funerals. Some people consider the Yoruba national dress to be the traditional dress of Nigerians in general. Traditional Yoruba garments include the *buba* (a loose, long-sleeved blouse worn by males and females), the *iro* (a long, wrap-over skirt worn swathed around a woman's hips and waist), the *agbada* (a loose robe worn by men on formal occasions), *sokotos* (loose-fitting drawstring trousers worn by men) and a *gele* (the iconic Nigerian cloth headdress worn by women). Igbo women traditionally wear various wraps. Everyday wraps are made from coarse fabrics while wraps for formal occasions are typically made from expensive, imported, highly ornate material. National dress for Igbo men consists of wraps and shirts made from cotton that are worn with sandals. Men belonging to the Hausa-Fulani people traditionally wear a long, wide-sleeved robe called a *babban riga*. This robe is the equivalent of the Yoruba's *agbada*. Hausa-Fulani men also sport a round cap called a *fula*. Hausa-Fulani women wear colorful wraps called *abaya* that they partner with matching blouses.

Some garments such as the *buba*, *iro*, *sokotos*, and *fula* are worn by Yoruba, Igbo, and Hausa-Fulani people as well as other Nigerians across the whole country. Other garments worn by most Nigerians include the *kaba* (a dress), a scarf tied diagonally across the body called an *iborun* or *ipele*, and an *abeti-aja* (a cap worn by men that has longer sides than a *fula*). In general Nigerian national dress is brightly colored and often features tie-dye patterns.

Nigerians usually eat with their right hands (never the left, which is considered dirty), and finger bowls are usually provided to enable people to wash their hands after eating. If finger bowls are present on a table, then it is a sign that a guest should expect to eat with his hands rather than with utensils. Although one must not eat with the left hand when dining in Nigeria, if given eating utensils they may be held in both hands. Also bear in mind that in Muslim homes males will normally eat separately from females.

If invited to dinner at a Nigerian's home, a person should bring a gift such as chocolates, fruit, or nuts to give to the host as a sign of gratitude. It is never okay in Nigeria to give or accept a gift with the left hand. When eating out in Nigeria, tipping is considered optional. The usual tipping rate is 5 percent. Another important thing to note about eating out in Nigeria is that restaurants rarely have washrooms. While big hotels or high-end eateries may have communal bathrooms, most restaurants do not have any such facilities. White foreigners (often referred to as *obiyo* by Nigerians) will usually be able to ask to use some form of bathroom, but if there is a facility, it will be extremely basic and might not be stocked with toilet paper.

Body language in Nigeria reflects the nation's belief in a hierarchical society. Thus it is necessary to show deference to elders and people of superior status. Respect is indicated either by bowing or lowering one's eyes. During a conversation or meeting, one should use facial expressions to indicate respect, pleasure, understanding, and concentration. Anyone who keeps their facial expression neutral might be considered rude and unlikable.

Nigerians typically do not pay attention to the concept of personal space, meaning Nigerians tend to stand very close together when talking or queuing. Though Westerners may find this lack of personal space unnerving, it is important not to push people away or request that they stand further back. Similarly, some Westerners feel disconcerted when Nigerians look into their eyes when speaking to them. However, many Nigerians living in major cities such as Abuja and Lagos tend not to make direct eye contact when in conversation, leading to accusations that they are not telling the truth or are acting shadily. In this case the Nigerian is merely showing a person respect by not staring. Also many Nigerians consider direct eye contact indicative of arrogance.

Major taboos in Nigeria concern body language. It is never acceptable to give or take gifts with the left hand or to present a business card with this hand. The so-called thumbs-up gesture that in the West indicates approval is considered a highly offensive gesture in Nigeria. Taboo topics of conversation include homosexuality and transvestism, which are both prosecutable offences in Nigeria. It is also not acceptable to use slang or to swear. Additionally, since Nigeria is such a religiously

Two men talk to each other in Lagos, Nigeria. During conversation Nigerians may employ facial expressions to indicate admiration, pleasure, comprehension, and satisfaction. (Fridah /iStockphoto.com)

diverse nation, it is best to avoid discussing religion—in particular one should not make generalizations about religions because these may touch upon sensitive issues.

In addition, although a visitor may overhear a Nigerian complaining about their country, it is never acceptable for a foreigner to do so. A visitor should remain polite and respectful when discussing Nigeria. Similarly it is also frowned upon for a foreigner to wear Nigerian traditional clothing. Nigerians are immensely proud of their traditional clothes and do not like it when visitors dress in it.

Victoria Williams

Further Reading

"Dress and Social Etiquette." http://www.abujacity.com/abuja_and_beyond/dress-and -social-etiquette.html. Accessed January 7, 2017.

Marot, Christine. "Learn More about Nigerian Etiquette." *Welcome South Africa: News.* April 27, 2015. http://welcome.southafrica.net/news/entry/learn-more-about-nigerian -etiquette. Accessed January 7, 2017.

"National Dress of Nigeria. Colorful Clothing of Nigerian Tribes." March 2, 2015. http:// nationalclothing.org/25-nationalclothing/africa/nigeria/27-national-dress-of-nigeria -colorful-clothing-of-nigerian-tribes.html. Accessed January 7, 2017.

Williams, Lizzie. *Nigeria*, 3rd ed. Chalfont St Peter, UK: Brandt Travel Guides, 2012.

P

PACIFIC ISLANDERS

The stretch of planet Earth between Asia and North and South America is dominated by the Pacific Ocean. Land is an afterthought; still, more than 25,000 islands dot the world's largest ocean. The islands range in size from New Guinea (178,000 square miles) to Micronesian coral atolls of less than 0.2 square miles. Cultural anthropologists refer to this area as Oceania, or the Pacific Islands, and it is home to widely different cultural groups and more than 1,500 distinct languages. The Pacific Islands are subdivided into three distinct culture areas: Polynesia, Micronesia, and Melanesia, each with its own broad cultural and linguistic similarities. Altogether, the region encompasses the most culturally and linguistically diverse area on Earth.

The first humans entered this region more than 35,000 years ago, and the last major migrations arrived about 3,500 years ago. Taking into account the pronounced cultural diversity of this region, its settlement history, and the vastness of its size, one would not expect to find many beliefs or customs common throughout. However, certain similarities are found throughout much of this region as they pertain to customs associated directly with belief systems.

The belief that spirits protect the living is common to most Pacific Island cultures, but it also is believed these same spirits will punish those who fail to follow customs and honor traditional prohibitions. In Western society, we consider "etiquette" as defining the rules of behavior considered correct or proper in social life. Generally, rules of etiquette pertaining to daily social interaction are not embedded into Western belief systems. In contrast, in most Pacific Island cultures, rules of etiquette and customs cannot be separated from the relevant belief system. In Western society a person who acts contrary to proper etiquette will likely be ridiculed, shunned, or perhaps punished. In Pacific Island cultures, it is believed that the individual acting contrary to custom or traditional behavior will face the anger of the offended spirit or ancestral ghost. In other words, breaking a custom or form of etiquette is not seen as "bad manners" in Pacific Island societies; it is seen as sacrilegious.

Proper behavior among many Pacific Island cultures is rooted into a belief system that categorizes the world into things that are sacred (pure) or profane (polluted). In order to establish this sacred/profane binary, the object, which can be any living organism or an inorganic object, must be compared to another. For example, a particular food might be considered sacred to certain members of a society while being viewed as profane to others in the same society. Thus, proper etiquette related to this particular food would vary, depending on the members of the same society who come into contact with it.

The Polynesian term *mana* captures this phenomenon. *Mana* has proven to be a difficult term to describe in English. It is something of a metaphysical concept whereby a person or thing can have spiritual empowerment. Something or someone can have a lot of *mana* or a little *mana*, which then determines the protocols for proper behavior. Even though the word *mana* is Polynesian, similar beliefs in this kind of spiritual empowerment also are found throughout Melanesia and Micronesia.

Traditional Polynesian society employed a highly stratified and ranked social system. At the top of the system were the paramount chiefs (*ali'i*); at the bottom were common people (*maka' ainana*). In relation to one another, the high chiefs had an abundance of *mana*, whereas the commoners had little to none. *Mana* laid the foundation for how the commoners had to behave when interacting with the chiefs. It also demanded certain forms of behavior from the chiefs when dealing with commoners. Such proscribed behavior was referred to as *kapu* or *tapu* (forbidden). In essence, *tapus* are prohibitions found in daily social interaction. Breaking a *tapu* is not considered an immoral act. Rather, it is an act that is contrary to the proper way to live. The Polynesian word *tapu* made its ways into the English language as *taboo*. In Western society, etiquette and taboo go hand-in-glove during the socialization process.

In Polynesian cultures, a person, place, or thing could be designated as *tapu* to certain members of the society. For example, under punishment with death, it was *tapu* for a commoner to step on the shadow of a high chief. All those in the presence of a high chief had to kneel since they could not be in a position that was equal to or higher than the chief.

Tapus were closely connected to foods and eating behaviors. In ancient Hawaii, men and women (even women of highest rank) were forbidden to eat together. Separate cooking vessels were used for each gender. While a man was consuming a meal, it was *tapu* for a woman to approach him. Menstruating women had a number of *tapus* placed upon them, since menstrual blood was believed to harm or lessen *mana*. The *mana–tapu* system in Polynesian society functioned to regulate daily activities and maintain order. By not observing the required etiquette in any given activity resulted in punishment by a spirit, god, or high chief.

The island of Yap, Micronesia, lies approximately 4,000 miles to the east of Polynesia. Despite the extreme distance and independent cultural development, the Yapese concepts of *tabugul* (pure or sacred) and *mathangeluwol* (forbidden) are quite similar to those described above for Polynesia. The opposite of *tabugul* (pure) in Yap is *ta'ay* (polluted). People, food, objects, and land are considered pure or polluted in the context of rank and social status of the individual. A man is considered pure when compared to his wife who is polluted. However, a high-ranking woman is considered pure when compared to a low-ranking man. A high-ranking man is allowed to walk across land that is considered pure, yet a low-ranking man is forbidden to cross such land. The *tabugul–ta'ay* system in Yap determines daily etiquette and social behavior in ways similar to the Polynesian *mana–tapu* system.

High-ranked Yapese chiefs enjoy more rights and privileges than the lowest ranked Yapese. It is forbidden for a low-ranked Yapese to touch a chief since it would diminish the sacredness of the chief. Chiefs could pass food down to a woman or a low-ranked man, but the reverse was forbidden. Just as in Polynesia, men and women could never eat together, and food for a husband and wife needed to be cooked in separate pots. The traditional Yapese house was divided into pure and polluted sections, reinforcing the mandatory observation of etiquette by all who entered, further refined by age, rank, and sex. In Yap, the ocean is seen as pure, while the land is seen as polluting. When a man planned to go to sea, it was necessary for him to behave in certain ways to lessen his own polluting aspects before entering the pure world of the sea. For example, he could not have sexual intercourse for several days before going to sea. When a man returned from the sea, he underwent a ritual cleansing process prior to returning home. Breaking any of these forbidden ways would result in punishment by the spirits or ancestral ghosts.

The polluting aspects of menstrual blood, a commonly held belief throughout the Pacific Islands, play a central role in defining day-to-day Yapese activities. Within the pure–polluted belief system, the Yapese consider nothing to be more polluting than menstrual blood. Each village in Yap has a menstrual hut where a menstruating woman is required to go during her menses. Subsequent to their first menses, teenage girls are subject to constraints including forbidden foods, forbidden social interaction with their brothers, separate living and eating quarters, and restrictions for entering the sea, touching objects that belonged to their father or brother, and walking onto forbidden land.

Similar to the restrictions a high chief had to follow in Hawaii because of the great amount of *mana* he possessed, Yapese individuals who were considered to be on the high end of the *tabugul* range faced daily limits too. The more pure a high-ranking Yapese was thought to be, the more caution he had to take ensuring that his pureness was not diminished by coming into contact with people, places, or things considered to be polluting. High-ranked Yapese could not eat certain foods, could not be close to a menstruating woman, and could not come into physical contact with a low-ranked person. The Yapese who were considered "specialists," such as sorcerers, magicians, healers, navigators, and highly valued craftsmen, were required to live a pure or sacred life. These specializations required close contact with the spirits, and those in contact with the spirits must remain pure.

Melanesia, the third region of the Pacific Islands, is likely the most diverse cultural area on Earth. At least 1,000 languages are found in Melanesia. Consequently, making any generalizations about customs and forms of etiquette common to the entire region is a daunting task. Nevertheless, taboos associated with menstrual blood are virtually universal among Melanesian societies. Most Melanesian villages have menstrual huts where menstruating women are required to go. Menstrual blood and food cannot come into contact. As a result, women must always take care to ensure they are not in a polluting state before entering a garden, cooking food for husbands, touching any vessels associated with the preparation of food, or having sexual intercourse. Even when not menstruating, women's daily lives were subject to restrictions. In some Melanesian societies, a woman was never allowed to touch her husband's bow, eat certain foods, or enter a men's house. Men were forbidden to have sex before embarking on an important journey or beginning significant tasks. A man could not enter the dwelling where his wife was giving birth for at least five days afterward—birth was considered a polluting event. In other words, both men and women were responsible for adhering on a daily basis to the social etiquette required by their specific belief system.

Why so many restrictions associated with menstrual blood? The people who lived in Melanesia, Micronesia, and Polynesia perceived menstrual blood as behaving contrary to what they understood about blood. Blood came from a cut, which was visible, as a result of an injury. Menstrual blood did not. Since menstrual blood appeared to be outside of the natural order of things, it was considered to be impure and polluting. This belief, common to Pacific Island societies, resulted in myriad examples of prohibitions on menstrual blood and menstruating women.

Most restrictions associated with daily life among Pacific Island peoples were connected to rite-of-passage ceremonies. When an individual went through such a ceremony or state of being, he or she was transitioning from one status or role in life to another, as in unmarried to married, life to death, unborn to born, and pre-menses to menses. Such transitions were out of harmony with the prior state; thus, the individual had to exercise caution until harmony was reestablished. In order to restore harmony and balance, behaviors and norms were observed and enforced by the spirts and ghosts who oversaw the traditional ways. Why were some social acts of behavior considered proper while others were considered improper? In Oceania, such violations were not seen simply as "bad manners." Rather, the violation was considered to be an offense against the very way of life of the people.

Richard A. Marksbury

Further Reading

Akin, David M. "Concealment, Confession, and Innovation in Kwaio Women's Taboo." *American Ethnologist* 30, no. 3 (2003): 381–400.

Beckforth, Martha. *Hawaiian Mythology.* Honolulu: University of Hawaii Press, 1976.

Fischer, John L., and Ann M. Fischer. *The Eastern Carolines.* New Haven, CT: Human Relations Area Files, 1970.

McDowell, Nancy. "The Significance of Cultural Context: A Note on Food Taboos in Bun." *Journal of Anthropological Research* 35, no. 2 (1979): 231–37.

Oliver, Douglas. *Native Cultures of the Pacific Islands.* Honolulu: University of Hawaii Press, 1989.

Roosman, Raden S. "Coconut, Breadfruit, and Taro in Pacific Oral Literature." *Journal of the Polynesian Society* 79, no. 2 (1970): 219–30.

PAKISTAN

Pakistan is a federal parliamentary republic located in South Asia. It is the sixth-most populous country in the world with a population of around 200 million people. Pakistan is bordered by India, Afghanistan, Iran, and China, with coastlines on the Arabian Sea and the Gulf of Oman. Pakistan is separated from Tajikistan by the Wakhan Corridor (a narrow strip of land in northeastern Afghanistan that reaches into China). Pakistan is an overwhelmingly Islamic country with 97 percent of the population being Muslim (77 percent Sunni, 20 percent Shiite). The rest of Pakistan's population are Christian, Hindu, or Sikh, or belong to another religious minority. Many languages are spoken in Pakistan (including Punjabi, Pashtu, and Guajrati) but Urdu is the only official language of Pakistan. Nevertheless English is the language used by both the Pakistani elite and the country's government. Pakistani society is inherently hierarchical and patriarchal with people given respect due to age and position. Older people are granted respect automatically and are deemed wise. For this reason elders and people in senior positions are expected to make decisions for groups.

Pakistani etiquette is influenced by Islamic and South Asian modes of behavior as well as the country's British colonial history. In Pakistan, etiquette also reflects the fact that Pakistani society is both patriarchal and hierarchical. Etiquette varies in Pakistan depending on location, as rural areas tend to uphold traditional feudal and patriarchal values more so than urban areas that are populated by the middle classes and immigrants.

The standard greeting said during both informal and formal introductions at any time of night or day is "Us-salam-o-alaikum," which translates as "Peace be upon you." When a younger person meets an older person, the younger person is expected to initiate the greeting, as older people are always greeted first in Pakistan. "Us-salam-o-alaikum" may also be used to bid someone farewell, though more usual ways of saying goodbye include "Allah hafiz" and "Khuda hafiz," both of which mean "May God protect you" or "May God be your guardian."

Titles are a complex element of Pakistani greetings, and they are considered very important as they confer respect. Moreover it is usual to use a person's title followed by their surname until one has been invited to use the person's first name. In fact,

---

Culture Shock! ⊕

Hajj

Hajj, meaning "pilgrimage," is an annual journey to Mecca in Saudi Arabia. The pilgrimage is a mandatory undertaking for all Muslims who are sufficiently financially and physically sound to do so. Performing hajj is the fifth pillar of Islam and the most important demonstration of a person's Islamic faith, with around 2 million Muslims performing hajj annually. Hajj lasts for five days and occurs only from the 9–13 Dhu Al-Hijah, which is the twelfth month of the Islamic lunar calendar. Muslims who undertake hajj do so believing they will be rewarded with entry into Paradise after death. Performing hajj is the religious highlight of any Muslim's life, for the pilgrimage reinforces their understanding of their connection to Allah. By taking part in hajj a Muslim knows that they have followed in the footsteps of the Prophet, and has also acted as part of the united Muslim nation (*ummah*).

Victoria Williams

first names are not normally used except among very close friends. Furthermore it is thought very rude for a younger person to address an older person by their first name. Thus it is important to address a Pakistani correctly. Pakistanis who speak Urdu also use special words to address someone depending on their age and status within an extended family. For example, *mamu* and *momani* are the titles given to an uncle and his wife, *phoopi* and *phoopa* are used to address an aunt and her husband, the soubriquet *chacha* and *chachi* is given to a father's younger brother and his wife, and *dada* and *dadi* are used to address a paternal grandfather and grandmother. In addition, elder brothers are referred to as *bhaijan* while elder sisters are called either *apajan* or *bajijan*. Family names are important in Pakistan as they often reveal information about people's class, ethnic heritage, job, and status. In general it is best to ask someone how he or she would like to be addressed.

In Pakistan introductions usually take place between people of the same sex, though middle-class people tend to tolerate mixed-sex greetings, meaning that a man may greet a woman and vice versa. In general, however, it is not acceptable for men and women to touch. If a woman enters into physical contact with a man she will most likely be considered to have displayed wantonness and to have shamed her family. Similarly, married Pakistani couples tend not to demonstrate affection in public, as doing so is considered immoral. When two men greet each other they will typically shake hands, but if they become close friends they may hug each other as well as shaking hands. Women tend to greet each other by hugging and kissing. In the most conservative Pakistani communities segregation of the sexes (purdah) may be observed. Purdah means that from the age of eight years a girl may not show her face in public and must live behind a curtain or veil. The only people allowed to see a female living in purdah are her female relatives, close male relatives, and her husband. If the female does venture outside of her home, then she is required to wear a burqa.

Introductions can take quite a long time to complete in Pakistan, as Pakistanis tend to pepper their introductions with conversation regarding health, work, and family. In business situations in particular it may be necessary to use third-party introductions, as Pakistanis prefer to do business with people they trust. Once introductions have been made in a business situation, business cards are normally exchanged. These cards should mention all professional honors and advanced university achievements, because in Pakistan great significance is placed upon educational qualifications and they are seen as status symbols. When exchanging business cards it is important to present the cards using only the right hand or using both hands together.

In Pakistan most people dress conservatively and modestly. Despite Pakistan's warm climate, people, especially women, do not reveal much skin. Most people (males and females) wear a traditional *shalwar kameez* that consists of a *shalwar* (loose trousers) and a *kameez* (long shirt). The *shalwar kameez* worn by females are usually brightly colored and decorated with embroidery and sequins, while the *shalwar kameez* worn by males tend to be white or gray in color. In urban areas some people (particularly younger people) may wear Western-style clothing such as jeans and a top. A number of Pakistani men wear a hat or turban though the exact style depends on where in Pakistan the man lives. Pakistani women wear a wide scarf called a *dupatta*, with which they cover their hair and shoulders in order to preserve their modesty. It is sometimes thought that it is customary to remove one's shoes when entering a Pakistani's home. However, this is not necessarily the case as removing shoes is a Hindu or Arab custom that is becoming prevalent in Pakistan and in Pakistani immigrant households worldwide. It is, however, essential to remove shoes when entering a mosque in Pakistan.

Pakistan has a long tradition of providing hospitality to guests. If someone visits a Pakistani's home during lunch or dinnertime, it is expected that the visitor will be given a full meal that includes all the best food available to the household. If a guest arrives at some other time then they should be given tea, fresh fruit, and snacks. The etiquette of food sharing is ingrained in Pakistani society to the extent that not having something to offer a guest is considered a source of huge embarrassment, while keeping a food item to oneself and not sharing it with others is thought the height of bad manners. It is very usual for a guest to be invited to stay in the host's home overnight with children taught to give up their bedrooms to guests. Most middle-class Pakistani households keep extra bed linen in case a guest should wish to stay over. It is considered an insult to both the host and the guest if a visitor from out of town has to stay in a hotel.

Pakistanis tend to take a relaxed attitude to time, especially with regards to social events. In Pakistan it is normal to arrive about 15 minutes late to a dinner or small social event, while it is usual to arrive an hour late to a party. When one arrives it is important to greet elders first. Similarly one should not start eating until the eldest people present start to eat. Guests, however, are served their food first with the oldest guest served first and the youngest guest served last. In cities and among Westernized families, some people eat using utensils with the fork held in the left hand and used to push food onto the spoon that is held in the right hand. However, most Pakistanis, especially those living in rural areas, eat with their right hands. It is also common for Pakistani people to eat their food from knee-high tables while sitting on the floor. Guests are often encouraged to take second and even third helpings of food—telling a host that one has eaten enough is considered merely a polite gesture and is not believed.

If a visitor is invited to a Pakistani home, it is customary to give a small present such as flowers or chocolates to the hostess. Men should not give flowers to a hostess, however, and the flowers should not be white in color as white flowers are associated with weddings. If a man does give a gift to the hostess, then he must say that the gift comes from another female such as his wife, or a female relative. It is best not to give alcohol as a gift in Pakistan as alcohol is technically banned for Muslims, even though the ban is not enforced stringently. Pakistanis belonging to other religions have to apply for alcohol permits. The guest must present any gift using both hands. Gift-giving in general is looked on favorably in Pakistan with gifts given to mark birthdays, weddings, births, graduations, engagements, the return from hajj (pilgrimage to Mecca), and other celebratory occasions.

When in conversation Pakistanis typically stand very close together and may encroach on what a Westerner feels is their own personal space. It is considered rude to back away from someone when they stand what seems to be too close. Pakistanis are indirect communicators and employ indirect eye contact. Similarly, many Pakistanis speak in a meandering way and prefer to be asked questions to which they can give vague replies. Indeed, a Pakistani might only speak in a direct way to someone with whom they have a lengthy personal relationship. Many Pakistanis also employ much hyperbole and tend to flatter people and things in what may seem (to a Westerner) an over-the-top manner. The compliments given by Pakistanis are not, however, direct, as direct compliments are perceived as insincere. Instead, any compliment is usually accompanied by a phrase such as "Masha Allah," meaning "By the grace of God." When returning a compliment it is important to do so indirectly.

Because verbal communication is often indirect, a Pakistani may not say "Please" or "Thank you" but rather they will express their gratitude through conducting themselves in a humble manner or way of speaking. Indeed there is no single word in Urdu for "please." Instead Urdu contains verbs meaning "please come" (*aeeyay*), "please go" (*jaeeyay*), and "please do" (*kijiyay*). Business meetings are usually conducted in English, though if emotions become roused then Pakistanis may revert to speaking Urdu. Taboo topics of conversation in Pakistan include sex, childbirth, and pregnancy—this in line with the Pakistani preference for modesty. Swearing (particularly in front of elders) is also taboo. Taboo actions include eating pork and wearing revealing clothes. Areas that were once considered taboo, such as divorce and discussing mental illness, are increasingly not taboo.

The Pakistani preference for building personal relationships with the people with whom they do business means they prefer to do business in person. Consequently Pakistanis view the telephone as too impersonal a tool to use in business communication and instead attend business meetings. These should be arranged around a month in advance and scheduled for the late morning or afternoon. It is also a good idea not to schedule meetings to take place during the Islamic holy month of Ramadan. This is because during this period workdays in Pakistan are shortened and a Muslim host would be required to fast and so would not be able to offer tea as a sign of hospitality to their guest.

Respect for elders is a universally important aspect of Pakistani etiquette. Treating elders with reverence extends to all areas of Pakistani life from seeking parental approval for marriages to giving up seats for older people on public transport. Children are taught from a very early age to defer to older people in all things, and it is considered extremely impolite for a child to disobey or argue with elders.

Victoria Williams

Further Reading

Bedell, Jane M. *Teens in Pakistan*. Mankato, MN: Compass Point Books, 2009.
Commisceo Global Consultancy. "Pakistan Guide." 2016. http://www.commisceo-global .com/country-guides/pakistan-guide. Accessed January 7, 2017.

Kamal, Rabia. "Pakistani Americans: Social Etiquette and Customs," in Jonathan H. X. Lee
    and Kathleen M. Nadeau, eds., *Encyclopedia of Asian American Folklore and Folklife*, vol. 3,
    991–92. Santa Barbara, CA: ABC-CLIO, 2011.
Mohiuddin, Yasmeen Niaz. *Pakistan: A Global Studies Handbook*. Santa Barbara, CA: ABC-
    CLIO, 2007.

PALESTINE

Palestine is a de facto sovereign state located in the West Bank and Gaza areas of
the Middle East bordering Israel, Jordan, and Egypt. The people living in Palestine
are mainly Muslim though there is also a significant number of Christian Palestinians. Palestinian etiquette and customs are very similar to that in the rest of the
Arab world, especially the other nearby countries of Israel, Lebanon, Jordan, and
Syria. Traditional modes of Palestinian behavior are also enacted by Palestinians
who have migrated abroad.

Palestinians are typically taught from childhood to be polite and to respect their
elders. When Palestinians meet each other they will normally shake hands or greet
each other with kisses. The Palestinian kiss greeting sees a Palestinian kiss someone on the cheeks three times by alternating between the two cheeks starting with
the right cheek. Alternatively, a Palestinian may perform two rapid kisses to each
cheek followed by a third long kiss to the first cheek. Both Palestinian men and
women perform kiss greetings.

Palestinians are Arabic speakers. When Palestinians greet each other they
may say "Marhaba" or "Ahlan" (Hello), to which one replies "Marhabtayn" or "Ahl-
ayn." Other greetings include "As-salam alaykum" (Peace be with you), to which
the standard reply is "Wa 'alaykum as salam" (And to you peace). When bidding
farewell it is usual for Palestinians to say "Ma'assalama." This translates as "Go with
peace" but is the Palestinian equivalent to "Goodbye."

Palestinians are well known for their hospitality. Neighbors usually become
friends with each other because Palestinians often live in one place all their lives,
meaning neighbors build lifelong friendships. Palestinians are very generous when
it comes to hospitality, with even very low-income families living in villages or
refugee camps more than willing to offer food and drink to strangers. It is common
for Palestinians to invite strangers into their homes and shops by saying "Tfaddaloo." This is the Arabic word for "Please," as in please come in and be welcome. A
Palestinian will often say "Tfaddaloo" repeatedly until the offer is taken up, though
after the offer is declined for a third time the would-be host will usually stop
asking. If one wishes to accept the offer one should say "Ahlan wa sahlan" in answer to "Tfaddaloo" as this is the Arabic for welcome. After this the guest may be
offered tea or coffee to drink. The coffee served in Palestine is Arabic coffee flavored with cardamom. Palestinians normally drink their coffee *saada* (unsweetened) but when making it for non-Palestinians they will usually add a little sugar.
In contrast, the tea drunk by Palestinians is extremely sweet. When given a drink,
a guest should thank the host by saying "Shukran" (Thank you) to which the host
may answer "Afwan" (You are welcome). When talking, Palestinians tend to stand

much closer together than Westerners do—so close in fact that strangers may touch when talking.

Palestinian society is considered very conservative by Western standards. Romantic social interactions are not permitted traditionally in Palestine, with the concept of dating being a fairly alien concept to Palestinians. Instead, if a Palestinian man and woman like each other, it is traditional for the man to declare his intentions to the woman's relatives. Social dating does not take place in Palestine, as any courting must occur only with the aim of leading to marriage. Though attitudes to dating are slowly coming round to the idea, dating is still not the social norm.

Foreign visitors to Palestine during the late nineteenth and early twentieth centuries often noted the diverse costumes worn by Palestinians. Up until the 1940s, a woman's economic and marital status and where she lived was easily determined by what the woman wore and how her clothes were decorated (if at all). Today, traditional Palestinian dress is worn alongside Islamic garments and Western fashions. The black and white checked kaffiyeh (or keffiyeh) is a gender-neutral headwrap that is nonetheless usually worn by men, and is sometimes associated with Palestinian political resistance. Women's traditional dresses are colorful, and while worn on a daily basis by some village women, are also made for weddings and other special occasions. Some of the most commonly worn Palestinian clothes include a *thob* (a loose robe with sleeves), a *qabbeh* (the square, ornate chest panel of the *thob*, which is often handed down from mother to daughter), *libas* or *shirwal* (trousers), a *jubbeh* (a jacket worn by both men and women), and a *shambar* (a large veil worn by women in Hebron and southern Palestine).

The women in each region of Palestine traditionally have their own distinctive style of headdresses that are usually embellished with gold or silver coins taken from their bride price money. In this case the more coins a headdress displays, the greater the wealth and status of the woman who wears it. One type of traditional Palestinian headdress is the *sha'weh*. This is a unique conical hat worn by married women living in Bethlehem, Lifta, and Ain Karm in the District of Jerusalem, as well as in Beit Jala and Beit Sahur in Bethlehem District. Another distinctive headdress is the embroidered cap, the *smadeh*, which is worn by women living in Ramallah. This has a row of coins attached to its brim that represents the wearer's wealth, and can act as a source of cash in emergencies. In Hebron both men and women wear an *araqiyyeh*, a small, close-fitting cotton cap. Originally this cap was intended to catch sweat, with the cap's name deriving from the Arabic word for sweat (*araq*). Nowadays when worn by a woman an *araqiyyeh* will have coins around its brim that signify the woman's bridal money.

Foods traditionally eaten in Palestine include falafel (fried patties made from chickpeas or fava beans), *hummus* (chickpea spread/dip), tabbouleh (bulgur wheat and vegetable salad), stuffed vine leaves, and the lentil and rice dish *mjaddarah*. Palestinians enjoy these foods as they are nutritious, economical, and tasty. Some Palestinians have Bedouin heritage and eat dishes such as *mansaf*, which consists of *shraq* (layers of very thin bread) that are covered with rice, chunks of lamb or goat, goats' milk yogurt, pine nuts, and almonds. This dish is served on large platters from which people help themselves to by taking the food and rolling it with their right hand. After most Palestinian dinners, tea or coffee will be served. The coffee will be served in very small cups, while tea will be flavored with mint or a type of sage called wild *miramiya*.

Victoria Williams

Further Reading

Advameg. "Palestinians." *Countries and Their Cultures*. 2017. http://www.everyculture.com /wc/Germany-to-Jamaica/Palestinians.html. Accessed January 10, 2017.

Farsoun, Samih K. *Culture and Customs of the Palestinians*. Westport, CT: Greenwood Press, 2004.

Miri. "The ABC of Palestinian Hospitality." *Green Olive Collective*. 2007–2014. http://blog .toursinenglish.com/2012/02/palestinian-hospitality.html. Accessed January 10, 2017.

Shomali, Majdi. "Land, Heritage and Identity of the Palestinian People." *Palestine-Israel Journal* 8, no. 4 (2001) and 9, no. 1 (2002). http://www.pij.org/details.php?id=804. Accessed January 10, 2017.

Travel Palestine. "Traditional Costumes." *Travel Palestine*. http://travelpalestine.ps/about /culture-heritage/traditional-costumes/. Accessed January 10, 2017.

PAPUA NEW GUINEA

Papua New Guinea is a Pacific Island nation of continuous change, with the majority of its 7 million residents living in rural, sparsely populated regions. The country gained independence from Australia in 1975 and has a diverse population with over 800 tribal languages, most of which continue to be spoken today. Despite Western influences in areas such as education, religion, economics, technology, and medicine, most Papua New Guineans continue to maintain traditional ways of living. They incorporate their traditional values with new forms of information and technology that are suitable to their collective needs. Residents are members of various Christian religions, with children attending schools where they are taught by Western missionaries. Men and women play soccer or rugby, and people participate in string bands and play other types of music. At local markets in bigger cities, women sell food and handcrafted items, like the *bilum* string bag. Most Papua New Guineans are no strangers to mobile and Internet technology and regularly communicate with people nationally and internationally. Violence remains high in both urban and rural communities and includes gang activity, intertribal warfare, and incidents of sexual and domestic abuse.

Both Papua New Guinean men and women are generally friendly and will engage with newcomers, often hugging friends and colleagues and other visitors whom they meet. Usually, individuals do not call family members by their given names, but will refer to the individual as *mama*, *papa*, *sister*, or *brother*, depending on the relationship to the person with whom they speak. Using the term for "mother" (*mama*) might refer to a person's actual biological mother, or any of her sisters, and the same goes for the father (*papa*) and his brothers. Using the *tok pison* (pidgin language) term *wantok* refers to any individual who identifies as Papua New Guinean, speaks the same language, is a neighbor or friend, or who has something in common with the speaker. Gift-giving and reciprocity among Papua New Guineans occurs regularly and often. Gifts should be given discreetly and if given a gift, the person receiving the gift should respond similarly in a timely manner. To forget to reciprocate a gift would be considered rude.

Papua New Guineans typically dress in both traditional and Western clothing. In everyday life, they usually wear Western clothing, especially in the more populated areas. For women, this usually includes oversized dresses and loose-fitting pants and shirts that they purchase from larger cities. Men also wear looser-style clothing such as shorts, T-shirts, and baseball caps. Visitors to Papua New Guinea should wear similar loose-fitting clothing. Traditional dress and clothing is worn during special occasions, such as marriage ceremonies, *singsings*, and cultural festivals. Traditional clothing and costumes may be made from natural fibers and objects such as ink-dyed chicken feathers; colorful parrot, cassowary, or bird of paradise feathers; and orchid leaves. Other native flowers, beads, coral shells, and opossum fur might be sewn into skirts and adorn the body. Men will often paint each other's faces in tribal colors and patterns. The *bilum* string bag is one of the few personal objects that an individual might be seen carrying, containing their most needed possessions. It might be given as a gift, sold at the local market, or used by mothers to carry infants. Traditionally the *bilum* bag is made from bamboo tree bark. Today, however, colorful Western yarn is used to create elaborate patterns and the bags are even sold internationally.

Papua New Guinean culture includes food taboos, gender taboos, and taboos that exist at certain times of the year or during particular events. These taboos vary among communities and may exist during funerals, marriage ceremonies, initiation rites, and other rites of passage. Subjects that are often taboo to discuss in everyday life might be played out publicly during festivals or theater performances, often in a comedic fashion. It is important to note that food taboos exist throughout all communities in Papua New Guinea and differ between tribal groups. Sometimes even neighboring tribes have and maintain different food taboos, so food that is considered taboo in one area might be traded with a community where the same taboo does not exist. The best food often goes to young, unmarried males who have the fewest food taboos. The most food taboos exist for menstruating and pregnant women, but other taboos also exist that depend on marital and gender status. Generally, foods to avoid are those from organisms that live in or burrow in the soil. Menstruating women might not consume bananas and other plantains, fresh meat, and red fruit. In some communities, menstruating women live in huts outside the main community, and if a woman steps over food, it is immediately thought to be contaminated. Taboos on where a person sits to eat might also exist. Male initiation taboos exist, which often see males refrain from eating certain foods that are associated with the female gender. These should be avoided in order to fully participate in the male initiation rites of passage that continue to exist in certain areas, even if they are not publicly discussed. Initiation rites are almost always taboo for outsiders to attend, especially for women and foreigners. Men might refrain from sexual intercourse or fast before hunting or fishing expeditions, depending on the village. Some areas of Papua New Guinea also consider it taboo to eat in public though the eating of betel nuts (a stimulant) is a social activity even in areas where there are strong food taboos about eating in front of others.

With over 800 tribal languages, most people usually speak their tribal language, *tok pison*, and more increasingly, English. *Tok pison* is used on a national level and is spoken in public, government, newspapers, radio, and television. Learning to speak *tok pison* to Papua New Guineans will show an interest in their language and culture. A *singsing* or celebration provides the opportunity for Papua New Guineans to gather, celebrate, sing, and dance for special occasions. A *singsing* often sees members of a village come together to celebrate events like marriage ceremonies, public works and government projects, and other important cultural events that occur both in the village and in the larger cities. Both men and women participate and might march in step as they sing in the village community space. The *singsing* might also include a group of youths gathered together who make up songs that they perform, or they might perform a more traditional form of singing in preparation for a wedding event, such as an all-night *singsing*. Papua New Guineans compose and sing about many different topics, including death, types of animals they are close to or that inhabit their villages, and other natural items. They make up songs as they walk and travel that relate to nature, rivers, and the weather. They sing songs that incorporate traditional values and myths. These songs might be sung during marriage ceremonies, funerals, and cultural festivals and events.

In Papua New Guinea marriages are thought to build relations between individuals, families, villages, and clans. A typical wedding in the highlands region might last up to four days or longer depending on the family and location of the wedding. Often, members of both the bride's and groom's families participate in the wedding events together as a collective, or singularly. Marriage ceremonies might include all-night *singsings*, bride price ceremonies, and numerous *mumus*. *Mumus* are a way to prepare food for a large group of people and often occur during cultural festivities, wedding ceremonies, death ceremonies, and any other time large groups of people gather. Both the bride and the groom will be instructed by elder members of their families on how to be a proper spouse, and they might even be ceremoniously "hit" with bamboo branches.

On the final day of the ceremonies, another large *mumu* will take place and typically begins in the early hours of the morning. The bride and close members of her family will be elaborately decorated wearing traditional headdresses and costumes, made mostly of natural materials, like cassowary feathers and opossum fur, and Western colored beads. The bride price will be displayed on the grounds in which the final marriage ceremony takes place so all members of the bride's family can inspect the gifts. The bride price typically includes large sums of cash (*kina*), foodstuff, dresses and clothing, and objects for the newlyweds' new house. The bride and her family will walk to the groom's land to be received by the groom and his family, in which she will now become a part. There is a food exchange, and the final symbolic symbol that seals the marriage is the receiving and cutting of the sugarcane (this might occur one week after the wedding ceremony to seal the marriage). Often, members of the bride's family will stay with her as she adjusts to living in her new family, with her parents being the last to leave a month or two after the wedding ceremonies. This way the woman slowly gets used to living in her new home.

Due to Western missionary influence, most of the residents in Papua New Guinea are Christian. Syncretism occurs for many Papua New Guineans who choose a Christian religion while at the same time they participate in traditional norms, ideas, and rituals. For many Papuans, however, sorcery is a part of their lives, and it is thought that no mistakes are forgotten. On the Trobriand Islands (an archipelago of coral atolls lying off the east coast of Papua New Guinea) most sorcerers are men, though women may also be thought capable of sorcery. It is believed that sorcery occurs through objects that are passed between people, so it is inherent to be aware of personal items at all times. For most Papua New Guineans, it would be taboo to discuss issues relating to sorcery and witchcraft to outsiders.

For many communities, death halts all activities, sometimes for many months and years. Wailing, particular forms of art and face painting, magic rituals, and other activities all occur after death. Women may carry mementos of the dead to continue their mourning. The dead usually are not buried with objects unless they are a person of importance, but this varies between communities. After death, there might be restrictions for the family and spouse. Family members might have to stay inside their mourning house, eat no "good" food, or even be fed by other family members. Often, mourners may not participate in work of any kind, and for the first few days after a death, a spouse is not allowed to talk, smoke, or chew betel nut. The spouse may also not be permitted to touch food and other close family members might also engage in these restrictions. Names of the deceased are typically not spoken by members of the community, and those who live far away must mourn upon their return to the community.

Katie Englert

Further Reading

Englert, Katie. "SingSings." http://www.anthropologiesproject.org/2012/01/singsings.html. Accessed June 16, 2015.

Hunter, John. *Lonely Planet Papua New Guinea Pidgin Phrasebook*. South Yarra, VIC: Lonely Planet Publications, 1986.

Knauft, Bruce. *The Gebusi—Lives Transformed in a Rainforest World*. New York: McGraw-Hill, 2005.

Logan, Sarah. "Rausim! Digital Politics in Papua New Guinea." Discussion podcast in *State, Society, & Governance in Melanesia Program*, Australian National University. http://asiapacific.anu.edu.au/news-events/podcasts/rausim-digital-politics-papua-new-guinea#.VY2SGu1Viko. Accessed on June 2, 2015.

Meyer-Rochow, Victor B. "Food Taboos: Their Origins and Purposes." *Journal of Ethnobiology and Ethnomedicine* 5, no. 18 (2009). http://www.ncbi.nlm.nih.gov/pmc/articles/PMC2711054/. Accessed June 16, 2015.

Weiner, Annette B. *The Trobrianders of Papua New Guinea, in Case Studies in Cultural Anthropology*. New York: Thomson & Wadsworth, 1988.

PASHTUNS

The Pashtuns (*Pathans*, *Pukhtuns*) with their unique historical, cultural, social, and political background occupy a prominent niche among the peoples of Afghanistan as well as Pakistan. Their traditional loci of habitat constitute the so-called Pashtunistan (Pukhtunistan)—bordering regions between the southeastern parts of Afghanistan and northwestern parts of Pakistan—homeland of the Pashtuns. The number of Pashtuns is estimated at between 40–45 million. In Afghanistan they comprise almost 40 percent of the population and are the major ethnic minority. In Pakistan Pashtuns comprise about 15 percent of the country's population. There are Pashtuns living also in Iran (mainly refugees) and Tajikistan.

The question of Pashtun origins has caused considerable debates, but there is no doubt that Pashto—the mother tongue of all Pashtuns—belongs to the southeastern branch of the Iranian language family. Thus, the core of the Pashtun ethnic unit is undoubtedly of Iranian descent, despite that numerous legends and folk stories based on Pashtun oral tradition ascribe various backgrounds (including legends of Arabic, Jewish, Coptic, Greek, etc., descent) to them. As Russian scholar Gankovskij has noted, the Pashtuns most likely were a "union of largely East-Iranian tribes which became the initial ethnic stratum of the Pashtun ethnogenesis, dating from the middle of the first millennium CE and connected with the dissolution of the Epthalites (White Huns) confederacy."

Pashto language has a number of dialects, but roughly it can be divided into two main dialect branches, the so-called soft—Southern (Qandahari) and hard—Northern (with local varieties of Jalalabad, Peshawar districts, etc.). Pashto is one of the two official state languages in Afghanistan, the second being Dari (a variety of Classical Persian, often called Afghani Persian). The language plays an essential role for the Pashtun identity and alongside the Pashtun behavioral code—a set of ethical rules—is the backbone for what being a Pashtun means.

Pashtuns are predominantly Sunni Muslims of Hanafi *mazhab* (school), although there is also a small number of Shiites of the Twelver Imami branch (the *Torai* subtribe in FATA—Federally Administered Tribal Areas—of Pakistan, and *Bangash* tribe in Khyber Pakhtunkhwa, also in Pakistan). Being a Muslim, particularly a Sunni, is an essential condition for being a real Pashtun. The righteous Pashtun, as every Muslim, has to follow the five pillars of Islam—*shahadah* (the creed of the belief—there is no God but Allah, and Muhammad is Allah's messenger), *salat* (the prayer), *zakat* (almsgiving), *ruzah* (fasting during the holy month of Ramadan), and *hajj* (the pilgrimage to Mecca). It is noteworthy that certain aspects of everyday Pashtun life, especially the rule of *badal* (revenge) according to the code of honor, are in contradiction with Islamic belief, which prohibits the killing of a Muslim unless by mistake. Yet this phenomenon itself stresses the complexity of the Pashtun life. As other Muslims, Pashtuns also celebrate the Eid ul-Fitr or Eid ul-Ramadan (*Qamqai Akhta*) after the end of the fasting during the holy month of Ramadan, as well as Eid ul-Adha, the Islamic New Year. The majority of Pashtuns strictly follow the Islamic principles of hygiene and modest behavior, including chastity until marriage for girls and women, and maintaining halal food practices.

Pashtun women usually wear *chadri*, in more traditional rural areas—a burqa, which covers not only the entire body, but also the face. Men usually wear *shalwar kameez*—a long tunic that reaches the knees over a loose trousers. Occasionally men wear *wasket*—a vest over the tunic. During the cold weather they cover themselves with huge woolen blankets. The headgear is called turban or *lungi*—a long cotton shawl that is usually rolled around the head. *Lungi* are sometimes used also as a supporting tool while sitting a long time on the floor: it is rolled around the waist and tied in front of the knees, thus serving as a leaning facility. Men occasionally wear also a *pawkul*—a traditional cap in the Chitral region of Pakistan (*pawkul* became quite an iconic attribute of the mujahedeen during the Soviet invasion in Afghanistan).

The traditional Pashtun society is based on tribal structure with both a segmentary lineage system and spatial group elements. Although the lion's share of the Pashtuns already prefer the settled lifestyle with sedentary elements to the once-prevailing nomadic and seminomadic way of life, certain features of their behavior go back to the so-called tribalism.

Generally Pashtuns are considered to be very independent, proud, and courageous people with a strict sense of equality and honor. As the Pashtun proverb stresses, "Only the man who follows *Pashtunwali* [the code of honor] can be called a Pashtun." *Pashtunwali* or *Pakhtunwali* (the way of the Pashtuns) is an unwritten code of ethical and behavioral rules. This is something that the Pashtuns consider as a guarantee for their distinctiveness from other ethnic groups. The main aspects of Pashtunwali refer to notions such as *melmastia* (hospitality), *nanawati* (asylum right, as well as mercy upon a person who has violated certain rules), *badal* (blood revenge, retaliation), *ghayrat* (defense of honor and property), and *namus* (defense of women and their honor). The wide spectrum of these rules include also *tureh* (bravery, lit. "sword"), *imandari* (righteousness), the necessity of consultation with senior tribesmen, equality, loyalty to and respect for the elders, and several other virtues.

Melmastia or the principle of hospitality ascribes the role of provider to the host. The guest is accepted to the household formally, but the attitude towards him is rather friendly. The host and his male kin show the utmost respect to the guest, which is firmly connected with the notion of honor.

Nanawati (lit. "going inside") is the right of asylum practiced during feuds not only between remote tribes but also between close kin. When the long-lasting blood revenge reaches an unbearable point, the *nanawati* principle neutralizes further hostility: a neighbor or a relative who is not directly involved in the feud enters the house of one of the fighting parties and announces *nanawati*—reconciliation. For settling the conflict often an exchange of women or girls takes place—a practice that is being gradually banned in the areas where the state legal system operates at full strength.

Badal is perhaps the central point of the Pashtunwali. *Badal* usually is exercised when there is an affair involving a woman, property, or land, i.e., something that is closely related to *nang*—honor. An assault to one's honor should be reciprocated by blood. In minor cases, though, negotiations might resolve the problem and help avoid the *badal*. At the same time *badal* also means compensation and reciprocation, thus being exercised in terms of answering to the support and help when needed. The compensation, also in cases of mistaken revenges, is usually determined by the *Loya Jirga*—a council of tribal chiefs, elders, and respected personalities. *Loya Jirga* is also responsible for decision making regarding any activity in the community on a village level or when an entire tribe is going to be involved.

The virtue *Ghayrat* has several meanings ranging from dignity, bravery, and zealousness to generosity, modesty, and anger. All of these attributes are incorporated in *ghayrat*, and if a person bears them, he approaches the closest to the "ideal Pashtun."

Pashtuns have still preserved the traditional endogamous system within their society, where the most preferable mate for the marriage is the parallel cousin, the father's brother's daughter or father's brother's son for men and women respectively. The Pashtun family, especially in rural areas, is preserved in its traditional extended version—the husband, wife, married sons with their wives and children, unmarried daughters. Women are usually secluded, and it is a matter of great shame (*haram*) for a Pashtun when an outsider tries to get close to his family matters, particularly when showing any interest in female relatives: the family's privacy is crucial for any Pashtun.

Most marriages are arranged, sometimes even in quite earlier age of the husband-to-be boys and wife-to-be girls by their parents. *Wulwar*, the so-called bride price, is paid by the groom's family, which, in fact, is a part of an economic exchange. *Khawkul*, the dowry, fixed in the marriage contract is sometimes equal to the price of the *wulwar*. The special role of the middleman or middle woman is played by the *wasta*, a close kin who negotiates the conditions of the marriage. It is the responsibility of the *wasta* to negotiate the bride price, which among certain Pashtun tribes can be either *kotara* (a fixed bride price, and the marriage is just about finding spouses) or *mosamma* (the bride price is announced by the bride's father, and the marriage is more about affinity) depending on the nature of the marriage. Although the Pashtun folklore is quite rich in love songs and ballads, love affairs between male and female before the marriage are practically taboo.

Childbirth is an important event in the life cycle of any Pashtun, especially when the newborn is a boy. Babies are not named until the third day after birth; by this they avoid being known to the evil spirits (jinn) who might haunt them. Quite a festivity is usually organized when the time of the boy's circumcision arrives. During the early years both boys and girls are cared for by the mothers and the close female relatives in the family.

The death and funeral ceremonies among the Pashtuns are identical to the practices within the milieu of the Islamic tradition. The corpse of a deceased man is washed by his male relatives, accompanied with the proclamation by a mullah: "We come from God, to God we return." A woman's corpse is prepared for the funeral in the same way, though after the funeral the head and feet stones over the grave of the male deceased are put perpendicular to the body, whereas the same stones in the case of a female are parallel to the body.

Vahe S. Boyajian

Further Reading

Adamec, Ludwig W. *Historical Dictionary of Afghanistan.* Lanham, MD: Scarecrow, 1997.

Ahmed, Akbar. *Millennium and Charisma among Pathans.* London: Routledge, 1976.

Azoy, Whitney. *Buzkashi: Game and Power in Afghanistan.* Philadelphia: University of Pennsylvania Press, 1982.

Barth, Fredrik. *Political Leadership among Swat Pathans.* London: Athlone, 1959.

Dupree, Louis. *Afghanistan.* Karachi: Oxford University Press, 2002.

Gankovskij, Jurij. *History of Afghanistan.* Moscow: Progress Publishers, 1982.

Lindholm, Charles. *Generosity and Jealousy: The Swat Pukhtun of Northern Pakaistan.* New York: Columbia University Press, 1982.

Rzehak, Lutz. "Doing Pashto: Pashtunwali as the Ideal of Honourable Behaviour and Tribal Life among the Pashtuns." *Afghanistan Analyst Network,* March 2011.

Steul, Willi. *Pashtunwali: Ein Ehrenkodex und Seine Rechtliche Relevanz.* Wiesbaden: Franz Steiner, 1981.

Tapper, Nancy. *Bartered Brides: Politics, Gender and Marriage in an Afghan Tribal Society.* Cambridge: Cambridge University Press, 1991.

Vogelsang, Willem. *The Afghans.* Oxford: Blackwell, 2002.

PERU

Peru is a beautiful country with a diverse cultural makeup. The geographical regions of the coast, the mountains, and the jungle are home to cultures that, although they share the same nationality, are sufficiently distinct that we should bear in mind their differences when considering specific dos and don'ts in social and professional settings. Tourism remains concentrated in the southern half of Peru, and Peru is a popular destination for tourists from around the globe, so cultural norms and customs may seem more relaxed in the larger, busier tourist cities. Notwithstanding their friendly and welcoming nature, Peruvians are acutely aware of the cultural differences between themselves and their guests and they appreciate the effort to respect and follow their cultural customs.

Greetings in Peru tend to be more intimate than what is customary in the United States. Men shake hands when introduced, and when men and women are introduced, it is common to greet with a kiss on the right cheek, although the kiss is most often over the right shoulder as right cheeks touch briefly and gently. Female friends will often greet with a more pronounced kiss on the right cheek as well as a hug. Men shake hands firmly, albeit not as firmly as is customary in the United States. Closer male friends may often greet each other with a brief hug and pat on the back. Each day, a visitor should greet his Peruvian host with "Buenos días" if it is before noon, "Buenas tardes" if it is after noon, or "Buenas noches" if it is the evening. This simple but formal greeting each day is expected, and failure to begin a conversation with it is seen as brash and rude.

Because tourism is now a major part of Peruvian culture, it is common to see people from all around the world in all types of dress, especially in the major tourist areas like Miraflores in Lima, Arequipa, and Cuzco. Peruvians tend to dress quite conservatively, wearing nice khakis or dress pants, collared shirts, and leather dress shoes. Jeans, T-shirts, and tennis shoes are uncommon among Peruvian adults, and shorts and tank-tops are reserved for the beach and frowned upon in nicer restaurants, museums, and churches.

In general, Peruvians are proud of their rich and diverse heritage, so whether they live on the coast, in the jungle, or in the highlands, they will be eager to tell the history of their community, the region, or even the nation. Peruvians are extremely proud of their *pisco* (a strong liqueur made from grapes), their cuisine, and their history. Peruvians might talk about politics, especially past corruption in politics, but it is best to avoid open or direct criticism of the political establishment so as to not offend, regardless of their personal political bias.

In recent years, Peru has invested a great deal in supporting and improving the tourist industry. Whether people are directly employed in tourism or not, most Peruvians welcome foreign tourists eagerly and are willing to help them fulfil any need they may have. Most people are happy to give directions or recommend a restaurant or other service if a visitor needs some guidance. Some people might offer to accompany a visitor to his destination, acting as a guide, but these offers are generally made with the expectation that a tip will be given to the person for the favor. A polite but firm, "No, gracias" is usually sufficient to reject the offer of accompaniment.

When invited to dine in the home of a Peruvian family, a guest can expect to be treated as a guest of honor. It is nice to bring a small gift to the host, something small like a box of chocolates, flowers, or perhaps a bottle of wine. One should not make the gift overly extravagant, as the host may feel the need to reciprocate. They will likely prepare a lot of food and continue to serve their guests throughout the entire meal. It is important to pace oneself, eating small portions of everything, even the fresh fruit that is generally served as a dessert after the meal. When dining, it is considered proper to keep one's hands above the table, but entire forearms or elbows should not be on the table.

Although there are several fast food chain restaurants in the major cities in Peru, the true Peruvian dining experience is found in the local eateries. In the major tourist cities, restaurants closer to the main attractions will have higher prices, but can also generally be trusted to serve food that is prepared correctly and safely. When dining at a restaurant, guests should not be in a rush to get in and get out. Food is meant to be enjoyed over casual conversation and not to be rushed, and it is customary to spend at least an hour for lunch and as many as two hours for dinner. The waiter will begin by offering something to drink. Water is always bottled, and there is usually a choice between sparkling "agua con gas" or "natural." Soft drinks are commonly consumed at meals, as well as wine in finer establishments, which is available by the glass or the bottle. Coffee (espresso) is a customary drink for after dinner to aid as a digestive.

When dining at a restaurant with a Peruvian companion or companions, it is polite to offer to pay for everyone's meal. Dutch dining (where each pays his own) is uncommon and unless agreed upon well in advance of the meal may be considered impolite. If a group does decide to split the check, it is improper to ask the waiter for separate checks. A receipt for the meal may be requested, which will be offered either "por consumo" (the total amount of the check) or "detallada" (a detailed breakdown of each item ordered). Leaving a 10 percent tip for the waiter is considered generous.

In many tourist restaurants, the proprietor will hire live entertainment. Depending on the establishment, the owner may include a service fee for the entertainment on a patron's bill, or guests of the establishment may be encouraged to tip the performers. Most musical groups will have their own CDs for sale and will visit each table hoping someone will purchase one. In open-air establishments (most commonly when tables are on a patio open to the street), artisans and vendors will actively try and sell their merchandise while patrons are eating. Showing interest in one person will result in having to entertain sellers throughout the meal. Usually the proprietor does not allow vendors to approach the customers seated at the table, so it is best to avoid eye contact with a seller or politely shake your head no if they approach. They will be more than willing to show off their wares after guests have left the restaurant.

When shopping for handicrafts or other souvenir items in the markets, haggling is customary and expected. Vendors will always quote a higher price than what they are willing to sell their merchandise for, but shoppers should not insult the vendor by offering an unreasonable, low-ball offer. It is wise to ask about prices at several shops or stands in the market to get a general idea of the price of the items. Shoppers are always welcome to inquire for a price without the commitment to buy. However, once the haggling process begins, the sale is considered to be initiated. If the vendor is unwilling to accept an offer, shoppers retain the right to discontinue the discussion and walk away politely, but if a vendor accepts the offer, it is expected that the shopper make good on that offer and complete the purchase.

Taxis in Peru do not operate with a meter, but rather the price of a taxi ride is negotiated between the traveler and the taxi driver prior to the passenger entering the vehicle. It can be expected that a nonnative will be quoted a higher fare than a Peruvian will, so if possible, Peruvian travel companions should negotiate the price for a group. If a visitor is traveling without a Peruvian companion, it is wise to ask shop owners or employees for a ballpark figure of what a taxi fare might cost so negotiations can begin with a fair target in mind. There are many private car owners who will pose as taxis to supplement their income. Most are willing to provide the taxi service as any official taxi would, but there are some who take advantage of this opportunity to rob tourists or other unsuspecting travelers. Wherever possible, and especially when taking longer cab rides (from the hotel to the airport, for example), visitors should ask the hotel staff to call and prearrange a taxi, as it will be safer and less expensive. Above all, Peruvians are generally friendly, open, and accommodating. They are eager to befriend anyone who is genuinely interested in their country and culture. Peruvians have embraced social media and use sites to network, so a connection made can easily become a lasting professional relationship or friendship.

Scott R. Infanger

Further Reading

Circles of Excellence for Corporate Education. "Cultural Clues, Do's and Taboos: Communication Guidelines for PERU." http://www.circlesofexcellence.com/blog/2013/05/cultural-clues-dos-taboos-communication-guidelines-for-peru/. Accessed August 29, 2015.

Cultural Crossroads: Enriching Cultural Journeys. "Do's and Don'ts in Peru." http://www
.culturalcrossroads.com/cross/info/PeruDosAndDonts.html. Accessed August 29, 2015.
Ferreira, César, and Eduardo Dargent-Chamot. *Culture and Customs of Perú*. Westport, CT:
Greenwood, 2003.

THE PHILIPPINES

The Philippines is a diverse archipelago in southeastern Asia with approximately 100 million people spread over more than 7,000 islands. Myriad indigenous ethnic groups, a colonial past with Spain and the United States, and a large Chinese influence that has immigrated and acculturated have influenced the development of a Filipino culture that, while not entirely homogeneous, has led to the development of *Sikolohiyang Pilipino* (Filipino psychology). Filipino psychology is a distinct branch of non-Western psychology that addresses the Filipino mentality prevalent in the country's social norms and etiquette. Understanding the basics of Filipino psychology lends itself to knowing how best to act in the country as well as behaviors to avoid.

At a fundamental level, Filipinos typically share the value of *kapwa*, the idea that every person must be treated as a human being. At its most advanced level, *kapwa* breaks down into two categories, that of being a social insider and a social outsider, which can alter how a person is treated socially. Since etiquette concerns behaviors that lend themselves to fitting into a society, the focus here is on the behaviors and taboos aligned with social insiders, the people who fit into the culture and society. Thus, treating a person respectfully and according to their age and social status is critical to proper etiquette. Etiquette in the Philippines complies with the country's core social values. The key to acting correctly and considerately is to be respectful and treat everyone as a human being. At the same time, it is important not to be critical of others and to maintain an easygoing and patient demeanor. Not to do so breaks many social taboos, which can create tension, long-standing grudges, and lead to conflict. These values function across the country and, while there may be slight variation across the islands, are universal within the country.

In all social interactions, greetings are important. Greetings range from informal hellos to more ritualistic greetings given to elders. Often, Filipinos will greet each other by raising their eyebrows up and down once while smiling to indicate hello. Another type of greeting occurs when meeting with an elder, for a younger person will often bow slightly, take the elder's hand while palm down, and either kiss it or touch the palm to his or her forehead. This greeting is the *mano* and is a gesture of respect. Greetings that are more universal include greeting another person with the time of day by saying "Good morning," "Good day," or "Good evening." When parting, especially from an elder or from a hosted social event, it is important to bid farewell prior to departure. In a business situation, greetings and farewells may be more formal but expected as part of the *kapwa* value system. In addition to greetings, it is polite to refer to another person by their title, such as Mister or Missus (Mrs.), until invited to address the person on a first-name basis. The Philippines is a collective society, meaning that a person's actions reflect not only on the individual, but also on the person's family and the community. This concept is also bound to *kapwa*, in the sense that there must be a sense of togetherness and harmony that binds human beings. In terms of etiquette, *kapwa* means there is extreme emphasis on establishing and maintaining personal relationships, which includes having nuanced and proper interpersonal communication skills. A respected person typically speaks softly, smiles and laughs frequently as appropriate, dresses modestly, and is always patient and considerate. Conversations about the family and other people are common because they help build rapport and knowledge, spread news, and heighten the sense of community. Families are the backbone of Filipino society, with Filipinos honoring and supporting their large extended families. Families consume the majority of energy in the Philippines and are therefore important conversational topics. Though talk about other people can feel like gossip, it is generally to discover mutual acquaintances, which can be a marker of social status. Personal questions, the type that may be overly personal in a Western context, such as marital status and number of children, are typical in personal relationships and are not invasive or intended to offend.

Social events require the most nuanced etiquette. First, there is an understanding that whoever invites guests agrees to pay for them. It is also typical to show up 15–30 minutes late for social events, especially when they take place in a private home. Showing up at the exact start time makes a guest look greedy and reflects poorly on the person. In contrast, for nonsocial appointments such as at a doctor's office, showing up late is bad form. Food is a critical part of social interaction. Upon the arrival of a guest in a home or an office setting, it is typical to offer them food. Navigating the acceptance of such an offer is not always easy, but usually the best practice is to indicate that one has already eaten, the equivalent of a "No, thank you." If the offer is made a third time, it is polite to accept. Conversely, when eating in front of someone even in an unexpected circumstance, there is the expectation to ask a new arrival to share. Asking one time is acceptable, but a sincere offer must occur at least three times. These rules change for parties or large hosted gatherings because socially a host must serve food.

Food is a requisite staple at social events. Hosts typically serve food banquet style, whereas social events at a restaurant are family style. Filipinos take great pride in their food. Eating local foods, such as the delicacy *balut*, a cooked undeveloped duck egg, will endear the locals and make it easier to become part of the community. Alcohol is also usually available. While many Filipinos drink, being drunk is a social taboo. Drunkenness at a party leads to a loss of social status and raises the chances that the inebriated person will not receive future invitations. For traditional meals, most people eat with their hands. The proper way to eat requires using the right hand. The eating technique involves picking up a small bit of rice with the index finger, middle finger, and thumb finger, and then rolling it into a small ball without rolling it over the palm. Once rolled, the ball is dipped into the sauce, mixed with a little of the vegetables or protein, and then eaten. The left hand rests in the lap and not on the table. When finished, a small portion of food should be left on the plate. If the meal is family style, it is important to refrain from taking the last portion from the central plate. Toothpicks, when provided, have their own

Traditional food served banquet style at a baptism celebration in Lapu-Lapu, the Philippines. Social events hosted in private homes typically involve food served banquet style, whereas at restaurants food is served family style. (Bjarki Reyr/Alamy Stock Photo)

etiquette. The right hand holds the toothpick while gently scraping the teeth while at the same time the left hand covers the mouth like a mask. After the meal, one needs to be cautions in complimenting the chef. Most homes in the middle class and above hire a cook. Therefore, compliments to the chef can slight the host. On a similar note, gifts to the host that include food or alcohol can signal to other guests that the giver believed the host provided insufficient food and beverage. To avoid problems, gifts should be wrapped where appropriate and the host will open the gifts in private after the event. Presents and favors are another core feature of Filipino culture. A culturally embedded system of reciprocation called *utang ng loob* exists in the Philippines, where someone who receives a gift (or asks a favor) is indebted to the person who gave the gift (or performed the favor), and the recipient must repay the debt. The *utang ng loob* system is often circular and can sometimes escalate as gifts and favors become larger over time. However, this type of reciprocation is excellent for building and maintaining personal relationships. Refusing to reciprocate often creates tension and leads to a loss of face and social standing.

An additional key concept in Filipino society is the idea that a person always needs to be mindful of *hiya* (shame). In the Philippines, Filipinos expend great effort to never shame or embarrass another person in front of others. Causing a person to suffer from *hiya* is a major taboo because it harms that person as well as the person who caused the infraction. In order to avoid *hiya*, it is important never to lose one's temper in public, not to show frustration or anger through words or body language, and not to express negative sentiment aloud. Behaviors to avoid include not standing with hands on hips, which is a sign of outrage, and trying not to stare, as staring indicates rudeness and aggression despite the fact that local peoples may stare at foreigners out of curiosity. It is never acceptable to snap fingers to get someone's attention, nor is it appropriate to use the hand to point. If it is necessary to beckon someone over, the socially acceptable means is to use the entire hand with the palm facing downward in a scooping motion. In tense situations where it is necessary to address a concern or frustration with another person, the conversation is held privately to permit that person to save face, or not have his or her reputation damaged in public. *Hiya* often functions parallel to the concept of *amor-proprio*, or self-esteem: damaging a person's self-esteem by insulting them can invite conflict and lead to the long-term holding of grudge. Treating a person as a human being, as described by *kapwa*, requires that interpersonal situations seek to build self-esteem and prevent shame or embarrassment.

There are several points of etiquette that fall in line with Filipino core values that may be confusing for non-Filipinos. The first revolves around how "yes," "no," and "maybe" are used to answer questions. "No" is seldom an answer to a question because it is not a pleasing answer and can invoke the concepts of *amor-proprio* and *hiya*. "Maybe" is a more frequent answer, though it usually means no in a way less likely to offend. "Yes" is the most common answer because it pleases the recipient and makes all parties look good. However, it is no guarantee. For example, when inviting people to a social event verbally, the most common response is that the person will attend. The "yes" can be an affirmation, but it can also signify that the invitee does not want to offend by stating uncertainty about the invitation. For purposes of etiquette, it is critical to understand what these responses indicate when said and when they are given. To confirm an invitation, it is usually necessary to make the invitation multiple times, with three affirmative responses signifying actual plans to attend. A better strategy would be to convey the invitation an additional time in writing and/or through a confirmed guest acquainted with the invitee, so that person can convey the message that the invitee's presence is expected.

One of the newer challenges to Filipino society is how the rising popularity of electronic gadgets and online communications affect the expected social values. *Kapwa* applies to cyber culture and netiquette. However, due to a sense of anonymity and a detachment from the normal sense of community, trolling and other insulting behaviors occur more frequently online than in person. The best practice is to ignore online users who are trying to annoy and insult. Another, perhaps more important, reason to do so is that the Philippines heavily regulates the Internet. In 2012, the government signed the Cybercrime Prevention Act into law. Though the Supreme Court decided some provisions were unconstitutional in 2014, the portions regarding the criminalization of online libel remain in effect, making it vital to be cautious when posting online.

Laura Steckman

Further Reading

Bulatao, J. C. "Hiya." *Philippines Studies* 12, no. 3 (1964): 424–38.

Pe-Pua, R., and E. Protacio-Marcelino. "Sikolohiyang Pilipino (Filipino Psychology): A Legacy of Virgilio G. Enriquez." *Asian Journal of Psychology* 3 (2000): 49–71.

Posadas, D., and J. Posadas. *Etiquette Guide to the Philippines: Know the Rules that Make the Difference!* North Clarendon, VT: Tuttle Publishing, 2011.

Roces, A., and G. Roses. *CultureShock! Philippines: A Survival Guide to Customs and Etiquette.* Singapore: Marshall Cavendish International, 2013.

POLAND

Poland is located in Central Europe along the Baltic Sea. It is bordered by Germany, the Czech Republic, Slovakia, Ukraine, Belarus, and Lithuania, as well as Kaliningrad Oblast, a Russian exclave. Poland was invaded by Germany in 1939, beginning World War II. Nazi German forces constructed numerous extermination camps across Poland, including Auschwitz-Birkenau, Sobibór, and Treblinka. Around 90 percent of Poland's Jewish population was killed in the Holocaust, along with over 2.5 million other ethnic Poles. The country later functioned as a satellite state of the Soviet Union. The Polish People's Republic was founded in 1952, with considerable Soviet influence, as a communist state. The "Solidarity" movement, which began as a labor union, developed into a political power that contributed to the fall of Communism in Poland and to the country's first democratic elections since World War II. Over 90 percent of Poland's 38 million residents are ethnically Polish, and the country is considered to be devoutly Roman Catholic. Roman Catholicism is important in Poland and Polish culture is rooted in its religious heritage, dating back to 966 CE.

In Poland, people generally greet one another by shaking hands and maintaining eye contact. A man should wait for a woman to extend her hand before offering a handshake. Kissing a woman's hand is generally only done by older businessmen and should not be attempted. It is also typical to greet people when entering or exiting an elevator. It is customary to use a formal address, to include earned titles such as "Doctor" or "Professor," when speaking to another person until invited to use a first name. Men are addressed as "Pan" and women as "Pani" along with their surname, the equivalent of the English "Mr." or "Mrs."

Polish dress is traditionally conservative, owing in part to the country's Roman Catholic heritage. When conducting business, it is appropriate for men to wear business suits and ties and for women to wear dresses or suits. Bright colors and patterns should be avoided. Other visitors to Poland should avoid extremely casual dress, such as shorts and sneakers or workout clothes. Modesty in appearance, to include clothing and jewelry, is highly valued.

It is customary for visitors to arrive around 15 minutes late, but not later than that. In some homes, it is customary to remove one's shoes, so a visitor should look to the host for guidance. If the host is wearing slippers, guests should remove their shoes. Hosts often offer visitors slippers for their comfort. Visitors also traditionally bring a small gift, such as flowers or wine, to give to the host, as well as a handwritten thank you note.

Polish dining etiquette is quite formal, from the order and arrangement of seating to the custom that men stand when a woman enters the room. Guests should wait to be seated by their host. Toasts are quite common in Poland and are generally made with strong alcohol that should be consumed in one gulp. Eye contact should be maintained from the moment the glass leaves the table until it is placed back down. Traditionally, the host offers the first toast, with other visitors and guests reciprocating as the meal continues. The most popular toast is "Na zdrowie," which means "To your health." The host begins eating first followed by the guests. Guests are expected to take second helpings, so take a small amount of food initially to leave room for more. In some cases, soups are served in small bowls without spoons and should be sipped like a drink. Wrists should be rested on the table when eating. When dining in a casual restaurant, it is customary to share a table. However, conversation with the strangers sharing the table is not necessary. Tipping in restaurants is not expected as a 10 percent service charge is generally already included in a dining bill. When dining out, avoid saying "Thank you" when paying for your meal before change is given. Saying "Thank you" implies that the waiting staff may keep the change.

Polish cuisine is generally rich in meat, winter vegetables, and noodles with dishes often quite rich and made using large amounts of heavy cream. The most well-known Polish foods include pierogi (a dumpling often filled with meat or potatoes), kielbasa (a type of sausage), and *bigos* (a meat and cabbage stew). Bread is a key component of Polish cuisine, and most Polish breads utilize a rye or wheat base. Polish onion syrup is a traditional cough remedy that is still widely used. Horsemeat, widely considered taboo in many parts of Europe, is eaten in Poland. Most people in Poland do not eat meat on Fridays during Lent and fast during particular holy days during this time period. Some people in Poland abstain from meat every Friday throughout the year.

While bars are common in Poland, drinking in public places such as streets or parks is illegal. Vodka is the most common alcoholic drink in Poland. It is customary, when toasting, to consume hard liquor and to consume the drink in one gulp.

Polish body language is generally reserved, particularly when meeting strangers, and when meeting people for the first time, the host is expected to introduce everyone present. It is considered bad manners to put your hands in your pockets. It is also considered rude to sit with your ankle resting on your opposite knee or to point your index finger to your forehead. Direct eye contact is important in Poland, particularly during a toast. It is customary to make considerable small talk before a business meeting. English is widely spoken in Poland, but it is helpful for visitors to learn a few key Polish phrases before traveling.

Due to the country's Roman Catholic heritage, the family is of utmost importance in Poland with extended families often remaining close-knit. Families in Poland are relatively large, particularly compared to other parts of Europe, with an average of 2.8 people per household.

While same-sex relationships are not legally recognized in Poland, Poland's laws do protect against discrimination based on sexual orientation and Poland has never outlawed homosexuality. Despite increasing tolerance, particularly among young people, homosexuality should generally be avoided as a topic of discussion when in Poland. While views on homosexual relationships are changing, most Polish people still hold to a traditional view of marriage, and adoption by gay couples is not allowed though a single homosexual person may adopt a child. Discussions of sex or sexual innuendo are generally inappropriate, particularly in mixed company of varying ages. Visitors to Poland should also avoid discussing the Holocaust, World War II, or Poland's relationship with neighboring countries. Modesty is highly valued in Poland, and is considered taboo to ask how much money someone earns, even between friends. It is also considered impolite to ask a woman about her age. Discussions of politics or religion are also generally avoided. While many Polish people consider themselves to be Catholic, rates of church attendance are much lower. That said, the church is still a respected institution, hence conservative dress is expected in churches and shorts are not allowed. Shoulders should also be covered, and women should wear long skirts. There are 13 public holidays in Poland, most connected to religious holidays including a two-day Christmas holiday. Despite the predominance of Catholicism, religion is not a common topic of conversation. Insulting the Roman Catholic Church or the pope is considered taboo in Poland. Pope John Paul II was born in Poland and is widely revered across the country. Most businesses are closed on Sunday for religious reasons.

Cremation is permitted in Poland, but was formerly considered to be taboo by the Roman Catholic Church, and thus less than 10 percent of people are cremated, with a more traditional burial generally preferred. A wake generally precedes a funeral, where mourners are expected to gather by the casket and offer condolences. The wake is followed by a funeral, often conducted in a Catholic Church. Yellow chrysanthemums are generally used for funerals, and are thus considered to be taboo as gifts at other times.

Caitlin C. Finlayson

Further Reading

Baker, Mark, Tim Richards, and Marc Di Duca. *Lonely Planet: Poland*. Oakland: Lonely Planet, 2012.
Central Intelligence Agency. "Poland." *The World Factbook*. https://www.cia.gov/library/publications/the-world-factbook/geos/pl.html. Accessed January 5, 2015.
Polish National Tourist Office. http://www.poland.travel/en/. Accessed January 5, 2015.
Steves, Rick, and Cameron Hewitt. *Rick Steves' Snapshot Kraków, Warsaw & Gdansk*. Berkeley, CA: Avalon Travel Publishing, 2014.
Turp, Craig. *Eyewitness Travel: Poland*. New York: Dorling Kindersley, 2013.

PORTUGAL

Portugal is located in southwest Europe where the country makes up part of the Iberian Peninsula. Portugal is the westernmost country of mainland Europe as it is bordered by the Atlantic Ocean to the west and by Spain to the east and north. The Portugal–Spain border is 754 miles long, making it the longest uninterrupted border within the European Union. The Portuguese people also live in the Atlantic archipelagos of the Azores and Madeira, though these are autonomous regions of Portugal that have their own regional governments. Portugal is a founding member

Culture Shock! ⊕

The Barcelos Cockerel

The Barcelos Cockerel is the unofficial Portuguese mascot and a recurring motif in Portuguese design. According to legend, the citizens of Barcelos thought an innocent Spanish pilgrim who was traveling through their city was guilty of committing a crime. The pilgrim was arrested and condemned to death, prompting the pilgrim to ask to be taken to the judge who had sentenced him. This wish was granted and the pilgrim swore to the judge that the proof of his innocence was that a cooked cockerel would crow at the hour of his death. The judged doubted the pilgrim's statement of innocence, but did not eat the cooked bird. As the pilgrim was about to be hanged, the cockerel appeared and crowed just as the pilgrim had predicted. The judge realized the pilgrim was innocent, and the pilgrim was released. Later, the pilgrim returned to Barcelos where he crafted a crucifix dedicated to the Virgin Mary and St. James, whom the pilgrim believed were responsible for the miracle of the crowing cockerel.

Victoria Williams

of NATO as well as a member of the United Nations and the European Union. Portugal's population numbers around 11 million people, 94 percent of whom are Roman Catholic.

Portuguese society is hierarchical and is structured around the concept of the family as the basis of social stability. The Catholic Church is respected throughout the country, while both the church and the family are especially important in rural areas. In general the Portuguese are an inherently conservative people who are resistant to change and wary of innovation. The Portuguese consider good manners to be a sign of respect for others and so view them as important.

Although recently Portugal has become more informal in its greeting etiquette, polite forms of address are still employed. People who have been to university are addressed by phrases such as *Senhor Doutor* (Mr. Dr.), while an educated woman or a woman who commands respect for some other reason may be addressed as *Dona* together with her first name, for example as *Dona Rosa*. The Portuguese distinguish between the more correct terms *o senhor* and *a senhora*, which are formal ways of saying "you" and thereby convey respect to strangers, and the more informal version of "you," *tu*, which is used when speaking to someone with whom one is intimate. When greeting someone informally a Portuguese person will likely say "Olá," meaning "Hello." However, the Portuguese tend to speak formally to people when greeting them initially and when talking to elders, as they feel doing so expresses veneration. More formal greeting phrases include "Bom dia" (Good day), which is considered slightly more formal than simply saying "Olá" and is said until around noon; "Boa tarde" (Good afternoon), which is used after midday until around sunset; and "Boa noite" (both "Good evening" and "Good night"), which is used as a greeting after sunset. In order to make "Olá" seem more formal or to make "Bom dia," "Boa tarde," and "Boa noite" seem less formal, the Portuguese may mix the phrases together to make another greeting, for example "Olá, bom dia" (Hello, good day).

When two Portuguese strangers meet, they will usually shake hands enthusiastically. In more informal situations, men who know each other will shake hands, embrace, and slap each other on the back, while women will greet each other with air-kisses to both cheeks. Older Portuguese men may take off their hat when greeting a woman and may also kiss a woman's hand in greeting. In general Portuguese gestures of farewell are the same as the greeting gestures. Children are taught to respect their elders and will stand when an older person enters or leaves a room. Children also remove their hats when entering a house.

The Portuguese take pride in their appearance, with the urban middle and upper classes dressing quite formally and expensively in everyday life, as they tend to view clothes and accessories as a way to indicate their social status. In some rural and coastal areas people also wear traditional dress that varies between locations. For example, in the seaside town of Esposende women customarily wear pink cotton skirts with white shirts, green or red shawls around their shoulders, black shawls around their waists, and black headscarves or narrow-brimmed hats on their heads. Esposende's men traditionally wear a black suit with a red sash. Though outside of urban areas the Portuguese wear traditional attire less and less, some element of the clothing is usually worn every day even if it is mixed with more modern garments. In areas with significant tourist trades, such as the southern Algarve region, locals wear their traditional clothes in order to satisfy tourist demands to experience authentic Portuguese culture.

In Portugal breakfast is usually eaten at 8 a.m. and is Continental style. Lunch is eaten around 12.30 p.m. and dinner is eaten between 11 p.m. and midnight. Portuguese food is influenced by Mediterranean cuisine and also features a great deal of fish both fresh (such as sardines) and preserved, such as the omnipresent salt cod (*bacalhau*), as well as meat and vegetables. The Portuguese also use a lot of spices in their food, especially hot chilies, cinnamon, saffron, vanilla, and black pepper. The Portuguese take great pride in their wines with port, a fortified wine produced in the upper Douro River area, being a major export. In rural areas port is offered to illustrious guests, such as the parish priest, to mark special occasions. Also in rural areas, it is traditional for men to stop by their local café before heading to the pastures in order to enjoy a shot of brandy (*pinga*).

In Portugal, if one is invited to a party or some other large social gathering, it is acceptable to arrive 30 to 60 minutes later than the scheduled arrival time. However, if one is invited to dinner at someone's house, one should not arrive more than 15 minutes late, and arriving late for business meetings is not generally acceptable. Dress codes for dinner parties are much the same as that for business events, so it is usual for people to dress conservatively and smartly. It is, however, considered rude to discuss business matters outside of work.

Portuguese dinner party etiquette is typically formal. The dinner's host may show everyone to their seat at the dinner table, and guests should stay standing until invited to sit. Similarly nobody should start to eat until the host announces "Bom apetite." Table manners in Portugal are Continental style with the fork held in the left hand and the knife held in the right hand. In Portugal few foods are eaten with the hands, meaning fruit and cheese should be eaten with utensils.

It is considered courteous to bring a gift for the dinner's hostess. Typical gifts include flowers, chocolates, or wine. However, any chocolates should be of good quality and wine should only be given if you know the type of wine the hostess prefers. Any flowers given should not have 13 blooms, as this is considered unlucky. Similarly lilies and chrysanthemums should not be given as the Portuguese associate these flowers with funerals. Red flowers are not normally given as gifts in Portugal as the Portuguese associate the color red with political revolutions.

The Portuguese tend to be naturally reserved and frown upon loud or overly boisterous behavior. Despite their natural reticence, however, the Portuguese prefer to meet face-to-face when it comes to business matters. Therefore the Portuguese will arrange meetings rather than communicate by writing, e-mail, or telephone, as the Portuguese view these modes of communication as being too impersonal a way to get to know a potential colleague or business partner.

Victoria Williams

Further Reading

Brettell, Caroline B. "Portugal." *Countries and Their Cultures*. http://www.everyculture.com/No-Sa/Portugal.html. Accessed January 17, 2017.

Commisceo Global Consultancy. "Portugal Guide." http://www.commisceo-global.com/country-guides/portugal-guide. Accessed January 17, 2017.

Condra, Jill, ed. *Encyclopedia of National Dress: Traditional Clothing Around the World*. Santa Barbara, CA: ABC-CLIO, 2013.

Guedes De Queiroz, Sandy. *Culture Smart! Portugal: The Essential Guide to Customs & Culture*. London: Kuperard, 2006.

Poelzl, Volker. *CultureShock! Portugal: A Survival Guide to Customs and Etiquette*, 3rd ed. Tarrytown, NY: Marshall Cavendish, 2009.

PUNJAB

The region of Punjab is shared between India and Pakistan. Punjab in India is considered a state, whereas Punjab in Pakistan is a province. This occurred after the partition of the subcontinent, with Pakistan receiving the larger portion of Punjab, with more than four times more landmass than India received. Both regions, regardless of borders, share common languages of Punjabi, Sindhi, and English.

It is important to note that both Punjabi Indians and Punjabi Pakistani have similar habits and customs, with major differentiation coming from religious practices and some cultural nuances. Both India and Pakistan are hierarchical societies and most commonly thought of as patriarchal societies. Thus, Punjabis in both countries often greet members of the same sex, unless dealing with the middle class or those they have a relationship with. Both men and women generally shake hands or hug (if they have a relationship) and ask about a person's heath, family, and business/work/academic success.

There are different verbal greetings depending on an individual's religion. Those who follow the Sikh religion say "Sat Sri Akaal" when meeting someone, which roughly translates to "God is the ultimate truth." Another common gesture in India is to touch an elder's (always superior in age and position) feet to show respect and subservience. Conversely, Punjabi Muslims would say "As-salamu alaykum," which translates to "Peace be upon you," and Punjabi Hindus would say "Namaste" or "Namaskar," translating to "I bow to the divine in you." Both "Sat Sri Akaal" and "As-salamu alaykum" are religion specific and would not be used as liberally as "Namaste," which is more commonly used by all people.

The appearance and dress of Punjabis depends on the location and religion, but both Indian and Pakistani Punjabis generally wear *shalwar kameez*. The *shalwar* are loose trousers, resembling pajamas with the legs wide at the top and narrow at the ankle. The *kameez* is a long shirt or tunic with a collar. The appearance and dress is different for Punjabi Sikhs and Muslims, as both abide by their respective religious dress codes. All Sikhs, regardless of sex, are initiated in a ceremony called "Amrit Sanchar"; once this happens, they need to abide by a strict dress code. This binds them as people who are committed to the Sikh ways of life and to the various gurus that make up the religion.

According to the Guru Granth Sahib (holy book with teachings from Guru Nanak and other Gurus), the Sikh dress code comprises five articles of clothing, known as the "Five Ks." *Kesh*, literally meaning "uncut hair," is the most important aspect of Sikhism, though some believe the turban (Keski) is a more significant aspect of the religion. Sikhs are to maintain and not cut any hair from their body. *Kanga* is a comb Sikhs must carry around to groom hair. This serves an important purpose, as Sikhs are not allowed to cut their hair, so combing removes dead hair and keeps one clean. *Kara* is a steel bangle or bracelet that Sikhs wear as a sign of being truthful and morally conscientious, and following their holy scripture. However, it should be noted that people from Gujarat also wear similar bangles, which are not affiliated with Sikhism. *Kachera* are shorts that Sikhs wear, usually as underwear, which historically meant that Sikhs are not bogged down with heavy clothing especially at a time of war. *Kirpan* used to mean a sword but nowadays it means a small knife or dagger. This is important because historically the Sikhs have been prosecuted for their beliefs, and the *Kirpan* is fundamentally used for self-defense or for protection and never for criminal behavior.

Indian and Pakistani Punjabi people have similar hospitality and table manners, and major differences are only with the types of food consumed (for religious reasons). Most Punjabi households do not wear shoes indoors, as they are considered unclean and also because all houses have a religious shrine or room where prayer takes place. People are also expected to dress conservatively when invited to a gathering or occasion.

Traditionally, Punjabis eat with their right hand only, although more Westernized families eat with cutlery. Punjabis in both countries tend to have more meat in their diet than Indians, as well as vegetables such as spinach and mustard leaves. Traditionally this was because many worked in agriculture and needed a high-energy diet that could sustain them for laborious work.

Punjabi body language plays a major role in communicating feelings without speech and is similar to those in the rest of India and Pakistan. This is mostly done by facial cues or hand gestures. A common gesture includes a loose, side-to-side head nod meaning "Yes," "Understood," or "In agreement." Avoid direct eye contact: it is a sign of respect to look away from someone's face. Similarly, any pointing of the finger during a greeting should be avoided because of its accusatory connotation. Punjabi people beckon with their hand and point with the chin, not finger. Placing hands on hips is considered an argumentative posture and is discouraged.

Note there are a multitude of taboos in India and Pakistan, though there are not any quintessentially Punjabi in nature. Those mentioned here are some that are observed all over India and Pakistan.

Dinesh Asudo Punjabi

Further Reading

Bhatti, H. S., and Daniel M. Michon. "Folk Practices in Punjab." *Journal of Philosophy in Schools* 11, no. 2 (2004): 138–54.

Grewal, J. S. *The Sikhs of the Punjab*. Cambridge: Cambridge University Press, 1998.

Grewal, J. S. *Social and Cultural History of the Punjab: Prehistoric, Ancient and Early Medieval*. New Delhi: Manohar, 2004.

Joshi, Manoj. *Passport India: Your Pocket Guide to Indian Business, Customs & Etiquette*. Petaluma, CA: World Trade Press, 1997.

Malhotra, Anshu, and Farina Mir. *Punjab Reconsidered. History, Culture, and Practice*. Oxford: Oxford University Press, 2012.

Rajmohan, Gandhi. *Punjab: A History from Aurangzeb to Mountbatten*. New Delhi: Aleph Book Company, 2013.

Veach, Sarah, and Katy Williamson. "Punjabi: Culture and Language Manual." Texas State University, 2011. http://languagemanuals.weebly.com/uploads/4/8/5/3/4853169/punjabi.pdf.

Q

QUECHUA

The Quechua people are primarily the descendants of the Inca, whose empire *Tahuantinsuyo* (Land of the Four Quarters) reached its peak in the fifteenth century and ultimately fell to the Spanish conquest in 1535. The Quechua primarily live in the Andean nations of South America (Peru, Bolivia, Ecuador, Chile, and Colombia) and are known by several different names in each of those countries. The Quechua people speak several different dialects even within the political boundaries of the nations they live in and the dialects differ enough that Quechua speakers from the highlands of Peru likely are unable to communicate with Quechua speakers of Ecuador, Bolivia, or even other parts of Peru. The Quechua have adopted much of the Spanish culture evident in the modern nations they call home, but maintain a strong cultural identity with unique customs and traditions.

Generally, the Quechua people live in remote villages far away from major metropolitan centers and popular tourist destinations. This isolation leads to tight communities, called *ayllus*, which primarily consist of extended families often numbering in the several dozens to well over a hundred people. Within the community, Quechua practice the *mink'a*, a shared labor in which everyone joins to work on a project for the benefit of the community as a whole (as in the construction of a school or community center), and the *ayni*, which is a more personal, "I help you today with your project and you will help me tomorrow with mine" kind of arrangement. This latter arrangement is most commonly seen as families build or improve their homes in the village. Economically, Quechua communities most often depend on subsistence farming and handicraft, with the men most commonly spending their time working as farmers, shepherds, or miners and the women focusing on weaving and other artisanal endeavors. In areas where tourism is common, men will subsidize their family income by working as porters or assistants to tour companies.

When greeting a Quechua person in Peru, it is customary to say, "Rimaykullayki" (pronounced reem-eye-cool-yeye-key). If you are feeling daring, you may want to ask, "Anillanchu?" (pronounced annie-yan-choo), which means, "How are you?" Most Quechua will appreciate the gesture and will respond with "Anillanmi." Since Quechua, known as *Runasimi* in the Quechua tongue, was not written prior to the Spanish conquest, much of the vocabulary was lost once Spanish was imposed on the people during the colonial period. Careful listening will allow a Spanish speaker to identify several words from the Spanish language that have been adopted back into Quechua. This also means that a visitor to a Quechua home or community generally can communicate in Spanish, but most often it is with the children who attend Spanish-language schools. Although the Quechua language is recognized as an official language in Peru, Bolivia, and Ecuador, and is taught in some of the Quechua villages, Spanish remains the primary language of instruction. Additionally, the remoteness of many of the Quechua communities results in a lack of government funds to build or support schools in the village, so students have to travel significant distances to attend secondary school. Many of the poorer Quechua people are illiterate after having lost their ability to read and write after completing primary school and returning to work in the fields and farms to help with the family economy.

The Quechua are easily identifiable by their bright-colored ponchos (worn by the men) and skirts (worn by the women). Each village has a common color scheme and weaving patterns as a motif in their textiles that identify them and their region or town. Men and boys will often wear a *chullo*, or knitted hat with ear flaps, and women will wear a felt bowler hat. More often than not, Quechua women will also be seen wearing a large red blanket tied around their shoulders with an infant or small child sitting comfortably inside. When the women are not carrying children on their backs, they use the same length of fabric to carry handicrafts, produce, or bundles of firewood. The thick woolen skirts and ponchos provide warmth in the cooler climates of the high plains and mountains.

Since tourism has become a major contributor to many of the national economies, often Quechua women will dress themselves and their children in their finest traditional attire and sit on the sidewalks in tourist cities like Cuzco and offer photo opportunities to the tourists. Quechua children will frequently perform a song and dance in both Spanish and Quechua with the expectation that they will be paid for their performance, while the mother knits, weaves, or sells trinkets or candy to the passersby. It is also quite common to see women and children carrying a lamb or baby alpaca that has been groomed and dressed with a knit cap or collar that tourists are encouraged to hold and pose with for their photos. Tourists are expected, however, to pay for the photo opportunity, and small children will often pursue an offending tourist who is caught sneaking a photograph for several blocks, all the while clamoring loudly for payment.

Because of the tourist industry, many Quechua traditions are being preserved or reinvented, the most famous being the annual Inti Raymi Festival in Cuzco, Peru, which celebrates the birth of the sun each year at the June (southern hemisphere winter) solstice. The Inti Raymi Festival attracts tens of thousands of spectators to the Inca ruins at Sacsayhuaman above Cuzco to see the celebration, including the sacrifice of a black llama, all of which is performed in Quechua. This immensely popular celebration brings many Quechua artisans to Cuzco, where they are able to sell their handicrafts to the tourists. Although there are often vendors who will sell original, handmade merchandise, much of the goods available outside of the major tourist attractions are mass produced and commercially available throughout the region. It is reasonable and expected to negotiate a fair price for an item of interest, but one should always take care to show respect to the vendor by not insulting him or her with an absurdly low offer. If you feel a price is too high, simply indicate that with a gentle shake of the head or wave of the hand to say no. If you cannot agree on a price, it is acceptable to walk away from the bargaining. Be forewarned, however, that competition for clients is often quite fierce and sales may be limited, so the vendor will persist long after you have abandoned the idea of buying anything.

Meals among the Quechua people almost always include some form of potato, corn, or grain, especially quinoa, or a combination of these staples. Guinea pig is eaten regularly as a source of protein, and many Quechua families cohabit with dozens of guinea pigs, called *cuy* (pronounced kwee), that run free within the confines of the kitchen area of the home. Most Quechua homes have either hard-packed dirt or cement floors, and the guinea pigs are a convenient way to dispose of vegetable scraps. Alternatively, families will construct a small pen with miniature adobe houses in the corner of a room to keep the *cuy* contained. In addition to guinea pig, chicken, lamb, alpaca, pork, and occasionally beef are also eaten as sources of protein. Fish is a common staple in communities along rivers and lakes, especially Lake Titicaca, which is located on the border of Peru and Bolivia.

Most Quechua people have adopted Catholicism as their primary religion while maintaining their belief in the deities of their ancestors. Although the Christian Quechua people attend mass and venerate the Virgin Mary and the patron saint of their city, province, or region, many of them still firmly believe in the *pachamama*, or Mother Earth, as well as the *apus*, gods that reside in the mountains. Religious rites and celebrations are often a combination of both traditions, with the Christian sacraments and ordinances being conducted in the church, but the family celebration giving equal attention to the ancient beliefs and occasionally rituals. Alcohol, especially *chicha*, a fermented corn-based beverage, is commonly served at celebrations, and after the initial offering to *pachamama*, libations flow freely. Many Quechua villages will have a shaman who is as much a spiritual advisor as a medicine man. Even as Evangelical Christianity has seen tremendous growth among the Quechua people, the traditional beliefs in the *apus* and *pachamama* remain quite strong.

Marriage and family in many Quechua communities is typically arranged, not necessarily by parents choosing who their children will marry, but when a couple decides that they would like to marry, the families arrange a trial marriage in which the couple is provisionally married and lives together as husband and wife. Unless the bride's *ayllu* is short on able-bodied men, the bride joins her husband's *ayllu*. If, after the provisional period is over (usually one year), the couple decides they are compatible and want to remain together, then they celebrate the official marriage ceremony. Conversely, if they decide during the initial period that they are incompatible, the union is dissolved and the bride returns to her family and resumes her life as it was before the marriage arrangement began.

Scott R. Infanger

Further Reading

Bolin, Inge. *Growing up in a Culture of Respect: Child Rearing in Highland Peru*. Austin: University of Texas Press, 2006.

Countries and Their Cultures. "Quechua," http://www.everyculture.com/wc/Norway-to -Russia/Quechua.html. Accessed February, 11, 2016.

Peoples of the World Foundation. "Quichua." http://www.peoplesoftheworld.org/text?people =Quichua. Accessed February, 11, 2016.

R

ROMA

The Roma have a history, a heritage, and are subject to global economic and political forces. Whether they are indigenous, immigrants, migrants, or refugees, Roma rely on their cultural attributes to adapt to their society. Like the Jews following the captivity of Babylon and Africans during the transatlantic slave trade, the Roma are historically diasporic; their ancestors were dispersed involuntarily from India to other countries of the world. Accordingly, the Roma constitute a population that shares ancestral origins, but does not share a single culture. Roma communities express cultural practices and beliefs relative to the country in which they live, and the economic niche that they occupy within it. Linguists have determined that the Roma are of Indian extraction. More than 1,000 years ago violent raids forced the ancestors of contemporary Roma out of their homeland. Their migrations through Persia and the Caucasus brought them to the Byzantine Empire, and ultimately to the Balkans and Western Europe. Roma are also known as Gypsies, Tsiganoi, Vlach, Sinti/Manouche, Cale, and Romanichals. They live throughout Europe, Asia, Australia, New Zealand, North and South Africa, and the Americas. The Roma population, estimated at about 12 million, is considered the largest racialized minority group in the European Union. The U.S. government recognized Roma as an official minority group in 1972. Today approximately 1 million Roma reside in the United States.

Language is the unifying cultural feature of all Roma. Since Roma are geographically dispersed, they speak a variety of Romanes, a linguistic system associated with the Indo-Aryan branch of the Indo-European language derived from Sanskrit. Roma language reinforces at once a shared sense of national identity and a separation between Roma and all others. Spoken Romani is interspersed with words from the dominant language, as well as other languages of commerce, e.g., English, French, or German. Through the International Romani Union (IRU) Roma intellectuals and activists promote a writing system of Romanes. An online course called RomaniNet inspires students of Gypsy studies to learn the language. The Roma traditionally believe in supernatural powers, spirits, ghosts, and curses. They also typically participate in the organized, mainstream religion of the country in which they live, including Christianity, Hinduism, and Islam. Religious pilgrimages, which they turn into opportunities for earning an income and as reunions with relatives and friends, are common. In countries where Christianity is the dominant religion, Roma celebrate Christmas on December 25, and Easter in April or May. Adults may also fast on these holidays and eat special foods.

Limited direct experience with Roma leads many people to perceive Roma as categorically exotic, mystical, romantic, talented, dangerous, or criminal. Such stereotypes reinforce popular misconceptions and a universal mistrust of all Gypsies. Roma are misunderstood and, therefore, discriminated against due chiefly to their historical and structural position as "outsiders." Ignorance of their history fuels prejudice against their economic strategies, customs, housing arrangements, dress codes, and other visible or imagined acts and values. Historical persecution and limited options for earning a living subject many Roma groups to nomadic, often precarious living conditions. Males have worked as entertainers and tool makers, while women have relied on fortune-telling to help support their household. Seasonal travel and temporary settlements are required for the Roma who work as migrant workers. That said, there are Roma academics, doctors, lawyers, and other professionals who live in integrated urban and suburban neighborhoods. On the whole, however, Roma lifestyles also vary depending on the economic and technological advancement across, and within, countries. Some Roma are nomadic while others lead more settled lives. Etiquette within the Roma community prohibits any form of exploitation for financial gain, and economic transactions for profit are reserved exclusively for non-Roma. While instances of Roma women with infants begging on the streets are common, asking for alms from fellow Roma is considered a disgrace. Fortune-telling is a popular subsistence strategy for many Roma women, but this is an activity that the women never practice within their own community.

Roma tend to be gregarious, and welcome impromptu visits by relatives, neighbors, or friends to socialize. Greetings are congenial, and include phrases of good will and good health. Generosity, including the exchange of gifts, is considered a noble quality; relatives are prepared to assist family members and friends with money or other material resources, such as food, clothing, or use of a car or horse as needed. Youths treat elders within and outside their family with high regard. They value seniors' wisdom, and address elders as "old man" and "old woman," both of which are terms of respect. The young seek out elders for conflict resolution or advice; they also show their appreciation by serving them first, waiting for them to speak first, and to have the last word in a serious conversation.

Roma dress codes vary according to terms of propriety associated with particular tribal groups, gender, age, and marital status. Married women keep their hair long and wear it in a variety of casual buns that are often accessorized with a hair ornament that may vary from a glittery comb to a pencil. Elderly women tend to braid their hair and cover their head with a scarf. Women in travelling communities are typically seen in full, often colorful, ankle-length skirts and low-cut blouses, while urban women may be dressed in longer, tight skirts and T-shirts that may depict a designer logo or other advertising image. Women wear jewelry, including gold earrings, necklaces, and bracelets, as such jewelry is regarded as a source of mobile property that the women can simultaneously display in public and protect from thieves. Teenage girls emphasize their femininity to prospective husbands and parents-in-law by appearing publicly in attractive, fashionable clothing, wearing makeup, and mimicking hair they see on television, film, and magazines. Men tend to adopt the dress code of non-Roma men of their age, while teenage boys dress in suits, fashionable shirts, and trousers. Older men may wear a scarf around their necks, or a hat and vest affiliated with particular communities or clans.

Most Roma apply strict rules of cleanliness to preparing, serving, and eating food. Some groups maintain separate eating utensils for members of their in-group who share the laws of hygiene. Among the Roma living in Athens, the capital of Greece, it is customary for men to dine at the table while women gather around a clean tablecloth placed on the kitchen floor rather than a table. The Roma diet differs depending on the mainstream cuisine of the country of residence and the foods to which they have access through their work. Common among nomadic and sedentary groups are vegetable stews. Families in homes with fully equipped kitchens have elaborate dietary practices, including grilled and baked fish, beef, lamb, pork, and poultry. A favorite and delicious Roma dish is cabbage rolls stuffed with ground beef and rice, cooked in a savory tomato sauce and spiced with bits of hot peppers. Following a meal, eating utensils, kitchen appliances, and the floor are cleaned thoroughly in accordance with purity taboos, and leftover food is discarded since it is considered taboo. Another food taboo among some Roma tribes precludes the eating of horsemeat. This is because the Roma view horses as a useful means of transportation.

Roma regulate their way of life through the distinction between clean/pure (*vujo*) and polluted/defiled (*merime*). They apply this perspective to the body, illness, sexuality, living quarters, food, material possessions, conversation, and social conduct. Roma perceive the inside and upper body as pure. In contrast, they consider the lower part of the body unclean and for this reason avoid clothing that exposes the legs. Moreover, Roma people wash clothes that cover the upper body separately from skirts and trousers. Women's and men's clothes are washed separately. To maintain purity, Roma handle separately the clothes of elders from those that younger, sexually active adults wear. Pubescent boys and girls are considered categorically pure.

Roma people are also typically generous emotionally as evidenced by their unconditional availability to be present with any individual or family in joy or sadness. It is common to comfort children and elders by hugging them. Physical affection may be displayed between women and between men, while interactions between men and women tend to be demure. Women are to avoid eye contact with men, flirt, or communicate in any way that may be interpreted as sexual. Ideally women are not to speak publicly about sexuality, swear, or tell jokes with sexual innuendos. Other Roma taboos focus on pregnant and menstruating women, for some Roma communities consider pregnant women and those who are menstruating as impure. This taboo means that the women are forbidden from socializing outside of the house, cooking, or having contact with men. Among evangelical Roma, after giving birth women will not participate in religious rituals for a period of up to three months. Following this period of isolation the new mother will wash her hands and the baby's face with water, a ceremony that marks the woman's reintegration in her community. Women keep their tents, caravans, houses, and courtyards spotless, and lavatories are built outside of the main living quarters. Those who violate the pollution taboos are reprimanded, tolerated, or ostracized by the community for a period of time before they are reintegrated. Roma consider all *gadge* (non-Gypsies) impure because they don't share this system of beliefs.

The extended family is the primary form of social organization within Roma communities. Mating rituals begin in early adolescence, and most Roma marry at 15–18 years of age. Marriage is a marker of adulthood, strengthened further by parenthood. Arranged marriages are common, although romantic relationships between a boy and girl may precede formal marital negotiations with marriages arranged by fathers or among acquaintances at fairs and pilgrimages. Typically the groom's father requests the bride's hand in marriage from her father, to whom he pays a bride price in the form of money, gold, and property. Proper etiquette requires that a formal marriage proposal be accepted, as rejection is considered humiliating. Roma people consider another important occasion, death, to be impure. For this reason Roma avoid touching the body of the deceased, though elderly women are expected to prepare a dead body so that it may be shown to mourners during a vigil. All Roma hold a vigil for the dead that in some communities may last 14 days. Relatives and friends remain with the deceased from the moment of death until the burial. Friends will travel from far to support the grieving family and ask the deceased for forgiveness. Doing so assures that the dead will not return as evil spirits to punish them for any harm they may have caused them. All members of the dead's extended family, including children, are expected to participate in funerals and memorials. Some Roma place money or tools in the coffin, and may burn, discard, or give away the remainder of the deceased's possessions after the burial, consistent with their laws of purity.

Kathryn A. Kozaitis

Further Reading

Hancock, Ian. "The Emergence of a Union Dialect of North American Vlax Romani, and Its Implications for an International Standard." *International Journal of the Sociology of Language* 99 (1993): 91–123.

Kozaitis, Kathryn A. "Foreigners among Foreigners: Conscious Adaptation among the Roma of Athens, Greece." *Urban Anthropology and Studies of Cultural Systems and World Economic Development* 26 (1997): 165–99.

Matras, Yaron. *The Romani Gypsies.* Cambridge, MA: Harvard University Press, 2015.

Okely, Judith. *The Traveller Gypsies.* Cambridge: Cambridge University Press, 1983.

Silverman, Carol. *Romani Routes: Cultural Politics and Balkan Music in Diaspora.* Oxford: Oxford University Press, 2012.

Stewart, Michael. *The Time of the Gypsies.* Boulder, CO: Westview, 1997.

Sutherland, Anne. *Gypsies: The Hidden Americans.* Long Grove, IL: Waveland, 1986.

RUSSIA

Nikolai Gogol, an early genius of Russian letters, speculated on the savage coarseness concealed in refined manners, and explored this theme in such stories as "How the Two Ivans Quarreled." Gogol's pronouncement may seem harsh, but etiquette and taboos do act as a subtle means to form group identity, as well as to maintain that identity in relation to different groups. In Russia, regard for the family unit, including the individual gendered roles within a given family, is a central pillar of ethnic identity, and thus it is not surprising to find much of proper social behavior in Russia revolves around this theme.

A first meeting in Russia generally involves a certain amount of ceremony. A serious demeanor is expected, and if one smiles too much or tries to hug someone, it might be perceived as overly emotional or foolish. Verbal greetings make use of the formal вы (vy) form in both choice of pronouns and the conjugation of verbs, and this mode of speech will continue until you are invited to use the informal ты (ty) form. Thus, the traditional greeting "Zdravstvujte!" (literally, Be healthy!) rather than the informal "Zdravstvuj." On being introduced to children, however, the ты form is appropriate.

In addition, Russians use patronymics when addressing each other in formal situations as a means of demonstrating respect. Patronymics are created by taking an individual's father's first name, and adding the appropriate gendered suffix. For example, a brother and sister, let's say Boris and Yelena, whose father's name is Ivan would be Boris Ivanovich and Yelena Ivanovna respectively. Many Russians will forgive a foreigner's forgetting to use a patronymic, but it is always better to include it.

When making an acquaintance, shaking hands is traditional among men, and the older man should be the first to extend his hand. Among those of equal age, a handshake ought to be initiated by the man with more social authority. On the street, men who are friends will often greet each other with just a handshake and no verbal salute. Women tend to not shake hands, especially with men, and may be considered forward if they initiate a handshake. One should never shake hands across a doorway of any kind, as doing so is seen as a means for bad luck to enter. In older times, the threshold of a home was often the dwelling place of the *domovoi*, an ancestral house spirit, who would not take kindly to such behavior. While belief in folk spirits has passed, the prohibition concerning doorways remains. So much so, in fact, that it is bad luck to exchange anything through the entrance of a home. When ordering a pizza in Russia, one will either need to step outside or invite the delivery person inside in order to receive it.

Russians typically like to dress up, and for official events such as academic conferences, as well as attending church, it is mandatory. However, this social pressure to dress up extends to simpler occasions such as going to the cinema. Women are expected to dress in a traditionally feminine fashion. Indeed, in the dead of winter it is common to see the ice-covered sidewalks pierced by dozens of holes from women's stiletto heels.

Hospitality in Russia can be overwhelming to the unaware. If a guest is invited to someone's home, he or she should always bring a gift for the host. Every Russian knows the expression "Don't show up with empty hands." Flowers should always be given in an odd amount, as even numbers of flowers are associated with funerals and the deceased. It is important to arrive on time, as tardiness is considered disrespectful. When a guest arrives, he should take off his shoes immediately upon entering the host's home. In some cases, especially in villages, a host may offer a pair of slippers to use.

Russians tend to be fond of giving gifts, and if a guest expresses admiration for something in the host's home, it may be sincerely offered to the guest as a gift. It might be something the host can ill afford to part with, and it is perfectly acceptable to politely refuse. When borrowing something from someone, it is expected that it will be returned accompanied by a small gift. For example, if a person borrows a coffee pot, it should be returned filled with candy. Never give watches or clocks as gifts, nor scarves or knives, as these gifts have negative connotations. If this is done inadvertently, the gift-giver will probably receive a small token payment in return to nullify the ill omen involved.

When sitting down for a meal in a host's home, a guest should expect to make an evening of it, even if that meal is lunch. At the table, guests ought to wait for their host to invite them to begin eating, and should not depart before the guest of honor. Diners should not sit with their elbows on the table, or eat from a knife, but should expect to eat cake with a spoon. It is fine to ask for second helpings, although a host will likely replenish plates before guests can do so. Refusing food, and especially vodka and cognac, may be perceived as rudeness. Some excuses for doing so are considered as valid, such as training for a sports competition or feeling unwell. If a guest tells his host he is ill, he should expect to be offered advice, medications, and home remedies.

Russian drinking culture is rather sophisticated, and boasts a highly developed system of toasts. This is not surprising when it is considered that Prince Vladimir of Kievan Rus' embraced Christianity in the late tenth century because it had no taboos against drinking. Drinking in Russia is often incorporated into a meal, but when it is not, *zakuski* (drinking snacks) will always be present. Russians will always eat a little something after having a shot of alcohol, and will consider those who do not uncultivated. When someone pours a drink for a guest, the guest should keep his glass on the table. When drinking in honor of someone deceased, the glasses should not be clinked or raised too high. A single woman, however, should make sure that the last glass she clinks in a toast is with that of a man, preferably a single one. Empty bottles should be placed under the table.

Russians say that simply drinking alcohol is deplorable drunkenness, but drinking with toasts is an occasion! Everyone in a given gathering is expected to make at least one toast, but the first toast is the prerogative of the host. This toast is in honor of the meeting of all who are gathered. The second toast is given in honor of the hosts, but it can be to someone's parents as the occasion demands. The third toast is to love, and glasses are held in the left hand. This particular toast is subject to much regional variation, such as men needing to drink from a glass placed on the crook of their elbow. Additional toasts are made to fit the circumstances. Notice how the order of the toasts fits their subject—one meeting, two hosts (a husband and wife, traditionally), and three for love, suggesting a couple with a child.

While Russians can often act with unbridled enthusiasm, on the street a more serious demeanor is the norm. Russians have a wide range of established bodily gestures, but their use is not considered respectful in formal situations. The Russian sense of personal space is typically much smaller than that of the average American, and thus Russians will tend to stand closer to someone with whom they are speaking. On public transport Russians will tend to sit down in the first available place rather than seek out a more isolated spot. Queues in Russia may seem like a chaotic crowd as people tend not to form a line but instead inquire as to who is last before joining in.

The standard American greeting "How's it going?" is not the throwaway expression it is in the United States. If a visitor asks it of a Russian, he should expect to hear a sincere answer. As mentioned, formal forms of address are used until one has been invited to use the informal. Even teachers will often use the formal form with students if they are teenagers or older. On the internet, the вы form is the default setting as you may not be aware of the status of the person with whom you are chatting. When in doubt, use вы. It is considered rude to refer to someone present, especially an elder, by a pronoun. Always use a name or title when speaking about anyone present.

Traditionally Russians tend to marry when young, often in their late teens and early twenties. Long engagements are not common. Instead, couples tend to register with the state authorities, and then celebrate their wedding at the end of the 30-day waiting period. After this legal marriage, some couples choose to wait a considerable time, even decades, before having their church marriage. As divorce is strictly forbidden in the Russian Orthodox Church, this allows couples time to work out their relationship. Wedding rings are generally made of gold, and are worn on the right hand. A woman is not allowed to marry her sister's husband's brother—it is believed that the consequences of such a marriage will be catastrophic.

Once a couple is married they are expected to have children. Couples who elect not to have children are often considered to be mentally unsound, and family members may coerce them to seek therapy.

The Russian Orthodox Church is by far the most prominent religion in Russia. Practitioners of the Orthodox faith, and in particular women, are subject to various rules. In an Orthodox church, women should sit on the left-hand side, while men sit on the right. Married women are allowed to sit on the right-hand side if they are accompanying their husbands. As in other Abrahamic religions, women are expected to cover their hair while in church and wear long skirts. Men should not cover their heads. A woman may not enter the church for 40 days after giving birth, as she is considered unclean at this time, and vulnerable to evil spirits. Women may enter a church while menstruating, although it is not encouraged, but they must not touch anything while inside. Outside of the church, women are expected to obey their husbands.

Like all cultures, Russians have many customs surrounding death and ill luck, and a host of behaviors to avert them. When referring to the deceased, euphemisms such as "the departed" are commonly used, and it is proper to add something like "God rest their soul" as well. Russians will not wish someone a happy birthday or celebrate their own before the actual date of that birthday. To do otherwise is to tempt fortune and thus cause the premature death of the individual. The 40th birthday is not usually celebrated. In Orthodox belief, the soul is judged 40 days after death, and to rejoice on your 40th birthday is to court early judgement and death.

Russians avoid removing things from their homes after the sun has set, including taking out the trash. If something is taken out after dusk it is believed that the good luck of the house will depart along with it. Bad luck can also be passed through money, and many cashiers will ask customers to place it on the counter to prevent its transmission.

Nowadays—with the exception of profanity, which is quite rich in Russia—there are no words that are inherently taboo. This was not always the case. For example, the Russian word for bear, *medved*, is actually a euphemism that literally means "the one who knows honey," the real name of the bear being taboo. This taboo was so strong that the original word for bear is now lost.

Jeffry Pretes

Further Reading

"The Basics of the Best Russian Drinking Toasts." *Russia Beyond the Headlines*. Rossiyskaya Gazeta. http://rbth.com/blogs/2013/12/26/the_basics_of_the_best_russian_drinking _toasts_32961.html. Accessed June 13, 2015.

Dabars, Zita D., and Liliia Leonidovna. Vokhmina. *The Russian Way: Aspects of Behavior, Attitudes, and Customs of the Russians*. Chicago: McGraw-Hill, 2002.

Figes, Orlando. *Natasha's Dance: A Cultural History of Russia*. New York: Picador, 2002.

"Manners and Customs of the Russians." Russia IC. Guarant-InfoCentre. http://www.russia -ic.com/culture_art/traditions/337. Accessed June 10, 2015.

Ryan, W. F. *The Bathhouse at Midnight: An Historical Survey of Magic and Divination in Russia*. Stroud: Sutton, 1999.

Trommelen, Edwin, and David Stephenson. *Davai!: The Russians and Their Vodka*. Montpelier, VT: Russian Life, 2012.

S

SCANDINAVIA

Scandinavia is usually understood to include the countries of Denmark, Sweden, Norway, and Iceland, which share a common Viking heritage, as well as Finland, whose historical culture is very different. These five countries are better known in the region as the Nordic countries. While individual differences exist among these countries, there are broad patterns of etiquette common among all five.

Scandinavia is characterized by shared cultural traits such as a strong belief in equality and egalitarianism, a sense of collective purpose, an avoidance of flashiness and attention grabbing, a strong environmental ethos, and an emphasis on efficiency. These values shape various aspects of etiquette and taboos as practiced in Scandinavia.

In accord with Scandinavia's egalitarian principles, greetings will tend to involve a round of handshakes among all participants, regardless of age, gender, and social status. On more formal occasions, a further round of handshaking may be appropriate upon leaving. When shaking hands, Scandinavians maintain eye contact. The people of Scandinavia favor directness in communication. Thus, traditional American greetings such as "How are you?" may be taken quite seriously, especially in Denmark and Norway. In the United States, one of the first questions asked of a stranger is "What do you do?" This kind of question is generally seen as prying and intrusive at a first meeting in Scandinavia. Instead, a person should wait for others to talk more about themselves, but one should be aware that for Scandinavians talking too much about oneself can be considered boastful and pretentious. Often introductions may begin on a first-name basis, but honorifics combined with surnames are used at times with individuals of high social standing, and as a rule with elders. In any case a person's title (especially important in the case of Doctor, Professor, or Engineer) or the local equivalent of Mr. or Ms. should be used until one is asked to use a person's first name. In Iceland, surnames are not as fixed as in most of Europe, and an individual's surname may be his or her father's name with *son* or *dottir* added as a suffix. Famously, Icelanders are listed under their first names in telephone directories.

Dress is generally casual, particularly among Norwegians and Danes, though "casual" means something different than how that term is used in describing American dress: Scandinavian casual means neat, well dressed, and tasteful, without going overboard in formal accessories or styles of clothing. For formal occasions formal dress is expected. Scandinavians usually avoid bright colors and prefer more somber earth tones in their clothing, but there are exceptions, especially among the young. Scandinavians generally keep a low but neat profile, without using flashy jewelry or accessories. Scandinavians usually remove their shoes while at home, and guests will also be expected to remove theirs as well.

When invited to a Scandinavian home for a meal or party, guests should be sure to arrive punctually, as any lateness is considered disrespectful. Also, guests do not arrive early, but strive to arrive exactly on time. Dinners tend to be in the early evening, but guests are expected to stay for an hour or more after the meal. Seating arrangements around the table tend to be predetermined, and the host will indicate each person's place. The host and hostess will be seated at opposite ends of the table, with the male guest of honor at the side of the hostess, and the female guest of honor at the host's side. In Finland, all the women in attendance may be seated on one side of the table with the men opposite and the hosts at the ends. Guests should not start eating before the host invites everyone to do so, or before the host has begun to eat. European table manners are the norm, with the fork always held in the left hand. The only food permissible to be eaten with one's hands is bread, and lettuce in salads should be curled around the fork, not cut. Even sandwiches and pizza are eaten with utensils. Hands should always be visible—placed on the table or above when not eating. In Finland and Iceland it is acceptable to lay one's wrists on the table. Dishes are passed around the table, often to the left, and guests are expected to help themselves. In Sweden, if passing something such as salt to a fellow guest it should be handed to them directly, whereas in Finland it should be placed on the table within reach. In restaurants one can draw the server's attention by making eye contact or raising a hand slightly, but should not wave or shout.

Most Scandinavians (especially Finns) love coffee and will drink it after (never during) meals and at set morning and afternoon times. In any gathering it is always the host who will propose the first toast. In Denmark, Sweden, and Norway the most common toast is "Skoal!," whereas in Finland it will be "Kippis!" It is customary to always maintain eye contact during a toast with each individual in the party. A guest should not reach for his glass until the host has finished with their toast. After this initial toast guests may drink as they normally would. It is expected that guests will propose their own toast, and this may be to the hosts. However, this is not considered proper in Finland, but the male guest of honor is expected to thank the hosts immediately after the meal on behalf of all the guests. This is common in Norway and Sweden as well. Toasts will be made with wine or spirits, but generally not with beer.

When visiting someone's home, it is customary to always bring a gift for the hosts. Chocolates, wine or spirits, and flowers are the traditional gifts. Flowers should always be given in odd numbers, and it is not appropriate to give flowers associated with funerals, such as lilies and other white flowers. Additionally, yellow flowers should not be given in Finland for the same reasons, nor should red roses be given in Sweden outside of a romantic relationship. In Norway, flowers can be delivered in the morning so that they may grace the dinner table that evening. Any wrapped gifts should be opened when received. For the Sami, Scandinavia's indigenous people, gift-giving within the local community is a means to maintain group solidarity. When visiting someone in their home, one should not wander around or request a tour of the house. Most parts of a Scandinavian home are considered

Culture Shock! ⊕

The Art of *Hygge*

The Danish word *hygge* (pronounced "hoo-ga") derives from the Norwegian word for well-being and is often translated into English as "coziness." However, *hygge* is more than mere coziness. Rather *hygge* is a relaxed lifestyle concept based on the ideal of doing simple things that gladden the soul, being free of life's irritations, and taking pleasure from gentle pleasures, such as entertaining friends and family while enjoying candlelight, coffee, and cake. The adjectival form of *hygge*, *hyggeligt*, is the word offered as a compliment to a host after an enjoyable time spent at their home. *Hygge* has recently become very trendy in the United Kingdom, with some Danish language schools in England offering classes in how to live a *hygge* lifestyle.

Victoria Williams

private and off-limits, including the kitchen. If the family knows the guest well, then he or she maybe be invited to these spaces.

Scandinavians are usually direct in conversation and avoid small talk and chit-chat. Especially in Finland and Sweden, people value their privacy even in public, and do not make conversation with strangers on public transit, while waiting in lines, or on the street. People tend to keep a serious demeanor in public places—appearing cool and calm at all times is important. Boasting and unruly behavior are very much frowned upon, though bear in mind that Scandinavians are tolerant of the customs of others, and if a visitor behaves in moderation and without excess he will get along well with them.

Some gestures that are common in the United States are considered rude in Scandinavia. These include making the "OK" gesture by linking thumb and index finger (considered obscene), making a "V" with the fingers with the palm facing in (the equivalent of raising a single middle finger), and crooking your finger to summon someone (obscene; instead, you should hold your hand out with palm down, and move your four fingers back and forth). In Finland, crossing your arms in front of your body can be interpreted as a standoffish and even hostile gesture.

In general, Scandinavians avoid backslapping, hugging, and other similar gestures until a close relationship is established. While handshaking is a common greeting practice, other physical displays are not acceptable outside of close family circles or with intimate friends. In general it is good to respect personal space. Scandinavians are also comfortable with silences, and do not expect these to be filled with small talk. Scandinavians, especially Swedes and Finns, may pause thoughtfully before replying to questions or statements. Conversations are usually held in low or medium tones, without elaborate gestures, and never in loud voices. While Scandinavians generally have an informal approach without elaborate ceremony, they do respect politeness and appreciate a sense of seriousness. Slouching, gum chewing, and other such behaviors are frowned upon.

Scandinavia is a largely secular place, and church participation and attendance are relatively low. Consequently, formal marriage is increasingly less common, and many Scandinavians live with a partner outside a formal married relationship. It is therefore unwise to bring up the topic of marriage or inquire into a person's marital status. Likewise do not inquire too much about a person's family, but wait for them to tell you what they want you to know.

Scandinavians tend to respect rules and see themselves as very law abiding. They frown upon those that willingly subvert rules, even to the point of refusing to cross streets against traffic signals. Do not touch produce in grocery stores or handle any kind of product too roughly (for example, in a store ask for assistance before opening a box to see the item inside). Scandinavians are extremely environmentally conscious, so do not do anything that can be construed as antienvironment, such as littering. Always knock before opening a closed door, and leave doors as you found them after passing through.

The sauna (bathhouse) is an integral part of Finnish life, and has been so for hundreds of years. Refusing an invitation to the sauna, while not an insult, should be avoided whenever possible. Most invitations to a Finnish home, whether for dinner or for a party, will include a sauna, as will business parties held at hotels. Most hotels have a sauna with separate evening times for male and female guests. All Finnish homes will have their own sauna and in apartment buildings there will either be a sauna in each apartment or a larger one that is shared among tenants,

Men enjoy a sauna in Finland. Most homes and apartments in Finland have either a private sauna or access to a sauna. An invitation to a home usually includes an invitation to the sauna. (age fotostock/Alamy Stock Photo)

with each tenant having a few hours per week as their private time. Most Finns go into the sauna naked. When entering a sauna, one should remove one's clothing in an outer room, take a quick shower (located adjacent to the sauna proper), and then enter the sauna. It is also possible to shower upon leaving before getting dressed. Saunas are usually gendered; women will go into the sauna together, and after they have finished then men will have their sauna time. Mixed saunas, where men and women enter together, are not uncommon; however, the sauna is a strictly nonsexual space. In general, it is a good idea to know the situation at a given sauna before you go. In any event, a towel is needed to sit down on while in the steam room. Sauna conversation ought to avoid controversial topics. Always be respectful of others as well as the sauna itself. Otherwise you risk offending the *saunatonttu*—the sauna's tutelary spirit.

Michael Pretes

Further Reading

Booth, Michael. *The Almost Nearly Perfect People: Behind the Myth of the Scandinavian Utopia.* New York: Picador, 2014.

Kingsley, Patrick. *How to Be Danish: A Journey to the Cultural Heart of Denmark.* New York: Marble Arch Press, 2012.

Lacy, Terry G. *Ring of Seasons: Iceland, Its Culture and History.* Ann Arbor: University of Michigan Press, 2000.

Lewis, Richard D. *Finland: Cultural Lone Wolf.* Yarmouth, ME: Intercultural Press, 2005.

Nordstrom, Byron J. *Culture and Customs of Sweden.* Santa Barbara, CA: Greenwood, 2010.

Notaker, Henry. *Food Culture in Scandinavia.* Santa Barbara, CA: Greenwood, 2009.

O'Leary, Margaret Hayford. *Culture and Customs of Norway.* Santa Barbara, CA: Greenwood, 2010.

SINGAPORE

Singapore is a multiethnic society, home to a diverse collection of cultural and religious beliefs and practices. Due to centuries of immigration, Singapore's population is made up of Chinese (about 75 percent), Malay (14 percent), and Indian (9 percent) communities. In addition, there are a number of smaller ethnic groups, including Eurasians, Arabs, and Europeans. The major religions of Singapore are Buddhism, Taoism, Islam, Christianity, and Hinduism. While the Malay community is almost exclusively Muslim, the Indian community comprises followers of Hinduism as well as Sikhism, Islam, and Christianity (Catholics as well as Protestants). The Chinese community is predominantly Buddhist or Taoist, but with an increasing number of Christians. This great cultural and religious diversity is reflected in different rules of etiquette and taboos across Singaporean society.

When addressing people older than yourself in Singapore it is customary to use an honorific title, such as "aunt" and "uncle," or "Mr." and "Madam" (only for married women, with their maiden surname). The terms "uncle" and "aunt" are widely used and should be understood as a sign of respect and have nothing to do with the actual age of the person; hence a person may be called "aunt" (or "aunty") whether she is 25 or 85 years old. Age and generation likewise determine the order of introductions, so older persons are introduced first. Family members and siblings often address each other by kinship terms, such as "older sister" or "younger brother." Younger siblings, however, are often addressed by first name. Peers address each other by first name.

Shaking hands is the most common form of greeting in modern Singapore. It is not proper to greet with a kiss or hug. In fact, kissing and hugging are not common even among family members and friends. The left hand is never used to greet someone of Malay or Indian descent, since the left hand is considered unclean. Greeting customs may vary between the ethnic groups. Malays sometimes place their right hand over their heart after greeting others. Malays and Indians may choose not to shake hands with members of the opposite gender. Instead they greet them by bowing the head. The traditional Malay greeting is called *salaam*, whereby the men stretch out both arms to touch each other's hands and then bring their hands back across their chest. When women *salaam* they often kneel first, before reaching for the hands. Women and men do not *salaam* with each other. In formal situations, such as business meetings, it is customary to exchange business cards. Business cards are usually offered and accepted with both hands, and it is polite to spend some time looking at the card before carefully putting it away.

Singaporeans are quite relaxed when it comes to attire. Smart casual dress works in most situations. Today most Singaporeans wear so-called Western clothing, although each ethnic group has its own traditional attire (for example, the Chinese *cheongsam* dress, the Indian sari, the Malay *kebaya* blouse-dress, and the Sikh turban). These are mostly worn on special occasions, such as weddings or other celebrations. The Sikh turban is permanent daily attire. Women of Malay descent often wear a headscarf, but far from all Singaporean Malay women adhere to this custom. The same goes for the hat worn by Muslim men. Certain dress codes apply when visiting places of worship.

It is not easy to describe Singaporean cuisine as the food served in Singapore is the result of myriad coexisting food traditions: Chinese, Malay, Indian, Peranakan or Straits Chinese food, among others. What can be said, however, is that Singaporeans take food seriously. Most Singaporeans know exactly where to go to find the tastiest Hainanese chicken rice, *roti prata* (an Indian flat bread served with curry), *laksa* (rice vermicelli in curry gravy), or chili crab. Food and table manners differ depending on the ethnicity of the host. Chinese eat with chopsticks and a small spoon for soup, while Malays and Indians usually eat with a spoon and/or their hands. One should never use the left hand to eat if the host is of Malay or Indian descent. Western-style knives and forks are common at restaurants, but using a spoon and fork is more usual. But regardless of ethnic group, it is the universal practice to set food dishes out on the table to be shared by all. Dining out is popular in Singapore, and it is easy to understand why. Singapore is widely considered a food paradise, where one can find any dish to satisfy any craving, be it Chinese, Japanese, Mexican, or Lebanese. For casual occasions, there are numerous hawker centers and indoor food courts, where you can get a good meal at very low cost. For more formal occasions, there are plenty of regular restaurants. Food is a beloved pastime for most Singaporeans, and many are happy to provide useful recommendations for particular types of food experiences to visitors.

When invited to dinner at a restaurant, the guest should let the host order all the dishes. The idea of reciprocity is important in Singaporean culture, so splitting the dinner bill is uncommon. The host pays the bill and it is expected that next time you will reciprocate the treat. Tipping is not customary in Singapore and is, in fact, discouraged by the government, but most restaurant establishments add a service charge. When visiting a Singaporean home, shoes should be removed and left by the entrance. If invited to dinner, it is polite to bring a gift to the host, such as flowers, fruit, or a small present. Gift-giving is an important marker of reciprocity and a demonstration of relationship. Gifts are normally not opened when received. One should not be surprised if a person initially refuses a gift before accepting it; this is usually an act of politeness, so the recipient does not appear greedy. In Singapore, it is customary to give money as a gift at weddings, birthdays, and at major festivals, such as the Chinese New Year or the Muslim Hari Raya Puasa (the end of Ramadan). There are certain cultural differences with regard to gift-giving. Red is an auspicious color in Chinese culture, hence Chinese commonly exchange red envelopes containing money (called *hongbao* in Mandarin). Malays use green envelopes and Indians prefer envelopes in yellow or any bright color. If a guest attends a Chinese wedding banquet, he tries to estimate the cost of each guest's dinner, and puts the equivalent sum or more in the envelope. It is customary to put only even numbers (e.g., 80, 100, 120 Singaporean dollars) in the envelope, because even numbers are considered auspicious in Chinese culture. In Indian culture, on the contrary, odd numbers are considered lucky. Avoid giving alcohol, items made of pigskin, or food containing pork to a Muslim Singaporean. Likewise, avoid giving items or food containing beef to Hindus. One should use the right hand when giving or receiving a gift from a person of Malay or Indian descent.

Singaporeans are usually subtle and indirect in their verbal and nonverbal communications. Body language and facial expressions are important. It is considered impolite to make strong statements that may lead to open confrontation. Likewise, Singaporeans do not express affection in public. It is impolite to point at someone with the index finger and to touch a person's head. Pointing at objects is often done with the thumb or pursed lips.

The family is central to Singaporean life, both as cultural tradition and a unit of support. Singapore is allegedly an "antiwelfare" state, where the family assumes primary responsibility for the care of elderly and younger family members. Neglected elderly parents are entitled to take their adult children to court if they do not provide necessary support. Regardless of these political and judicial dimensions, the family is an important cultural institution across all ethnic groups. According to the Chinese notion of filial piety, adult children are expected to reciprocate their parents' care by providing material as well as practical support. Whereas extended family living arrangements are less popular with the younger generation, which tends to prefer the nuclear household, it is still common for old parents to reside with one of their children. Likewise, the number of single households remains small. The term *filial piety* is of Chinese origin but the ideas and practices of intergenerational support and reciprocity apply to the Malay and Indian communities as well.

Singapore is home to a great diversity of religious practices and beliefs. While the state is secular, religion plays an important role in the lives of most Singaporeans. Different places of worship have different rules of etiquette. When entering a mosque, the place of worship for followers of Islam, footwear should be removed. Female visitors should wear a headscarf and robe (most mosques provide such attire for female visitors). The women's section is behind that of the men, and sometimes curtained off. Visitors to Hindu temples are expected to remove their shoes and wash their hands and feet before entering. Clothing should be modest and suitable for sitting on the floor, as is customary. Devotees usually bring flowers, food, and incense sticks as offerings for the gods. Visitors should avoid pointing their feet toward the deities or any sacred objects. In Singapore it is not uncommon for Buddhists to visit Taoist temples and vice versa, hence the etiquette is quite similar. As with Hinduism, offerings of food and flowers and the burning of incense are common practice. Visitors should not touch Buddha statues and avoid pointing at people or things in the temple, as this is considered disrespectful. Use an upturned open palm gesture instead. In some, but not all, Buddhist and Taoist temples in Singapore, visitors are expected to remove their shoes. Most churches in Singapore are Catholic or Protestant. Unlike mosques and temples, Christian churches provide pews where visitors can sit during prayer or services. Visitors are not expected to remove their shoes. There is no particular dress code but, as in other places of worship, clothing should be modest.

In multireligious and multiethnic Singapore, perceptions of death vary. Chinese hold funeral wakes ranging from three to seven days—but always an odd number, since even numbers are associated with joy. During the wake, family and friends are expected to pay their respects to the deceased. Cash contributions are presented in white envelopes, since white is the color of mourning. Malays do not hold wakes, since according to Islam the body should be buried as soon as possible after death. Indians do not hold wakes either.

Religion and race are considered politically sensitive subjects in Singapore and are best avoided in conversation. The strict monitoring of these subjects is aimed at preserving religious harmony. The Maintenance of Religious Harmony Act (passed in 1990) allows the government to take actions against any person or group whose actions or speech could harm racial or religious harmony. It should be noted that Singapore is in general known for its strict punishments for even trivial breaches, such as littering and vandalism. Singapore is also known for its strict monitoring of mainstream media. The country ranks low in the press freedom indexes, such as the Reporters Without Borders World Press Freedom Index (in 2015 Singapore ranked 153 out of 180 countries in terms of press freedom).

Singaporeans are very active users of social media. The impact of social media was particularly evident in the 2011 Singapore General Election, when the Internet became a platform where ordinary Singaporeans expressed their political opinions. The Media Development Authority has attempted to regulate social media through various licensing requirements, and bloggers risk being sued for defamatory remarks. This was evinced in 2014 when a blogger was sued and found guilty of defaming the prime minister.

Kristina Göransson

Further Reading

Bravo-Bhasin, Marión. *CultureShock! Singapore: A Survival Guide to Customs and Etiquette*, 3rd ed. Tarrytown, NY: Marshall Cavendish, 2012.

Göransson, Kristina. *The Binding Tie: Chinese Intergenerational Relations in Modern Singapore.* Honolulu: University of Hawai'i Press, 2009.

Lai, Ah Eng. *Meanings of Multiethnicity: A Case-Study of Ethnicity and Ethnic Relations in Singapore.* Kuala Lumpur: Oxford University Press, 1995.

Lai, Ah Eng, ed. *Religious Diversity in Singapore.* Singapore: Institute of Southeast Asian Studies jointly with Institute of Policy Studies, 2008.

Milligan, Angela. *Culture Smart! Singapore: The Essential Guide to Customs and Culture.* London: Kuperard, 2004.

Ong, Jin Hui, Chee Kiong Tong, and Ern Ser Tan, eds. *Understanding Singapore Society.* Singapore: Times Academic Press, 1997.

SOUTH KOREA

The Korean kingdom, called the *Gojoseon*, emerged as the first recognizable state of the Korean people about 2300 BCE. The people and culture of Korea have a rich history and heritage. South Korea was established as a modern nation in 1948.

In order to understand South Korean cultural etiquette and taboos, a person needs to have knowledge of two major influences in South Korea: Confucianism and the Korean concept of *kibun*. In South Korea, Confucianism serves to guide social relationships between individuals in South Korean society. Confucianism has also influenced South Korean etiquette concerning ideas of duty, loyalty, honor, and respect for others. *Kibun* is the idea of a person's feelings of harmony, peace, and well-being that are so important in Korean culture.

Greetings in South Korea have certain rules. The more formal the setting, the more formal the greeting. Typical greetings consist of a bow at an approximately 45-degree angle. The person of lower status—typically based on one's age or job—generally initiates the bow. When people greet each other they do not slap each other on the back or hug each other. Hugging is reserved for couples and is usually done in private. If a man is speaking with another man he may put his hand on the other man's knee to show that he likes the other man as a friend and that he respects him. Following a bow greeting the person will say "Ban-geop-seum-nida," which means "Pleased to meet you." The person who is the most senior in the greeting will typically initiate a handshake after the exchange of bows. In South Korea it is customary to always shake with the right hand, and the handshake should be a soft handshake rather than a hard clasp. When shaking hands, the left hand should be placed near or under the right elbow to show mutual respect and honor for the other person because displaying respect and honor is a key teaching in Confucianism.

When addressing another person, one does not call the person by his or her first name but rather by his or her family name or last name. If two people are close in age and good friends, they may call one another by their respective first names. In business settings, a person is called by his or her title such as "boss." Also in a business context, two people will exchange business cards during a greeting. The business cards will be placed on a table for several minutes before being stored away as a means of acknowledging the importance of the other person.

South Koreans typically love to get dressed up for social occasions. In business settings, a suit and tie for men and dress shoes are expected. When one is invited to a house for dinner as a guest, one should dress for the occasion by wearing rather formal attire. In South Korea it is considered very important to wear clean socks at all times. This is because when a person enters a home, school, restaurant, temple, or old building, etiquette calls for the person to remove his or her shoes, thereby revealing their socks. Wearing dirty socks is, therefore, taboo in South Korea. In a place of one's employment shoes are not removed as a general rule. At most occasions in South Korean culture, modesty in dress is the societal norm. Shorts and jeans are not considered appropriate attire in most South Korean gatherings.

Hospitality and table manner etiquette are very important, especially in formal and business settings. In a home the role of the host and hostess is to provide the most delicious meal possible for their guests. The role of the guest is to eat everything that is served to them and hopefully ask for seconds. When a person's boss invites one to dinner, along with a gathering of other people, one should never eat until the boss has begun eating. When using chopsticks, a person should never stick the chopsticks into a bowl of food; rather, the chopsticks should be placed on the side of the plate or bowl. Kimchi is the national dish in South Korea. It is a hot and spicy mixture of fermented and pickled vegetables. Meat dishes such as *bulgogi* (barbecued meat) and *kalbi* (short ribs) are some of the most popular foods among both South Koreans and foreigners. South Korea has no food taboos, although Buddhist monks may observe some food taboos or practice vegetarianism. It is customary in South Korea that everyone at the dining table will drink alcohol or the traditional South Korean rice wine called soju. Drinking is part and parcel of the South Korean social fabric, and it is expected at dinner and when gathering with colleagues after work. When drinks are served it is important to remember that a person never pours his own drink. Instead, the drink is poured by the other people at the table to that person's right. In like manner, if one notices that a person's glass of wine is getting low, they will pour the drink for the other person at the table. When filling the glass at the table, the right hand is used with the support of the left hand underneath the elbow. When the meals and drinking are finished, the boss will pay the bill or the oldest person at the table will pay for the meals and drinks.

South Korean body language is rather reserved and modest. In public speaking South Koreans tend to avoid flamboyant gestures, or what others might call "talking with one's hands." When calling for a waiter or waitress to a come to a table in a restaurant, the palm of a person's hand is held face down instead of face up, and a person motions to their server using a "dog paddle" kind of motion using their palm and all of their fingers.

Verbal communication in South Korea always involves what is called "honorific language" or the highest and most polite form of speech when two adults meet and speak to each other for the first time. When two people know each other very well, they may relax their language with one another and forego the honorific speech. Verbal communication typically revolves around conversations about sports, the health of one's family, and personal hobbies. Subjects that should be avoided in general conversation include politics, the Korean War, socialism, communism, or personal family matters. Also, it is important that a person should not confuse or compare South Korea with other Asian countries, especially Japan. If a person is given a compliment, she should not respond with "Thank you" as this is not thought to be modest—which is another influence of Confucianism. In conversations a person should not be surprised to be asked personal questions such as one's age or salary.

When two people get married in South Korea it is a family affair. The families of both the bride and the groom must give their consent to the marriage. Not to seek the family consent is taboo. It is also taboo to marry someone of the same last name, especially if the man and woman are from the same locality. The influences of Western culture have impacted many modern-day South Korean wedding ceremonies; however, South Korean wedding ceremonies with traditional South Korean clothing and Confucian practices are still observed in the country. In most South Korean weddings, wooden Mandarin ducks are used as a symbol for longevity, loyalty, and commitment in marriage since South Koreans believe that Mandarin ducks mate for life.

Traditionally, South Korea has been a male-dominated society. In South Korean culture, it is the duty of a woman to bear her husband children, especially a son. If a South Korean woman does not bear her husband a son, it is not considered to be good for the family. A son is desired in a family in order to carry on the family name and also to care for his parents once they reach old age.

When a person dies in South Korea there is a three-day ceremony that is held to honor and remember that person's life. The body of the deceased is cleaned but not embalmed. South Koreans do not embalm the bodies of their deceased as this is thought to disturb the balance or *kibun* of the body, even in death. The body is then dressed in a suit or a dress and placed into a casket. South Koreans do not cremate the bodies of the deceased, based on teachings in Confucianism. The casket is then placed into a white tent and a black curtain is hung in the tent in front of the casket. The living are expected to pay their respects to the deceased. When a parent dies, etiquette dictates that the oldest son act as master of ceremonies for the funeral service.

Each year, South Koreans perform a three-day observation called *Chuseok*, which is the South Korean version of Thanksgiving. The occasion is intended to honor ancestors. South Koreans observe *Chuseok* on the 15th day of the eighth month of the lunar calendar. During *Chuseok*, South Korean family members go to the gravesites of their deceased family members and have a three-day meal on the actual gravesite in order to honor their ancestors. It is taboo if a person does not honor his or her family's ancestors in South Korean culture.

David H. Campbell

Further Reading
Crane, Paul S. *Korean Patterns*. Seoul: Royal Asiatic Society Korea Branch, 1974.
De Mente, Boyé Lafayette. *The Korean Mind: Understanding Contemporary Korean Culture*. North Clarendon, VT: Tuttle Publishing, 2012.
Korea.net—Gateway to Korea. "The Beginnings of the Country's History (Prehistoric Times—Gojoseon)." http://www.korea.net/AboutKorea/History/The-Beginnings-of-the-Countrys-History. Accessed June 27, 2015.

SOUTHERN AFRICA

Southern Africa is a general term for the southern region of Africa, which includes the countries of Namibia, Botswana, Lesotho, Swaziland, and South Africa. Other southern countries that are sometimes added are Angola, Malawi, Mozambique, Zimbabwe, and Zambia. The region is filled with rules of etiquette and taboos that are nuanced according to various tribes. The cultural differences are most seen between urban and rural areas. Rural areas tend to continue traditional African customs while urban areas have embraced more Western ones. Sharing information in the form of a narrative story is a natural type of communication in Southern Africa. Rules regarding etiquette and taboos are passed along in similar fashion.

The overwhelming rule of etiquette for Southern Africa, including rural and urban areas, is sensitivity to the African definition of time. Time is event oriented. Africans are more concerned about the event taking place than the timing of the event. Rushing through greetings, meals, or other events could be interpreted as rude and disinterested behavior. Be prepared to stop and take the appropriate amount of time to enjoy the event. Also do not be too driven by deadlines or schedules. What is most important is that the event takes place and not that it started or ended on time.

The most important African custom is meeting and greeting one another. Learning a few African phrases used in the greeting process will be appreciated. The emphasis in the greeting custom is the content that is shared. The exchange follows a few simple guidelines that can vary slightly between tribes. Africans are usually willing to forgive a few greeting missteps as long as the exchange provides a detailed review.

In contrast, the Western custom can be very quick and superficial. A few simple words can be exchanged as two people walk past each other. One may even ask, "How are you?" without a sincere desire to stop and share any events that may answer the question. Both parties are, however, very content to continue walking past each other without any further explanation. Africans would likely take offense to this style of greeting.

Within the African custom of meeting and greeting, one is expected to stop and greet one another. Many tribes will quickly grip the hand twice while shaking hands. Others will also place the left hand on the right forearm as a sign of respect. Persons of the same gender will continue to hold hands until the conversation is complete. Opposite genders may end the handshake quicker or even offer a quick nod instead. Regardless, continue forward in the conversation.

Some greetings might take an extended time. Greeting conversations can cover any personal event such as work, health, spouse, and family. Provide plenty of opportunities for Africans to share as much as they desire, but be prepared to offer the same. Both parties in the greeting are expected to update the other about personal events with a great level of detail.

If you recognize someone, take the time to walk over and initiate the greeting custom. It is considered rude to avoid or walk past someone familiar. Taking the time to greet someone properly will make a lasting impression and smooth over cultural mistakes.

In a rural setting, a formal introduction and greeting to the village chief needs to be made prior to any business venture or event planning. Strangers walking through the village and organizing gatherings will be viewed with suspicion. Initial greetings should be made by key leaders. The chief is considered the most important person in the village and should be the focus of the first visit.

Western attire such as pants, shirts, and dresses are worn throughout Southern Africa, though traditional African wardrobe is still worn by a few tribes. Africans in rural areas tend to lean very conservative in appearance and dress. In particular, women are expected to wear skirts or dresses. Clothing that is very short, tight, or revealing is discouraged. Clothing has to be very functional in rural areas of Southern Africa where extended periods of walking are commonplace. Urban areas are more progressive with updated clothing and styles on display, especially within larger cities.

The most important meal of the day is dinner. Breakfast and lunch should be served with smaller portions, with the largest given during the evening meal. In rural areas, a traditional *mielie* meal is made from crushed maize with a firm consistency similar to mashed potatoes. The *mielie* meal is served with a side of meat. One is expected to use hands and not utensils to eat the traditional meal. Meals in urban areas may include Western-style foods with eating utensils. Foods should be passed and received with right hands only. Placing the eating utensils together on the plate is a sign that one is finished with the meal. In both rural and urban areas, guests are served first and then the men. Children are served next, and women are served last. In some tribes, women and children will gather and eat separately.

Africans have a very close personal space. In rural areas, close friends of the same gender might even hold hands as they engage in a conversation or walk together through the village. Although the personal space is much smaller, overt physical gestures like slapping a person on the back, grabbing someone's arm, or shaking someone with a side hug are discouraged. Constant joking and rough horseplay are not bridges to friendships.

Long periods of silence are completely acceptable. Sitting together and enjoying the day is a great relationship builder. Eye contact should be comfortable but not extended. Prolonged eye contact can be interpreted as hostile.

If gifts or items are exchanged, use the right hand to present or accept. As a sign of respect, place the left hand on the right forearm as the item is exchanged. Extend both hands to receive a large item, if necessary, but avoid using only the left hand. Gifts should be opened immediately in the presence of the giver.

Oral traditions are practiced as a form of passing along cultural and family heritage. As a type of oral tradition, stories can take the form of music, dance, and singing. The ability to play any musical instrument is highly regarded. In particular, the African drum has played an integral part of tribal identity and communication. An entire village can express emotions through the African drum, such as anger, mourning, or celebration.

Families are the cornerstones to African culture. A village is a local gathering of families. A tribe represents a larger ethnic and spiritual gathering of similar villages and family members. Tribes share wealth, food, and resources with all members and are identified by totems. Most tribal totems are in the form of an animal. An animal totem also has the task of being a spiritual guide for the village. Care must be taken not to handle totems because of their religious nature.

Courting rituals vary from arranged marriages to romantic marriages. The bridegroom must pay a *lobola*, or price, to the bride's father for his daughter's hand in marriage. In rural areas, the *lobola* is paid in the form of cattle. Urban residents will use cash instead. The bride's grandparents can also be given additional gifts, such as blankets and clothing. Polygamy is an acceptable practice if the *lobola* can be afforded. A husband with many wives is seen as influential and wealthy.

The wedding event can last several days with relatives arriving throughout the week. Traditional weddings are held at night during a full moon. The bride's parents do not attend the ceremony. With the influence of Christianity, a more Western style of daytime weddings, including the giving away of the bride by the father, is becoming more common. In cases of divorce, the *lobola* is returned to the husband. Extended family members usually become involved in the proceedings to save the marriage and to keep from returning the *lobola*.

In rural areas, women have traditional roles within the home and family. The additional wives in a polygamous marriage would share in the household responsibilities. Men are seen more as protectors and providers.

Pregnant women hold a special place in the tribe. Care must be taken not to rub the stomach of a pregnant woman. Rubbing the stomach can be interpreted as a sexual gesture within some tribes. In the case of a pregnant woman, some tribes believe that touching a pregnant woman's stomach can pass bad spirits to the new child. Unwed pregnant mothers are sometimes described as "falling pregnant." The reference is similar to someone catching an unexpected virus and "falling ill."

From an early age, children are encouraged to become active members in the communal lifestyle described as tribalism. Children are raised, taught, and disciplined by any member of the village. They are viewed as belonging to the village. Older generations are to be respected as they are the primary shapers of tribal identity. Young children are expected to sit and listen as elders share stories about their village and tribe. As the children grow to have their own families, they will share the same stories with their youth.

Many Southern Africans identify their religious beliefs by family, village, and tribe. Music, singing, and dancing are also integral parts of religious expressions. Avoid making disparaging remarks about religious practices, members, and religious figures, as spirituality is part of the African identity.

Christianity is practiced widely throughout Southern Africa with Pentecostalism being the most common form. To a smaller degree, other major world religions are also present, such as Islam, Baha'i, and Hinduism. Many African countries have established worship centers in urban areas where they are afforded legal and zoning protections. Rural areas are less formal and focus on gathering times in the village center.

Traditional African beliefs center on ancestor worship. The physical and spirit world interact together and influence daily living. Small offerings are given to dead ancestors when seeking affirmation for a decision or relief from a difficult event. Even for Africans that identify with a major world religion, many will continue the practice of ancestor worship. Any discussions about parents or grandparents, especially if deceased, should be respectful and positive.

Along with ancestor worship, another aspect of traditional African beliefs that is still practiced is witchcraft. A witch can inflict a variety of illnesses, injuries, and bad fortune. For a price, a diviner can remove the curse and find the responsible witch, who is then subject to village justice.

Worship with masks and body paintings is not a common traditional practice unless part of a holiday or special ceremonial event. With the mask, the wearer represents a spirit being communicating to the people. The African drum and an intricate dance play a prominent part in the spirit being sharing a message to the people.

The village chief is the primary gatekeeper of allowed religious services in rural settings. Organizing religious gatherings without prior permission from the chief will be poorly attended and possibly discouraged. Worship events can last several hours in duration and include music, singing, and dancing. Entire generations will attend and worship together. The worship service is scheduled as an event and not for a particular time. People can walk in and join with the others at any point. Being late to a worship service is not an offense of etiquette.

While everyday attire consists of shirts and blue jeans, people are expected to dress more formally for a religious service. Men will wear dress shirts and leather shoes. Women will also wear nicer dresses and skirts. Religious leaders will wear coats and ties. Although a common practice in urban worship centers, more formal attire is also seen in many rural villages.

Death is not considered the end of life within African culture. Death is understood as a passage from the physical world into the spirit world. The departed one has left his or her physical body and taken up a spiritual one. The spiritual body will take the form of either an ancestor or an animal totem that is ready to guide the village members.

The burial event can take several days as relatives travel to pay their respects to the family. An animal is sacrificed in the burial ritual to avoid further calamity. To keep the departed spirit from returning to the home, the body is removed through a side door or a hole in the wall. The procession to the cemetery will wander back and forth along the path to further confuse the departed spirit. Singles and children are not allowed to attend the burial ceremony.

The bereaved family members will be expected to go through a period of mourning. Some tribes expect the widows to spend this time alone. After a period of mourning, the bringing-home ritual is initiated as part of ancestor worship. The departed spirit has finished the transition to an ancestor and is ready to return to the home. The ancestor is represented by dirt gathered from the gravesite. The grave dirt is placed inside a bottle and brought back to the home. Some tribes will organize a formal procession for the bringing-home ceremony. Once in the home, the new ancestor is ready to guide the remaining family members. The bottles can be placed on display in bedrooms or on window sills. They should not be handled, as they are viewed as spiritual artifacts.

Arnold Arredondo

Further Reading

Holt-Biddle, David. *Culture Smart! South Africa: The Essential Guide to Customs & Culture.* Edited by Geoffrey Chesler. New York: Random House Distribution Services, 2010.

Main, Michael. *Culture Smart! Botswana: The Essential Guide to Customs & Culture.* Edited by Geoffrey Chesler. New York: Random House Distribution Services, 2010.

Rissik, Dee. 2011. *CultureShock! South Africa: A Survival Guide to Customs and Etiquette.* Tarrytown, NY: Marshall Cavendish Corporation.

Whiting, Sharri. 2008. *Culture Smart! Namibia: The Essential Guide to Customs & Culture.* Edited by Geoffrey Chesler. New York: Random House Distribution Services.

SPAIN

Spain's etiquette can vary significantly from that of other Western cultures. Much like Spaniards themselves, the etiquette of Spain can appear to outsiders at best as paradoxical, at worst, offensive, particularly to those who lack an understanding of Spain's social norms.

In Spain the familiar Spanish greetings "Buenos días" (Good morning), "Buenas tardes" (Good afternoon), and "Buenas noches" (Good night) are said frequently. The expression ¿Qué tal? (What's new?) exemplifies Spain's relaxed etiquette, in the sense that it is both formal and informal. In other words, ¿Qué tal? can be used to approach a close family member or a friend, but it can also be used when talking to a superior or an unknown person. When talking to a stranger or to a superior, Spaniards use an entirely different verb tense than when speaking to a friend or equal; the formal pronoun of *usted* (the polite form of you as opposed to the informal you or *tú*) accompanies the formal verb tense. When addressing a Spaniard, *Señor* (Mr.), *Señora* (Mrs.), or *Señorita* (Miss) should precede the surname of the person to whom you are speaking. In a more polite way, *Don* (male) or *Doña* (female) are used with the given name. Teenagers or adolescents are an exception to this social rule, and they are simply called by their given names. In Spain names are rooted in tradition. Many given names in Spain are based on Catholic saints or

Christian names, though this is changing in the modern era. Family names follow a specific pattern based on lineage. A typical Spanish full name consists of at least three words: one given name (although Spaniards tend to have double given names) plus two surnames. Spanish surnames can be confusing because a Spaniard always has a double surname: the first surname is the father's surname and the second is their mother's father's surname. When two people marry, the partners both maintain their original surname. In this way neither loses their family lineage.

Nonverbal greetings in Spain are changing over time. A traditional Spanish greeting usually consists of a kiss on both cheeks. Due to globalization, however, in a private gathering, it is not uncommon to see the standard international handshake. However, a kiss on both cheeks is still the norm in Spain after leaving a party. While women usually kiss both men and women, men only kiss women, and may give a hug to another man as a friendly expression.

Overall, Spaniards dress very fashionably. Even completing a simple task of running errands or going to the grocery requires a respectable outfit. Women are usually expected to have hair and makeup completed. For men, a nice pair of jeans or slacks and a dress shirt is a common norm. One can walk thought the streets of a more cosmopolitan city and easily spot the latest trends and brand names, whether it is women's latest shoe trends or the current men's brand shirts, as the city dwellers will most likely be wearing them. Conservative dress is expected for business meetings or for employees of government offices. Wearing flip-flops and beachwear is reserved strictly for the beach. Also, wearing the more relaxed exercise clothing such as yoga pants or running shoes outside of the gym would be considered taboo by Spanish standards. Likewise, even in contemporary times, certain dress is expected for mass. Wearing a hat in church would be considered offensive, and modest clothes would be expected for women; shorts or tank tops should be avoided.

Spaniards are passionate about food, and dining in Spain constitutes a general knowledge of the local etiquette. Table manners in Spain are overall relaxed although several rules can be observed. For instance, Spaniards always eat around a table, and eating in front of the TV or "on the go" is relatively unheard of. Wrists are always kept on the table and never rest in laps. "Buen provecho" or "Que aproveche" are the Spanish way to say "Good appetite." Bread is omnipresent in all meals, and usually is not cut with a knife but broken with the hands. Dipping bread into any sauce is also common and expected. Putting bread directly onto the table as opposed to a bread plate is also the Spanish norm. The only meal where Spaniards put butter on their bread is breakfast, which is a very light meal. During a social or private gathering, if you have been offered a glass of wine, it is common among Spaniards to wait until the host has already taken his drink, and it normally goes with the expression ¡Salud! which is a sort of blessing for good health.

Tapas, appetizers or snacks, are usually served quite informally before lunch or dinner. Because it consists of a small portion of food, tapas are normally eaten standing up at the bar. The main meal of the day in Spain is lunch, which is usually eaten around 2 p.m. Spanish culture also has a word, *sobremesa*, which refers to a very distinctive Spanish custom of enjoying a conversation after lunch. *Sobremesa* usually happens on weekends or during a particular celebration or even for a business reunion. In essence *sobremesa* is the leisure time that occurs immediately after lunch, and normally it consists of coffee or tea and sweets. The main difference with the *merienda* (a snack in the afternoon) is that *sobremesa* does not involve heavy food and does not occur as regularly as the *merienda*. In other words, *sobremesa* is more of a drink or digestive and the importance is in the conversation, while the *merienda* always contains more substance such as a sandwich (*bocadillo*), the famous *churros con chocolate* (sugared fried dough dipped in thick hot chocolate), or sweets, cakes or cookies with coffee, tea, or *cola-cao* (chocolate milk). Dinner in Spain is normally light; it may last easily until midnight in the summer, and never occurs before 8 p.m. In fact, during the summer season it is very common to see Spaniards enjoying an ice cream at midnight.

The idea of splitting the bill according to the number of people is still unheard of in certain areas of Spain. Even during times of economic crisis, the custom of pub crawling, which in Spain is known as *ir de copas* or *ir de tapas*, still consists of one person who pays for the first whole round, and then the Spanish etiquette is that someone else will pay for the next round, until everyone has contributed. Interestingly, foreigners are treated differently in this regard, in the sense that most Spaniards will invite their international guest for drinks as a way of welcoming them to the Spanish culture.

While Spanish dining may appear to be a relaxed affair, there are some cultural taboos to be aware of. Rushing a meal, especially lunch or dinner, can be considered offensive. In fact it is uncommon for a waiter to bring the bill to the table until it is requested, even if the meal has been concluded for quite a while. The waiter wants to avoid giving the clientele the feeling of being rushed. The practice of tipping is still relatively unusual among Spaniards. Tipping the waiter in restaurants is optional since the service industry (cafeterias, hotels, and restaurants) already add a service charge, which is shown on the bill as *servicio incluido*. If you want to add a tip on top of this, 10 percent is considered generous. More than 10 percent would be considered offensive. Other professions, including taxi drivers, barbers, and hairdressers, normally expect at least one euro on top of the bill.

Food commands great respect in Spain, thus asking for food "to go" or eating in the car or on the move is not the social norm. Similarly drive-throughs are relatively rare even in the more globalized cities of Spain. Eating is considered a social event as much as a functional one, and a person is expected to take the time to stop and enjoy even the most casual meal. While dining out with a group, it is considered polite to leave the table if you receive a phone call. Texting at a meal might cause offense to others seated as well. Finally, as a guest in a Spaniard's house, the idea of "helping yourself" to food in the refrigerator would be considered offensive. A guest is expected to eat the food prepared for him by the owner of the house, no matter how extended his stay may be.

The concept of space varies tremendously in Spain. For instance, Spaniards tend to live in a very clean house, although they behave differently while they are outside. This is evident with regard to the Spanish liking for eating *pipas* (sunflower seeds), for in Spain people will eat the seeds while in a park or at the beach and will often spit out the hulls without cleaning them up. Similarly in rural bars it is still possible to see Spaniards spitting out olive stones and shrimp shells onto the floor in a casual manner. Also, some Spanish cities are difficult to walk in because of the amount of dog and even horse excrement left on the pavement. Walking in Spain can also inform the foreigner about certain Spanish habits, including bad manners. Holding doors open for others is not a traditional custom in Spain. Also, forming lines in public, when queuing for a bus or admittance into a show, is often abandoned in exchange for a more casual, and sometimes chaotic, grouping.

Spaniards are typically very welcoming people who love to talk, especially around the topics of food and weather, arguably two of the most common subjects in the country apart from politics. It is not uncommon for Spaniards to become so involved in their conversations that they unintentionally appear to be upset or to be arguing to those who are not familiar with their customs. For instance, Spanish citizens talk much louder than the average English speaker; Spaniards are very expressive in the way they manifest their opinions. Spanish discussions usually involve certain mannerisms such as gesturing frequently with their hands when they talk. Also, Spanish social norms tend to require less personal space between two people than those in other parts of the world. Having multiple discussions with different people at the same time is also fairly common. Since Spain is a "loud" country, noise actually constitutes an integral part of the ambiance in any conversation regardless if it takes place in a public or private setting. Under this context, it

A group of older men discusses politics in Seville, Spain. The often loud and expressive conversational style typical in Spanish culture may come across as argumentative to those unfamiliar with Spanish social norms. (minemero/iStockphoto.com)

can be fascinating or irritating to witness a debate carried out by Spaniards. It is not uncommon for this particular Spanish way of conversation to take place while the television or radio is blustering in the background.

Not only does the manner of communicating for Spaniards differ from that of English speakers, but also the way in which they utilize phrases and formulate their sentences differs. One noticeable distinction is that Spaniards do not say "Please" and "Thank you" as often as native English speakers. If a Spaniard is thanked, he/she will often dismiss it with "De nada," which translates to mean literally "Of nothing." The Spanish language dictates that requests are structured in command form. So in contrast to the English speaker asking, "May I have a drink of water?" or "Can you please pass the bread?" Spaniards use the more direct command form, "Give me a drink of water," or "Pass the bread." In fact, to translate the polite English way of asking for something sounds very strange to a Spaniard. On the other hand, Spaniards are not without obligatory courteous phrases of their own.

Fiestas (festivals), both religious and secular, are a strong component of the Spanish way of living and, therefore, they are an integral component of Spain's tradition. Spain has more festivals than days in a year, and every festival is different and has strong regional roots. For example, the festivity of *Semana Santa*, or Easter, requires the following of certain etiquette and customs, including eating fish during Lent, or attending processions, which are celebrated very formally in the streets. On the other hand, other festivals, like *La Tomatina* (in Buñol, Valencia), which has been in existence since the 1940s and consists of throwing tomatoes at each other, have unknown origins. In regards to individual celebrations, the Spaniards recognize a person's birthday (*cumpleaños*) in addition to a person's saint day. A saint day is based on a person's Christian name and corresponds with their saint's feast day (*Santo* or *Dia del Santo*). A small gift, a card, or at least a call is expected and much appreciated for both occasions.

Another Spanish tradition that is very much ingrained in the Spanish psyche is the popular siesta or short nap, which usually happens immediately after lunch, and it is compulsory during summer time due to the heat. Total silence is expected by everyone in the house, and nobody visits or calls over the phone during those hours. In rural areas it is very rare to see a Spaniard in the street at 4 p.m. in summer, especially in the south of Spain where summers are unbearably hot, easily reaching 100°F average temperature. However, the custom of the siesta is also changing because of globalization.

Spaniards are fun-loving people who enjoy life copiously. Their relaxed way of communicating can be best exemplified by the word *mañana*, which has a double meaning: literally it translates to "tomorrow" or "morning." Yet said with a dismissive wave of the hand, it means "not now," exemplifying the philosophy, "Why do today what you can put off until tomorrow?" On the other hand, Spaniards' careful attention to food, festivals, and fashion attests to a particular way of living and thinking that characterizes Spain for what it is: a warm, diverse culture.

Enrique Ávila López

Further Reading

Graff, Mari Louise. *CultureShock! Spain: A Survival Guide to Customs and Etiquette*. Portland: Graphic Arts Books, 2005.

Hampshire, David. *Living and Working in Spain*, 8th ed. London: Survival Books, 2009.

Knowles, Laura. *Countries Around the World: Spain*. Chicago: Charlotte Guillain, 2012.

SPANISH-SPEAKING CARIBBEAN: PUERTO RICO AND THE DOMINICAN REPUBLIC

Puerto Rican culture has been influenced by the indigenous Taínos, the native population of the island they called Borinquen; by the Spanish who conquered the island in 1493; and by the Africans who were brought as slaves. The presence of those three cultures is alive in the language, the food, the religious practices and traditions. After the United States defeated Spain in the Spanish-American war in 1898, Puerto Rico became a free territory of the United States (a commonwealth). Nowadays, contemporary American culture has influenced much of the island life, but Puerto Ricans remain proud of their Spanish heritage.

Puerto Ricans have been U.S. citizens since 1917, and they enjoy many—but not all—of the privileges citizenship entails. The issue of Puerto Rico's political status has been an ongoing debate for over 50 years. Yet in spite of their colonial situation and U.S. citizenship, Puerto Ricans regard themselves as citizens of the nation of Puerto Rico. The island is a blend of Spanish traditions, creole culture, and recent Americanization. Most Puerto Ricans are broadly familiar with mainland U.S. culture and behavior.

Puerto Ricans, even if very friendly and hospitable, can also be traditional and conservative. Awareness of the local etiquette and cultural sensitivity is necessary. When meeting people greetings are usually done with a polite "Hola" (Hello) and "Como esta usted?" (How are you?). People will also shake hands. Women and friends exchange kisses on the cheek. In business situations people normally use both English and Spanish since Puerto Rico is a bilingual society. Business cards are usually printed in both languages. Before asking a person for directions, it is better to be polite, take time to greet the person first, then explain the situation and ask for help, all without a rush, more like a conversation. They find it rude to be asked in a hurry.

Puerto Ricans celebrate *Noche Buena* (Christmas Eve) and Epiphany (*Dia de Los Reyes*) on January 6, the day in which the Three Kings are said to have arrived bearing gifts for the Christ child. Sometime during the night, after the children fall asleep, Los Reyes arrive and quietly leave their gifts for the children. Later in the day family and friends get together for dinner and celebration.

Taíno and African influences are seen in the use of condiments, tropical fruits, rice, beans, and yucca. The Spanish introduced wheat, pork, cattle, chickens, and their own culinary techniques. Meals follow the Spanish custom of a continental breakfast with bread, coffee with milk, and juice; a large lunch with a meat, plantain, and rice and beans; and a simple supper. However, in Puerto Rican cities, the American way of having a fast food lunch and a large dinner has become popular.

Puerto Rican traditional food, or *comida criolla*, is enriched by the culinary heritage of the Taínos, the Spaniards, and the Africans. The very distinctive flavors of Puerto Rican food lies in the use of *sofrito*, a combination of ingredients and spices such as vegetable oil colored with annatto seeds, garlic, cilantro, oregano, and sweet peppers, used to give a distinctive flavor to traditional dishes. Puerto Ricans enjoy leisurely lunches and dinner. They tend to dine late.

One of the most traditional dishes is *asopao*, a hearty soup made with chicken or fish, flavored with garlic, oregano, chili peppers, onions, tomatoes, chorizo, ham, and more. Rice is a very important component of every meal and is prepared in many different ways.

The traditional Christmas menu includes *pernil* or *lechón* (roast pork), *arroz con gandules* (rice with pigeon peas), *pasteles* (plantain or yucca tamales), and sweet delicacies such as *arroz con leche* (coconut rice pudding), *tembleque* (coconut milk pudding), and *bienmesabe* (coconut pudding). The American holiday of Thanksgiving is celebrated, but the food is prepared according to Puerto Rican tastes. The turkey is seasoned with adobo, a local mix of seasonings made from crushed peppercorns, oregano, garlic, salt, oil and onion, and either lime juice or vinegar.

Christopher Columbus arrived at an island named Quisqueya by the indigenous Taínos in 1492. Columbus renamed the island *La Española*, which became known as Hispaniola. Santo Domingo became the first city founded by European conquerors in the Americas. In 1509, Diego Colon, the oldest son of Columbus, arrived in Santo Domingo as the first viceroy of the New World. In the nineteenth century, La Hispaniola fell under the dominion of France (1800–1809), which already had control of the western part of the island (Haiti). In 1804, the black African slaves in Haiti rebelled against France and founded the first free republic in the Americas. In 1822, Santo Domingo was invaded by the Haitian general Toussaint L'Ouverture. Haiti had control for 22 years until 1844, when Santo Domingo overthrew the Haitian rulers. This history of conflict created an anti-Haitian sentiment in the Dominican Republic, a sentiment that lasts to this day.

In both the Dominican Republic and Puerto Rico, the family is a cohesive force, the fundamental social unit in which maternal lineage is not overshadowed by paternal lineage. People usually carry their father's and mother's surnames. Extended family is the primary family structure. The individual derives a social network from and in times of need leans heavily on the extended family.

It is customary among people from rural areas who have been living abroad to come back to visit bringing presents for everybody in their town, as is celebrated in the merengue song "Volvio Juanita," which plays on radios in the Dominican Republic mainly in December, when expatriates return home for the holidays, bearing gifts.

The Dominican Republic is fundamentally a multiracial society. As is the case in the rest of the Caribbean, there has been a process of miscegenation or race mixing known as *mestizage*. Gradations of light to dark skin color, rather than pure racial types, tend to define racial identities. Social stratification is influenced not only by economic status but also by racial issues inherit from colonial times. There has been an emphasis on whitening or hiding African characteristics and extolling the virtues of Hispanic culture and the phenotypic features of the white race and the Taíno Indians. Exalting Taíno heritage, nonwhite Dominicans began to call themselves *indios* in reference to their color.

Dominicans share Taíno, Spanish, and African influences and traditions in their food preferences. *Mangu*, a dish of mashed green plantains with butter or olive oil served with salami, fried cheese, or pickled onions is considered the official Dominican breakfast. It was brought to the island by West African slaves during the Spanish colonial times.

Rice is not only one of the most important crops, but also a critical part of the Dominican diet. The main meal is served at midday. Most Dominicans will have rice and beans as well as some form of animal protein: beef, pork, goat, or chicken, for lunch every day. This trilogy is known as the "flag." The white rice and red beans remind people of the colors of the Dominican flag, hence the name.

The typical drinks of the country are *mabi* and *mamajuana*. Both of these drinks are prepared by fermenting several roots. It is customary that every time a bottle of any alcohol is opened, a little bit of its contents must be spilled on the floor as an offering to the ancestors.

Families have lunch and dinner together. Dominicans are very hospitable people. They tend to talk out in a loud manner but they are very friendly. They will invite you to have dinner in their home just after meeting you. At the table bad luck follows if you pass a salt shaker to the hands of another person. It is considered bad manners to leave the table before the meal is over. Meals always end with a dessert that is usually very sweet and a *cafecito* (a coffee).

There are a few taboos associated with food, especially during pregnancy. Pregnant woman should not eat pineapple or seafood, and they should not swim in the ocean: these things could cause them to lose their baby. After she has given birth, a woman is not allowed to wash her hair for a few days. In the handling and care of a newborn infant there are also many beliefs and taboos. *Mal de Ojo* or the "evil eye" is feared by the mothers of infants. Babies usually wear protective talismans in the form of bracelets or a pin (with a tiny piece of red coral and a black stone) against the intended harm. It is believed that if someone gives the infant an admiring look, a stare, or a compliment, it can bring sickness and even death to the infant.

Nancy Noguera

Further Reading

Ayala, Cesar J., and Rafael Bernabe. *Puerto Rico in the American Century: A History since 1898*. Chapel Hill: University of North Carolina Press, 2007.

Moya Pons, Frank. *The Dominican Republic: A National History*. New York: Hispaniola Books, 1998.

Pico, Fernando. *History of Puerto Rico. A Panorama of Its People*. Princeton, NJ: Markus Wiener, 2006.

Roorda, Eric Paul, Lauren H. Derby, and Raymundo Gonzalez. *The Dominican Republic Reader: History, Culture, Politics*. Durham, NC: Duke University Press, 2014.

Sagas, Ernesto, and Orlando Inoa. *The Dominican People: A Documentary History*. Princeton, NJ: Markus Wiener, 2006.

T

TAJIKISTAN

Tajikistan is a mountainous, landlocked country of Central Asia bordered by Afghanistan, Uzbekistan, Kyrgyzstan, and China. The Wakhan Corridor separates Tajikistan from Pakistan. The population of Tajikistan is estimated to number around 8 million. The main ethnic group is the Tajiks, a Persian people who speak Tajik, a Persian dialect. The Tajiks include the Pamiris of Badakhshan, a small number of Yaghnobi people, and a fairly large minority group of Ismailis. Other people living in Tajikistan include Russians and Uzbeks, though numbers of these are decreasing as people migrate away from Tajikistan. All people who live in Tajikistan are known as Tajikistanis. Officially Tajikistan is a secular state, but the country has a large Muslim population divided into two primary groups: Hanafi Sunnis and Ismaili Shiites. Of these the Hanafi Sunnis are the largest group making up around 90 percent of the country's Islamic population. The country also has a minority Bukharan and Ashkenazi Jewish population, while other religious groups living in Tajikistan include Russian Orthodox, Seventh Day Adventists, Catholics, and Baptists. In addition, Zoroastrianism has influenced the country's traditions and superstitions. When visiting Tajikistan it is worth remembering that many Tajikistanis know very little about Western culture.

Tajik society is based on concepts of hospitality and respect for others. In particular the elderly are held in great esteem and always treated with the utmost respect. When greeting each other everyone will stand in acknowledgement. Handshakes are the standard polite greetings between men. Handshakes are accompanied by another gesture intended to demonstrate that the men hold each other in high regard—the men place their left hand over their heart and bow slightly as they shake hands. Today people who know each other well will typically hug and kiss each other on the cheeks as a greeting and may hold each other's hand while talking.

A man must never enter a home that is inhabited only by women. Similarly a girl must never be left alone in the company of a boy, and dating is a rarity. At large social events, men and women are usually separated. In business situations it is acceptable to address work colleagues by their first names, but people higher up the business hierarchy should be addressed by titles such as *Muallim* (teacher), *Khujain* (boss), *Ustod* (master), or *Rais* (chief). In the workplace, hierarchy is extremely important, so if Tajik is being spoken, the formal version of "you," *shumo*, should be used. When in doubt about how to address Tajik colleagues, it is okay to simply ask them. Some Tajikistanis still use the Soviet greeting protocol whereby people are addressed using their first and middle names. It is rare for someone to be introduced as *Janob* (Mr.) or *Khomun* (Ms.)—these terms are mainly employed at official events or on very formal occasions. Other customary Tajik honorifics include the religious titles *Pir*, *Domulloh*, *Eshon*, and *Kahlifa*, and *Okhon* (meaning teacher). In informal settings people will call older men *Aka* (meaning elder brother) while younger men are referred to as *Dodar* (meaning younger brother). Similarly a younger woman is called *Apa* (elder sister) with a younger woman known as *Khohar* (younger sister). The term *Khola* is applied to any woman whom is believed to be the same age as a person's mother, while a man who is believed to be the same age as a person's mother should be addressed as *Amak*.

From childhood many Tajikistani women are taught the attributes that will help them find a husband, including modesty. In rural areas of Tajikistan teenage girls wear a garment called a hijab, which covers their head and possibly part of their face too. Girls who wear the hijab usually belong to the extremely conservative Pamiri (Iranian ethnic) communities. Most Tajik girls and young women wear either colorful headscarves or a *tupi* (or *topi*), a gold- or silver-colored, four-cornered hat. Tajik women also wear a modest, traditional dress called a *curta* together with *aezor* or *pajomah* trousers in a contrasting color. If not wearing this traditional outfit then girls will wear full-length skirts or dresses but hardly ever trousers. Only a few non-Muslim girls living in the Tajik capital city, Dushanbe, will wear trousers. When visiting Tajikistan Westerners should dress conservatively. Tajik boys and men tend to wear more Western-style clothing including jeans and slacks with white shirts. Shorts are acceptable for small children and when playing soccer. Such is the harsh climate of Tajikistan that both men and women also wear thick fur hats known as *shopkas*. In the workplace Tajikistanis wear very formal, conservative attire. Men generally dress in Western clothing such as a suit and tie while women sport traditional dress. In cities, however, people are increasingly seen wearing a combination of traditional and Western clothing.

The Tajikistanis are famous for their hospitality. Table etiquette, particularly the etiquette of the tea ceremony, is very important to Tajikistanis because they see table manners as indicative of an individual's upbringing, ethnicity, class, and age. Tajikistanis drink green tea, and it is usual for the youngest person present to pour the tea for everyone else. Alternatively a host will pour the tea for his or her guests as a sign of respect. The correct etiquette for pouring the tea sees freshly made tea twice poured into cups and then twice emptied back into the teapot. This is thought to help the tea brew. At any meal the most revered person present is known as the *aksakal*, whose responsibility it is to motion for the meal to start and finish and to lead everyone in conversation. When Tajikistanis eat out they usually do so at an eatery known as *anash-khanas*, where people sit on mats, cushions, or rugs placed on the floor around low tables. Here Tajikistanis socialize with their friends and family and also broker business deals. Meals taken at an *anash-khana* are expected to be leisurely and may take several hours to complete. As is the case in many countries with large Muslim populations, food and drink are served and enjoyed using only the right hand, with the left hand regarded as impure. Another taboo action is to reject food that has been offered. Instead, if the guest does not want to eat something that has been offered, he should take a little of the food and eat a tiny bit of it as a sign of respect. Otherwise it will be understood that the guest is either ill and unable to eat or already full.

In general Tajiks are conscious of personal space and are careful not to encroach on each other when sitting or standing. This does vary slightly, however, between rural and urban locations, between different classes of people, and between those educated locally or elsewhere. Under Soviet rule physical contact in public was acceptable, meaning people used to greet each other by hugging and kissing each other on the cheek. Today, however, Tajikistan is more religious than it was in Soviet times, meaning people are now more conscious about touching. That said, friends may still touch though they will usually keep equidistant when speaking, while still being sure to maintain their personal space. Tajikistanis consider eye contact a good way to judge if a person is honest, with an inability to maintain steady eye contact taken as a sign of a problem that needs resolving. Overly direct eye contact may also be taken as challenging behavior, especially by macho young Tajik men.

Tajik body language is dynamic, with many physical gestures used when talking. Placing your hand to your chest denotes respect and agreement. Outright taboo physical gestures include placing the thumb between the index finger and middle finger or placing the index finger to the forehead. When speaking to a Tajikistani of the same sex it is acceptable to make physical contact, but if speaking to a Tajikistani of the opposite sex, any physical contact may be taken as a flirtatious gesture. It is worth remembering that it is strictly taboo for a man to flirt with a woman during a first meeting.

When speaking, Tajikistanis tend to talk without worrying if the conversational volume is annoying those around them. Even so, soft voices are thought indicative of good manners (*adab*). Directness in speech is permitted, so long as this does not result in impolite speech. Tajikistanis look upon favorably any foreigner who shows knowledge of their country, leading to good relations. Safe topics of conversation in Tajikistan include asking people about their family and life in general—Tajikistanis will usually reply honestly. Tajikistanis also like to laugh, though they will never start a conversation with a joke. Humor is particularly evident at mealtimes, allowing relationships to develop. Conversely Tajikistanis typically do not like any show of arrogance when talking, so bragging and boasting are taboo. Discussion of Islam is probably best avoided, as some Tajikistanis are more sensitive about this topic than others. The Islam found in Tajikistan is fairly secular—probably both because Tajikistan is officially a secular republic and because Tajikistan was formerly a Soviet republic. However, it is best not to chance offending a Tajikistani by discussing the religion to which they may belong. It is also best not to discuss the recent violent civil war that took place (1992–1997), destroying much of the country's infrastructure. Similarly it is ill advised to joke in public or be generally disparaging about the current Tajik authorities.

Victoria Williams

Further Reading

Abazov, Rafis. *Cultures of the World: Tajikistan*. New York: Marshall Cavendish Benchmark, 2006.

Global Affairs Canada. "Cultural Information—Tajikistan." https://www.international.gc.ca
    /cil-cai/country_insights-apercus_pays/ci-ic_tj.aspx?lang=eng.
Wagner, Rowan E. "Tajikistan." In Jeffrey Jensen Arnett, ed., *International Encyclopedia of
    Adolescence A-J, Index, Volume 1*, 981–88. New York: Routledge, 2007.

TAMILS

The Tamil name comes from *Damila*, the name of a non-Aryan people mentioned in early Buddhist and Jain records. The Tamil have roots in western India, Pakistan, and areas farther to the west. Many Tamils settled in northern Sri Lanka in ancient times. Significant Tamil emigration began in the eighteenth century, when the British colonial government sent many poor Tamils as indentured laborers to far-off parts of the Empire, especially Malaya, South Africa, Fiji, and the Caribbean. There was also a large emigration of Sri Lankan Tamils in the 1980s in order to escape ethnic conflict. These recent emigrants have most often fled to Australia, Europe, North America, and Southeast Asia. Today, the largest concentration of Tamils outside southern Asia is in Toronto, Canada. There are about 77 million Tamil people living around the world. They are one of the largest and oldest of the existing ethno-linguistic cultural groups of people in the modern world to exist without a state of their own.

The Tamil culture is very conscious of social order and status. In families, the father or oldest man is generally considered the leader of the family. Both Tamil Nadu and Sri Lanka are hierarchical societies, and professional titles are important. If one does not have a professional title, use the honorific title "Sir" or "Madam." Tamils typically greet each other by saying "Vanakkam," which means, "May you be blessed with a long life." Physical contact is generally not a part of communication (especially between men and women); however, among close friends holding hands or putting arms around each other is a way of expressing friendship.

It is important to note that Tamils live under a highly gendered Indian society, where women have more pressure on them to uphold traditions and are often held to standards higher than those set for Tamil men. Tamil culture also views women through a lens of idealized concepts on how they should look and dress. These concepts and traditions are being challenged by younger Tamils, but many still conform to these when it comes to auspicious occasions such as marriages, family functions, and professional events such as job interviews.

Men have no restrictions in the way they dress, often wearing traditional clothes such as a *dhoti*, a loose, pantaloons style of clothing, which is usually one large piece of cloth that is wrapped around the lower body and folded in pleats. Tamil men always cover their legs, especially above the knees. This is seen as a sign of respect and dignity, but unlike women, they are not coerced to do this. Women are usually expected to dress conservatively and often represent a social role, position, or hierarchy, for instance, someone from a lower caste will not resemble someone from a higher caste, based on their clothes. Similarly, a woman's social role is part of how she dresses; for instance, a married women would wear a *thali* (not to be mistaken with traditional Indian steel plates), a thread that the groom ties around the bride's neck (which denotes similar connotations as a wedding band). The sari is seen as the ideal piece of clothing for women who are married or of marriageable age. Tamil parents will often begin to dress their daughter in a sari when she attains puberty. Colors, designs, and style of saris are also important factors: a simple sari with not many patterns usually indicates lower class, while a colorful, patterned, embroidered sari represents middle or high class. Tamil literature and philosophy see married women as a manifestation of a celestial mother, with god-like qualities that help protect her family.

Tamils have a great affinity for their elders and, like most Indians, they live in joint family households, meaning that more than one generation of family members live in the same house or locale. Sending elders away to a retirement home is still seen as a taboo in Tamil culture. The elders of the family act as the primary decision makers and are usually relied upon to take care of the children. Most Tamil families are patriarchal by nature, wherein the eldest man in the family gives advice on issues such as finance, religious practices, social norms, and marriage, among others.

Please note that there are numerous taboos in India and Sri Lanka, though there are not any quintessentially Tamil in nature. These are some that are observed by Tamils all over India and Sri Lanka. Tamil people tend to prefer using their right hand, as using the left hand is considered inauspicious. A majority of South Indian schools will encourage children to change their behavior in accordance to the cultural norm.

There are dietary restrictions depending on one's religion; most Hindus do not eat beef, while Muslims do not consume pork. Many Tamils prefer to be vegetarian, based on their religious and cultural beliefs.

There are some communities in South India that allow first cousin marriage. The rule is only "cross-cousins" can get married; "parallel-cousin" marriage is strictly forbidden as incest. A "cross-cousin" is a child of one's parents' opposite-sex siblings, i.e., mother's brother's child or father's sister's child. Conversely, "parallel-cousin" is a child of one's parents' same-sex siblings, i.e., mother's sister's child or father's brother's child. This system of kinship is called the "Iroquois kinship" and is still popular among various groups such as the Anishinaabe of North America and some rural Chinese societies. Though this is very common among Hindus in India and Sri Lanka, it should be noted that more westernized Tamil families do not adhere to this custom.

Tamils tend to avoid topics or materials such as leather (cow), alcohol, pigskin, or dog, as it could insult one's religion. Hindus generally do not touch anything they deem important with their feet. When/if something is touched with feet, it is treated as dirty/untouchable and even insulting.

Dinesh Asudo Punjabi

Further Reading

Chitty, S. C. *The Castes, Customs, Manners and Literature of the Tamils.* New Delhi: Asian Educational Services, 1992.

Fuglerud, O. *Life on the Outside: Tamil Diaspora and Long Distance Nationalism.* London: Pluto Press, 1999.

Krishnan, A. *Tamil Culture: Religion, Culture and Literature*. New Delhi: Bharatiya Kala Prakashan, 2002.

Pandian, J. *Caste, Nationalism and Ethnicity: An Interpretation of Tamil Cultural History and Social Order*. Bombay: Popular Prakashan, 1987.

Ramaswamy, V. *Historical Dictionary of the Tamils*. Lanham, MD: Scarecrow Press, 2007.

Shanthi, G. *Folk-Customs in Tamil Nadu*. Delhi: Sharada, 2012.

THAILAND

Thai people have a specific etiquette that is based on Buddhist teachings that promote interpersonal and social harmony. According to these teachings, people are expected to remain calm in all situations. Becoming angry, screaming, yelling, and arguing are considered as lacking emotional control. Most rules of etiquette and some taboos are focused on preventing social embarrassment and preserving a person's reputation or, as Thai people say, "saving the face." Most Thai people practice Buddhism and spirit religion. Religious taboos include some gender-related restrictions. For example, women should not enter the sacred place in a temple or touch a monk.

Thai people typically greet each other by placing their hands together and slightly raising them upwards and, at the same time, slightly bowing their head.

A man gives a traditional Thai greeting, or *wai*, in Bangkok, Thailand. The proper response is to *wai* in return, although elders and people of higher class do not reciprocate the *wais* of those who are younger or of a lower class. (Akabei/iStockphoto.com)

This form of greeting is called *wai*. People should respond with the same gestures. Older and well-positioned people never *wai* to younger or inferior people; monks never respond to *wai*. People of lower rank are usually introduced first. Guests should never introduce themselves and are supposed to wait to be introduced to others. Thai people tend to smile a lot. In Thai culture, however, a smile could express different emotions, including fun, happiness, sadness, embarrassment, and an apology. In Thai culture, the head is considered a sacred part of the body and should not be touched. Apologies should follow after accidental touching; purposeful touching could be interpreted as insulting. Pointing out with your foot or even sitting with the legs stretched out and shoes pointing at someone is considered a taboo.

Modesty is expected from both men and women, and wearing low-cut tops, short skirts, and shorts is considered offensive. In particular wearing revealing clothes in a temple is considered taboo. In famous tourist areas, modest clothes are frequently available for rent by tourists who wish to visit a temple. Shoes should be taken off before entering temples. Formal wear is required for business meetings and for visits to government offices, police departments, and other offices. Apart from tourist resorts and beaches located in the central cities, most Thai people swim fully dressed. Nude or topless sunbathing is prohibited.

Food preparation is a traditional women's role except animal slaughtering; it is taboo for a woman to slaughter an animal. Food is usually consumed in a relaxed atmosphere, and freshly cooked dishes are served over time. People eat slowly, enjoying their meal. The dishes are placed on a garment or a rug spread out on the floor and people gather around the meal. Men usually sit in a cross-legged position, and women turn their legs to the side. In modern families, food is served on the dining table. People usually start eating whenever served, though guests are supposed to wait until they are invited by the owner to help themselves with a second serving and should never take the last portion from the main plate unless invited to do so. Leaving no food on one's plate is considered good manners, indicating that the food was enjoyed and the individual is full. Leaving chopsticks on a plate or in a bowl after a meal is considered bad luck and a sign of death.

Nowadays most Thai marriages are based on the individual's free will; however, parental blessing is always sought by a young couple wanting to wed. According to traditional beliefs, brides are expected to be virgins. Premarital sex is considered unacceptable, and, if it occurs, a couple is required to pay a reconciliation fine to restore their honor from the local spirits. In relation to dating, young people living in rural areas are expected to be modest and reserved; even holding hands in public is considered inappropriate. Dating couples residing in urban areas tend to follow Western norms, feeling less embarrassed and more comfortable expressing their affection in public.

The marriage process is usually initiated by a man and his family. A small dowry is paid by the groom to the bride's family in gratitude for raising their daughter. Similar to Western traditions, engagement consists of presenting a ring to the future bride and announcing the couple's intention to marry. In order to save money, engagement ceremonies may take place at the time of the wedding. After a marriage ceremony the groom usually moves to the bride's house in order to support his wife's family and to prevent the potential tensions between a mother-in-law and a daughter-in-law. Marriage between close relatives is a taboo. There are also taboos surrounding pregnancy; these are not followed nowadays in general, though they may be adhered to in order to satisfy elders. For example, one of the most common taboos suggests that the family members of a pregnant women should avoid killing a domestic animal. This taboo is related to a belief that a mother and a child may die at the time of childbirth if the family does not conform to this behavior. Other taboos preclude pregnant women from visiting sick people or attending funerals. Thai people see death as a sad event, though they also understand it to be the occasion when the dead person is reincarnated in a land free from illness and suffering. Funeral ceremonies are conducted by monks and involve chants, taking the coffin to the temple, and cremating the body. Black and white colors are considered the colors of death in Thailand, and mourners are expected to wear black and white when attending funerals.

Victoria Team

Further Reading

Andrews, Tim, and Sununta Siengthai. *The Changing Face of Management in Thailand*. New York: Routledge, 2009.

Cooper, Robert. *CultureShock! Thailand: A Survival Guide to Customs and Etiquette*, 9th ed. Tarrytown, NY: Marshall Cavendish, 2012.

Hoare, Timothy D. *Thailand: A Global Studies Handbook*. Santa Barbara, CA: ABC-CLIO, 2004.

Kislenko, Arne. *Culture and Customs of Thailand*. Westport, CT: Greenwood, 2004.

Knutson, Thomas J., Rosechongporn Komolsevin, Pat Chatiketu, and Val R. Smith. "A Cross-cultural Comparison of Thai and U.S. American Rhetorical Sensitivity: Implications for Intercultural Communication Effectiveness." *International Journal of Intercultural Relations* 27 (2003): 63–78.

Poulsen, Anders. *Childbirth and Tradition in Northeast Thailand*. Copenhagen: NIAS, 2007.

Segaller, Denis. *Thai Ways*. Chiang Mai: Silkworm Books, 2005.

TIBET

Situated high in the Himalayas, Tibet has the reputation of being a remote and isolated place. However, Tibetan civilization has both profoundly influenced other Asian cultures (including Mongolia, Nepal, Northern India, Bhutan, and China) and also adapted aspects of neighboring cultures, most notably India, China, and Persia. Heavily influenced by Buddhism, traditional Tibetan scholars divide their history based on the two waves of Buddhism entering into Tibet. The early dissemination of Buddhism occurred during the Tibetan empire period (seventh to ninth centuries). After Buddhism entered Tibet for the second time in the eleventh century, Tibetan culture began to be dominated by competing Buddhist traditions. Over the next 500 years, Tibetan Buddhist culture became an elite political tool in much of Asia.

The influence of Tibetan culture stretches far beyond the boundaries of the current political-administrative region called the Tibetan Autonomous Region in the

People's Republic of China. Since the incorporation of Tibet into China, Tibetan culture within China has undergone massive sociopolitical changes. Since 1959, the spiritual leader of Tibet, the Fourteenth Dalai Lama Tenzin Gyatso, has lived in exile in Dharamsala, India. In 2011 he turned all his political responsibilities over to the Tibetan Central Administration, effectively bringing a 369-year political tradition of Dalai Lama rule to an end.

While Buddhism lies at the heart of Tibetan culture, the indigenous religion, Bön, heavily influenced the development and practices of Buddhism in Tibet. Before Tibet became incorporated into the People's Republic of China, Tibetan areas were under the rule of local elites, with each mountain and valley (or parts thereof) boasting its own religious institutional authorities including Bön, Islam, and many competing Buddhist traditions: Kadam, Kagyu, Nyingma, Geluk, Sakya, Jonang, and Bodong. Each of the Buddhist institutions had renowned cultural centers, often located at large monastic complexes. Religious practice and artistic production are intricately linked in Tibetan culture to this day. Once only found at monasteries, Tibetan sacred paintings called *thangka* and Buddhist sculptures can now be seen in museums around the world. One of the holiest places for all Tibetan Buddhist traditions is the ancient Jokhang Temple in Lhasa, which houses a sacred statue of the Buddha Shakyamuni, that is known as the *Jowo*—the Venerable One. Islamic Tibetans known as Khache have lived on the Tibetan plateau for centuries with several major mosques located in Lhasa. In eastern Tibet, mosques tend to be located in populated river valleys, while Buddhist monasteries were built in remote areas such as high grasslands and mountains. For most, Buddhist practice and ritual life shaped the daily life and religion was not only a matter of belief, but the way one lived.

The reverential presentation of a long silk scarf called a *katak* as a greeting is an enduring symbol of Tibetan culture. The exact origins of presenting a *katak* to a lama (the Tibetan translation of the Sanskrit term *guru* meaning "teacher") remain unknown. Some Tibetan scholars maintain that this was originally a symbol of pure speech, one of the three main components to Buddhist practice along with the practices of pure mind and pure body. Different types of *katak* are used on varying occasions; they can be offered for sad events as well, such as in funerals or departures. When friends or family members return home after a long period of absence, many *katak* are presented. Although slight regional differences exist in the way that *katak* are given, the scarf should always be offered reverentially and never simply draped around someone's neck. The longer and the better quality of the material, the higher the prestige given to the recipient.

Tibetan clothing, dress, and accessories vary significantly from region to region across the plateau. *Chuba* is the common term for a uniquely Tibetan piece of clothing, traditionally made from either home-spun wool or sheepskin. The styles of *chuba* vary greatly depending upon gender, region, and social standing; strict dress codes were to be followed on ceremonial occasions in traditional Tibet. Nomads generally wear a sheepskin *chuba* with fleece on the inside. It is common to wear the *chuba* leaving the right shoulder and arm free, tied up by a belt. In the towns, women wear modest, dark-colored *chuba* over colorful, long-sleeved blouses revealing almost no skin; women indicate their marital status by wearing colorfully striped, woven wool aprons called *pangden*. Tibetan headdresses vary significantly from region to region. Women from wealthy households will frequently have jewels, such as coral or turquoise, woven into or attached to their hair. Women and men will wear massive jeweled necklaces, especially during the Litang Horse Festival. Hats in traditional Tibet were significant for indicating social standing or official rank. Monastic robes come from the Indian tradition, and generally are red and orange in color. Today many Tibetans wear traditional clothes only on special occasions.

When entering a home, Tibetans will frequently exchange outdoor boots for slippers. Similarly, it is common practice to remove one's shoes before entering a sacred space such as a Buddhist shrine or temple. Tibetan nomads or rural agriculturalists are known to open their homes to weary travelers when no inn is available. Tibetans will sit on the floor or on a *kang* (a heated, raised bed-couch common in eastern Tibet) around a table to share a meal. Monks and lay people rarely sit at the same table, and often men and women will take their meals in separate quarters depending on social status of the guests. The head of the table sits facing an entranceway. Wealthy households have a separate raised divan for dignitaries visiting the family. Tibetans will offer food and drink as a sign of hospitality and never leave a glass half-empty until the end of a meal. Fresh meat, especially the fattiest section of mutton or yak, will be offered to the guest of honor. When entering a sacred place or meeting a dignitary, Tibetans will hold their hands together in prayer as a sign of respect. Similarly, when entering a Buddhist temple or facing a religious object or person, it is common for people to prostrate or kowtow. Full body prostrations are common in Tibet, whereby one bends one's knees, comes to the ground, extends hands and legs completely outright, and then reverses the process to stand

---

Culture Shock! ⊕

Tibet's Yoghurt Festival

The Sho Dun or Shoton Festival, often referred to as the Yoghurt Festival, is an annual event held in Lhasa, the capital of Tibet. The festival is held in the summer, from the 15th to the 24th of the fifth lunar month, that usually falls around the middle of August. The festival began during the eleventh century as a religious occasion that saw locals offer yogurt to monks who had finished their retreats. During the seventeenth century, the festival began to include Buddhist rituals and performances of various types of entertainment including *Lhamo*, dramatic musical theater akin to opera. Another important aspect of the festival is the *thangka* unfolding ceremony that sees a giant painting of the Buddha (the *thangka*) unveiled at Drepung Monastery. The painting is some 598 square yards in size and is unveiled on the hillside on which the monastery sits.

Victoria Williams

upward. Devout Buddhists will do a certain number of prostrations in front of a holy Buddhist temple or statue (often three, but can be as many as ten thousand). Some will go on pilgrimage to Lhasa or a local temple prostrating the entire journey. It is considered impolite to show the bottom of your feet toward any holy object or person. Tibetans will use the thumbs-up sign to indicate a job well done, but the raising of the little finger indicates disappointment or dissatisfaction.

The traditional Tibetan year is based on a 12-month lunar calendar. Tibetan New Year celebrations will vary from region to region across the plateau. In general, festivities will last for two weeks, each day imbued with a special significance. Families are expected to dress in their finest clothes and set up an altar with New Year offerings including roasted barley grain, butter decorations, ceremonial rice, fried breads and cakes, a sheep's head decorated with colorful butter designs of sun and moon, barley beer called *chang*, and pots of green sprouting barley shoots. New prayer flags are hung outside in high places so that auspicious prayers are carried by the wind to be answered. People also decorate their homes with the eight auspicious symbols (conch shells, fish, umbrellas, etc.). In particular, kitchens will be decorated with these symbols or others as they are said to bring good luck. On the first day of the New Year, people will go to their local temple to make offerings and say prayers. Other holidays throughout the year include Buddha's Birthday and Enlightenment, the Horse Festival, the Yoghurt Festival, Buddha's Descent from Heaven, and Tsongkhapa's Anniversary. The entire way of traditional Tibetan life depended on the seasons of nomadic pastoralism and the festival calendar, though this is changing rapidly with modernization.

One of the most distinctive features of traditional Tibetan family life is the practice of polyandry, whereby one woman (or sometimes sisters) marry the brothers of a family. Women generally marry outside of the family, thereby becoming part of her husband's family. Under the polyandry system children are raised as family members, blurring the line between cousin and sibling. This is seen as a way to keep land within one extended family and to make sure that it is not divided up. Traditionally polyandry was most common among the wealthy landholders in Tibet. Today polyandry is practiced infrequently. Divorce is not unheard of in traditional Tibetan society, and would see a woman return to her biological family. If there were children involved, the son would remain with his father, while a daughter moves with the mother. There are generally no Tibetan taboos against remarrying.

People observing Tibetan culture often remark that Tibetans have a unique attitude toward death and do not feel remorse at the death of a loved one because of their deep belief in reincarnation, that the soul will find rebirth in another body. This assumption regarding the Tibetan view of death is largely a misinterpretation of the vast rituals and beliefs associated with Tibetan funerary customs, however. Tibetans mourn their departed loved ones deeply and profoundly. Tibetan Buddhists and Bön practitioners have long liturgical traditions for the dying and deceased. This vast corpus of liturgical materials has been condensed and summarized in English under the title *The Tibetan Book of the Dead*, and has even been adapted by some hospice movements in the United States and Europe. Buddhist priests will often perform *po-wa*, or the transfer of consciousness rite for the dying, which is believed to help the person find a positive rebirth through the process of death. The body of the recently deceased will generally not be moved for a certain period of time as it is believed to disrupt the process of rebirth. While death within a family is commonly a very private affair, the funeral of a high lama will draw crowds of thousands. Formerly only reserved for high lamas or aristocrats, the process of cremation has increased among the common people in modern times. Rarely, the most eminent of Buddhist lamas were embalmed and entombed in sacred vessels called *chörten*. Due to permafrost on the Tibetan plateau, it was common for Tibetans to have a so-called sky burial whereby the corpse of the deceased was fed to vultures and other large birds of prey. This practice is rapidly disappearing due to the increase in human population and subsequent encroachment on the birds' habitat as well as overall environmental degradation.

With global advances in technology, the Internet and social media are having a strong effect on the development of Tibetan-language culture, even breaking down some of the political divides between Tibetans in China and diaspora Tibetans living in India or the United States. There is an unprecedented increase in Tibetan-language blogs and Web sites. Tibetans have a long-standing tradition of intellectual debate that had been formalized in monasteries, but can now be found in secular forums such as the Internet. Topics of debate most often concern moral-ethical dilemmas such as vegetarianism or wearing animal skins.

Nicole Willock

Further Reading

Alexander, André. *The Temples of Lhasa: Tibetan Buddhist Architecture from the 7th to the 21st Centuries*. Chicago: Serindia Publications, 2005.

Bell, Charles. *Tibet Past & Present*. Oxford: Clarendon Press, 1924.

Li, Tao, and Hongying Jiang. *Series of Basic Information of Tibet of China: Tibetan Customs*. Beijing: China Intercontinental Press, 2003.

Norbu, Thubten Jigme, and Colin Turnbull. *Tibet: An Account of the History, the Religion and the People of Tibet*. New York: Simon and Schuster, 1968.

Ryavec, Karl. *A Historical Atlas of Tibet*. Chicago: Chicago University Press, 2015.

Schaeffer, Kurtis, Matthew T. Kapstein, and Gray Tuttle. *Sources of Tibetan Tradition*. New York: Columbia University, 2013.

Stein, R.A. *Tibetan Civilization*. Translated by J. E. Stapleton Driver. Stanford, CA: Stanford University Press, 1972.

Wangdu, Sagong. *A Hundred Customs and Traditions of Tibetan People*. Translated by Tenzin Tsepak. Dharamsala: Library of Tibetan Works and Archives, 2009.

TUAREG

The Tuareg are a predominantly pastoral nomadic society living in the Sahara desert and surrounding areas. Since decolonization and the subsequent nation-building process in the 1950s and 1960s the Tuareg have been attached to five states: Libya, Algeria, Niger, Mali, and Burkina Faso. In each of these countries the Tuaregs' political, economic, and social participation has developed differently. The Tuareg have been confronted with a rigorous Arabization policy in Libya and Algeria; in Niger,

Mali, and Burkina Faso they have been opposed to African elites. The Tuareg had to face different lingua franca, varying school systems, competitive economies, and diverse political ideologies, which additionally contributed to their heterogeneity.

The name Tuareg is a foreign designation, coming from the Arabic *tawariq*, which found entry into European languages and linguistics. The Tuaregs' emic names differ depending on the dialect of their language Tamasheq/Tamahaq: Imuhagh (Algeria, Libya), Imajeghen (Niger), Imushagh (Mali). Important is that Tuareg is already the plural, therefore one should abstain from using English pluralization—a single female Tuareg is known as a Targia, while a single man is called a Targi.

The Tuareg have developed a unique set of norms, values, and rules of conduct. Right behavior in public plays an important role in everyday life and centers on the umbrella terms *ashak*, honor/pride/dignity, and *tekerakit*, decency/respect/reservation. The requirements are gender-neutral; they concern men, women, and children likewise. The following examples of etiquette and taboos all cluster around *ashak* and *tekerakit*, in order to bestow respect and honor of oneself and the counterpart.

Greeting rituals among the Tuareg are of great importance, mainly in the nomadic surrounding. When people meet in the Sahara they shake their hands by touching repeatedly one's hand very softly and murmuring greetings such as "tagoday?" "maigendem/maigendek?" (How are you?); "mani aghiwan?" (How is your family?); "mani akhsawan?" (How are your animals?); and "mani tuske?" (What about the heat?). The questions are always responded with the standardized phrase "al-khayr ghass?" (Good only?). The greeting questions are repeated several times depending on how long one has not seen each other. In order to express respect to sitting elder people, one hunkers down and lowers one's gaze. Men especially do this towards elderly women and their parents-in-law.

When leaving, the visited person accompanies the guest a certain distance (*esigli*). Even in urban environments this very polite gesture towards appreciated guests is common. However, among family members greeting and leaving is not ritualized in that way. The Tuareg do not say, for example, "Good morning" to their partners they have spent the night with, and when men are leaving their camp they often say nothing, and do not mention where they are going and when they will be back.

Visually correct appearance and proper dress play a major role in Tuareg society and represent their conceptions of honor, decency, and morality (*ashak* and *tekerakit*). Clothing is a form of nonverbal communication, conveying messages concerning tribal affiliation, social class, family status, and age. Wearing traditional clothing among the Tuareg not only represents a person's respectability and dignity, but simultaneously embodies the supreme ideal of beauty, aesthetics, and attractiveness. A correctly wrapped *tagelmust* (*eshesh*), the man's face veil, is a sign of adulthood, a symbol of belonging, and an expression of social norms and values. It is a conception of social distance and degree of respect. Mostly in white or indigo (*aleshu*) it can be wrapped in different ways, depending on region, age, tribal affiliation, social class, or specific occasions. During a wedding, for example, a highly complex form (*anagad*) of the veil is used, while in everyday life it can be wrapped casually around the head.

A Tuareg man wears a *tagelmust* in the Algerian Sahara. The *tagelmust*, a man's face veil, is worn to signify adulthood, and the way it is wrapped varies with location, occasion, age, and other situations. (Hecke01/Dreamstime.com)

The wrapping of the *tagelmust* covers nearly the entire face, only leaving the eyes, and is pulled over the mouth. In the past men ate and drank under the veil; in recent times only very respectable elders still do so. The younger generation (*ishumar*) often uses the veil as an attractive fashion accessory in all colors. Traditionally men wear black trousers (*ikarbey*) framed by embroidery, and long robes (*tekatkat*). Due to the influence of the Hausa, stiff cotton fabrics patterned with strong colors (*bazin*) have become a traditional element.

Tuareg women wear depending on their region either *tasirnest* (wraparound garment), such as in Mali or Algeria, or a loosely fluttering embroidered top (*tekatkat*) and a wraparound skirt (*teri*) in Niger. They do not cover their head like other Muslims, but married women wear a headdress (*adeko, afar*), which underscores their honor and dignity and implies womanhood. Correct clothing in relation to social norms, morals, and values is reflected through many proverbs, such as "The dignity of a woman lies under her headdress" (*almastar n tamtot yela daw afar-net*), or "Tea without mint is like a man without trousers" (*eshahid wur narnar, elis wur ikarbey*).

At meals Tuareg men and women sit separated on the floor clustered around one bowl, and eat with a wooden spoon. Children usually eat separated, or share the meal with their mothers. Parents-in-law also eat separated. Not sharing the meal together relates to the code of respect and honor. If one is full, the spoon is supposed to stick in the sand or be left beside the bowl, and one leaves the bowl immediately in order to make room for others. Every visitor who arrives during mealtime is politely invited to take part, and even if he or she has already eaten or is full, hospitality and politeness claim that at least one spoon is tasted. Often visitors, although they are hungry, refuse to eat when they remark that food is not enough for the family members.

Hospitality is part of the Tuareg's code of conduct. Every visitor, no matter if he or she is a family member, friend, or unknown person, is offered water and given a place to rest. Food is prepared for guests as soon as they are welcomed and a Tuareg tea ritual is typically enacted. Usually three glasses of strong green Chinese tea with a lot of sugar are offered. A proverb reflects the decreasing intensity of the tea: the first is bitter, like life; the second sweet, like love; and the third one is light, like the breath of death. The third cup is often refined by mint (*an-narnar*) or herbs and offered to children as well. Belching after meals is normal, but passing gas in public is considered offensive. Similarly blowing one's nose in public is regarded as very impolite or even disgusting.

Ignorance is used to express refusal and denial. If unwanted people enter the house or tent, they will be completely ignored. This means a strong sign since Tuareg attach high importance to conversation (*eduwane*), and often recount happenings and incidents again and again. When visitors remain too silent, they are always encouraged to chat. Conviviality, cheerfulness, eloquence, and politeness are important factors in social interaction.

Right behavior in addition to honor, respect, and dignity correlates to a high degree with verbal and nonverbal communication and body language. Most importantly this concerns emotions: demonstrating them in public is a taboo, no matter if it is a time of extreme joy or absolute anger. The Tuareg speak quietly and gently, and never argue or insult somebody in public. They also lower their gaze as a sign of respect towards elders, or pull their veil over their mouth while laughing as a sign of respect. The Tuareg are always supposed to demonstrate dignity and reserve and to save face. Only children are able to show pleasure and joy, or anger and grief. Communication between family and tribal members underlies formal regulations. Cross-cousins (e.g., the child of the mother's brother) have a jocular relationship (*tabubezza*); thereby the rules of decency and shame are suspended. Cross-cousins may abuse, flout, or tease each other without consequences. Parallel-cousins (e.g., paternal uncle's child), on the contrary, act and react with extreme respect and reserve. This system is reflected on the tribal level: some tribes follow a joking relation (*tukshut*), while others have a reserved, almost fearful one (*tamajaq*).

The Tuareg language Tamasheq/Tamahaq (an Afro-Asiatic Berber language) has no concrete word for taboo. Normally the Arabic equivalent *haram* (holy, forbidden) is used to express it. Paraphrases such as a lack of honor, pride, or dignity (*iban ashak*), or a lack of decency, respect, or reserve (*iban tekerakit*) are used as well. Etiquette frowned upon by the Tuareg are associated with appearances and behavior. For example, exaggerated expressions of beauty are avoided as they are believed to trigger the evil eye (*tehot/togelshit*). In order to say, for example, "Oh what a nice, beautiful girl," people add the Arabic expression *ma'shallah*. This phrase is used to fight off envy, jealousy, or distrust, which are all thought to trigger the evil eye.

The Tuareg are Muslims (Sunnis, mostly belonging to the Maliki jurisprudence school) and so even though many Tuareg practice a liberal Islam and do not follow all strict regulations, Islamic rules and regulations apply in some areas. For instance the Tuareg adhere to all Islamic taboos concerning food. Eating pork meat and drinking alcohol are taboo. Depending on the region and the influence of their neighbors (Arabs, Hausa) eating other animals may also be forbidden. In Niger and

Mali, for example, many Tuareg consider eating camels as a taboo, since they are their main economic wealth, while in Libya camel meat is quite popular. Others, mainly traditional elder people, consider eating fish or chicken as a taboo. Dog meat is also taboo. The Tuareg follow Islamic taboos concerning blood. This means that the Tuareg do not eat blood (in the form of black pudding), and since menstruation blood is thought able to harm religious amulets, men always wash their clothes separately from those of women. Also sexual intercourse during menstruation is taboo. Demonstrating emotions and sexual relations in public are taboo. This includes kissing, holding hands (except among same-sex people), talking about sexual affairs, or speaking about genitals or genital diseases in any public conversation. Mentioning sexual concerns in private, especially in the presence of elder women, is also regarded as taboo. Violence and sexual force against women or other defenseless people are an absolute taboo. Homosexuality is also extremely taboo.

Taboos concerning marriage and family require a short introduction into the social system of the Tuareg. The traditional Tuareg society differs among different sociopolitical levels, ranging from high-status groups, religious ones, subordinate status groups, craftsmen, to offspring of former slaves. This system exists in limited forms today, but the shaping and its importance have developed differently depending on tribes and regions. Common among all Tuareg is that craftsmen (*inadan*) marry only in their stratum (endogamous marriage); for all others marrying one from the *inadan* is taboo. For many members of a high-status group it is also a taboo to marry someone from a lower group. This is especially true for women since any children resulting from the marriage would automatically belong to the man's family under Islamic law and therefore would lose their higher status. One of the most important taboos concern illegitimate children, in particular an illegitimate child from an offspring of a former slave. Taboos concern also the way of addressing parents and parents-in-law. Normally one avoids their names, by generally using the respectful terms for elders and leaders (*amghar/tamghart*).

Tuareg taboos focused on death are influenced by Islam and also pre-Islamic beliefs. In practice this means that suicide is absolutely forbidden behavior and a dead Tuareg person must be buried as cremation is a taboo. Once a person passes away, his or her name will be mentioned only with the preceding phrase *n-shashela*. Some Tuareg groups avoid mentioning names of dead persons completely and consider pictures of dead persons a taboo.

Ines Kohl

Further Reading

Kohl, Ines. *Beautiful Modern Nomads: Bordercrossing Tuareg between Niger, Algeria and Libya.* Berlin: Reimer, 2009.

Kohl, Ines, and Anja Fischer (eds). *Tuareg Society within a Globalized World: Saharan Life in Transition.* London: I. B. Tauris Academic Studies, 2010.

Kohl, Ines. "Libya's 'Major Minorities': Berber, Tuareg, and Tubu. Multiple Narratives of Citizenship, Language and Border Control." *Middle Eastern Critique* 23, no. 4, (2014) 423–38.

TURKEY

Turkey is a country of rich heritage: from ancient Anatolia, in the hands of Greek, Roman, Byzantine empires, to being taken over bit by bit by the seminomadic Turkoman tribes from the East to become the mighty Ottoman Empire. With each of these changing hands, religion in Turkey also changed, from being Christian during the Roman Empire, to the gradual takeover by the Muslim Turks. This was a slow process and as Douglas Howard has stated, "the Muslim and Christian communities of Anatolia did not live entirely separate existences. Interaction of Muslims and Christians—including intermarriage—at all levels of society, from the peasantry to the family of the sultans, was ongoing." After becoming a republic in 1923, Turkey was re-formed into a secular state by Mustafa Kemal.

These gradual changes over centuries have informed modern Turkey and made it what it is today, a country that, although having no declared religion, has a large population of Muslims—99.8 percent in fact. The majority are Sunnis with Alevi (Shiite) and Sufi minorities. Indeed, Turkey is a cultural gateway from the West to Islam (and courted as such politically by the West) as well as literally being the gateway from Europe to Asia; one side of Istanbul sits in the continent of Asia, and one in Europe. With its location and rich layering of histories, it is no wonder that Turkey is a mix of cultures.

One of the keys to understanding modern Turkey is the great influence of Mustafa Kemal, who has the honorary name of Ataturk, meaning "Father of the Turks," bestowed by the National Assembly. He was a brilliant soldier who fought in World War I, under the command of the sultan of the Ottoman Empire. The empire offered themselves to the Allies, but were turned away, and although initially neutral, sided with Austria-Hungary and Germany. After World War I the sultan was forced to sign the Treaty of Sevres by the Allies as retribution, which effectively carved up the Ottoman Empire and put it into French, Italian, and British hands. Ataturk disagreed with this decision, which led to him giving up his titles in the Ottoman Army and joining the insurgency gathered around the Black Sea to overthrow the Sultan and fight for an independent and unified Ottoman Empire. The Greeks tried to enforce the Treaty of Sevres, ordering 100,000 into Anatolia to support the Greeks living there. Ataturk's answer was to order his soldiers to march to Aegean with the words, "I offer you the choice: death or the sea." The Turks took back Izmir, and over the next three years drove all foreign forces from their lands, signing a separate agreement with the USSR forcing the Allies to renegotiate the retribution terms, in the Treaty of Lausanne, essentially claiming back the Ottoman Empire as their own.

The Republic of Turkey was essentially founded by Mustafa Kemal Ataturk, and even in modern-day Turkey no child is allowed to be given his name, and it is a serious insult to make jokes about the flag, the national anthem, or Ataturk. It is also an offense to make a garment out of the flag.

Turkey is composed of seven different regions, each of which vary in their customs and culture. The regions closer to the sea are more progressive than the ones further inland, particularly in relation to women.

Turkish culture values respect and honor. Titles are applied when meeting people to be polite, such as Mister (*Bey*), Lady (*Hanim*), Teacher, or Expert to show respect. Seniority is particularly valued, and young people will visit their elders on holidays first, and often will leave the room to smoke when with the older generation, to be respectful of them. Friends of the same sex may shake hands or kiss each other on the cheek, but men and women generally do not show affection in public. Two men will kiss each other on the cheek as a greeting, or may link arms walking down the street. Men will generally only shake a woman's hand if extended to them, and a loose handshake is preferred, unless they are of the same family or old friends. Indeed, all handshakes should be looser than a Western handshake, as too firm a shake is seen as aggressive or arrogant. Turning your back on someone of importance is very insulting to them, and after meeting them you should back away, rather than turn.

Ataturk gave women the right to vote in 1930, earlier than in many European countries, but the largely Muslim culture dictates the roles and clothing of women away from the larger cities. In Istanbul one will see women covered with headscarves, but also office workers in miniskirts. Closer to the Iranian border where there are mostly farmers, women's roles are much more conservative, and they are expected to dress accordingly with headscarves and long coats, even in summer. This is very apparent when going to mosques, where women should always wear a headscarf and clothing that covers the arms and is not low cut. In Istanbul women are allowed to visit the mosque when not in use for prayer, but in rural areas they will often be confined to its secret chambers. Both men and women remove shoes going into the mosque.

If in doubt that what one is saying might be insulting to someone, the general rule is to be polite, and say nothing to rock the boat. This also applies to invitations to someone's house. It is polite to say yes, or to blame being unable to go on an outside force or reason, in order to save the host from embarrassment. When visiting peoples' homes, the guest always brings a gift. These should be wrapped, and left at the host's hallway or table, so as not to draw attention to them. Alcohol is not entirely suitable as Turkey is an Islamic country, but flowers and sweets are common. There is also a culture of bestowing the guest with anything they admire, so for a visitor it is wise to be careful not to compliment the host on an item in their home too much, else it might be given to them.

Generally, shoes are removed when entering someone's house or mosque, as the soles of the shoes are seen as dirty. When sitting on the floor in someone's home, it is impolite to sit cross-legged or to show the undersides of one's feet to someone, and one should stand up as new guests arrive to greet them. When offered food, the host will serve guests. Finger food should be eaten with the right hand, as in Islamic cultures the left hand is seen as unclean. When not eating, it is polite to keep one's hands out of one's pockets, keeping them either by one's side or engaging them in conversation. At the end of the meal guests put their knife and fork together to signal they are finished. The host may press guests to have extra helpings; to indicate fullness, a guest should place his right palm down on his chest as a way of expressing gratitude for the food and saying he is full. When the dinner is

Women in burqas stroll past women in Western clothes on Istikal Caddesi, one of Istanbul's most popular shopping avenues. The influence of traditional Islamic culture on women's fashion is less pronounced in cities than in rural areas. (Amy Laughinghouse/Dreamstime.com)

over, it is polite to stay and chat. When a guest is ready to leave, it is polite to drop hints about leaving first rather than abruptly ending the evening.

In terms of food, pork is not generally eaten, due to its prohibition in Islam, but alcohol consumption is more socially acceptable than in other Islamic countries. Other food taboos include seafood, except fish for the Yureks; members of the Alevi sect do not eat rabbit; and Turks in the northwest providence of Balikevir do not eat snails.

It is not unacceptable to be late, and business meetings in particular always start with tea or coffee. When hosting, it is important to offer guests food or drink before partaking yourself. In terms of social relationships, frankness and honesty are not necessarily seen as positive attributes if they go against the harmony of a relationship. If directness causes someone to be insulted or lose face, they may not be forgiven and the person speaking out may be ostracized in order to restore the honor of the family.

The Turkish often seem very confident, and if something is done often, there will be no admission of wrong-doing; blame is shifted to outside forces, again in the name of saving face and dignity. This dignity is also preserved when asking for favors, which is done through a third party, so that if the person refuses, the person asking will not lose face. Indeed, saying "No" outright is not really part of the culture; it is better to have a nicer way of letting someone down gently.

It is unusual for women to live alone, and instead they will be invited into a relative's house or a relative will join them. Improper behavior can result in family ostracism or a male relative acting as an executioner. In terms of going out, if women are walking home alone late at night, they should be careful not to attract attention to themselves, as it is assumed they are trying to invite male company. Western women can be misunderstood for their openness, and particularly in rural areas, women should not smile or make light conversation or flirt with men they do not know, as it will be taken the wrong way. In rural areas there is also more delineation between women's areas and men's areas. Coffee shops, known as *kahve* (literally, "coffee") are men's areas and women are not welcome. Typically women congregate in the home, or homes of their friends, to socialize.

As part of Ataturk's Turkishization program, citizens were legally required to speak and write in Turkish. Until 1991 publications, radio broadcasts, and public speaking in any non-Turkish language was prohibited.

President Recep Tayyip Erdoğan has been actively trying to restrict the freedom of speech on the Internet. Twitter and Facebook have been known to be blocked in Turkey, especially after terrorist attacks such as the Ankara blast. Over 100,000 Web sites are blocked from within Turkey. It is forbidden to insult the president over social media, and the use of Twitter to criticize or retweet other journalists' articles criticizing the state has resulted in being detained after house calls, job losses, and in some cases arrest and jail time, such as for Hayri Tunç, then a reporter for online news portal Jiyan.

Honor links to the family's good name and is also tied to the women of the household, who should be modest and show virtuous behavior. It is still taboo in parts of Turkey for a woman to not be a virgin before marriage. Men also do not generally marry up in class. Although divorce is not seen as an Islamic sin, there are strict grounds for divorce. It can only be obtained by one of six reasons: adultery; plot against life, grave assaults, and insults; crime or a dishonorable life; desertion; mental infirmity; and incompatibility. These can be difficult to prove due to the amount of evidence required.

When a person dies there are typically three stages that must be performed. The person should be buried right away, but in daylight, and washed by a professional washer first. Only male washers may wash male deceased and female washers the female deceased. The eyes of the deceased are closed, clothing is taken off, hands are placed by the side, the head is turned towards Mecca, often a metal knife is placed on the belly, and the body is shrouded in white and placed in a coffin. The Koran is read at the bedside. At the funeral the coffin is wrapped in a green cloth, and pall bearers clear a path. It is taboo to cross in front of the coffin while it is being transported. The deceased is mourned with celebratory events on the 40th day and 52nd day following their passing.

Claire Townsend

Further Reading

Abazov, Rafis. *Culture and Customs of Turkey*. Westport, CT: Greenwood, 2009.
Bernard, Doug. "Turkey Moves to Block Internet Access." VOA, January 4, 2017. http://www.voanews.com/a/turkey-moves-to-block-internet-access-/3662886.html.

Bowen, Ronda. "Birth and Death—Traditions, Ceremonies and Rituals in Turkey." Bright Hub Education. March 2, 2012. http://www.brighthubeducation.com/social-studies -help/15601-birth-and-death-traditions-in-turkey/.

Howard, Douglas A. *The History of Turkey*. Westport, CT: Greenwood, 2001. http://www .everyculture.com/To-Z/Turkey.html.

McPherson, Charlotte. *Culture Smart! Turkey*. London: Kuperard, 2005.

Property Turkey. "Best Regions of Turkey for Expat Living." http://www.propertyturkey .com/blog-turkey/best-regions-of-turkey-for-expat-living.

Sozeri, Efe Kerem. "The Reality of Life Under Turkey's Internet Censorship Machine. " *The Daily Dot*, July 5, 2016. https://www.dailydot.com/layer8/turkey-censorship-real-life/.

Turkish Cultural Foundation. "Death Tradition." http://www.turkishculture.org/lifestyles /ceremonies/death-and-funeral-544.htm?type=1.

Worley, Will. "Turkish Government 'Blocks Twitter and Facebook' as Part of Alleged Media Ban Following Ankara Blast." *The Independent*, March 13, 2016. http://www.independ ent.co.uk/news/world/europe/ankara-explosion-turkey-twitter-facebook-ban-a6929 136.html.

U

UKRAINE

Ukraine is a country in eastern Europe, sharing a border with Russia. Ukrainians typically believe in the power of words and the power of actions. Although Soviet authorities worked hard to eradicate beliefs they considered superstitious, many Ukrainians are convinced that what one does and says evokes a supernatural response. If anything, growing Westernization is affecting what might be called a magical worldview much more than Soviet practice ever did, and beliefs about the power of words and deeds is dying in urban settings, even as it maintains a foothold in rural areas. Still, urban Ukrainians will practice virtually all of the behaviors and observe all of the taboos detailed below.

When meeting someone, the older person should address the younger one first and the younger person, unless given permission to deviate from standard behavior, should speak to the older person using the more formal version of the second-person pronoun: *vy* instead of *ty*. In many parts of Ukraine respect for elders in the form of pronoun choice applies to parents as well as strangers, although elsewhere, and especially in urban settings, all members of the immediate family are addressed using the familiar form. Usage with more distant kin such as aunts and uncles varies.

When greeting someone, one should never touch the other person across a barrier. Reaching out to a visitor coming to one's home and shaking hands across the threshold is taboo; both people should be either inside the door or outside. Shaking hands across a doorway means that the relationship between the two people will be severed and they will have no contact for seven years. People coming to one's home should be offered food and drink and it is considered most impolite not to make such an offer and equally impolite to refuse. In general, boundaries, whether between the inside and the outside of the house or between the inside and the outside of the body, are considered extremely potent and should be treated with care. Many people, especially in rural areas, will cross themselves before eating. Picking one's teeth and otherwise reaching inside the mouth is considered vulgar. While in rural settings everyone seated at a table may eat from a common serving dish, but the utensil that actually goes into a person's mouth must be his or her own. Spoons and forks are not shared and soldiers carried their own utensils inside their boots when they went to war. When sitting at a table, one should sit along one of the sides. Sitting at a corner is considered unlucky and a person who is foolish enough to sit in this manner will not find love for seven years.

Modesty is a contentious issue. Westerners who see Ukrainians often consider them provocatively dressed. Women might wear see-through garments to the office or when walking down the street. By the same token, the covering of the hair was widely practiced by married women and many village women still insist on wearing their kerchief or *khustka*. What Westerners find strange is what might be called the contemporary evolution of lack of body shame. In the past and in some rural areas today, family members regularly see each other naked in the bath, often a separate structure that, once heated, is used by the entire family: men, women, and children. People would, and in some areas still do, go to public baths and appear naked in front of strangers. On beaches today one often sees women with less-than-ideal bodies in bikinis and elderly and pot-bellied men in speedo-type bathing suits. People who are not related and not of the same sex share sleeping compartments on trains without anyone feeling threatened or embarrassed.

What is considered a threat is uncontrolled desire, typically manifested through excessive praise. When one sees a child, calling that child beautiful or pointing out his or her accomplishments will make parents uncomfortable and cause them to spirit the child away. Objects praised by others are often given away to the person uttering the laudatory words for fear that the speaker may desire the object and adversely affect its owner. People traditionally fear the evil eye. A person who wants something she or he cannot have may inadvertently or intentionally cast the evil eye. Some people are said to have a gaze that harms others even when desire is not present. They are expected to avoid looking at vulnerable people such as infants. While excessive praise of children is considered suspicious, letting complete strangers care for one's children is not. On public transportation, strangers will hold a child on their lap until the family reaches their destination.

A mixture of fear of jinxing a desired outcome and taboos against expression of desire means that baby showers do not exist and no gift may be bought for a child until after he or she is born. Stories about foolish purchases of baby gifts prior to the actual birth abound. Pregnancy is considered a dangerous state and expectant mothers are supposed to avoid sewing on Fridays, the day of St. Paraskeva, lest their babies be born with webbed fingers or toes. Fathers-to-be are also subject to taboos and must avoid using sharp objects on holidays to prevent the birth of a child with a cleft palate. The concept of being careful around boundaries, combined with the taboos on praising good things, means newborns and their mothers are sequestered for 40 days. While few people meet the requirement of not appearing in public for that length of time, Ukrainian women typically will not post baby pictures online or take the infant to their place of work to show friends and office mates.

The wedding couple, because they are crossing the threshold between single and married life, are considered vulnerable to hexing and the evil eye. To protect the couple, pins are inserted into the clothing of both the bride and the groom. There is no prohibition against the groom seeing the bride on the day of the wedding prior to the ceremony. The process of his picking up the bride for the trip to church is complex, however, and often involves bargaining and "paying" for access to the bride. This is usually done at the doorway to the bride's home, and the person in charge of collecting money is the maid of honour or *druzhka*. A great deal of fortune-telling accompanies the wedding. During the wedding ceremony the bride and groom stand on a ritual towel called a *rushnyk*. It is believed that whichever member of the couple steps on the towel first will dominate in the marriage. In other areas, both members of the bridal pair take a bite out of the wedding bread or *korovai*. The person who takes the bigger bite will be the dominant spouse. The ritual towel not only separates the couple from all others during the wedding ceremony, it is used to tie their hands together and ensure their union once the ceremony is complete. The couple are both vulnerable and potent and, when a drought affects a village, a bride walking down the street can sprinkle water and cause the rains to come.

Many taboos surround death and the body of the deceased. Opinions on whether relatives should maintain a vigil over a dying person vary. Once a person is dead, the body is washed and this can be done only by postmenopausal women; premenopausal women who touch a dead body will become infertile. The water used to wash the body is considered dangerous and must be disposed of in such a way that no living thing will step where the water has been poured. Usually this is done by having the water run down a fence and immediately into the ground under it. All things that touch the body are dangerous and must be either buried with the deceased or burned. There are rumors, however, of people stealing "dead" water and using it to "deaden" pain or to cause harm to enemies. The body of the deceased must lie in state in the home for at least one night, a practice still observed in villages, and friends and relatives keep watch over the body because, should an animal such as a cat jump over the deceased, there is danger that the soul will enter that animal. Lamentation is practiced in many areas and is believed to be very powerful; it must be done over a dead body only because it might otherwise cause a living person to die. Once the body is removed from the home, it is carried in a funeral procession to the church and then to the graveyard. Crossing the path of a funeral procession is taboo, and so is looking at it through an opening such as a window. The consequences of violating these taboos are sickness and possible death. Burial in the graveyard is limited to those who have lived and died properly. Unbaptized infants are typically buried outside the graveyard or at least separately from "normal" dead persons. Suicides cannot receive proper burial and are interred apart, though this practice is now being relaxed and a funeral ritual plus reburial is allowed after a year has elapsed. People who die before their time, as the result of an accident, illness, or because they are killed in battle, receive special rites to ensure their repose. These include a death wedding for unmarried persons. Bringing a dozen roses to a funeral or to an event commemorating the deceased is praiseworthy, but giving an even number of flowers to a living person is taboo because even numbers signify completion and should be used only when life is done.

Homes are typically blessed with and protected by icons that are displayed in a special corner opposite the door. Icons were forbidden during the Soviet period, but most people simply hid theirs and did not discard them. The belief in a house spirit or *domovyk* survives even in urban settings, and people moving from one apartment to another will invite their house spirit to change domiciles with them. Pleasing the house spirit ensures household harmony and prosperity and is done by keeping the house tidy and making small food offerings to the *domovyk*. When leaving on a trip, it is proper to sit down for a few moments to say goodbye to the *domovyk*, and even people who do not believe in spirits observe the custom of sitting before travel. Once a person has left the house, he or she cannot go back; returning after departure brings bad luck. Most out-buildings such as the barn are believed to have their own spirit who must be similarly respected. Natural features such as forests, rivers, and lakes are also believed to have their own caretaker beings. These interact with humans to a lesser degree than household spirits, their primary function being to keep people from violating norms such as fishing out of season, or being greedy and hunting with abandon, or gathering too many berries or mushrooms.

Religious taboos apply to icons and any and all items sanctified by the church. These must be treated with respect and can be disposed of only by a church official. People often carry icons on their person, and many drivers of public transportation use them to protect their vehicles. The opposite of the veneration of icons is their use in black magic. Rumors speak of the desecration of icons to gain special powers or wealth.

Natalie Kononenko

Further Reading

Boriak, Olena. "The Anthropology of Birth in Russia and Ukraine: The Midwife in Traditional Ukrainian Culture: Ritual, Folklore and Mythology." *SEEFA Journal* 7, no. 2 (2002): 20–49. https://journals.ku.edu/index.php/folklorica/article/view/3723/3564.

Havryliuk, Natalia. "The Structure and Function of Funeral Rituals and Customs in Ukraine." *Folklorica* 8, no. 2 (2003): 7–23. https://journals.ku.edu/index.php/folklorica/article/view/3738/3577.

Kononenko, Natalie. *Slavic Folklore: A Handbook*. Westport, CT: Greenwood, 2007.

Kononenko, Natalie. "When Traditional Improvisation Is Prohibited: Ukrainian Funeral Laments and Burial Practices." In Gabriel Solis and Bruno Nettl, eds., *Musical Improvisation: Art Education and Society*, 52–71. Urbana: University of Illinois Press, 2009.

UYGHURS

The Uyghurs (also written as Uighurs) are a Turkic ethnic group living in Eastern and Central Asia. Most Uyghurs live in China's Xinjiang Uyghur Autonomous Region, though there is a sizeable Uyghur diaspora to be found living in the other Central Asian countries of Kazakhstan, Kyrgyzstan, and Uzbekistan, as well as in Turkey. Smaller Uyghur communities also exist in Afghanistan, Germany, Belgium, the Netherlands, Norway, Sweden, Russia, Saudi Arabia, Australia, Canada, and the United States. The Uyghurs are the second-largest Chinese Muslim ethnic group after the Hui, with most modern Uyghurs being Sunni Muslims. While modern Uyghurs self-identify as Muslim, observance of the religion varies geographically. In Xinjiang province there are repeated outbreaks of ethnic unrest and violence, with many Uyghurs striving to establish their own independent state within China.

Central Asian culture is typically extremely forgiving of foreigners who do not demonstrate correct local etiquette, but at the same time the Uyghurs are impressed

Culture Shock! 🌐

China's Mandela: Professor Ilham Tohti

In September 2014 the Uyghur intellectual Professor Ilham Tohti, who has been likened to Nelson Mandela by some commentators, was sentenced to life in prison for what the Chinese authorities viewed as his advocacy of Uyghur separatism. From 1999 to 2003 Tohti was barred from lecturing, and authorities hampered his ability to publish. In response to this Tohti turned to the Internet to increase public awareness of Uyghur issues. In 2006 Tohti established a Web site intended to promote understanding between the Uyghurs and the Han Chinese that also investigated social issues concerning the Uyghurs and Han. Over time this Web site was taken offline periodically, and its contributors harassed. In 2009 Tohti was detained by Chinese authorities but was released after requests from the Obama administration. In January 2014 Tohti was detained again and sentenced to life imprisonment. The same year Tohti was awarded the PEN/Barbara Goldsmith Freedom to Write Award (an American human rights award for writers striving for freedom of expression). In 2016 Tohti was awarded the Martin Ennals Award for Human Rights Defenders.

Victoria Williams

if a visitor can show some knowledge of, and respect for, their culture. The Uyghurs are a naturally friendly people who demonstrate great courtesy to others, meaning that when they encounter strangers the outsiders are greeted warmly. When Uyghurs meet up with their friends and relatives, they will normally shake hands. Typical Uyghur greetings include "Yakhshi musiz" (Are you well?) and "Bu nimä" (What is this?). The most common Uyghur greeting gestures for both men and women are handshakes and hugs, but men should wait to see if the woman initiates the physical contact before shaking her hand or embracing her. In the west of the Xinjiang region, handshakes are common among all people while close friends will kiss each other on the cheek. Again when a man meets a woman it is best if he lets the woman initiate any physical contact and nod to acknowledge her.

Uyghur men typically wear a shirt together with a *qiapan* (a long, buttonless robe), the collar of which wraps across the body from the right and that reaches down to the knees. Women tend to wear colorful, sleeveless blouses and flamboyant waistcoats. Many Uyghur women spin silk, cotton, and wool producing golden brocade fabric that is frequently made into costumes and hats. Many Uyghurs customarily wear an ornately embroidered, square (or rounded) cap called a *doppa* as well as long leather boots. The Uyghurs also like to wear jewelry such as bracelets, rings, and earrings made from silver or porcelain.

Young, unmarried Uyghur women wear their hair in many very long braids (usually eight or ten but sometimes more). The Uyghurs traditionally believe that the longer a woman's hair, the more beautiful the woman is. In general, Uyghurs living in the southern region, particularly in the city of Kashgar, are more conservatively Muslim than elsewhere. This is evinced by the fact that Uyghur women living in this area traditionally wear a full veil made of brown cloth that covers their head completely. This form of dress is particularly common in Kashgar. In other areas, such as in the ancient city of Turpan, women merely cover their hair with scarves. Recently Chinese authorities have placed certain restrictions on Uyghur dress and appearance. Today young Uyghur men living in Xingjiang are forbidden to have long beards, while some women also face limitations if they wish to wear an Islamic veil.

Many mosques in Urumqi (the capital of the Xinjiang province) and throughout the Xinjiang region are open to the paying public, with tourists permitted to enter whether or not they are Muslim. Women tourists may wish to cover their heads out of respect when visiting a mosque, but they are unlikely to be asked to do so. It is, however, necessary for all visitors to remove their shoes when entering mosques' prayer halls.

The Uyghurs take great pride in providing hospitality to guests with hosts inviting friends, relatives, and even strangers to social events including weddings and informal gatherings. Most Uyghur food is based around flour including grilled *nang* (bread), baked buns (*samsa*), fried flour twists (*sangza*), and *lengmen* (or *läghmän*) noodles that are made from flour, water, and salt. Other common dishes include rice dishes (*polu* or *polo*) featuring mutton or beef as well as vegetables and fruit. *Polu* is particularly associated with social gatherings as it is often eaten on occasions related to rites of passage, including weddings and funerals. The Uyghurs love to eat fruit and also enjoy drinking green or black tea. It should be noted, however, that very recently Chinese authorities have begun to crack down on Uyghur cultural gatherings that involve numbers of men debating, listening to music, and eating together to the extent that today such meetings occur rarely in China.

When entering a Uyghur home it is very important to remove one's shoes in order to prevent dirt from outside being brought into the home. This is true whether one is entering a more modern house or a yurt (the tent dwelling of a nomad). Also when entering a yurt it is important not to step on the threshold, as this is considered taboo. A guest to a Uyghur home may also be expected to wash their hands before they eat, though this custom is less common in the homes of the more Westernized Uyghurs. If a guest is expected to wash his hands before eating, he should wash them three times, with the host pouring the water over the guest's hands and into a basin. Once the hands have been washed three times, the guest must allow the hands to drip dry rather than shake the water from them. He may also be offered a towel on which to dry his hands.

A Uyghur host will usually lead guests to the eating area. The Uyghur sit cross-legged on the floor to eat around a table. The Uyghur normally prefer to eat with their hands. Many items of Uyghur cuisine are bite-sized, but when an item is larger than this, for example as is Uyghur bread, then you should break the food into smaller pieces and then eat the pieces rather than biting into the entire bread. In Uyghur culture eating everything on the plate is taken as an indication that the guest is still hungry, so if one has eaten enough, one should leave some food on the plate. This will not prevent a host from offering more to eat, but it may slow down the rate at which the extra food is offered. A Uyghur host will often offer a guest tea to drink. When drinking the tea it is polite to use both hands to bring the cup to the mouth.

If eating in a Uyghur restaurant it is usually necessary to pay when ordering the food, rather than after eating the meal. Unlike when eating in a Uyghur home, cutlery is normally provided in Uyghur restaurants. Typically the cutlery will include spoons and chopsticks, and one will not be expected to eat with his hands.

In recent times the Uyghurs have had to be careful when communicating for fear of being punished by the Chinese authorities. The Uyghurs in northwestern China have long migrated to the neighboring countries of Central Asia in order to avoid the restrictions placed on their freedom by the Chinese government. Nowadays, as China's influence increases across Central Asia, campaigning for an independent Uyghur state within Xinjiang (which would be called Uighuristan) is becoming a near impossibility. The last attempt by the Uyghur to establish an independent homeland state inside China was thwarted by the Chinese in 1949. This led to in excess of 60,000 Uyghurs migrating into Central Asia over subsequent years. This migration has resulted in around 350,000 Uyghurs residing in formerly Soviet areas of Central Asia, particularly in Kazakhstan. Until recently these Uyghurs living outside of China were able to express their support for an independent Uyghur state within China. However, this situation is changing, as China is extending its influence in Central Asia by bankrolling investment in the area and establishing trade zones. Thus today much of Kazakhstan's Uyghur society is controlled by the Chinese, meaning that the Uyghurs do not feel free to express their desire for an independent state for fear of punishment. Chinese authorities are also said to be increasingly policing the expression of Uyghur identity, both online and in print, meaning that people risk imprisonment for opposing Chinese policies related to the Uyghurs.

Victoria Williams

Further Reading

Fang, Huawen. *Traditional Chinese Folk Customs*. Newcastle upon Tyne, UK: Cambridge Scholars, 2015.

Martin Ennals Awards. "Ilham Tohti 2016 Martin Ennals Award Laureate for Human Rights Defenders." October 11, 2016. http://www.martinennalsaward.org/?p=1078. Accessed January 9, 2017.

Phillips, Tom. "Ilham Tohti, Uighur Imprisoned for Life By China, Wins Major Human Rights Prize." *The Guardian: World: China*. October 11, 2016. https://www.theguardian.com/world/2016/oct/11/ilham-tohti-uighur-china-wins-nobel-martin-ennals-human-rights-award. Accessed January 9, 2017.

Qobil, Rustam. "Dreaming of Uighuristan." *BBC News Magazine*. April 16, 2015. http://www.bbc.co.uk/news/magazine-32337643. Accessed January 9, 2017.

Rudelson, Justin Jon. *Oasis Identities: Uyghur Nationalism Along China's Silk Road*. New York: Columbia University Press, 1997.

Summers, Josh. "A Lesson on Central Asian Etiquette for Uyghur and Kazakh." *Far West China*. April 11, 2013. https://www.farwestchina.com/2013/04/a-lesson-on-central-asian-etiquette-for-uyghur-and-kazakh.html. Accessed January 9, 2017.

Tate, Mary Kate, and Nate Tate. *Feeding the Dragon: A Culinary Travelogue Through China with Recipes.* Kansas City: Andrews McMeel, 2011.

Bellér-Hann, Ildikó, M. Cristina Cesàro, Rachel Harris, and Joanne Smith Finley. *Situating the Uyghurs Between China and Central Asia.* Abingdon, UK: Routledge, 2016.

UZBEKISTAN

Uzbekistan is a landlocked Central Asian country bordered by five other landlocked nations: Kazakhstan, Tajikistan, Kyrgyzstan, Afghanistan, and Turkmenistan. Uzbekistan is a constitutional democratic republic with a diverse ethnic population. The official language of Uzbekistan is Uzbek, which is spoken by around 85 percent of the people. Russian is also widely spoken, as Uzbekistan is a former bordered constituent republic of the Soviet Union. Today the majority of people in Uzbekistan, about 84 percent, are ethnically Uzbek (the largest Turkic ethnic group in Central Asia), with 5 percent of the population being Russian, 4 percent ethnically Tajiks, and 3 percent Kazakhs. The remaining population comprises other ethnic minorities. The majority of Uzbeks are Muslim.

Generally speaking Uzbekistan is a country steeped in traditions, though these traditions vary depending on location and people's ethnicity and class. On the whole ethnic Uzbeks and other Muslim ethnicities within the country hold tighter to their traditions and etiquette than do ethnic Russians and people from ethnic groups that have a European heritage. Uzbeks living in cities are the least traditional people living in Uzbekistan, while people living in rural communities are the most traditional in terms of etiquette, customs, and dress. This having been said, there are a few universal elements to etiquette in Uzbekistan.

Elders, especially those in positions of authority, are treated with the utmost respect in Uzbekistan. For this reason young Uzbeks will normally address older Uzbek men as *aka*, or elder brother, whether the man is well known to them or a stranger. This greeting is used in order to show respect and deference. As well as proclaiming *aka*, a young Uzbek will also place their right hand across their heart in order to signal that their respect is genuine. At social events, elders are always the first to be served food and will be given the honor of making the first toast. Anyone who does not show great respect to their elders is considered ill-mannered and uncivilized by Uzbek society. A common greeting said in Uzbekistan is "Salom alaikum," which translates as "Peace be upon you" but is the equivalent of "Hello." In formal situations handshakes are usually performed, though you should wait to see if a person of the opposite sex initiates the gesture by extending their hand first. When meeting to discuss business it is necessary to have business cards available, as it is usual to exchange the cards when meeting potential business partners.

The way in which people dress varies greatly across Uzbekistan and depends on people's ethnic background, religion, social class, and economic standing. However, all Uzbek peoples take great pride in their appearance. In particular the way in which women dress is dependent on factors such as ethnicity and religion. Ethnic Uzbek and Tajik women dress very modestly, and those living in rural areas also wear a scarf over their head when out in public. Since Uzbekistan gained independence from the Soviet Union some women have also started to wear a veil known as a *paranja*. These are also worn in Afghanistan and Pakistan. Dress codes do not apply to non-Muslim women and those with Slavic heritage who are allowed to dress pretty much how they like. Men in Uzbekistan tend to wear shirts and slacks with sandals, though in business situations most will wear a suit and tie with loafers. Both men and women in Uzbekistan like to wear their finest clothes to celebrations and other social events.

Mosques and other holy places often have their own dress code and it is essential that visitors heed these regulations. If in doubt about what to wear to a sacred space, it is better to ask a local person's advice rather than appear disrespectful. Dress requirements typically state that shoes must be removed, women must cover their heads, and trousers and skirts should be full-length. In Uzbekistan, shorts and revealing tops are not generally encouraged and are deemed unacceptable to wear at religious sites. In addition, when visiting a holy place visitors may be expected to wash their hands and faces. Some religious buildings also only allow one gender to enter.

Uzbeks regard hospitality towards guests as very important. If one is invited to an Uzbek house, it is expected that the visitor will bring a small gift to give to the host. An ideal gift is a souvenir of the guest's homeland such as a picture book. Failing this other suitable gifts include a bunch of flowers or a box of local candy. A bottle of good vodka or wine is also an acceptable gift if the guest knows for sure that the host drinks alcohol.

Sometimes an Uzbek will invite someone to their home for what they call a cup of tea. This is usually a euphemism for an entire meal, not just a drink. If a guest is invited to a home that is most likely short of food, then it is considered polite to

---

Culture Shock! ⊕

Beshik-tuyi Cradle Ceremony

Beshik-tuyi (wooden cradle) is an ancient, widespread ritual concerned with the first time a baby is put in a cradle. The ritual takes place soon after a baby is born and involves all of a baby's family and their friends. Relatives of the baby's mother present the *beshik* (cradle), cakes, candy, and toys to the baby's parents and grandparents. Next the baby's grandfather puts the *beshik* on his right shoulder before handing it to his son who places the cradle on his right shoulder before giving it to the baby's mother. Once all the guests have assembled around a table, they enjoy the candy that has been brought by the baby's grandmother while older female guests swaddle the baby before putting it in the *beshik*. The baby is then carried to another room where the guests visit the baby and give him or her gifts. The guests also throw sugarlumps into the cradle and wish the baby well. Traditionally guests also coated their faces in white flour so that their thoughts of the baby would be pure.

Victoria Williams

bring as much food as the guest thinks is necessary. The food the guest brings is regarded as a gift to the host, and though the host will probably refuse it at the first time of offering, they will accept it eventually. When entering a house in Uzbekistan, guests must remove their shoes at the door. This is true not just of ethnic Uzbek homes but also homes owned by ethnic Russians and applies to both houses and yurts (tents covered in skin that are the dwelling place of Central Asian nomads). Since Uzbekistan is a desert country, taking off outdoor shoes means that dirt and dust from outside does not enter the home. Visitors do not have to go barefoot, however, as in Uzbekistan dwellings will contain a mix of assorted slippers and sandals for visitors to put on once they have entered the abode. In addition, visitors must not shake hands or kiss their host on the cheek while straddling a threshold or standing in an entranceway, as this is considered to bring bad luck.

In the most traditional households men and women dine and entertain separately. Although there are no strict rules about women being seen by people other than relatives (as occurs in purdah), Uzbeks often feel more relaxed when socializing with people of their own sex. This social convention does not usually apply to foreign women, however, who are able to sit with both men and women. If during a meal alcohol is provided, it is considered rude to refuse to drink. Similarly, a guest may be asked to give a toast, which should include thanks and praise directed to the host.

Another important element of dining etiquette in traditional Muslim homes in Uzbekistan is that it is taboo to eat or pass food to someone using the left hand, as

Men celebrate a birthday in the village of Gigikhana, Uzbekistan. In the most traditional Uzbek households men and women eat separately because they feel more at ease mixing with people of their own sex. (Vova Pomortzeff/Alamy Stock Photo)

the left hand is associated with bodily functions—most especially using the toilet. It is particularly important not to eat the Uzbek national dish, *plov*, with the left hand. *Plov*, which is eaten on special occasions, consists typically of rice, carrots, meat, and cumin and is cooked by men in a special pot called a *kazan*. Once the *plov* is cooked it is transferred to a communal platter called a *lyagan* from which everyone eats. *Plov* is usually eaten using the right hand rather than eating utensils. As a guest it is imperative to eat the food that is served, for it is rude to refuse a dish due to personal preferences. This may mean eating foods that are not usually included in Western diets—for example, in Khoresm (a region that also falls partly in Kazakhstan and Turkmenistan) a guest of honor will often be presented with a sheep's head. At formal dinners cutlery may be used, in which case it is held Continental style with the knife in the right hand and the fork in the left hand.

Just as the left hand is regarded as dirty, so Uzbeks also view feet as unclean. For this reason it is never acceptable to bring feet close to a dining table or area where food is served. This is particularly true if the food is being served in the traditional Uzbek way—from a large tablecloth placed on the floor. When sitting around the tablecloth, people are careful to keep their feet tucked under them so that the feet do not go anywhere near the food. Another example of behavior considered bad table manners occurs when someone tries to blow their nose during a meal, or indeed, while in any public place. If a visitor must blow his nose, he should find a private area to do so.

At the end of a meal, it is important to demonstrate gratitude to the host by bringing one's hands together in front of one's face, then moving them downwards in a way that suggests washing the face. This gesture is the sign for everyone present to leave the dining table, and it is thought very rude for someone to continue to eat after someone has made this gesture. At the end of a meal it is usual for an Uzbek host to serve tea, often accompanied by sweets or small cakes. The tea served in Uzbekistan tends to be unsweetened green or black tea. Before serving tea to their guests a host will fill each cup with water three times before emptying the water into the teapot holding the tea leaves. This ensures that the tea is well combined with the water and that everyone's tea is of equal strength. Elders and guests will be handed their tea by the host, who will fill their cups only half full as a sign of his esteem. The thinking behind this gesture is that by only half filling the cups, the elders and guests will ask for tea frequently in order to quench their thirst, thereby allowing the host to display his hospitality skills and act in a servile manner to his guests. A more prosaic reason for the half-filled cups is that the teacups (*piala*) used in Uzbekistan are small and without handles (they are held from underneath) so half filling the cups means that guests do not burn their fingers when trying to drink.

Business in Uzbekistan is very reliant on personal relationships, so Uzbeks consider it necessary to get to know their potential business partners. This may make it necessary for a foreigner wishing to do business in Uzbekistan to visit an Uzbek's home in order to get to know their family, socializing, getting drunk over glasses of vodka, and sharing saunas as well as attending business meetings. Indeed, whether a potential business partner likes to spend time with a person may be the determining factor in whether one clinches a business deal.

As is the case in many countries, it is considered polite to ask locals' permission to photograph them. Also in Uzbekistan it is wise not to photograph anything connected to the military or government as this could lead to officials confiscating the camera. The government also limits Internet use in Uzbekistan. While Uzbeks are very keen on using the Internet, with WiFi easy to find and cybercafés quite a common sight, visitors may find that some Web sites are blocked. Virtual private network (VPN) access that can be used to access some region-restricted Web sites is needed to read most foreign news sites. Uzbek authorities control very tightly what people can access online, and there are frequent outages of Skype and YouTube.

Uzbeks typically like to engage in small talk, and when in conversation with an Uzbek it is best to keep to uncontroversial subjects such as family, children, weddings, the weather, and education. Other popular topics include work, including salaries and money—Uzbeks like to know about exchange rates and to discuss the value of material goods. Politics is an increasingly discussed topic in Uzbekistan (mainly because of the influence of the Internet) with many Uzbeks siding with Russian political policies—this may well be due to the fact that Uzbekistan was once Soviet. Local politics are also discussed, but in a somewhat obtuse way as Uzbeks are inherently wary of condemning authority. In Uzbekistan taboo behavior is influenced by religion. For example, in addition to not using one's left hand when eating or blowing one's nose during meals, it is also taboo to display affection in public. Muslim Uzbeks of the opposite sex do not display physical affection towards one another—this is especially true of unmarried people and most especially unmarried women.

Victoria Williams

Further Reading

Hanks, Reuel R. *Central Asia: A Global Studies Handbook*. Santa Barbara, CA: ABC-CLIO, 2005.

Ibbotson, Sophie, and Max Lovell-Hoare. *Uzbekistan*, 2nd ed. Chalfont St Giles, UK: Bradt Travel Guides, 2016.

Ulko, Alex. *Culture Smart! Uzbekistan: The Essential Guide to Customs & Culture*. London: Kuperard, 2017.

V

VENEZUELA

Situated on the northern coast of South America, Venezuela is the sixth-largest country in the region. In 1999 it was renamed the Bolivarian Republic of Venezuela. The country's official language is Spanish. The country is known for its petroleum industry, holding some of the world's largest oil reserves. It is one of the most urban countries in Latin America. The majority of the population (93.5 percent) is concentrated in the north, especially in the capital city Caracas, and in other main cities, such as Valencia, Maracaibo, Barquisimeto, and Ciudad Guayana.

Family is one of the most important social aspects of Venezuela. The extended family often forms a significant role in the daily lives of many Venezuelans, playing a part in child-rearing and in caring for the old. However, Venezuela nowadays is a country going through a severe economic and social crisis. In the past, parents sought to transmit to their children a sense of respect for family members, good manners, deference, decorum, and public behavior that has been eroded by the crisis. It is common to see adult children continue to live with their parents until marriage. Getting together for holidays, family celebrations like baptisms, birthdays, graduations, and weddings is an important part of Venezuelans' social lives. Most middle-class women are college educated, and often are able to pursue careers in the sciences and the humanities. Many women hold high elective or appointive offices. Traditionally, in the lower-class sectors women head households and usually work to support the family.

Venezuelans are known for their gregarious nature; their optimism and open-mindedness is evident in the way they greet each other. When meeting female family members or friends, the customary greeting is a mutual kiss on one check usually accompanied with the onomatopoeic sound of "muak." Between men, adult family members, and friends a greeting often means a strong-gripped handshake while slapping each other on the back. A hug is also used between men. Among business colleagues and more formal interactions, a handshake and direct eye contact are the more common practices.

Appearance is taken seriously in Venezuela—a country that holds the Guinness World Record as the country with the highest number of international beauty pageant victories, while also ranking among the top countries in the world for plastic surgery procedures. Clothing follows American and European styles, but women tend to wear tight pants, skirts, and dresses.

Some rules of etiquette can indeed lead to more enjoyable communication and social interactions. It is common in offices and business to be offered a *cafecito*, a small cup of black coffee. Venezuelans pride themselves on being coffee connoisseurs. In any bakery, diner, or eatery, big espresso machines can be found. Customers order quite a few variations of coffee. One of them is *guayoyo*, a brewed and filtered, sweet, watered-down black coffee. From the espresso machine coffee is served often in small or middle-sized cups, Italian style. This can be served straight black called *negro*, or *negrito*, depending on the size; *marron* or *marroncito*, a double shot of *espresso* with more or less milk; *café con leche*, meaning more milk than espresso; and *tetero*, hot milk with a dash of coffee.

When invited to lunch or dinner at a private home it is customary to bring a small gift, usually a bottle of wine, flowers, or chocolates. Most Venezuelans are punctual for business, but they usually arrive at private gatherings 15 to 30 minutes after the indicated start time. Printed invitations for formal gatherings will always give the hour the party starts, but never the ending time. Dictating a time at which a guest is expected to leave is considered rude in a country where entertaining is socially important, and hosts try very hard to please their guests. Usually, the way to indicate that the party is over is playing the famous Venezuelan song "Alma Llanera," the country's second national anthem. When the table is set, the fork is on the left side of the plate and a knife on the right in the traditional Continental way. A fork or tea spoon at the top of the plate is provided for dessert. Guests must wait until everyone is seated and served before beginning to eat. Usually the host will say "Buen provecho" (the equivalent of "Enjoy your meal") and people will immediately respond with "Gracias, igualmente" (Thanks, same to you). Hands should be visible when eating, and elbows should not rest on the table. Utensils are used to eat hamburgers, pizza, and fruits.

In Venezuela *el desayuno*, or breakfast, consists of fruit juice, coffee with milk or *café con leche*, eggs, *arepa* (a round cornmeal patty either fried or grilled and served with a variety of savory fillings), or bread. *El almuerzo*, or lunch, is usually served between noon and 2 p.m. and is the main meal of the day. A traditional lunch consists of a soup, a main dish with some meat or fish, rice, fried plantains, and sometimes a dessert. It is often finished with coffee. Most people in small cities and towns still eat lunch at home, but in the larger cities people eat at work, from street vendors, or in restaurants called *areperas*, where the most distinctive Venezuelan food is served. The national dish is *pabellon criollo*, a traditionally large portion of black beans, white rice, shredded meat or *carne mechada*, and sweet fried plantains. Other popular typical dishes are *empanadas* (deep-fried filled pastries), *tequeños* (long, small rolls filled with hot white cheese), and *pan de jamon* (a ham bread). *Hallacas*, a traditional Christmas corn tamale wrapped in banana leaves, is representative of the multicultural heritage of the country since it has European ingredients (such as olives, chicken, pork, and almonds), spread over indigenous cornmeal dough and wrapped the African way in banana leaves. In the afternoon *la merienda*, a light snack of coffee and rolls or sandwiches, is typically served to children once they arrive from school. In the evening, from 6:00 p.m. to as late as 9:00 p.m., *la cena*, or dinner, is served as the last meal of the day.

There are very few taboos regarding food. Most of these deal with the foods that pregnant women should refrain from eating, such as seafood. In some regions menstruating women are advised not to drink ice-cold beverages and to avoid whisking egg whites because the whites simply will not foam or froth when whipped by a menstruating woman.

Venezuelans typically have a smaller sense of personal space than many other cultures. People are generally very friendly and stand close to each other while speaking, even in business situations. It is not unusual to hold the arm or elbow of the other person while conversing. Venezuelans have an assortment of gestures and facial expressions to communicate, for example pointing with a puckering of the lips towards something or nodding the head to indicate agreement.

Nancy Noguera

Further Reading

Salas, Miguel Tinker. *Venezuela: What Everybody Needs to Know.* New York: Oxford University Press, 2015.

Skidmore, Thomas, and Peter H. Smith. *Modern Latin America*, 7th ed. New York: Oxford University Press, 2010.

Taver, Michael, and Julia C. Frederick. *The History of Venezuela.* Westport, CT: Greenwood, 2005.

VIETNAM

Vietnam is a country located in southeast Asia, bordering Cambodia, Laos, and China. It has a population of almost 90 million people. Social customs in Vietnam have changed since the Vietnam War. Generally Vietnamese in the large cities are less formal than they were a generation ago, but rural villagers are still fairly conservative in their manners, so it is important to observe not only how people interact with oneself but also with each other. People in Vietnam are usually friendly and polite, but at the same time, very formal. They typically expect everyone to behave this way, especially in recognizing each person's position in a social network that factors in age, gender, and social importance. The American habit of treating everyone equally with no need to defer to anyone is considered simpleminded and insulting. Social importance is normally due to a person's position and importance in a particular social network, be it family, governmental body, company, church, club, and the like. This can be difficult to evaluate correctly before a visitor knows people, so when meeting someone, one should pay attention to the person's age in relationship to one's own age and to the details of how other people are speaking with the person.

The importance of elders is central. Every family, no matter their religious beliefs, has a family altar in their living room where framed photographs of deceased parents, grandparents, and other relatives are displayed. Family members who have died remain very important to the living. It is felt that the elders' spirits continue to care about their family and want to be included and remembered on a regular basis. Anyone who claims to have no family or not to care about their family is considered ungrateful and unfortunate.

The Vietnamese language creates a fictive family of everyone with whom a speaker is connected. It is practically impossible to say or write any sentence in

Vietnamese that does not show the speaker's status in regard to the person spoken about. One uses the basic words for family relatives as pronouns (rather than the English "you") when talking to or talking about anyone. These terms are mostly differentiated by gender and age. Thus, in speaking to anyone, one always has at least 10 pronouns to choose from. These pronouns are covered in any basic Vietnamese textbook and are extremely important. Correctly addressing elders is especially important.

One should not begin any sort of conversation in a brusque fashion, as this seems like one is ignoring the importance of the relationships between people. It is very important to establish connection with people. One should not merely be talking business with someone whom one respects, or who is older, or who out-ranks him. It is important to exchange greetings before beginning to talk about anything. It is customary to keep about three feet of distance, and one should bow the head somewhat when greeting someone, especially an elder. A younger person shows respect for an elder by keeping their arms crossed and by not looking directly at the older person. It is important not to hug or touch someone when greeting or saying goodbye, unless the person is a close friend or family. Bear hugs are not appropriate. Also, it is as important to say goodbye as it is to begin with a greeting. The same salutation with the correct pronoun is used for both, for example "Chào bà" or "Chào ông." When greeting monks or other people at a temple, it is customary to place one's palms together and nod the head. This symbolizes saluting the spirit of that person, and they return this gesture.

Women are usually modest in their dress—even though much of Vietnam has hot temperatures. Older women rarely wear shorts or even dresses above their knees. The traditional and popular Vietnamese costume, the *áo dài*, covers a woman from neck to wrists to ankles. When visiting older people, a temple, church, or any important place (such as Ho Chi Minh's tomb) even sleeveless shirts or shorts may be considered inappropriate. In some of these places, improperly dressed women must rent or borrow shawls or wraps in order to enter. Young children can wear short clothes without problem. Men may wear shorts (usually loose ones), but it is better to wear long pants. Modesty also extends to a separation of the sexes in many churches or temples. Men sit on one side of the room and women on the other side. Children may sit with either parent, or sometimes they sit with their class in the front rows.

When a guest is invited to eat with others in Vietnam, after the blessing (if it is a Christian group) and before eating, younger people at the table should respect the elders by inviting them to eat. The elder nods and may reply. Then either a younger person will serve the elder or they serve themselves and begin eating, after which younger people follow suit. An elder may graciously serve younger people near them. A younger person at the table never begins to eat first. The basic idea is that a guest never grabs, and always waits to be invited to eat. This holds true even at parties, where it is considered out of place to serve oneself from the snack trays or to mix oneself a drink. At a meal, each place will usually have a plate or a large soup bowl, a small bowl for rice, chopsticks, a short porcelain spoon for soup, and a napkin. The napkin should be left beside the plate during the meal and used to wipe fingers—and perhaps one's face—during the meal. During the meal and at the end it is customary to put one's chopsticks down across the top of the plate or beside the soup bowl on the table. Most dishes are brought to the table in large bowls and people serve themselves by the eldest going first, followed in turn by younger ranks. When serving oneself, the large serving spoons beside the serving bowls should be used. If there is no serving implement, it is okay to turn the chopsticks around so that the thicker end of the chopsticks (that doesn't touch the mouth) are used to serve the food. At a family meal, the family members may use their chopsticks to serve from the main bowls, but that is because they are in intimate company.

Vietnamese meals are to be enjoyed, so there is less attention on table manners and more on how much guests show they are enjoying the food. It is good to enjoy the meal, but also important to take time to enjoy the food and talk to the people—however, not with a mouth full of food. It is polite to take small bites so you can savor the food rather than gulp it down. Hosts may offer a fork to those not adept at using chopsticks, and it is fine to accept. Most place settings do not include knives, so it is appropriate to pick the food up with chopsticks or fork and bite it. That being said, noodles dripping from the mouth (which one bites and lets drop back into the bowl), slurping soup, and burping are all within bounds (but only for men!) because the emphasis is on praising the meal and the cooks by one's enthusiastic eating and words. The host will probably energetically try to give a guest more helpings, and one can accept if hungry enough to eat this much. Otherwise one must equally, forcefully refuse several times, explaining how full one is, how great the food is, and how one cannot eat any more. This type of dialogue is also true for gifts that the host may offer during a visit. It is assumed that the recipient always refuses the first few times and only acquiesces if they actually want to accept. Do not feel browbeaten into eating more or accepting a gift that seems out of bounds. The hosts are trying to show their hospitality and generosity, and one must respond by being an equally thoughtful guest. When invited to a home for a meal, it is courteous to bring a gift of fresh fruits, pastries, and/or tea. Vietnamese people tend to eat fruits for dessert and drink tea after a meal. Pastries are considered to be a sweet treat for a special occasion.

When eating in restaurants, the person who suggests eating out is expected to pick up the tab. Dividing the cost of the meal is considered very parsimonious, but the guest should make an offer to pay. People may argue over paying the bill before one person wins, and it is polite to enter into the fray, especially for someone of higher status. There is no formal rule on tipping in Vietnam and most people do not practice this, especially in rural areas. However, more Westernized people and most tourists do leave a small tip for the servers (or taxi drivers).

Anyone being complimented—host, cook, anyone—will always disparage themselves. This is not a lack of self-esteem but a practice of modesty. When giving compliments, one must do so enthusiastically and probably a bit over the top from what is customary in other countries, and then protest and argue when the other person denies doing anything worthy of notice. To let someone talk about how inferior their work is and then be silent means that one agrees with these statements.

This custom of always disparaging oneself and always being indirect is a social norm.

When talking with someone toward whom one wants to extend respect, pay attention but do not murmur "Um-mm" or "Okay" as you listen. The respectful response is to say "Dạ," which sounds a lot like a nasal "Yeah" in English but it is the correct way to show attention. However, if people are listening and murmuring what sounds like "Yeah, yeah," it means they are politely listening but not necessarily that they agree. Vietnamese people expect conversation to be friendly and cheerful, without angry or curt tones of voice. To defuse a tense or potentially embarrassing situation, both men and women will smile and laugh—but not because they are unaware of what is going on. Hearing a man giggle may seem odd, but one should read smiles and laughter in terms of politeness and social acuity. In fact, it may feel disconcerting to have a tense discussion on a serious subject during which people are bravely smiling. They are not being oblivious to the situation but are trying to respond well for the sake of the group. Private feelings are only shared very privately.

One should be very careful with criticism and insults. Vietnamese practically never criticize those older or of higher status than themselves, and if one feels it necessary to speak up, things should be phrased very carefully ("I think perhaps it might be better to . . ." or "There might be a problem if . . ."). On the other hand, elders and more powerful people regularly criticize those under them. This is not necessarily received well by the recipient but rarely shown directly. Someone who feels insulted may hold a grudge for a long time and only communicate their aggrieved feelings by (what to Americans seem like) very subtle signs. If one is trying to correct or guide a student, younger colleague, or junior employee, talk with them privately and in terms of concern for their future or improving their work.

Body language reflects modesty, self-control, and knowledge of one's place in society. Even babies are carried carefully with their arms held in and their head positioned properly, and toddlers are taught to stand solemnly with their arms crossed and looking down when in public. Friends and family touch each other a fair bit while they are talking together, and it is common to see girls, women, boys, or men walking along hand in hand or arm in arm—but never man and woman in public. Public displays of romantic affection are out of bounds and embarrassing.

Vietnamese sexual stereotypes might be compared to American attitudes in the 1940s and 1950s. Women may run their households, but in public a man is expected to be the leader. This can make it difficult for Vietnamese men to work under an American woman as boss. An American woman working with any man must always be aware of this. Modesty is important at work and all social encounters. Married women do not flirt with anyone unless he is a very close family friend. Any man–woman relationship such as boss and secretary is considered sensitive and very open to scrutiny. Personal relations and business do not mix at all. A boss is a boss, an employee is of lower rank, and they are definitely not peers or colleagues. Infidelity is not acceptable in general—but it is far more accepted for men than for women. Women are always expected to keep their family intact—no matter what—for the sake of the children.

E-mails are usually formal in Vietnamese, and if the e-mails are to a respected elder or someone of status, they are written in the manner of formal business letters. Friends may write to each other very casually, but if one does not know someone well, it is best to write in a formal and polite way.

When someone dies, the news spreads, and friends and family call and visit, bringing condolences, offers of help, and food. If bringing a meal to a Buddhist family, one should bring a vegetarian dish even if the family normally eats meat. White is the color of mourning, so at a funeral the immediate family (parents, spouse, children) wear white robes with long white hoods. Family and close friends carry flowers at the funeral. Family and close friends can send flowers, but friends usually contribute money to help pay for funeral costs.

In summary, while in Vietnam act as politely and formally as with one's own grandparents and aged relatives, unless with close friends. It is wise to explain anything that may be misunderstood cross-culturally. It is better to belabor a point rather than to find out later one has unwittingly hurt or insulted someone by acting friendly and breezy. Vietnamese people know that foreigners were not brought up like them, but showing that one is trying to understand and appreciate their culture is usually greatly appreciated.

Cam-Thanh Tran and Kathleen Carlin

Further Reading

Crawford, Ann. *Customs and Culture of Vietnam*. Rutland, VT: Tuttle, 1966.

Fitzgerald, Frances. *Vietnam, Spirits of the Earth*. Boston: Bulfinch/Little Brown, 2001.

Jamieson, Neil. *Understanding Vietnam*. Berkeley: University of California, 1993.

McLeod, Mark W., and Nguyen Thi Dieu. *Culture and Customs of Vietnam*. Westport, CT: Greenwood, 2001.

Whitmore, John, ed. *An Introduction to Indochinese History, Culture, Language, and Life*. Ann Arbor, MI: Center for South and Southeast Asian Studies, 1979.

W

WESTERN AFRICA

The term "West Africa" or "Western Africa" refers to a group of countries in the western part of Sub-Saharan Africa. It is made up of 16 countries—Benin, Burkina Faso, Cape Verde, Côte d'Ivoire (Ivory Coast), Gambia, Ghana, Guinea, Guinea-Bissau, Liberia, Mali, Mauritania, Niger, Nigeria, Senegal, Sierra Leone, and Togo—spread out over $614,0178 \text{ km}^2$ and inhabited by approximately 338 million people. These populations use many local languages in addition to the official languages inherited from the old colonial powers, namely France, Great Britain, and Portugal. These territories exhibit wide geographical and cultural variety while sharing common heritage and influences. The continued existence of various social habits points to the unity existing among West African sociocultural systems. This is exemplified by what socio-anthropologists call *cousinage*—cultural practices based on humorous insults. The best-known form of cousinage is the one that allows the members from the same community or from different ethnic groups to mock one another publicly without any serious consequences. Far from engendering conflict, these verbal fights actually help relieve social tensions. This ancestral system of prevention of social tension through laughter can be found all over Western Africa under different names: Sinankunya in Mali, Rakiré with the Mossi of Burkina Faso, Toukpê in the Côte d'Ivoire, Massir with the Serer people, and Kal with the Wolof people of Senegal.

The rules of socially acceptable behavior in West Africa depend on an individual's social status and mirror the structures of society. These rules are a crucial factor in the maintenance of order and balance in the group.

There are a number of elements to West African greeting practices. More than a simple means of establishing contact, greetings constitute recognition of one's social status and are deeply ritualized. Greetings can last several minutes since one has to enquire about the whole family of the person one has met. Greeting gestures are indicators of social status. The right handshake accompanied by a snapping of the fingers, which can be observed over most of West Africa, is admissible only among friends or people of equal social status. The right hand, symbolizing light and strength, is the only one acceptable. Beside handshaking, one can also kiss by coming forehead-to-forehead rather than cheek-to-cheek. This custom, however, is usually restricted to men of the same age. Between people of different social status or different ages, genuflexion with lowered head is expected because it is considered impolite to look an elder in the eye during greetings. Older people are considered wise and should be treated with deference.

Greetings go beyond simple formalities, gestures, and words. They correspond to social ethics that facilitate and reinforce relationships between the different

Culture Shock! ⊕

Trokosi: Female Ritual Servitude

In the cultural region known as Yorubaland consisting of Benin, Togo, and parts of Nigeria, as well as most parts of Ghana, a system of ritual servitude exists known as *trokosi* (from *tro*, "god," and *kosi*, "slave girl"). The practice sees a child (nearly always female) serve at a shrine under control of a priest as an act of atonement for a wrong-doing committed by somebody else, usually a male relative. In the past some girls entered into *trokosi* voluntarily, as the role was considered prestigious. Today, however, *trokosi* is commonly considered a form of slavery. Though a *trokosi* period is usually limited theoretically to three to five years, in actuality many girls spend their entire lives living under *trokosi*. This is because there is a strong social stigma attached to girls who have served under *trokosi*. This social scorn means families refuse to take back their daughters once their sentence is served. The exact number of girls living under *trokosi* today is unknown, though estimates suggest there were over 3,000 girls living in ritual servitude at the start of the twenty-first century.

Victoria Williams

members of a society or group. A greeting is considered a token of socialization, integration, and harmony. As such greetings can also contain thanks, wishes, congratulations, condolences, and expressions of compassion.

Despite several constants, clothing styles do differ according to ethnic origin, sex, and social class throughout West Africa. Clothing, therefore, acts as a token of social and cultural identity. It is important that appearances remain elegant under all circumstances. During gatherings such as parties, traditional outfits are worn. These outfits often comprise a headpiece for both men and women and are made from fabric that is often colorful and richly adorned. One can distinguish between handmade fabric such as the *bogolanfini* (Malian cotton fabric dyed using mud) and the indigo, and industrially produced printed fabric such as batik and *bazin* (brocade material). In everyday life the loincloth remains the garment of choice especially among women who are expected to exercise greater caution than men in the way they dress. Women's garments are meant to display some body parts and hide others, thereby indirectly illustrating socially admitted clothing rules.

The peoples of Western African are reputed to be very hospitable. The traditions of hospitality are governed by one principle: the visitor or stranger must be treated with dignity, otherwise the host's honor is at stake. Usually the first thing a host does when welcoming a visitor is to present that person with a drink before inquiring about the reason of a visit, which is often unannounced. The table is the place where hospitality is best expressed. The meal is often communal and regulated by numerous rules. Men and women usually eat separately. Children who have not reached adulthood eat with their mothers. The meal is taken sitting on a mat on the floor. Traditionally, the meal is eaten by hand, which renders it necessary to clean one's hands before and after the meal. This washing is performed in a water basin provided for that purpose. It is strictly forbidden to put one's left hand in the common dish.

Such rules tend to disappear in larger cities where people's lifestyles have become more Westernized. It is, however, still expected to show hospitality during a meal by inviting others to join in. It is not unusual to receive invitations to join in a meal by those eating outside. Politeness dictates that one should refuse the invitation. When invited for lunch or dinner, one should always leave a few morsels on the plate to indicate satiety even if the host insists on the dish being finished.

Evil forces are seen as the cause of all the calamities capable of disrupting family or even the country's life—diseases, penury, misery, and natural disasters. Therefore the relations that people have with these forces are based on the search for harmony. Numerous precautions are taken to avoid disruption. Consequently, numerous taboos are respected in everyday life regarding food, the dead, communal life, and so on. These taboos vary according to sex, age, moments of the day, and functions and have both educational and symbolic value.

There are many taboos surrounding food. These taboos have more to do with belief and tradition than hygiene. The imposing of a taboo usually comes about out of respect for an animal or plant that is believed, according to ancestral myths, to have been of valuable service to an ancestor in the early history of the group. It might be forbidden to eat the meat of a specific animal because of its physical characteristics that one might inherit if one were to eat it. That is why in some regions people never eat horse or donkey meat lest they take on the animal's set of teeth. As far as fish is concerned, a taboo on catfish exists nearly everywhere in West Africa, especially among the Dogon of Mali, because it is under the shape of this fish that the first ancestors of this people appeared. Concerning plant products, it is forbidden to eat millet, sorghum, corn, manioc, or yam, the principal food supplies in West Africa, before the first harvests. The harvests lead to celebrations organized at fixed dates that allow the consumption of the season's products to start officially. Numerous food taboos focus on pregnant women. These taboos generally demonstrate a fear that specific qualities or characteristics may be transmitted from the consumed product to the mother-to-be or her baby. Because of a lack of protein, doctors and nutritionists have been calling for several years for an end to food taboos especially concerning vulnerable populations, namely, children and pregnant women. Doctors and nutritionists consider the taboos as having a mere symbolic and social function.

All over West Africa marriage entails obligations that validate it. Most ethnic groups see couples get married according to traditional customs that, beyond the union of two people, seal the alliance of two families or even two clans. It generally takes place before the religious or civil ceremony and represents the moment when the two families confirm the couple's union and grant them their blessing. Departing from this custom means certain failure in marital life. Most unions are arranged, especially in rural areas.

In some West African countries such as Burkina Faso and Côte d'Ivoire the dowry system is illegal, but the system is still in existence because it is one of the founding elements of a traditional wedding. To marry a woman, a man is expected to pay a dowry that is subject to transactions between the two families. The bride's family imposes a list of objects such as loincloths, bed covers, cooking utensils, beds, beer cases, palm wine, and alcohol. Recognized as ancestral and thus sacred, this custom is seen as a symbol of the solemnization of the union over and above its economic functions.

Furthermore, various marriage taboos also exist that are associated with social status. For instance in Manding societies (Senegal, Gambia, Mali, Guinea, Côte d'Ivoire), the union of people from different castes is not permitted. As names are tokens of social ranks, a marriage between a male member of a noble family such as a Keita, Coulibaly, or Ba with a female descendant of slaves or Griots such as a Sissokho, Kouyate, or Diabate is taboo.

It should be noted that the caste system found in West Africa is not comparable with the Indian system as exclusions generally concern only marriage. The existence of these West African taboos means couples often decline to marry because they feel that they must respect traditions rather than fulfil romantic desire. Marriage taboos are more prevalent in rural areas than in cities.

Fear and respect for the dead are still very vivid both in rural and urban areas, with many people still believing in the evil powers of dead people. Such beliefs gives rise to various taboos in order to avoid unleashing the wrath of the dead. Many peoples believe the spirit of the dead remains on earth for 40 days, so during that time it is compulsory to organize the funerals and to go into mourning. Funerals are organized according to rituals that vary according to different ethnic groups. It is deemed essential that people attend the funerals of relatives, as well as colleagues, neighbors, and even acquaintances. Not to attend a funeral would mean breaking a taboo—something that could cause suspicion. Since dying of natural causes is rarely considered the real cause of death, a person's failure to attend a funeral means that they may be suspected of having something to do with the deceased's demise. Mourning practices concern mainly widows. Widows are expected to remain alone in their hut or in one of the rooms of the house, sit on the floor, and eat very little until their husband's spirit is considered to have finally left the world of the living. Widows are also not supposed to do any work, especially housework. Food is prepared for widows, and they may not touch a member of the opposite sex unless it is a small boy.

Erick Cakpo

Further Reading

Mudimbe, Valentin. *Invention of Africa: Gnosis, Philosophy and the Order of Knowledge*. London: James Currey, 1990.

Sellier, Jean. *Atlas des peuples d'Afrique*. Paris: La Découverte, 2011.

Wilson, John Leighton. *Western Africa: Its History, Condition, and Prospects*. New York: Harper and Row, 1969.

Z

ZHUANG

After the establishment of the People's Republic of China (PRC), the term "Zhuang" was first used as an official nationality name or an umbrella term for Tai-speaking peoples who are distributed mainly over the southwestern part of China, the Sino-Vietnamese border. Nowadays, the Zhuang nationality is recognized as the largest minority group in China with a population of over 16 million. Most of them are concentrated in Guangxi while others are in Yunnan, Guangdong, Guizhou, and Hunan provinces. Although the Zhuang assimilated into Chinese culture and adopted Han customs and manners during the formation of the modern Chinese state, they were regarded as indigenous to the area and retained distinctive characteristics different from the Han.

The Zhuang have their own languages. Living within remote and isolated mountainous terrains of karst topography and poor communication networks led to vast variations in dialects and cultural diversity among the Zhuang. Chinese linguists divide the Zhuang languages into Northern Zhuang, with seven subdialects, and Southern Zhuang, with five subdialects respectively, but some linguists argue that the Zhuang "dialects" in China can be linguistically divided into many single languages. All the Zhuang languages are tonal, and use pitch to distinguish lexical or grammatical meaning. Basically, the vast majority of the Zhuang varieties have five to six tones.

The distinctive style of folk antiphonal singing and the "Song Market" are credited as cultural markers. Culturally the Zhuang perform a type of group antiphonal singing, where the singers are divided into male and female singing groups. In each group there is a lead vocalist and the other singers sing the chorus. They exchange quatrains in conversation until one pair cannot answer. Such contests show the singers' wit in debating issues and improvising lyrics. The lyrics are always verse, with strict rules of the metrical pattern, especially rhymes. The foot waist rhyme structure is of a particular style in Zhuang songs. It means the last syllable in the former line must rhyme with one of the syllables except the last syllable on the next line. The Zhuang songs also present some common Taic poetry features such as parallelism, elaboration, and grammatical efficiency. The music of Zhuang songs has a lot of harmony consisting of a major second, with resolution to the unison. In the past, it was customary for young men and women to gather together and sing in antiphonal style to one another during festivals and bring into play in such occasions the custom of finding a mate. Today the Zhuang song festival, Sanyuesan, is annually celebrated on the third day of the third lunar month and has been adopted as a public holiday in Guangxi.

To greet other people, the Zhuang usually ask "Where are you going?" or "Have you had a meal?" as they are a people who put value in hospitality. They enjoy preparing food and ask visitors to their village or home to eat at the same table. There is also dining etiquette for seating when a guest is invited to a Zhuang's home, where the host of a family will sit in the most honored position, which is at the head of the table in front of the ancestor altar, with the honored guests seated next to the host in order, with the more superior closer to the host, and to the right side first and to the left next. It is also a custom to welcome guests with chicken, duck, fish, pork, and alcohol as part of the meals. To continually urge the guests to drink liquor is an important manner for a host at a banquet. To refuse the liquor is not polite; if at the beginning one refuses one must continue to decline for the evening, or it is more impolite to refuse after that first drink. One must continue to drink throughout the night until they cannot drink any more. In some places, the host may invite the best singers from their own village to come and sing a call-and-response wine banquet song with their guests. If the guest can also sing songs of response to express their appreciation, then the banquet will reach a climax of social appreciation and respect.

The seniors are always respected in the Zhuang society. Grand birthday feasts are held by one's family, relatives, and friends to celebrate birthdays on 49, 61, and 73 years old, as well as every year's birthday above 80 years of age. An honorific system is used for expressing respect to the seniors or the elders. In some Southern Zhuang areas, the words "you" and "I" are never used between an elder and a younger. A younger or a junior must use the seniority (e.g., kinship terms like grandmother, uncle, and aunt), position, and status in a family, a clan, a village, a department, or a company to address an elder or a superior, instead of directly addressing the elder/superior's name or using the word "you." In addressing him- or herself, a younger or a junior must also call his or her own name or seniority, position, and status. Normally the juniors always offer their seats or priorities to the seniors in most situations, and follow the seniors' requests or assignments.

During the feast, the men and women eat at separate tables. It is customary that the men take charge of welcoming the guests with serious conversation and alcohol, while women and children eat at another table. This is because women and children can finish their meal soon and women can prepare and serve food to the men's tables.

Rice is the main food for the Zhuang, and rice wine is the main beverage when treating guests or celebrating important festivals. Vegetables and corn are grown abundantly by the Zhuang people, and as a result they are also the main foods for them. Corn porridge is a popular food for the Zhuang. They also have the habit of pickling vegetables. Sour vegetables, sour bamboo, salty radish, and kohlrabi are quite favored. During the winter, having a dinner by putting vegetables such as leaves of soybeans, leaves of sweet potatoes, young plants of pumpkins, flowers of pumpkins, and young plants of peas together with fresh chickens, ducks, and fish into boiling water is a very common way of preparing the meal.

Apart from rice as a staple food, glutinous rice is very important food for Zhuang rituals and festivals. Five-color glutinous rice soaking in natural dyes is a special offering to worship their ancestors for the New Year and the Zhuang tomb sweeping festival on the third day of the third month. Colored black, red, yellow, white, and purple by steeping with natural herbaceous plants such as day lily and maple leaf, the five-color rice represents a good year's harvest. It is a tradition to make glutinous rice dumplings during the New Year. As New Year is a festival when all family members go home and dine together, women of each household will cook glutinous rice with meat or bean filling wrapped in green leaves in a large triangle shape and distribute these to family members when they go away to work. In the Lantern Festival, married girls will come home and enjoy the delicacy of a giant rice dumpling with their parents to show filial piety. A different kind of glutinous rice dumpling is prepared during the fifth day of the fifth month festival.

Although food taboos are not numerous, there are still some cases in the Zhuang. Beef and dog were not eaten in the past since cattle and dogs are of great concern in the traditional agricultural society of Zhuang. Now the ordinary Zhuang people do not treat beef and dog meat as taboo anymore along with the Chinese influence, but the ritual specialists do insist on the traditional food taboos, or they will be thought to be punished by deities or their masters, and their religious rites will be treated as ineffective.

Although the ordinary Zhuang people eat snakes, a pregnant woman can never eat snakes, and her husband cannot even kill a snake because it is believed that eating or killing snakes would harm their child who is about to be born. A family that has a pregnant woman does not welcome an unrelated guest. If a straw hat is hung above the gate or the entrance of a room, it is best to avoid entering the room since a pregnant woman may be inside.

Funerals are important for the Zhuang, not only for expressing respect to the departed but also for the destiny of the bereaved. A funeral is divided into two stages—the first burial and the second burial. When a person dies, the first burial will be held under the Taoism or local religion burial custom. The elder relatives will not attend the younger departed's funeral; instead their children attend. Children change their dead parent into new clothes before the corpse is put in a coffin, and then spend nights around the coffin. The relatives will abstain from eating meat during the first funeral, while friends who come to the funeral do not have to fast from meat. The first burial is inhumation. After several years, as the corpse decomposes, the second burial is held. Timing of the second burial is critical as certain days and even the time of day have a critical impact on what a person does in the Zhuang society. The bereaved family will dig the grave from the first burial and open the coffin, under a Taoist or local sacrificial ceremony held by an invited ritual specialist. Any flesh that is left is cleaned off the bones. The bones will be taken to a site selected in advance. The skeleton is then placed sitting up inside a clay jar, and the jar is put into the sealed grave. The second burial is critically important because it is believed that the destiny of the family will be controlled by it, especially the ultimate site of the grave.

The Zhuang venerate their ancestral spirit, honor their extended family, and respect the elderly in their community. Traditionally, the Zhuang are polytheists. For the Zhuang living in rural areas where agriculture forms the primary means of a subsistence economy, they practice nature worship of the sun, the moon, the stars, thunder and lightning, and other objects such as giant rocks, old trees, and totems in the shape of a frog, snake, bird, crocodile, dog, cow, tiger, and dragon. The huge number of bronze drums found in Guangxi and Yunnan are crucial supporting evidence that the Zhuang's ancestors made use of the bronze drum as an instrument of authority or worship. The figure of frogs cast in the bronze drums has been recognized as a totem of the Zhuang. Until now, some Zhuang communities in Donglan County of Guangxi still have the bronze drums and celebrate the Frog Festival (*Maguai Jie*) and perform sacrificial rituals of the frog, which is considered as the goddess in charge of wind and rain, in order to pray for good weather, bumper harvests, and prosperity.

The Zhuang people value harmonious relations between human beings and nature. It is prohibitive to cut and even to show disrespect to big trees, especially the banyan and camphor. Dense forests in the deep mountains are treated as the homeland of various deities. A shrine of a village is normally built under a big banyan tree around the end of a village. "To love fields provides rice, and to love rivers provides fish" is a famous proverb of the Zhuang.

They believe that human beings, rice, water buffaloes, and a number of other domestic animals have a soul and that these souls have been put to flight by the breaking of some taboos. The absence of this soul causes sickness and lack of vitality. Zhuang people have their own indigenous ritual specialists to perform a wide range of household and communal rituals in the vernacular language. The characteristics of their rituals distinctively vary from place to place. The ritual specialists and shamans have played major, deep-rooted roles in Zhuang social life because they have the ability to communicate with the spirits, and can thus search for and call back lost souls.

Meanwhile, fertility is a critical element in rural Zhuang society. It is believed that a Goddess of Flowers has efficacious power on issues of the family, especially fertility. This goddess of creation and fertility occupies a very important position in Zhuang society. People go to worship and ask to have a son or get rid of difficulties in childbirth. When a child is born, a small shrine of the Goddess of Flowers has to be placed on the bedside of the woman who is in childbirth, for appreciating the power of the goddess as well as praying for the protection of the child.

It is noteworthy that the role of Zhuang women as ritual performers is quite unique. Compared to other nearby ethnic groups like the Yao, Miao, and Han, the status of Zhuang women is quite high, as evidenced by the courtship practices taking place in the song markets and the freedom of choice in marriage partners. Zhuang women occupy an important position in the family and society. This is reflected in the custom that the daughter who is married off must go back to her parents' house and bring back offerings to worship her ancestors there. Zhuang women are the main ritual performers in all ritual spaces, and they are actively engaged in claiming their ritual places and preserving their traditions.

Somrak Chaisingkananont and Hanbo Liao

Further Reading

Absolute China Tours. "Zhuang Nationality Cuisine, Reason to Love Guangxi." http://www
.absolutechinatours.com/china-travel/zhuang-nationality-cuisine.html.

Chaisingkananont, Somrak. "The Quest for Zhuang Identity: Cultural Politics of Promoting
the Buluotuo Cultural Festival in Guangxi, China." PhD dissertation, National University of Singapore, 2014.

Liao, Hanbo. 2015. "Yang Zhuang Poetry." Paper presented at the 25th Annual Meeting of
the Southeast Asian Linguistics Society, Chiang Mai.

Zhang, Junru (張均如), Liang Min (梁敏), Ouyang Jueya (歐陽覺亞), Zheng Yiqing (鄭貽青),
Li Xulian (李旭練), and Xie Jianyou (謝建猷). *Zhuangyu Fangyan Yanjiu* 壯語方言研究
[*Studies on Zhuang Dialects*]. Chengdu: Sichuan Ethnic Publishing House, 1999.

ZULU AND XHOSA

The Zulu and the Xhosa (pronounced with a "click" sound for the X, or with a
strongly aspirated "kh-" sound for those who are unable to click) are two of the largest ethnic groups in the diverse country of South Africa. More than three-fourths of
the population of South Africa's KwaZulu-Natal province, some 11,500,000 people
according to the 2011 South African census, speak isiZulu (the Zulu language) as
their first or "home" language, and in the neighboring Eastern Cape province more
than eight million people, over three-quarters of its population, speak isiXhosa (the
Xhosa language) as theirs. Zulu and Xhosa people also live in other parts of the
country, including the cosmopolitan metropolitan area of Johannesburg. Their etiquette and taboos, a product of this complex heritage, reflect a mixture of urban
and rural, contemporary and historical influences.

isiZulu and isiXhosa are closely related, often mutually intelligible languages, and
the people who speak them share many cultural traditions. Much of their etiquette
and taboos reflect customs that developed before the beginning of the twentieth
century, when both groups relied on a mixture of agriculture and livestock herding
for subsistence. During this period, women were generally responsible for farming
and men for livestock, a division of labor that often persists in rural areas today.
In particular, men were associated with cattle, which carried cultural and ritual significance as well as providing milk, meat, and other products. Society was organized
through multiple layers of family relationships. Ideally, households were polygamous, consisting of a man, his several wives, and their children, including adult sons
with their families and unmarried adult daughters. At the base was the house, consisting of a woman and her children; several such houses would be included in the
polygamous household led by a patriarch. People also belonged to clans, groups of
people claiming descent from a common ancestor, in which each lineage was ranked
according to the strength of its senior member's connection to that ancestor.

The ancestors of today's Zulu and Xhosa people lived in small villages led by
headmen, where most if not all of the residents belonged to the same clan. Groups
of villages were gathered into chiefdoms, and chiefdoms that were very successful
militarily or effective in recruiting new members could expand into large, centralized kingdoms. During the late eighteenth century and nineteenth century the

Zulu state developed in this way, and most modern Zulu speakers are descended from people who were once ruled by the Zulu kings. Xhosa-speaking people were never politically unified. Two groups, the amaGclaeka (Gclaeka people) and the amaRharhabe (Rharhabe people), claim descent from an ancestor named Xhosa but separated politically at the end of the eighteenth century.

Ubuntu, a philosophical concept often expressed in English through the phrase "a person is a person through other people," is at the foundation of Zulu and Xhosa approaches to social order. Social scientists describe both groups as culturally collectivist, meaning that they tend to place a high value on belonging and the common good. Among both the Xhosa and the Zulu, individuals are likely to think about their social roles in terms of how a person fits into the group, and to judge their own behavior more in terms of its impact on their relationships with others than in accordance with absolute principle or a moral law. The ideals of reciprocity and hierarchy, which govern etiquette and taboos, express the importance of relationships and the community.

Historically, everyday behavior in both groups was organized around these principles, and they are still an important part of polite behavior today. Zulu and Xhosa etiquette emphasizes the importance of deference to authority. Ideally, younger people should defer to elders, children to parents, women to men, wives to husbands, and commoners to chiefs. Historically, it was easy to tell where each individual stood in relation to others; a person's status was (and, on occasions when traditional attire is worn, still is) reflected in his or her clothing, personal adornments, and hairstyles, which changed along with age, marital status, and place in the social and political hierarchy.

In etiquette, the principles of hierarchy and reciprocity are expressed through behavior demonstrating mutual respect. Lower-ranking people show their respect for those of higher status by using appropriate phrases and behaviors; higher-ranking people are less constrained by ritual but should respond in ways that appropriately acknowledge the respect offered to them. This ideal was historically expressed through patterns of behavior often described as respectful avoidance. They were most noticeable in the behavior of young married women, because these women lived among their husbands' extended families but would only gradually be integrated into the family group. They were forbidden from drinking *amasi* (fermented milk, a traditional staple food among both Zulu and Xhosa) from the family herds until it was formally offered, generally after the birth of the first child, as a sign of acceptance into their new lineages. They were required to avoid their parents-in-law, particularly their fathers-in-law, even avoiding looking at them. The element of respectful avoidance that early observers of the Xhosa and the Zulu found most distinctive was the custom whereby women were obliged to avoid saying the names of their fathers-in-law and other male relatives or similar-sounding words. The necessary substitutions of synonyms or near-synonyms in conversation led some observers to conclude that women spoke a different form of the language than did men.

The ideal of respectful avoidance weighed most heavily upon such women, but applied to everyone in some degree. Chiefs' names, for example, were universally tabooed. Even the dead, who remained part of their lineages and clans in the form of ancestors, were granted this form of respect. Over their lifetimes people would acquire many names, both official and unofficial, and often reflecting their relation to others or their place in the community. The etiquette of personal address was and is a way of showing respect through acknowledgement of the two parties' relative positions in the group. Seniors and high-status people use the personal names of their juniors, who cannot reciprocate. This avoidance etiquette also applies to other circumstances; for example, children are taught to avoid gazing at their parents, and to remain seated in their parents' presence. Both within the family and in gatherings, juniors give way to their seniors, youth are taught never to interrupt, question, or speak harshly to their parents and other elders, and participants in communal occasions socialize with others of their own age and gender.

Sharing, especially within families and kin groups but also with visitors, is also an important element of reciprocity that is expressed in Zulu and Xhosa etiquette. Hospitality, especially to strangers, is a cherished custom, and children are taught at an early age that it is important to share what they have and shameful not to do so. Sharing and reciprocity reinforce bonds and allow people to complete tasks that are too large or laborious for a single worker or family to undertake. Among rural Xhosa people in today's Eastern Cape, for example, gatherings to drink home-brewed beer are an important expression of a community's cohesion. These gatherings grew out of the custom of communal work parties, where the women of the host family would brew beer for the people who came to help them as a way of encouraging people to participate and thanking those who did so. They have become such an important part of community life that even people whose religious beliefs prevent them from drinking the beer themselves will still brew it to share with others. The gatherings also reinforce the principle of hierarchy. The locations where participants drink their beer are determined by gender and age, and the male head of household, acting as host, seats his guests in an arrangement that reflects their relative status and distributes beer to them accordingly.

Social change has caused the ways in which the ideals that inform Xhosa and Zulu etiquette are expressed to evolve, with some traditional practices declining in importance. Young people, especially in urban areas, almost never use the language of respectful avoidance. The ideal of deference to one's elders was seriously challenged during the era of resistance to South African apartheid, the white-supremacist regime that ended in 1994, when young people staked out their own positions as political activists. Urbanization, decades of labor migrancy that separated men from their families, and widespread poverty among African people in South Africa have all served to undermine the traditional patriarchal family structure, while the philosophy of reciprocity and sharing within extended kin groups has come under stress due to economic inequality. But although some traditional forms of etiquette have become less common due to changing economic, social, and political circumstances, others—like the communal beer-drinking among the rural Xhosa—have emerged to become more prominent as Xhosa and Zulu people continue to behave in ways that express their core values. *Ubuntu* and the obligation to show respect remain important cultural ideals.

Much Xhosa and Zulu etiquette reinforces behavioral norms within the community and will not directly apply to visitors, but polite behavior for outsiders reflects the same underlying philosophy. Appropriate behavior for visitors also reflects the broader South African culture. Most South African etiquette that visitors will encounter is "Western" in its assumptions, generally similar to what one might find in a country such as the United States or the United Kingdom. As a visitor, it is recommended that you adhere to Western practices while also respecting African norms. English is widely used in business, education, and public life, but most Zulu and Xhosa people will respond positively to those who are seeking to learn their languages and will be helpful in response.

Traditionally, Zulu and Xhosa people did not maintain eye contact when speaking with those they considered to be elders or senior to them, nor did women maintain eye contact with men. This custom has faded; you will definitely not encounter it in a business environment and probably not in other places. Nonetheless, be aware of unspoken issues of relative social status. Using your access to financial resources to impose your will on others is generally bad manners, but in this case it is especially problematic when it transforms the context of a relationship from that of peers to one of unequal authority, or one's de facto position in an established hierarchy from junior to "senior." Be sure to make eye contact with peers, which communicates sincerity. Officially South Africa does not discriminate on the basis of gender, but at the same time men's behavior towards women, across its various ethnic groups, often remains paternalistic in attitude. Among all African ethnic groups in South Africa, men traditionally precede women when exiting or entering a room.

Among both Zulu and Xhosa, greetings and introductions are structured encounters that take place along ritualized lines. If you are offering a greeting in isiZulu or isiXhosa, use the plural form to indicate respect, even if you are speaking to a single person. Newcomers should wait to be introduced, and should greet their new acquaintances formally. If two people arrive in the same place simultaneously, either may greet the other; otherwise, the junior person should greet the senior person first. When you greet someone, regardless of whether you have met that person before, be sure to inquire about their health and well-being and that of their family as a way of expressing respect. They will do the same for you, and not making such inquiries is considered to be rude. There is an exception to this rule, however; the rise of pay-as-you-go cell phones as a common communication tool has created one situation where the polite thing is to be direct and to the point rather than using up minutes in ritualized inquiries. In this context, follow the lead of the person to whom you are speaking. When it is time to leave, the person who is departing should say goodbye first. When leaving a group, take leave of each person individually.

Make a point of addressing people politely and by name. In formal and business situations, personal and professional titles are an important part of address. In general, only close friends and family members address each other using first names, so wait to do so until you are asked. Married women are often addressed by their clan name. Upon marriage, women may adopt their husbands' surnames, but they keep their own clan names and use them, or an informal name associated with their clan, with the prefix "Ma-" (for "mother of") attached. Zulu and Xhosa men have praise names (*izithakazelo* in both languages) that are associated with their clans. All male members of a clan have the same *izithakazelo*. These names are only used by men; women don't call men by their *izithakazelo*. In general, men appreciate other men using their praise names in conversation.

Use your right hand rather than your left when picking things up or offering them to others, a preference common to most South African people. Do not use your feet to move things or touch anything with your feet other than the floor.

While white South Africans often entertain business acquaintances in their homes, African people in South Africa usually do so in restaurants, which operate along Western lines. If you are invited to someone's home, it is polite to bring a small gift. Visitors should be punctual. If, while visiting a rural area, you are invited to visit a Zulu homestead enclosed by a fence or wall, enter the homestead through its main gate and give praises to the owner of the homestead. Although dress in South Africa is generally casual outside of business environments, clothing is fairly conservative in rural areas, including in the Eastern Cape and KwaZulu-Natal. Tank tops, short shorts, and similar attire may be considered offensively revealing to local people.

In a home, or at a gathering, do not seat yourself, but wait for your host to seat you in a place that is appropriate to your position. In traditional formal meals, women served food to guests and elders from their knees, which was meant as a way of honoring the guests and their lineages. The guest, in turn, would honor the host's ancestors by receiving the proffered gift with both hands. Rural people will often dine in a traditional African way, divided into groups according to gender and age. If invited to participate in a traditional Xhosa or Zulu meal, the staple food served is likely to be a corn porridge similar to grits or polenta, called *puthu* in isiZulu, *ipapa* in isiXhosa, and *mealiepap* in South African English, served along with a vegetable or meat-and-vegetable dish. This cuisine is served in communal bowls from which it is eaten with the hands. Use your right hand to take some *puthu* or *ipapa* from the bowl, roll it into a ball with your fingers, and dip it into the accompanying stew. If you are invited to a rural home—either Zulu or Xhosa— where lack of access to communication technology means that you will arrive un- announced, avoid arriving at mealtime unless you have been invited to do so. Late morning and early evening are better times to arrive. If there is a cattle enclosure, keep in mind that these are traditionally the domain of men, and women visitors should not stray into them without the permission of their hosts.

Today, South Africa is increasingly a participant in global economic and social trends, a far cry from the isolated rural past in which the Zulu and Xhosa cultures developed. Its tremendous cultural and economic diversity means that the etiquette you should observe while interacting with Xhosa or Zulu people will depend on the circumstances. In brief, be sure to inform yourself about the culture of your hosts, remember that you are a guest in someone else's community, observe, and be patient. Learn as much as you can of your hosts' language, and remember that while English is considered to be a lingua franca for South Africa, less than half of the population speaks it fluently. Make sure to ask for clarification if you are unsure whether you are communicating clearly. South Africans collectively have a well-deserved reputation as welcoming to visitors; politeness, willingness to learn, and respect for the principles of etiquette will lead to a successful stay.

Sara C. Jorgensen

Further Reading

Afolayan, Funso. *Culture and Customs of South Africa*. Westport, CT: Greenwood, 2004.

Carton, Benedict, John Laband, and Jabulani Sithole, eds. *Zulu Identities: Being Zulu, Past and Present*. New York: Columbia University Press, 2009.

Holt-Biddle, David. *Culture Smart! South Africa: A Quick Guide to Customs and Etiquette*. London: Kuperard, 2007.

XhosaCulture. http://xhosaculture.co.za. Accessed May 9, 2015.

Selected Bibliography

Abrahamian, Levon, and Nancy Sweezy, eds. *Armenian Folk Arts, Culture, and Identity*. Bloomington: Indiana University Press, 2001.

Allman, Jean, ed. *Fashioning Africa: Power and the Politics of Dress*. Bloomington: Indiana University Press, 2004.

Al-Semmari, Fahd. *A History of the Arabian Peninsula*. London: I. B. Tauris, 2009.

Asselin, Gilles, and Ruth Mastron. *Au Contraire! Figuring Out the French*. 2nd ed. London: Nicholas Brealey, 2010.

Baranski, Zygmunt G., and Rebecca J. West, eds. *The Cambridge Companion to Modern Italian Culture*. Cambridge: Cambridge University Press, 2001.

Bellér-Hann, Ildikó, M. Cristina Cesàro, Rachel Harris, and Joanne Smith Finley. *Situating the Uyghurs Between China and Central Asia*. Abingdon, UK: Routledge, 2016.

Bent, J. Theodore, and Mabel Bent. *Southern Arabia*. London: Routledge, 2011.

Billingsley, Andre W. *Climbing Jacob's Ladder: The Enduring Legacy of African American Families*. New York: Simon and Schuster, 1992.

Bolin, Inge. *Growing up in a Culture of Respect: Child Rearing in Highland Peru*. Austin: University of Texas Press, 2006.

Booth, Michael. *The Almost Nearly Perfect People: Behind the Myth of the Scandinavian Utopia*. New York: Picador, 2014.

Bouchara, Abdelaziz, and Bouchra Qorchi. *The Role of Religion in Shaping Politeness During Greeting Encounters in Arabic: A Matter of Conflict or Understanding*. Hamburg: Anchor Academic, 2016.

Boyer, Paul S., ed. *The Oxford Companion to United States History*. Oxford: Oxford University Press, 2001.

Broome, Richard. *Aboriginal Australians: A History Since 1788*. Sydney: Allen and Unwin, 2010.

Buranbaeva, Oksana, and Vanja Mladineo. *Culture and Customs of Hungary*. Santa Barbara, CA: ABC-CLIO, 2011.

Chomsky, Aviva, Barry Carr, and Pamela Maria Smorkaloff, eds. *The Cuba Reader: History, Culture, Politics*. Durham, NC: Duke University Press, 2003.

Condra, Jill, ed. *Encyclopedia of National Dress: Traditional Clothing Around the World*. Santa Barbara, CA: ABC-CLIO, 2013.

Cooper, Robert. *CultureShock! Thailand: A Survival Guide to Customs and Etiquette*, 9th ed. Tarrytown, NY: Marshall Cavendish, 2012.

Crawford, David, and Rachel Newcomb. *Encountering Morocco: Fieldwork and Cultural Understanding*. Bloomington: Indiana University Press. 2013.

De Ferari, Guillermina. *Community and Culture in Post-Soviet Cuba*. New York: Routledge, 2014.

De Mente, Boyé Lafayette. *Etiquette Guide to Japan: Know the Rules That Make the Difference!* 3rd ed. Singapore: Tuttle Publishing, 2011.

De Mente, Boyé Lafayette. *The Korean Mind: Understanding Contemporary Korean Culture*. North Clarendon, VT: Tuttle, 2012.

Diran, Kevin. *How to Say It: Doing Business in Latin America: A Pocket Guide to the Culture, Customs and Etiquette*. New York: Prentice Hall, 2009.

Dresser, Norine. *Multicultural Manners: New Rules of Etiquette for a Changing Society*. New York: John Wiley & Sons, 1991.

Esbenshade, Richard S. *Cultures of the World: Hungary*. 2nd ed. Tarrytown, NY: Benchmark Books, 2005.

Falola, Toyin, and Daniel Jean-Jacques, eds. *Africa: An Encyclopedia of Culture and Society*. Santa Barbara, CA: ABC-CLIO, 2016.

Fang, Huawen. *Traditional Chinese Folk Customs*. Newcastle upon Tyne, UK: Cambridge Scholars, 2015.

Farsoun, Samih K. *Culture and Customs of the Palestinians*. Westport, CT: Greenwood Press, 2004.

Foster, Dean. *Global Etiquette Guide to Mexico and Latin America*. New York: John Wiley & Sons, 2002.

Galvan, Javier A. *Cultures and Customs of Bolivia*. Santa Barbara, CA: Greenwood, 2011.

Gerard-Sharp, Lisa, and Tim Perry. *Eyewitness Travel: Ireland*. London: Dorling Kindersley, 2014.

Gladney, Dru C. *Muslim Chinese: Ethnic Nationalism in the People's Republic*. Harvard East Asian Monographs 149. Cambridge, MA: Council of East Asian Studies at Harvard University, 1996.

Hampshire, David. *Living and Working in Spain*, 8th ed. London: Survival Books, 2009.

Hanks, Reuel R. *Central Asia: A Global Studies Handbook*. Santa Barbara, CA: ABC-CLIO, 2005.

Hill, David. *Dos and Don'ts in Cambodia*. Bangkok: Book Promotion and Service, 2005.

Hourani, Albert. *A History of the Arab People*. Cambridge, MA: Harvard University Press, 2002.

Hurtado, Osvaldo. *Portrait of a Nation: Culture and Progress in Ecuador*. Lanham, MD: Madison Books, 2010.

Ickes, Scott. *African-Brazilian Culture and Regional Identity in Bahia, Brazil*. Gainesville: University Press of Florida, 2013.

Jamieson, Neil. *Understanding Vietnam*. Berkeley: University of California, 1993.

Kaneko, Anne. *Japanese for All Occasions: The Right Word at the Right Time*. Singapore: Tuttle, 2015.

Lawrence, Anthony. *The Fragrant Chinese*. Hong Kong: Chinese University Press, 1993.

Leontis, Artemis. *Culture and Customs of Greece*. Santa Barbara, CA: ABC-CLIO, 2009.

Li, Tao, and Hongying Jiang. *Series of Basic Information of Tibet of China: Tibetan Customs*. Beijing: China Intercontinental, 2003.

Long, Lucy M., ed. *Ethnic American Food Today: A Cultural Encyclopedia*. Lanham, MD: Rowman & Littlefield, 2015.

Lord, Richard. *CultureShock! Germany: A Survival Guide to Customs and Etiquette*, 6th ed. Tarrytown, NY: Marshall Cavendish, 2011.

Macmillan Brown, John. *Maori and Polynesian, Their Origin, History, and Culture*. London: Forgotten Books, 2015.

Mannani, Manijeh, and Veronica Thompson. *Selves and Subjectivities: Reflections on Canadian Arts and Culture*. Edmonton: Alberta University Press, 2012.

Marsot, Afaf Lufti Al-Sayyid. *A History of Egypt: From the Arab Conquest to the Present*. New York: Cambridge University Press, 2007.

Martin, Jeanette S., and Lillian H. Chaney. *Passport to Success: The Essential Guide to Business Culture and Customs in America's Largest Trading Partners*. Westport, CT: Praeger, 2009.

Matras, Yaron. *The Romani Gypsies*. Cambridge, MA: Harvard University Press, 2015.

May, Timothy. *Culture and Customs of Mongolia*. Westport, CT: Greenwood, 2009.

McDougall, James, ed. *Nation, Society and Culture in North Africa*. London: Frank Cass, 2003.

Mezei, Kathy. *Translation Effects: The Shaping of Modern Canadian Culture*. Montreal: McGill-Queen's University Press, 2014.

Minahan, James B. *Ethnic Groups of South Asia and the Pacific: An Encyclopedia*. Santa Barbara, CA: ABC-CLIO, 2012.

Mohiuddin, Yasmeen Niaz. *Pakistan: A Global Studies Handbook*. Santa Barbara, CA: ABC-CLIO, 2007.

Monger, George P. *Marriage Customs of the World: An Encyclopedia of Dating Customs and Wedding Traditions*, 2nd ed. Santa Barbara, CA: ABC-CLIO, 2013.

Norbury, Paul. *Culture Smart! Britain: The Essential Guide to Customs & Culture*, 7th ed. London: Kuperard, 2010.

Nordstrom, Byron J. *Culture and Customs of Sweden*. Santa Barbara, CA: Greenwood, 2010.

Nydell, Margaret. *Understanding Arabs: A Guide for Modern Times*. London: Intercultural Press, 2005.

O'Leary, Margaret Hayford. *Culture and Customs of Norway*. Santa Barbara, CA: Greenwood, 2010.

Oliver, Douglas. *Native Cultures of the Pacific Islands*. Honolulu: University of Hawaii Press, 1989.

Ong, Jin Hui, Chee Kiong Tong, and Ern Ser Tan, eds. *Understanding Singapore Society*. Singapore: Times Academic Press, 1997.

Osman, Tarek. *Egypt on the Brink: From the Rise of Nasser to the Fall of Mubarak*. New Haven, CT: Yale University Press, 2013.

Randrianja, Solofo, and Stephen Ellis. *Madagascar: A Short History*. London: Hurst, 2009.

Roces, A., and G. Roses. *CultureShock! Philippines: A Survival Guide to Customs and Etiquette*. Singapore: Marshall Cavendish International, 2013.

Roraff, Susan, and Julie Krejci. *CultureShock! Austria: A Survival Guide to Customs and Etiquette*, 3rd ed. Tarrytown, NY: Marshall Cavendish, 2011.

Ruedy, John. *Modern Algeria: The Origins and Development of a Nation*. Bloomington: Indiana University Press, 2005.

Sabath, Ann Marie. *International Business Etiquette: Latin America*. Franklin Lakes, NJ: Career Press, 2000.

Salas, Miguel Tinker. *Venezuela: What Everybody Needs to Know*. New York: Oxford University Press, 2015.

Salzman, Philip Carl. *Culture and Conflict in the Middle East*. Amherst, NY: Humanity Books, 2007.

Saw Myat Yin. *Cultures of the World: Myanmar*. Singapore: Marshall Cavendish, 2011.

Skidmore, Thomas, and Peter H. Smith. *Modern Latin America*, 7th ed. New York: Oxford University Press, 2010.

Steele, Ross. *The French Way: The Keys to the Behavior, Attitudes, and Customs of the French*. New York: McGraw-Hill, 2006.

Teague, Gina, and Alan Beechey. *Culture Smart! USA: The Essential Guide to Customs & Culture*. London: Kuperard, 2013.

Titus, Paul, ed. *Marginality and Modernity: Ethnicity and Change in Post-Colonial Balochistan.* Oxford: Oxford University Press, 1997.

Turp, Craig. *Eyewitness Travel: Poland.* New York: Dorling Kindersley, 2013.

Ulko, Alex. *Culture Smart! Uzbekistan: The Essential Guide to Customs & Culture.* London: Kuperard, 2017.

Vance, Jonathan F. *A History of Canadian Culture.* Oxford: Oxford University Press, 2009.

Vincent, Jon. *Culture and Customs of Brazil.* Westport, CT: Greenwood, 2003.

Wallace, Vanessa A. *Buddhism in Mongolian History, Culture, and Society.* New York: Oxford University Press, 2015.

Weiner, Annette B. *The Trobrianders of Papua New Guinea, in Case Studies in Cultural Anthropology.* New York: Thomson & Wadsworth, 1988.

White, John. *The Ancient History of the Maori, His Mythology and Traditions.* New York: Cambridge University Press, 2011.

Wilson, John Leighton. *Western Africa: Its History, Condition, and Prospects.* New York: Harper and Row, 1969.

Zmukic, Lara. *Culture Smart! Serbia.* London: Kuperard, 2012.

Zubiri, Nancy. *A Travel Guide to Basque America: Families, Feasts, and Festivals,* 2nd ed. Reno: University of Nevada Press, 2006.

Index

Boldface indicates main entry.

About the Editors and Contributors

Editors

Ken Taylor, PhD, is a professor of urban missions at New Orleans Baptist Theological Seminary and pastor of Gentilly Baptist Church in New Orleans. He has a library science degree from Louisiana State University and has served as a library director. He holds a law degree from the University of Alabama and practiced law in Alabama. He has traveled widely, experiencing many different cultures.

Victoria Williams, PhD, is an independent writer living in London. She is author of ABC-CLIO's *Weird Sports and Wacky Games around the World: From Buzkashi to Zorbing* and *Celebrating Life Customs around the World: From Baby Showers to Funerals*. Williams has written on a range of other subjects for ABC-CLIO, including Hollywood film (*Movies in American History: An Encyclopedia*), Mesoamerican mythology (*Conflict in the Early Americas*), and American folklore (*American Myths, Legends, and Tall Tales: An Encyclopedia of American Folklore*). Williams's doctoral thesis (King's College, London) examined European fairy tales in nineteenth-century British art and literature and on film.

Contributors

Nadia Ali is a freelance writer who has contributed to other educational and academic works published by ABC-CLIO.

Arnold Arredondo is the dean of enrollment management at Baptist College of Health Sciences.

T. Eric Bates, PhD, is a part-time anthropology faculty member at Northern Kentucky University.

William O. Beeman is professor and chair of the Department of Anthropology, University of Minnesota, and an internationally known expert on the Middle East and the Islamic World, particularly Iran, the Gulf Region, and Central Asia.

Nabil Boudraa is associate professor of French and Francophone studies at Oregon State University. Nabil has also published books and articles in refereed journals on various topics including French and Francophone cinema, landscape in Edouard Glissant's work, minorities in North Africa, Albert Camus and Algeria, the language issue in the Maghreb, Berber culture, the use of history in Maghrebian literature, and William Faulkner and the Francophone World, among other topics.

Vahe S. Boyajian is a senior research fellow at the Department of Contemporary Anthropological Studies (Institute of Archaeology and Ethnography) at the National Academy of Sciences of Armenia, Yerevan, whose interests include Iranian ethno-linguistics with a special focus on Balochistan and Afghanistan.

Erick Cakpo is assistant professor of history of religions at University of Lorraine (France).

David H. Campbell is a Baptist pastor and an online instructor of intercultural studies at Liberty University.

Dr. Kathleen Carlin is a research anthropologist working with the Center for Studies of Displaced Populations at Tulane University.

Somrak Chaisingkananont is a researcher at the Princess Maha Chakri Sirindhorn Anthropology Centre, Thailand.

James I. Deutsch is program curator with the Center for Folklife and Cultural Heritage at the Smithsonian Institution and adjunct professor of American Studies at George Washington University.

Peter J. Dziedzic is a Fulbright fellow based in Fes, Morocco.

Katie Englert is part-time instructor of anthropology for Northern Kentucky University.

Caitlin C. Finlayson is an assistant professor of geography at the University of Mary Washington.

Kristina Göransson holds a PhD in social anthropology and is associate professor in the School of Social Work at Lund University, Sweden.

Nora Greani has a doctorate in anthropology from the École des haute études en sciences sociales and is an associate researcher to the LAHIC Laboratory in Paris.

Gerardo Del Guercio is formerly of the Royal Military College of Canada (St-Jean), Collège Jean-de-Brébeuf, and l'université de Montréal. He is the author of *The Fugitive Slave Law in The Life of Frederick Douglass, An American Slave* and *Harriet Beecher Stowe's Uncle Tom's Cabin: American Society Transforms Its Culture* (2013).

Anna Hamling is an associate professor in the Department of Culture and Media Studies at the University of New Brunswick.

Misti Nicole Harper is a lecturer for the Department of History and the African and African American Studies Program at the University of Arkansas.

Vincent K. Her is an associate professor of anthropology at the University of Wisconsin–La Crosse.

Ashley Humphrey is a PhD student in the School of Psychological Sciences and Monash Institute for Cognitive and Clinical Neurosciences at Monash University.

Scott Infanger is associate professor of Spanish and Latin American Studies at the University of North Alabama.

Sara C. Jorgensen is an independent scholar with a PhD in History.

Jeffrey C. Kaufmann was professor of anthropology at the University of Southern Mississippi. He currently writes and edits full time in Washington, D.C.

Candida Khan is a registered dietician in Trinidad and Tobago. Currently, Ms. Khan is working as a nutrition officer at National Schools Dietary Services Limited. She is preparing to complete her MSc. Nutrition at the University of the West Indies, Mona Campus, Jamaica.

Ines Kohl is affiliated with the Institute for Social Anthropology at the Austrian Academy of Sciences in Vienna.

Natalie Kononenko is professor and Kule Chair in Ukrainian Ethnography at the University of Alberta.

Francis Koti is professor and chair of the Department of Geography at the University of North Alabama.

Kathryn A. Kozaitis is associate professor and chair of Anthropology at Georgia State University.

Hanbo Liao is a PhD student of linguistics at the University of Hong Kong.

Enrique Ávila López, PhD, is cross-appointed full professor in the Departments of Humanities and General Education at Mount Royal University in Calgary, Canada.

Hasan Mahmud is an assistant professor of sociology at Northwestern University in Qatar.

Richard A. Marksbury is dean emeritus and associate professor of Asian Studies at Tulane University.

Carmen Martínez Novo is associate professor of anthropology at the University of Kentucky.

Blanca Montero-Philips is director of Providence Learning Center at New Orleans Baptist Theological Seminary and was born in Santa Cruz, Bolivia.

Nancy Noguera is an associate professor at Drew University in Madison, NJ.

Adama Ousmanou, PhD, is a senior lecturer at Maroua University, Cameroon. He specializes in the political, social, and religious history of Chad Basin. His present research, publications, and teachings focus on religions and ethnicity in the Chad basin. He is a member of Swiss Society for African Studies and former visiting fellow at the A.S.C., Basel University.

Howard D. Owens is professor of Christian ministry at Piedmont International University, Winston-Salem, NC, and teaches online for Liberty University, Lynchburg, VA, and Luther Rice College and Seminary, Lithonia, GA.

Cameron Phillips serves as a church planter and researcher in Bulgaria.

Dr. Philip A. Pinckard is professor of missions, New Orleans Baptist Theological Seminary.

Jeffry Pretes will complete his MA in linguistics at San Francisco State University in December 2017, and has previously studied at Khakas State University in Abakan, Russia.

Michael Pretes is professor of geography at the University of North Alabama.

Dinesh Asudo Punjabi is an electorate officer for the Oakleigh Electorate and teaching assistant at Monash University, Melbourne.

Marc Anthony Sanko is a PhD candidate in history at West Virginia University.

Laura Steckman, PhD, is a social scientist who studies how people and culture influence and interact with emerging technologies. She received master's degrees in education, Latin American studies, and Southeast Asian studies. Steckman holds an affiliation of Honorary Fellow with the University of Wisconsin–Madison's Center for Southeast Asian Studies.

Ed Steele is professor of music for Leavell College of New Orleans Theological Seminary.

Ronald Bruce St John is an independent scholar and author of five books on Libya, including *Libya: Continuity and Change*, 2nd ed. (2015).

Emily R. Sutcliffe is a cultural anthropology PhD candidate at the University of Pennsylvania.

Victoria Team is research associate in anthropology in the School of Social Sciences, Faculty of Arts, Monash University, and managing editor of international journal *Medical Anthropology: Cross-Cultural Studies in Health and Illness*.

Claire Townsend is a New York City–based costume designer and regularly researches other cultures' customs and traditions for her theatrical work.

Cam-Thanh Tran is assistant director of the Center for Studies of Displaced Populations at Tulane University.

Juliana Tzvetkova, MA, is professor of communication and language studies at Centennial College, Toronto, Canada, and the author of *Culture Smart! Bulgaria* (2015), and *Popular Culture in Europe* (2017).

Bill Warren is the Landrum P. Leavell, II, Professor of New Testament and Greek and the director of the H. Milton Haggard Center for New Testament Textual Studies at New Orleans Baptist Theological Seminary.

Nicole Willock is assistant professor of Asian religions with a specialization in Tibetan studies at Old Dominion University in Norfolk, Virginia.

Saw Myat Yin is a freelance writer and editor, and author of *CultureShock! A Survival Guide to Customs and Etiquette: Myanmar.*

Antonio N. Zavaleta is a retired professor of anthropology at the University of Texas at Brownsville.